Socialist Criminology

Theoretical and methodical foundations

ERICH BUCHHOLZ
RICHARD HARTMANN
JOHN LEKSCHAS
GERHARD STILLER

Translated from the German by
EWALD OSERS

SAXON **SH** HOUSE | LEXINGTON BOOKS

First published as Sozialistische Kriminologie
by Staatsverlag der DDR, Berlin
© E. Buchholz, R. Hartmann, J. Lekschas, G. Stiller

Published by

SAXON HOUSE, D. C. Heath Ltd.
Westmead, Farnborough, Hants., England

Jointly with

LEXINGTON BOOKS, D. C. Heath & Co.
Lexington, Mass., U.S.A.

$$\frac{H}{364.0943}$$

ISBN 0 347 01030 X
Library of Congress Catalog Card Number 74-3911
Printed in Great Britain by Unwin Brothers Limited
The Gresham Press, Old Woking, Surrey.
A member of the Staples Printing Group

Contents

Introduction   1

PART I   THEORETICAL FOUNDATIONS OF SOCIALIST
CRIMINOLOGY   25

    1   The Subject of Socialist Criminology   27

    2   Theory of the Causes of Criminality in Socialist Society   57

    3   Critique of Bourgeois Criminology   107

PART II   THE SOCIAL CONDITIONS OF CRIMINALITY IN
THE GERMAN DEMOCRATIC REPUBLIC   137

    4   Criminality as a Socially Conditioned Phenomenon in Capitalism and Socialism   139

    5   Some Specific Social Conditions of Criminality in the GDR   159

PART III   THE PERSONALITY OF THE OFFENDER AS AN
INDEPENDENT VARIABLE AMONG THE COMPLEX CAUSES OF CRIME AND THE TASKS OF
CRIMINOLOGY   185

    6   The Dialectical Process of Personality Development – The Foundations of Personality Research   189

    7   Freedom – Responsibility – Accountability – Their Significance in Criminology   201

    8   Criminological Personality Research and the Personality Analysis in Criminal Proceedings   223

PART IV   TECHNIQUE AND METHODOLOGY OF CRIMINOLOGICAL RESEARCH   245

    9   Theoretical Problems of Criminality Research   247

10 Procedures for the Investigation of Criminality and its Causes   303

Appendix to Part IV: Data Questionnaire   377

Index   407

Introduction

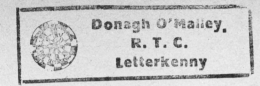
The central problem of socialist criminology, forming as it does an integral part of the socialist social sciences, is the question of the causes of the criminality which exists as a specific social phenomenon in our Republic. Criminality, as the sum total of criminal offences (major and minor offences within the meaning of Article 1 of the Criminal Code), is highly diversified and structured both in its qualitative and in its quantitative aspect. Proceeding from the socially determined character of this specific social phenomenon, our theoretical conclusions and practical experiences have been summed up in the causal concept developed in Part I of the present book. This causal concept is the result of many years of international debate and argument, as well as of the concerted thinking of socialist criminologists. As a methodological directive it has proved its worth and met with universal acceptance in our Republic; as far as we can judge it underlies all studies concerned with criminological problems. The concept reflects the realisation that the social phenomenon called criminality is, in the final analysis, a complex and complicated phenomenon, internally diversified and structured, a phenomenon which cannot be correctly or comprehensively understood in its origins and causes merely on the gnosiological plane in terms of purely linear causal relations. As we all know, historical and dialectical materialism enlarges our cognitive capacities. More particularly, dialectical determinism enables us, in the shape of such categories as possibility and reality, interaction, correlative relations and statistical laws, to penetrate more deeply into the problems of the causes of the phenomena and processes to be investigated. Its application enables us to discover any still partly operative stochastic connections between criminality on the one hand and any material and spiritual features (processes and phenomena) still surviving in our reality, and thus to arrive at appropriate probability statements. The general character and high degree of abstraction of the causal concept established by us must tend to widen our horizon. This is done in two separate directions — on the one hand, by an exposition of the complexity of the factors causing or determining the phenomenon of criminality and on the other by showing up the developed socialist system of society within which such complexes of material and spiritual character emerge as interference factors.

Especially fruitful in arriving at this realisation has been our co-opera-

1

tion with Marxist—Leninist philosophy. The development of the causal theory concept of socialist criminology as a methodological tool led to clarity about the fact that the central task in studying the causes of crime is the discovery of the statistical laws which operate, or operate in part, between the material and spiritual sets of conditions of social reality and certain criminal phenomena. It is only on the basis of such an understanding that we can define the social counterforces, and the social conditions corresponding to them, which, by a scientific guidance of social processes through the socialist State, the principal instrument of the working class led by the Socialist Unity Party of Germany and its allies, and with the assistance of socialist law, are capable of restricting the effectiveness of such identified and partially still operative specific laws or — provided the material and spiritual possibilities are present — entirely liquidating them by abolishing the conditions of their existence.

The task of discovering specific laws and regularities opens up a wide field for sociological case work and criminological fundamental research. In this context criminology will have to pay more attention than in the past to the relations between the partial statistical laws discovered by it and the fundamental kinetic laws of socialist society and must investigate them. Such investigations are also likely to provide new and deeper insights into *prediction* research concerned with the long-term development of measures and deployment of forces for the struggle waged by socialist society against criminality. This problem has been well formulated by Herbert Hörz:

> The question which criminological research has to answer is: How is the statistical concept to be utilised in order to arrive at a new understanding? There are clearly a number of points to bear in mind. Since on principle the importance of the statistical concept has been acknowledged, the task now is, firstly, to discover the laws of criminality operating within the system of social laws generally. From this, secondly, the probable distribution of groups of individual cases can be derived and this must provide the basis of administrative measures in the struggle against crime. Thirdly, a classification of accidental occurrences must be performed in order to show whether certain occurrences are manifestations of the existing system of social law or whether they are system-alien accidents whose essential effects have to be opposed. Scientific examination will in consequence be able to disregard the inessential external and internal chance occurrences because these inevitably distort the proportions and render more difficult a thorough examination of the other offences which, though of chance character, are essential.[1]

In the degree of its generalisation the concept of the cause has a heuristic (understanding-promoting) function in the scientific sense, as is proved by the criminological studies conducted on its basis. It represents, as it were, a methodological thread which runs through criminological research, orienting it towards the exploration and examination of essential connections and relations between external (objective) and internal (subjective) complexes of conditions. It acknowledges that criminality is the totality of society-endangering and anti-social actions by individuals acting deliberately and purposefully. Anything man does, Engels says, first goes through his head. That means that external influences which determine action are first subjectively refracted, as though by a prism, by the state of knowledge and the given experiences of the agent and eventually — in conjunction with various motives, material and spiritual aspirations, interests and purposes — determine his action. In other words, the external (objective) determinants impinge upon phenomena which themselves bear the character of heterogeneous 'systems', so that in the interaction of forces the effect of external determinants depends not only on their nature or character but also on the state of the consciousness of the agent upon whom they are acting. S. L. Rubinstein in his studies, more particularly in his work *Being and Consciousness*, has placed this interaction at the centre of his investigations.[2]

The knowledge-promoting effect of the causal concept can, moreover, be seen in the fact that it enables us to distinguish two fundamental aspects in criminological research — the social and the personal aspect. The social aspect guides appropriate empirical investigation towards an analysis of external conditions and, proceeding from the primacy of external determination of all social action, towards an understanding of shortcomings and weaknesses in personality — significant social spheres of coexistence, without negating the problem of personal conditions and any resulting personal responsibility for the opportunity of self-determination. The personal aspect focuses criminological research on the exploration of those personality features of offenders which combine, within the personal sphere, the external influences and internal conditions into criminogenic factors. This makes it possible by suitable comparative studies to identify attitudes and social behaviour dispositions, as well as thought and living habits which have developed in the process of social and personal development, and these in turn make it possible to draw conclusions about the system of social prevention, of early diagnosis, of treatment and of integration.

The method of proceeding from the above-named aspects has proved exceedingly fruitful because the complex and difficult determination of

3

the structure of criminal occurrences can thus be analysed by a procedure based on a *division of labour* and synthesised into an integral picture through theoretical thought. In consequence, we can distinguish two trends in criminological research — one examining criminality and its separate manifestations from the social aspect and the other from the personal aspect; only when these two are combined under a fundamental theoretical concept does this unity produce fruitful results. In such a division of labour it will have to be remembered that neither the external nor the internal relations can by themselves claim the attribute 'criminogenic', but that the two sets of conditions by combining in dialectical interdependence and interaction become operative as causes of criminality. In order to penetrate more deeply and more specifically into the problem of causes we apply the method of 'artificial isolation' of external and internal conditions and sets of conditions. But the results obtained by each of these procedures must not be absolutised. Any such absolutisation is bound to lead to mistakes, chiefly through over-simplified theoretical ideas about the effect of environment and personality. As far as practical work is concerned, the aforesaid means that crime prevention can never confine itself to merely attempting to change the external conditions without at the same time exerting an educational effect, just as it would be inadequate to act in a purely educational way without at the same time striving to eliminate any negative external influences. In other words, the concept of the causes of criminality developed in this study will be successfully applied only if the dialectics of external and internal factors in determining human action are borne in mind.

The basic methodological function of the causal concept and its interpretation in the light of Marxist—Leninist theory have, moreover, shown their fruitfulness in studies which, proceeding from these fundamental aspects, base themselves extensively on criminological hypotheses about determination and, as a result, have revealed three levels of factors: (a) permanently operative external conditions; (b) personality characteristics as internal conditions of relative constancy; (c) real conditions operating in the action situation.

In this connection we should like to draw attention to yet another important aspect of our study. The causal concept developed by us and its detailed justification has sprung from, among other things, a militant dialogue with revisionist views of the most diverse types. They all shared the assumption that socialism, in its nature, gave rise to criminality. The debate conducted in the relevant section of the present book was therefore and continues to be necessary. The experience of the international

4

working class movement has confirmed the correctness of such a firm and militant dialogue.

The concept of the theory of causes developed in this book does not, on the other hand, simplify the real problems connected with the origins of criminality. Nor was any attempt made to pass over in silence the genuine conflicts and human problems contained in general criminality. On the contrary, our concept of the causes has taken into consideration the experiences of socialist society in its confrontation with old, outdated phenomena and processes in social co-existence, in so far as they can influence the thinking, feeling and action of individuals, as well as the fact that old and outdated thinking and living habits and behaviour patterns continue stubbornly to survive and are even liable to be re-activated by a variety of influences. The building of the new society is not taking place without conflicts or contradictions. Nor is it taking place as an automatic process. It has always been linked with a militant confrontation with the survivals of· old social phenomena both of material and spiritual character.

P. N. Fedoseyev, member of the CPSU Central Committee and director of the Marxism—Leninism Institute under the CPSU Central Committee, at an international scientific conference organised by the SED Central Committee in June 1970 discussed these important theoretical and practical problems, which also have a bearing on the general causal concept held by socialist criminology. He observed:

> It is frequently said that after 50 years of Soviet rule one can no longer regard various negative phenomena in our reality as survivals of capitalism. It should be pointed out that we do not judge the processes of our evolution in such an over-simplified manner.
>
> Of course such phenomena as cupidity or idleness, bureaucracy or irresponsibility, nationalistic prejudices or intellectual—anarchist overbearing are survivals of the past. But they cannot simply be explained by circumstances which existed half a century ago. We must view the complicated dialectics of social evolution with all its contradictions. Lenin said that while antagonisms disappear under socialism the contradictions live on. The development of socialism must not be imagined as an absolute harmony of all aspects and all phenomena of social life. Under socialism, too, the evolution of society towards higher levels takes place amidst contradictions. Generally speaking, these contradictions between the new and the old, the progressive and the backwards, the positive and the negative, may be said to be part and parcel of the evolution of society. They are the contradictions of a living, growing organism.

As economic development progresses so the material prosperity of the working people increases. For the great mass of the population this is the prerequisite of a better life, of a cultural advancement. At the same time, however, distortions, survivals of an ownership ideology and rapacity are encountered in the behaviour of some individuals ...

We are not shutting our eyes to the fact that certain prejudices and wrong actions by individuals may be connected with difficulties in their lives, disturbed relationships, the grave consequences and upheavals of the last war, failures and sorrow in their personal lives, etc. But one cannot blame the unworthy behaviour of certain individuals upon objective relations let alone on the principles of socialism. Views and habits alien to us are connected not with the principles of socialism but with their distortion.[3]

Bourgeois criminology is repeatedly revealed in the present book in its class-related character. The outlines of the most diverse views are presented.[4] More recently there have also been attempts — especially under the influence of American sociology — to develop a variety of causal-theoretical concepts. There has been a concentration on the explanation and elaboration of formal psychological mechanisms which, in a sense, presupposed criminality to exist as a 'nature-given' specific social phenomenon with the result that, whether deliberately or unwittingly, any reference to the specifically criminogenic social system of the exploitative order of society is avoided.[5] This objectively manifest endeavour by monopoly bourgeoisie to disguise its anti-progressive and anti-human aims also leads to the view that bourgeois criminology has 'occasionally resigned itself to a higher crime quota'.[6] There are, for instance, sociologists who have made a virtue out of the necessity of a low crime detection percentage in the face of a mounting flood of criminal activity by putting forward the thesis 'that non-explanation of infringements of the norm has a beneficial effect by relieving the burden on criminal prosecution and maintaining the infrequency and hence the moral weight of punishment'.[7] On the other hand some authors, faced with the lack of success and the practical inefficacy of the studies of bourgeois criminologists, have raised the demand that if criminology wishes to keep its place as a science it is time for it 'to abandon the ascertainment of the causes of crime and the formulation of appropriate theories as the main task of criminology'.[8] In other words, in the 'name of science' it is proposed here to abandon the very thing that is the meaning and purpose of science — the search for laws and regularities in the social movements under review. The aim or task mapped out for such an amputated criminology is instead to discover 'the magnitude of the extent of crime (not expressed mathematically) which a particular country can withstand without serious disturbance'.[9] Joachim Hellmer quite openly proclaims the essence of such a theory: 'Society prefers the adjusted individual, even if he becomes an offender, to the rebellious one because he uses the facilities of society and therefore is not dangerous ...'[10]

We quote these statements in order to round off the picture presented in our study. They again concern the correctness of our fundamental judgement on the social character of bourgeois criminology. Its class interest is patently revealed in it. At the same time it hides behind the oft-proclaimed so-called 'freedom from value judgements' and an alleged 'scientific exactitude' approximating that of the natural sciences. This class interest gives rise to bias and narrow-mindedness, to an anxious endeavour to avoid any reference to the criminogenic character of the social system generally. Its class interest — as we were able to prove — is revealed also in its choice of subject matter, in the delineation of its tasks and objectives. It also conditions the specific shaping of its theoretical apparatus employed for achieving its limited tasks. Time and again it is therefore necessary, whenever important techniques and procedures of bourgeois science are adopted, to approach these critically and consistently from the viewpoint of Marxism—Leninism, bearing in mind our own social conditions, before we can authorise the acceptability, for our own socialist conditions, of some procedure borrowed from psychology, sociology or mathematics. Particular attention must be paid to the dispute with various so-called 'modern concepts and categories' of bourgeois criminology, such as those of 'crimes of affluence' and 'crime policy'.[11] These concepts, unless indeed they reflect the simplicity of some theoretician, are designed to manipulate people's minds. The concept of 'crimes of affluence' thus seriously aims at deluding the reader into believing that the growing criminality in the leading imperialist countries is due primarily to their material 'affluence'. The growing wave of criminality, according to these authors, is due not to the imperialist and militarist policy of their ruling circles, producing as it does a continuous disintegration of social interrelations, but allegedly to man's normal need for a better material and cultural life. It is thus argued that mankind is faced with the straight 'alternative' between either a high standard of living with a high crime rate or a low standard of living with a low crime rate. Thus — not so much in official scientific publications but in the propaganda which follows such 'theories' — the substantially lower crime rate in all socialist countries and the generally declining criminality trend is attributed to some alleged 'lack of affluence', an explanation intended to brainwash the public of the capitalist countries against socialism. Bourgeois criminology thus — whether the individual criminologist is conscious of this or not — with its concepts and categories merely provides ammunition for the monopolistic mind manipulators.

Part IV of the present book, whose general author is Gerhard Stiller, is concerned with highlighting this state of affairs, performing the necessary critique, and developing the basic ideas first touched upon in the preceding parts. It endorses what Kurt Hager, at the Ninth Meeting of the SED Central Committee in 1965, said on the subject of sociological research — viz. that an offensive dialogue with bourgeois science must embrace also a critique of its categories and concepts, 'although of course any rational problems and elements of the methods and techniques of bourgeois sociology are to be utilised for our own researches'. [12]

Socialist criminology sees the Marxist—Leninist concept of the causes of crime as its principal scientific foundation. This concept, moreover, must be formulated as a directive for action. Even though the first objective is an explanation of the origins of criminality, requiring ever new empirical investigations, this does not exhaust the nature or the goals of socialist criminology. Any new knowledge about social or personal reasons of criminal behaviour must ultimately lead to conclusions aimed at utilising the potentialities of socialist society, or indeed initiating such potentialities of severing and genuinely eliminating any identified internal and essential correlations between criminality and certain circumstances in actual life. In this sense criminological theory is a directive for action. This needs emphasising because the causal theory concept, as developed by socialist criminology, must not be understood *either* as a mechanical pattern capable of automatically explaining all criminal phenomena without further profound analytical research, *or* as a substitute for the creative endeavours and thoughts of scientists and workers in the field. This is how the question of the specific character and subject of socialist criminology has to be seen within the system of the socialist social sciences. The principal task outlined at the Seventh Congress of the SED by the party of the working class — the task of creating the fully developed social system of socialism — has already produced certain solutions in the field of dealing with criminality and other infringements of the law, and these have to be borne in mind in tackling the question in general. [13] Among these solutions is the comprehensive reorganisation of the law which assists socialist society and its State, as the principal instrument of the working class led by the party and of the other classes and strata of the working people allied with it, in its offensive against criminality and other infringements of the law. This offensive position is confirmed in Article 90 of the Constitution and in Article 3 of the Socialist Criminal Code. [14] These require socialist criminology to make its contribution, within the system of the socialist sciences, towards the conscious moulding of a socialist life style which would attain a higher degree of harmony between the objectives of the Constitution and social reality. This enlistment of criminology in the communal task mapped out by the Constitution in the form of a legal principle, moreover, demands that Marxist—Leninist social theory, which forms the basis of the policy of the working class, must be made the principal theoretical foundation of the further evolution of theory and practice. Only on this basis is criminology in a position to make its contribution as a science in three different respects:

Firstly it must, by its aetiological investigations and the information obtained by them, make a deliberate contribution to the organisation of the common struggle of society, its State and all its citizens against criminality and other infringements of the law. This is a complex common task in which criminology, mainly by detailed structural analyses and by the investigation of the structures determining criminality, contributes to the discovery of complex systems of solutions.

Secondly criminology must help to work out a specific pattern of the strategy and tactics of crime prevention and the struggle against crime by determining the best way of directing, organising and realising a mutual and optimally co-ordinated co-operation of all principal social forces involved in crime prevention and the struggle against crime. This contribution towards optimisation of the joint social effort as well as to the co-ordination of State measures and social activities must be made by its fundamental and its object-related research. This presupposes that all research is planned and conducted with a view to transferring its findings into social practice. It is here that — to borrow a term from industrial production — we need a technology for the transfer of the conclusions of the social sciences to the practical management of social processes.

Thirdly criminology must play its part in controlling the extent to which social effort is effectively organised, co-ordinated and realised, in line with its objective and plan, in order to achieve the aimed-at overall results. This will enable it, at the same time, to assess the correctness of its objective and its plan in the light of experience and ever-changing social conditions. This, in turn, presupposes that prediction work is conducted within criminological research itself.

The next question to be examined should be the place of criminology as part of a unified body of scientific disciplines. As a science — as we shall prove in Part I of this book — criminology develops under socialist

9

conditions from the soil of the laws governing specialisation and integration processes within the system of sciences. Related to the general scientific programme, criminology within the overall system of sciences is and remains an 'ancillary discipline', even though a most necessary one. This is not to imply any diminution of status or any avoidance of responsibility. It merely reflects the position of socialist criminology as a discipline within the system of socialist sciences, basically concentrated upon the problem of exploring the complexes of social and personal conditions governing really existing criminal phenomena (see Part I). That is its subject. As a science it supplies important information on shortcomings, weaknesses and obstacles in important and major spheres of social activity and in the development of a socialist personality. Utilisation of its statements and findings demands that, within the system of the socialist sciences, co-operation between appropriate disciplines is purposefully developed and their joint efforts in this way multiplied. It demands the construction of entire chains of co-operation among social science researchers and an appropriate type of scientific organisation. We shall return to this point later.

The question about the 'subject' of criminology must not be confused with that about its place in the system of socialist sciences. The continually growing promotion and development of socialist criminology as a science — and this seems to us more urgent than ever — largely depends on how clearly its range and scope are defined within the sphere of scientific disciplines.

Based upon the teachings of the classics of Marxism—Leninism as well as on its own experience and that of the international working class movement, the party of the working class has creatively developed the ideas of socialism as a new social order. Its theoretical generalisation has led it to the conclusion:

> that with the establishment of a firm socialist State power, the consolidation of the leading rôle of the working class and its party in all spheres of public life, and with the development of a scientifically founded socialist planned economy all those conditions have now arisen which make it possible and necessary to shape society's entire life 'according to an overall plan' and with an 'overall will' on the basis of the productive forces and production relations peculiar to socialist society, to produce, in consequence, a fully developed socialist system of society.

> Our practical experience and our theoretical work in the field of the social sciences have led us to the conclusion that *it will take a*

fairly long period of time to give shape to the fully developed system of socialism. We must invest massive resources to create new productive forces on a vast scale in order thus to realise the scientific revolution and bring the production relations of socialism to full flower. [15]

An integral part of this system is also the complex prevention of and struggle against criminality. It is being deliberately shaped by the principle of its indivisible unity and by fundamental normative acts of the socialist State power. Crime prevention and the struggle against crime are realised on the basis of democratic centralism in two main directions whose social elements are linked with one another by purposeful co-operation, sensible co-ordination and mutual information in dialectical interactions:

1   By an active shaping and creative moulding of socialist social relations through elaborately planned State measures and deliberately initiated social activities the material and spiritual room for decision in favour of criminal misbehaviour and hence the effects of identified objective and subjective complexes of determinants are being systematically restricted and reduced step by step.
2   Through the active prosecution and rejection of committed (major and minor) criminal offences by elucidation, ascertainment and application of criminal responsibility and, at the same time, utilisation of the new knowledge thus gained about the specific causes and conditions for the conscious control and organisation of social processes, measures are taken to re-educate the offender and generally instruct the public as well as raise the sense of responsibility for the liquidation of criminality.

These principal forms embrace the general trend of socialist society in its offensive against criminality and other infringements of the law. They are based on the social law operating in socialist society that a systematic and organised struggle must be waged against criminality, ensuring that the guidance and organisation of deliberate actions by the working people, their administrative and social forms of organisation and application lead to the realisation of this law and thus help it assert itself in all spheres of social life and action.

The integration of criminology into the overall evolution of socialist society requires that it should systematically and purposefully investigate the determinants and determining structures of criminality as well as its various main categories and manifestations in order thus to create the basis for a realistic and long-term opportunity for its social control and manipulation. Such long-term complex research must base itself on the

11

principal theoretical theses which are developed and explained in the present book and which form part of our basic beliefs. We shall list only a few of them here:

1 Criminality is a social and historical phenomenon.
2 Criminality is a phenomenon alien to the nature of socialism. It is diversified and to that extent represents a specific system of differentiated social phenomena of a negative character, phenomena which must be seen and investigated as, among other things, reflections of definite determinants. [16]

On the basis of these theses it is now necessary to penetrate more deeply and more specifically into this 'system of criminality'. This can be done in a way which sums up what we already know about the social character of criminality: [17] crimes against peace, war crimes and crimes against humanity form a separate major category of criminality. They are by their nature international political crimes of imperialism and militarism. This is proved, quite apart from the crimes of, for instance, German fascism, more recently also by the crimes of the imperialists, especially in Indo-China, in the Middle East and in the Latin American countries. Such crimes are the expression of a criminal foreign and domestic policy conducted by the monopolies. As is well known, socialist criminal law, consistently realising the principles of international criminal law, opposes such crimes most rigorously. This can be seen as the struggle waged by the socialist countries, under a universal principle of international law, for the preservation of the most elementary principles of humanity and as an act of humanist solidarity with those peoples of the world who are threatened by such crimes of imperialism or terrorised by imperialism. The main social causes of such crimes therefore lie in the existence of imperialism as a specific social system of the capitalist order desperately struggling against its inescapable collapse.

Crimes against the German Democratic Republic are crimes of a counter-revolutionary nature. These crimes have no social basis in our Republic, either objectively or subjectively. They are therefore possible only, as a matter of principle, as crimes carried into the GDR from without. This applies also to all the so-called unconnected cases which need not necessarily be directly linked with any action directed by imperialist secret services or other counter-revolutionary organisations. These crimes simply have to be judged as ideologically hostile effects of the activity of imperialism. The agent has here succumbed to deliberate manipulation by the overall imperialist system − a circumstance which does not reduce his own responsibility in any way. Crimes against the GDR do not spring from the GDR's own social structure. They are aspects of the class struggle waged by imperialism against socialism and are directly aimed at the GDR itself. They are committed either on its territory or else their effects become operative, or are intended so to become, on its territory. In that respect there are certain differences between the first-named main category of crimes and this one. The former need not directly affect the GDR. Indirectly, however, all such crimes — no matter who is directly affected — are directed also against the people of the GDR, because these crimes involve an intolerable negation of the principles underlying the existence of human society altogether. They demand international opposition and are therefore also declared insupportable under the principles of international law.

The successful and implacable prosecution and liquidation of that kind of criminality — as clearly emerges from the principal document of the Moscow Consultation [18] — is a decisive contribution by the working class in power, and by its allies, to the strengthening of the socialist world system and to the protection and consolidation of peace.

General crime covers a totality of (major and minor) criminal offences which are clearly differentiated from the two main categories listed above. They differ from the above crimes not only in the degree of gravity of the crimes covered by this concept but rather in the social character of this category of offences. The social character of the crimes in this group consists in the fact that various offenders, by committing more or less society-endangering and anti-social actions, disturb or gravely impair the co-existence of citizens, the relationship between State and citizen, between society and individual, and the rights and interests of the citizens generally. Such criminal actions, however, do not reflect any hostility to the social order existing in the GDR as such, but rather a more or less deeply rooted difficulty of the offender in integrating himself consciously, voluntarily and in a disciplined manner into socialist conditions and the social relations resulting from them. This applies also to offenders guilty of the gravest offences of general criminality, offences to which socialist society must react by imposing heavy punishment. [19]

It is from this social angle that we have to compare our general criminality with seemingly similar phenomena in the antagonistic social order. In such social conditions of life and existence general criminality represents a socially blind reaction by the isolated individual and is therefore the inevitable direct result of the general exploitative social system. It is obvious that such criminality as still exists under the conditions of socialism cannot, by definition, possess the character of social protest against the new human conditions and relations. This is not to say that it is impossible to live under socialist conditions without coming into conflict with them. But we may state — and this will be justified in detail in the present book — that general criminality is the expression of 'relics' or 'survivals' of the old social order.

To avoid misunderstandings or distortions it is necessary in this context to add an explanation of the function of these concepts in the theory of Marxist–Leninist criminology. Such misunderstandings or deliberate distortions frequently take the form of the 'accusation', especially from bourgeois circles, that our concepts of 'survival' and 'relic' represent an attempt to evade the 'specific' causes of criminality because we either do not recognise them or are reluctant to identify them. The concepts of 'survival' and 'relic' of the old order of society are not intended to denote a specific phenomenon of life in its specific nature, nor indeed would they be able to do so. They are not therefore used as substitutes for specific information on the factors of criminality. Their sole — though indispensable — function consists in reflecting the social character of those specific phenomena which we highlight as the causes of criminality. It is undoubtedly correct that one should not always or exclusively meditate on the social character of specific real-life phenomena, but that one should tackle them in their specific shape and form. But it is equally unacceptable to write only about the 'phenomenon' and not about its nature. We can only regard any such 'critique', which is clearly intent on making us keep silent about the social aspect of the causes of criminality, as an attempt to force socialist criminology on to the tracks of pure empiricism, i.e. to de-ideologise it. The solution of the problem therefore cannot be found either in 'pure meditation' while denying the phenomenon in its specific shape and individuality nor in disregarding its social content by considering solely its form. Only by consideration of the dialectical relation of content and form can a real scientific solution of the problem be found.

The following problem emerges from our necessarily sketchy outline of the three principal categories of criminality: the correct organisation of crime prevention and the struggle against crime requires not only knowledge of the nature of criminality and its general causes but also knowledge about its structure as a specific system of socially negative phenomena. Here lies a broad field of criminological research and it is here that we encounter a line of research that might be described as 'criminological structural analysis'. By the structure of criminality we mean the edifice of the various criminal phenomena, an edifice of several dimensions, in which criminality as a whole or certain parts of it may be found with relative constancy. The concept of 'structure of criminality' thus embraces the totality of essential relations of the phenomena covered by criminality.

Analysis of the structure of general criminality is one element in the system of criminological investigation. It is performed, among other things, with a view to gaining new knowledge, to meeting the demand for a specific examination of causes [20] and for specific time-related and space-related preventive and crime-fighting measures, [21] and also to exploring the information content of the statistics. [22] This line of criminological research has hitherto been somewhat neglected, and a few reflections on it would therefore seem to be in order. The structure of general criminality is determined by the valid criminal law. The thesis of bourgeois criminology that a distinction must be made between a 'criminal law' concept of criminality and a 'criminological' one has no validity for us (see Part I of this book). The criminal law instead has a decisive influence on the structure of general criminality. It lays down what is to be judged and assessed in law as a criminal action. It lays down that there is no such thing as criminality outside the criminal law; it defines the framework of the categories within the system of criminal offences and defines personal conditions for criminal responsibility. Admittedly it has to be borne in mind that the structure of real criminality, i.e. offences taking place in space and time, cannot be derived solely from the logical structure of the criminal code. Such a simplified procedure would be disregarding the special function of the criminal law; it would fail to protect citizens, society or the State against actual offences and it would expend effort on the provision of measures covering actions which admittedly might occur in certain circumstances but are in fact numerically very rare or indeed never occur at all.

The structure of general criminality as a multidimensional system is characterised by its differentiation into major and minor criminal offences within the meaning of Article 1 of the Criminal Code. This differentiation is significant inasmuch as the quantitative distribution of major and minor offences − seen from the point of view of society as a whole − may provide information on the extent to which major criminal offences still occur as grave eruptions from the rules of social co-existence or as attacks on elementary values of social life and co-existence. The minor criminal offences, on the other hand, are destructive not so much from the point of view of the specific individual action as in their totality, and therefore demand considerable breadth in the deployment of preventive and crime-fighting measures.

Another aspect which criminological structural analysis should concern itself with is the examination of the historical trend of general criminality altogether and within certain definite parameters. Such a historical aspect, as pointed out some time ago by the GDR Prosecutor General, [23] could be significant in revealing general tendencies which demand consideration with a view to prevention on a society-wide scale and also from territorial points of view. It hardly needs saying that in any such consideration the validity of the information content of the structural data must be determined as accurately as possible in order to prevent rash conclusions. [24]

Yet another aspect of structural analysis is the distribution of general criminality among various categories. It is a well-known fact that the bulk of all offences committed is concentrated within a relatively small percentage of the circumstances covered by criminal law. The remaining offences scarcely affect the structure. The category structure therefore raises certain problems and questions for analytical thought, and these might be made the basis of further criminological work. Combined with territorial parameters such as district, region, etc., such research, proceeding by way of crime topography, might, if correctly interpreted, likewise prove of the greatest importance for the specific definition of preventive and crime-fighting measures as well as for the concentration of the anti-crime effort. Such a structural analysis can, moreover, be bracketed with distribution in time, such as season, month, week or even time of day, and this — correlated with other parameters — may provide valuable information for time-oriented preventive and crime-fighting measures. Analogous information may be obtained on spatial distribution in a narrower sense. Thus a similar structural analysis revealed that criminal phenomena are concentrated in cities, especially large cities, so that particular attention has been and continues to be devoted by central and regional administrative bodies to appropriate topographical centres of gravity for crime prevention and crime-fighting. [25]

Structural analysis thus opens up a variety of approaches to the distribution of general criminality. It enables us to identify this distribution in certain main spheres of the individual's social life and actions. It makes it possible, moreover, to discover connections between modes of crime commission and between specific personal data such as age, sex, social origin, etc.

In planning the future of criminological structural analysis the aspects here quoted will have to be further developed, but space prohibits us from going into the details of the working hypotheses entailed, although these have already been touched upon in a number of unpublished studies. What is, however, obvious at once is that in its global structural pattern general criminality clearly is not an amorphous accumulation or a mere sum of individual actions. It represents a system with definite elements or subsystems whose essential relations evidently also display a measure of

16

stability; the task, therefore, is to discover the specific laws or systematically operating complexes of conditions which underlie this criminality. Criminological structural analysis thus conceived will have to take account of the findings, experience and data of socialist sociology and indeed will not be able to dispense with such comparative studies. It will also require an appropriate gnosiological apparatus using, wherever necessary, such tools as factor analysis, type analysis and discriminance analysis. In our view structural analysis — supplemented by appropriate longitudinal and cross-section analyses along the basic social and personal aspects mentioned above — may be expected to lead to an overall result that will enrich and fructify the State's and society's measures for preventing and fighting general criminality.

We thus regard criminological structural analysis as *one* specific line of research within the system of criminological research. As such a specific line it must be integrated into the general system of joint scientific work on the problems of crime prevention and the struggle against criminality and other infringements of the law.

The continually growing degree of the scientific character of the open confrontation with criminality, in line with the state of development of socialist society, is based upon a continually advancing political—ideological and scientific—organisational perfection of the guiding activity of the State. This includes the problem of defining the extent of the information necessary for the solution of the tasks of the socialist State power in consciously and systematically directing social processes of a material and spiritual nature. The collection, collation and processing of important data needed for crime prevention and crime fighting cannot be confined to those which contain direct information on criminality in the sense discussed above; they must extend wherever necessary to data covering the pre-stage of criminality. The discovery and correct determination of the necessary information is particularly important in this respect since prevention must include such phenomena of social risk as may, in due course, objectivise themselves as infringements of the law. It is becoming increasingly obvious that conventional means and methods of information gathering and processing can no longer by themselves ensure the best possible crime prevention and crime fighting. Methods of mathematical modelling, methods of precise parameter determination, especially for social and criminal risk situations, will have to be applied on an increasing scale, all the way to machine memorising and processing of the data. Criminology, like other disciplines, must take note of these new processes and adapt both its basic and its applied research to collecting the necessary information on such social risk phenomena by defining suitable criteria, especially from the point of view of the prevention of any social mis-development of juveniles. This in turn requires that criminology should improve its own apparatus of specific methods and techniques. This is discussed in Part IV of this book, where the necessary theoretical foundations of such work are outlined.

Closely connected with this is the application of new knowledge on the organisation of scientific work, an issue which is gaining increasing importance in step with the further evolution of the social system of socialism. It is a key problem for criminology, as for all other disciplines, continually to increase the social effectiveness of science and to make the most efficient and the most time- and effort-saving use of available potentialities. A brief attempt will be made to outline the problems involved and to hint at solutions still not available. [26] This is accompanied by the particular hope of the present authors that their readers will offer them their creative collaboration, especially in a field in which they themselves have only slight experience or are only about to consolidate their initial experiences.

The question of the socially most useful application of the findings of scientific criminology is largely also a problem of the relations of science and social practice. The effect which criminological science can exert upon practice depends largely on the prediction objectives which the party of the working class poses to the State and to society generally in connection with crime prevention and crime fighting. If — as is the case in the exploitative order — the premise of the eternal nature of criminality is maintained, then of course criminological science and practice cannot aim at or offer any constructive solutions for crime prevention or crime fighting.

The result is the relatively contemplative approach found in bourgeois criminology, an approach purely along roads which avoid touching on the social status quo. Joachim Hellmer, who specialises in questions of the struggle against criminality, thus arrives at proposals which, in their negative statement, speak for themselves without any need for further interpretation on our side. He sees the main aspect of the struggle against crime in a reform of the consciousness and in changes in the 'social value structure'. In this connection he states:

> One could bring the wife and mother back into the family, at least where there are children and juveniles; one could reduce the ceaseless propagation of more prosperity, larger fortunes and bigger consumption and hence the continuous talk of money, wage rates, pay, social product, taxes, etc.; one could reduce the massive pressure of

18

sales publicity and over-supply of goods; one might offer improved educational prospects; one could set up all-day schools ...; one could provide stimuli for the individual, above all for young people, to take on responsibilities in social groups, in their occupation, in charitable organisations, and in political life, starting from the municipality ... [27]

Criminological science and practice in the German Democratic Republic, basing itself upon the development of socialist social relations and the development of the personality of the socialist individual, in line with the objectives mapped out by the socialist Constitution, are striving to find constructive ways of further reducing criminality. In these endeavours effective and durable results are possible only if the demands of crime prevention and crime fighting are ever more efficiently integrated as a system into the social processes and the social evolution guided by the State and by society. On the basis of the general social evolution, therefore, efforts are being made in the GDR to integrate scientific research and practical crime prevention and crime fighting. These efforts have already opened up certain roads, though a number of problems are still awaiting satisfactory solutions.

1   It was necessary to integrate criminological research into the research system of the social sciences. This was achieved, among other things, by the decision of the Political Bureau of the SED Central Committee of 22 October 1968 on the further development of the Marxist—Leninist social sciences in the GDR and by the setting up of key research institutions which would guide research efforts towards specific focal problems and concert the work of different researchers. In the field of criminal law and criminological research concerned with crime prevention and crime fighting and for jurisprudence research generally this task of acting as a key research institution is discharged by the German Academy for Constitutional Law and Jurisprudence (DASR).

2   It is necessary to direct and focus all available capacities in the field of criminality research towards a unified and concerted thematic plan, i.e. to develop comprehensive research. This task is similarly being discharged, vis-à-vis the various research teams in the law departments of the universities, by the DASR. It functions as the principal customer and concludes appropriate research contracts with such research teams.

3   The research subjects — considering the predictive development tendencies of society generally — must spring from the needs of social practice. A system has therefore been developed under which the leading practical bodies directly responsible in law for the prevention of crime and

19

the struggle against crime will submit their proposals for a predictively oriented research programme adapted always to the general five-year long-term planning period. These plan proposals will then be discussed in the Council for Constitutional and Law Research of the GDR, passed on to the Council of Ministers in the form of a precise proposal and approved by the Council as a plan assignment. The results of the research conducted on this basis will be applied and justified by the practical bodies. Formulation of the need and assignment of the research task involve the obligation that the research programme is carried out as a co-operative task jointly by scientists and practitioners.

4 Researches into problems of criminality are effective only if they are broadly based both on scientific theory and on scientific organisation. Co-operation between scientists and field workers is one way of solving this problem theoretically and organisationally. Connected with this, however, is also the task of uniting the work of such disciplines as jurisprudence, philosophy, sociology, educational science, psychology and medicine. The results of such complex joint work enable such social measures and changes to be proposed as are optimally suited to the existing conditions of development and the demands of the system of socialist society; in this way losses through friction are avoided. In this respect we still possess untapped reserves which might be utilised by the development of scientific-organisational co-operation between diverse disciplines.

5 Effective research also demands a solution to the organisational problem of establishing a whole system for transmitting research results into practice. In this respect the first results have already been achieved inasmuch as the central organs of the socialist judiciary are under a statutory obligation to introduce into their practice any research results that have been successfully tested. Socialist criminal law implies such an obligation for all bodies and institutions of the State. An analogous regulation exists for juvenile research. In addition, this problem might be solved even more extensively if the system of further education were consistently used to make university staff familiar with the latest research results. The scientific potential of students and/or participants in postgraduate courses would also be more effectively developed by studies which are both research-related and practice-related. Our educational system should therefore be viewed also as involved in the direct transmission of research results into social practice.

6 Finally an optimal organisation of scientific effort demands the direct involvement of scientists also in controlling posts in central bodies. Thus, scientists are being enlisted by the managements of central bodies concerned with crime prevention and crime fighting to work in administrative

teams in those bodies. In this way the necessary flow of information between theory and practice is made even more direct and personal. At the same time an opportunity is being created for the utilisation of scientific discoveries through the direct work of scientists in such bodies.

The first major steps have thus been taken towards an effective organisation of criminological research. A number of important questions still await answers — such as the development of content criteria for a long-range strategic research concept which, by thorough fundamental research in the present, would make it possible to develop questions of significance for the future shaping of crime prevention and crime fighting. This applies also to various other problems which cannot here be specified. None the less the authors hope that their book will stimulate discussion and argument, and perhaps even contribute towards the solution of some problem or other. They look forward to reader reaction and will be grateful for any criticism.

Berlin
August 1970

The authors

Notes

[1] H. Hörz, 'Die Rolle statistischer Gesetze in den Gesellschaftswissenschaften und ihre Bedeutung für die Prognose', *Deutsche Zeitschrift für Philosophie*, 1968, Issue 3, pp. 327 ss.

[2] Cf. S.L. Rubinstein, *Sein und Bewusstsein*, Berlin 1962, esp. chapter III.

[3] F.N. Fedoseyev, 'Eine lenkende und führende Kraft — das ist unsere Partei', *Horizont*, 1970, no. 26, p. 9.

[4] Cf. esp. Part I, pp. 107 ss.

[5] Cf. also R. Hartmann, 'Die bürgerliche Kriminologie am Scheidewege', in: *Wissenschaftliche Zeitschrift der Humboldt-Universität, Gesellschafts- und Sprachwissenschaftliche Reihe*, Berlin 1968, Issue 5, pp. 653 ss.

[6] G. Kaiser, *Festschrift für Hans v. Hentig*, Hamburg 1967, p. 231. Kaiser reports that 'a high crime rate' is interpreted by some criminologists as an 'index of affluence' (J.B. Mays, *Crime and Social Structure*, London 1963, p. 201).

[7] Cf. H. Popitz, 'Über die Preventivwirkung des Nichtwissens', *Recht und Staat*, Tübingen 1968, no. 350.

[8] M. Lopez-Rey, 'Umfassendes Ziel der zeitgenössischen Kriminologie',

Kriminalistik, Hamburg 1968, December issue, p. 3.

[9] Ibid. (present authors' italics).

[10] J. Hellmer, 'Kriminalitätsentwicklung und -abwehr in der Demokratie', *Recht und Staat*, Tübingen 1969, no. 380, p. 19.

[11] On the concept of 'crime policy' cf. Gerhard Stiller, 'Aktuelle Schlussfolgerungen aus der Leninschen Lehre für die sozialistische Rechtstheorie', *Staat und Recht*, 1970, Issue 4, pp. 575 ss.

[12] K. Hager, 'Gesellschaftswissenschaften auf neuen Wegen', *Neues Deutschland* of 1 May 1965, B edition, p. 7.

[13] It is impossible to list all the solutions here. Specialised bibliographies listing such studies are published by the 'Walter Ulbricht' German Academy of Constitutional Law and Jurisprudence, DDR-1502 Potsdam-Babelsberg, Dokumentations- und Informationsstelle, and may be obtained from that address.

[14] Cf. 'Materialien der Sitzung des Verfassungs- und Rechtsausschusses der Volkskammer der DDR vom 26. November 1969', *Aus der Tätigkeit der Volkskammer und ihrer Ausschüsse*, Issue 16, 5th electoral period, Berlin 1969.

[15] F. Ebert, Friedrich Engels — Mitbegründer des wissenschaftlichen Sozialismus, *Materialien der 'Internationalen wissenschaftlichen Konferenz anlässlich der 150. Wiederkehr des Geburtstages von Friedrich Engels'*, Berlin 1970, p. 11, with a quotation from Walter Ulbricht in: *20 Jahre DDR*, Berlin 1969, pp. 32 ss.

[16] Cf. also the summing-up of the Marxist—Leninist overall concept in J. Streit, 'Probleme des Kampfes gegen die Kriminalität in der DDR', *Sozialistische Demokratie*, 1968, no. 38, pp. 3 ss.; also by the same author, 'Erfahrungen mit dem neuen Strafrecht der Deutschen Demokratischen Republik', *Sozialistische Demokratie*, 1970, no. 30, p. 3; cf. also E. Buchholz/R. Hartmann/I. Schaefer, 'Zum Wesen der Kriminalität in der DDR', *Neue Justiz*, 1969, no. 6, pp. 165 ss.

[17] Cf. also the study published by J. Lekschas even before the present book, 'Zur materiellen Eigenschaft der Straftaten', *Neue Justiz*, 1963, no. 24, pp. 779 ss.; the same author on the problem of international criminal law in: 'Materialien der Sitzung des Verfassungs- und Rechtsausschusses der Volkskammer der DDR vom 19. Juni 1969', *Aus der Tätigkeit der Volkskammer und ihrer Ausschüsse*, Issue 14, 5th electoral period, Berlin 1969, pp. 67 ss.

[18] On this subject cf. the main document, 'Die Aufgabe des Kampfes gegen den Imperialismus in der gegenwärtigen Etappe und die Aktionseinheit der kommunistischen und Arbeiterparteien, aller antiimperialistischen Kräfte' of 17 June 1969, in: *Internationale Beratung der kom-*

munistischen und Arbeiterparteien in Moskau – Dokumente, Dietz Verlag, Berlin 1969, p. 9.

[19] The question of the social character of a totality of social phenomena cannot be answered by reference to marginal cases. Criminal law, of course, must take note even of such marginal cases, as is proved by the regulations on non-accountability and diminished responsibility, etc.

[20] Cf. the demand of J. Streit, loc.cit.

[21] Cf. footnote 13.

[22] Cf. H. Harrland/M. Meyer/R. Hiller/H. Schwarz, *Kriminalstatistik-Leitfaden*, Berlin 1968.

[23] Cf. J. Streit, loc.cit.

[24] Cf. *Kriminalstatistik-Leitfaden*, loc.cit.

[25] As an example we refer to 'Grundlagen des Modells eines Systems der Kriminalitätsvorbeugung in kreisangehörigen Städten', *Neue Justiz*, 1968, no. 22. Further details may be found in the specialised bibliographies of the German Academy of Constitutional Law and Jurisprudence.

[26] We are here making use of arguments contained in an unpublished report drawn up by R. Hartmann, J. Lekschas and G. Stiller for the VIth International Congress of Criminologists (September 1970).

[27] J. Hellmer, loc.cit., p. 25.

PART I

Theoretical Foundations of Socialist Criminology

1   The Subject of Socialist Criminology

The development of socialist criminology

In order to define the subject of a science which has only recently been developing into a recognised independent scientific discipline, it is necessary to look more closely at the process of its emergence. John Desmond Bernal, in his work *Science in History*,[1] has demonstrated convincingly that the emergence of new sciences or branches of science is intimately linked with the historical development of society, with the emergence of new tasks which society is compelled to solve for the sake of its further development. From such new historical tasks springs the need for a scientific search for ways of solving them. In this connection it is often found that these new branches of science initially unfold as elements or constituent parts of another science and only become independent when a sufficient quantity and quality of new knowledge, together with independent methods of scientific work, have developed so that the independent existence of the new scientific discipline has become a condition for the further growth of the new line of study.

This general tendency in the development of sciences is reflected also in the emergence of socialist criminology. This — as may be observed also in other socialist countries[2] — is connected with the general social task of checking and progressively reducing both criminal behaviour and its causes in the process of the further evolution of socialist society. The more realistic this objective became on the basis of the development and consolidation of socialist social relations, the more urgent became the need to subject criminality, its structure and trends, as well as the causes of this negative and progress-impeding phenomenon, to a thorough examination. State and society require such scientific investigations in order to be able to conduct the struggle for the reduction of criminality more systematically and purposefully.

Socialist criminology, therefore, differs even in the social causes of its origin from bourgeois criminology which regards criminal behaviour as equally as permanent as society itself.[3] The development of bourgeois criminology is connected with the collapse of all those illusions about

27

bourgeois society which regarded this society as homogeneous and free from profound internal contradictions and which therefore concluded that criminality was no more than the wickedness of the individual.[4] In fact, however, criminality and its persistent increase reflected for the bourgeois system such disturbing contradictions that they called for an explanation. This need of the ruling circles and of the State thus gave rise to bourgeois criminology, whose 'objective' — if one may call it that — was, at the most, confined to explaining this phenomenon and developing proposals for the mitigation of the social conflicts reflected in criminal behaviour, but was not aimed at liquidating the phenomenon.

Socialist criminology thus differs from bourgeois criminology not merely in that it is the criminology of a qualitatively different social system — the socialist system — and that it is based on a different theoretical foundation — the Marxist—Leninist ideology — but also in its entirely novel task, which is to liquidate criminal behaviour. Hence socialist criminology should not be regarded as the continuation of bourgeois criminology on a higher level. Neither in its theoretical foundations, nor in its origin, nor yet in its method of interpreting the phenomena can it be understood as the successor of bourgeois criminology in a socialist political system.

Seen historically, the first beginnings of a Marxist criminology data back to 1845, the year in which Friedrich Engels published *The Position of the Working Class in England* — what in modern terminology would be described as a sociological study — and in this context discovered several essential laws on the origin and trend of criminality in capitalist society.[5]

In view of subsequent theoretical studies by Karl Marx and Friedrich Engels on problems of criminality and its causes, found in a whole series of their works, we are entitled to state that the foundations of a Marxist criminology, even though it did not then lay claim to this name, developed in parallel, as it were, to the emergence of a bourgeois criminology. This had its cause, on the one hand, in that an all-embracing social theory like Marxism could not in silence pass over such an elementary social phenomenon as criminality. On the other hand, crime in the early stages of the development of bourgeois society was a phenomenon which occurred with a high incidence among the proletariat, which was then developing into a class, and therefore necessarily attracted the attention of the theoreticians of the working class. Thirdly, there was an obligation on the working class, even while it was developing into a class — and, more particularly, developing its organisations — to overcome crime as a method of struggle against the ruling classes if it wanted to become the leading force in the nation.[6]

We can therefore record here the historically significant phenomenon that, even while it was still shaping itself into a class — i.e. roughly in the second third of the last century — the working class embarked on the struggle for overcoming criminality. By criminality we do not mean those patterns of behaviour which were persecuted as punishable acts by the feudal or bourgeois rulers because of their revolutionary, or even merely socially progressive, character. As Jean-Paul Marat pointed out early on, such patterns of action have essentially nothing in common with criminality. While the working class was subject to the rule of the exploiters, its efforts to free itself from criminality were naturally confined to preventing its own class comrades from seeking a way out of its crushing antagonisms by criminal behaviour. Such attempts, as Engels demonstrated by historical instances, could only do harm to individual workers and to the working class movement. If, then and later, workers nevertheless allowed themselves to be swept into criminal behaviour then they were doing so no longer as representatives of their class but as human beings who had been driven into desperation or been demoralised by the devastating antagonisms of the exploitative society.

A striking feature of this Marxist criminology was that it treated crime not just as a normative phenomenon of criminal law but as a problem of reality. The Marxist criminological considerations showed:

Criminality is explained as a social phenomenon by the limited state of productivity of human society and the resultant form of production in the shape of man's exploitation of man, as reflected in the private ownership of the means of production. This private ownership inevitably produces selfishness and individualism as the basic pattern of social behaviour in man. From private ownership inevitably springs alienation, conflict between individuals and an antagonism between individual and society.

Private ownership with its struggle of each against each, with its transformation of all human values into merchandise, leads to progressive demoralisation.

Although capitalism also results in a development of productive forces, exploitation and the chase after profits simultaneously result in an exacerbation of social contradictions so that the raising of social productivity is accompanied by progressive loneliness, isolation and alienation. The raising of the material prosperity of society and the growth of the national revenue cannot therefore lead to a drop in criminality but on the contrary cause a sharp exacerbation of all selfish and individualist patterns of behaviour, resulting in increased criminality.

The conclusion of these findings inevitably is the demand to overcome a society which of necessity produces criminality in a growing measure.

This finding represents the most remarkable achievement of Marxist criminology during the pre-socialist period. By standing squarely on the ground of strict scientific method it was found to lead to a revolutionary critique of society, i.e. the general Marxist doctrine of society.

Regarded in this light, socialist criminology is by no means devoid of tradition. But this tradition must not be sought in bourgeois criminology. Socialist criminology — and here we do not share the pessimism of the Hungarian criminologist Andras Szabó,[7] a man whom we regard as exceptionally meritorious — is not devoid of theoretically significant foundations. These foundations can be found in the general social theory of Marxism—Leninism, in the theory of the transition from capitalism to communism, in pre-socialist Marxist criminology and in the various socialist social sciences which concern themselves with human behaviour.

Like every other specialised branch of contemporary science, socialist criminology originated first within the body of another science. It has already been shown that the first Marxist criminological reflections were part and parcel of the general Marxist doctrine of society. They were — Engels's work is typical of this — embedded in the critique of bourgeois society generally even before the question of a specialised subject arose.

After the socialist revolution the findings of pre-socialist Marxist criminological reflections were absorbed into the socialist science of criminal law. Within this framework they existed as a general theory of the causes of criminal behaviour until the time came for them to develop into an independent criminology. From the moment, however, when socialist society first set itself the task of systematically and progressively overcoming criminality, their growth potential into a socialist criminology as an independent branch of scientific study began to be realised.

In the German Democratic Republic (GDR) its beginnings were the demand to investigate 'concretely the causes of crime', a demand raised in particular by Josef Streit in the discussion on *Class Struggle and Crime*.[8] Gradually the realisation gained ground that socialist judicial practice urgently required a scientific investigation of the causes of crime. The beginnings were studies by Axel Römer on homicidal offences, by Hans Weber and Gerhard Feix on sexual offences, by Kurt Grathenauer on offences against property committed by juveniles, by Günther Jäger on offences in the building industry, by Walter Griebe on offences against property in the countryside, by Otto Kraft on the poisoning of livestock,

30

by Gert Schwarz on squandering offences, by Karl-Martin Böhme on offences in railway transport, by Otto Dierl on offences in pit railway operation, by Kurt Manecke on offences in the field of labour protection,[9] by Walter Orschekowski, Kurt Manecke, Hans Sahre on thefts in HO department stores in Leipzig, [10] etc.

These studies — which were of not inconsiderable value for their time even though, unfortunately, the public took only limited notice of them — are characterised by the fact that they combine aspects of criminal law study and the first aspects of socialist criminology. In consequence, while presenting a relatively complex picture of the tasks posed, they also suggested that criminal law study and criminology could not in the long run continue as a unified science, except at the cost of examination in depth on both sides. The development of socialism, however, demanded on the one hand a higher quality of judicial practice — with particular reference to the study of criminal law and criminal procedure — and on the other the development of a system of administrative and social measures designed to overcome criminality and its causes, a task involving in particular the participation of socialist criminology and other social sciences. Parallel with this development within the domain of criminal law study, medicine (more precisely, psychiatry) in the GDR was trying to comprehend scientifically the phenomenon of criminal behaviour, the principal names in this field being Hans Szewczyk, Hanns Schwarz, Gerhard Göllnitz and Karl-Heinz Mehlan.

A particular stimulus to the development of socialist criminology came from the study of juvenile behaviour. It was here that legislative practice discovered, sooner than in other fields, that juvenile criminality could not be a subject merely for criminal lawyers and also that it was virtually impossible to try to understand its nature solely on the basis and with the methods of criminal law study. For that reason some complex scientific work started in this area at a relatively early date, and this proved more productive than any specialised single-discipline research. This was shown clearly in the studies of Richard Hartmann. But this stage of the development is still characterised by a quantitative compilation of the findings of different lines of research rather than by unified criminological investigation.

Criminological research in the GDR received important help and stimulus from the Party's criticism of the work of criminal law research in 1962 and from the GDR State Council's decree of 4 April 1963 on the fundamental tasks and working methods of judicial organs. This decree, which was immensely important for all practical and scientific development, proclaimed the consistent and systematic struggle 'for the overcoming of criminality, one of the ugliest after-effects of the exploitative society finally liquidated in the German Democratic Republic and of that society's wolfish laws' (Section 1; Principles) as a task to be discharged by the State in the scientific guidance of society. In this context the Prosecutor General was charged with the responsibility for 'analysis of criminality and its trends, the causes and circumstances of major and minor criminal offences [*Verbrechen und Vergehen*] as well as the operation and the acievements of the struggle against criminal acts'. It was laid down that this task was to be discharged 'in collaboration with other judicial and investigatory central organs and with scientific institutions'. The setting up of a Department for Scientific Criminality Research and a corresponding advisory council under the Prosecutor General, as well as the improvement of criminal statistics, were major steps which decisively influenced criminological research in the GDR.

The fundamental theoretical reorientation which followed gave rise to such studies as Erich Buchholz's on theft and Gerhard Knobloch's on the personality of offenders against socialist property; these already showed a stronger emphasis on empirical research into criminal behaviour and, more particularly, tested document analysis and the use of observation forms in investigations as criminal research methods. [11] These first beginnings of criminological work were followed by further 'empirical' researches into criminal behaviour; these were the subject of a number of research papers. At the same time, major practical efforts were put in hand to analyse criminality and its causes and to categorise trends in criminality under a number of different headings. Particularly successful was the development of new criminal statistical records, a development not yet completed but one which already shows that with it the GDR will receive the most up-to-date scientific criminal statistics and hence an outstanding tool for conducting the struggle against criminality.

The time had come to turn to the foundations of further criminological research. Naturally the theory of the causes of criminality had to stand at the beginning of these studies, providing as it did the theoretical basis for the planning and scope of research into the causes of criminality. This task was tackled first in a number of contributions to specialised periodicals, all of which clearly reflected an endeavour to adopt a new dialectical-materialist point of view as against earlier views. Important as the findings of these studies were, they did not yet lead to any useful guideline for further investigation, largely because of a clinging to the view that criminality is principally due to ideological causes. [12]

The first conspicuous success was the study by Hartmann and John Lekschas, *Notes on the Theory of Causes, Conditions and Circumstances of Criminality in the GDR.* This developed the state of the discussion on the causes of criminality as it was at the beginning of 1964, and more particularly as it was set out in the work of Soviet and Czechoslovak jurists and criminal law theoreticians in the GDR, and — proceeding from the newest findings of Marxist philosophy — the attempt was made to develop a unified theoretical concept of the causes of criminality in a socialist society.

The next stage was the development of the methods of criminological research. Valuable groundwork had been done by Harri Harrland with his study of criminal statistics.[13] A further step was the application and testing of statistical correlation calculations in the work of Arno Lutzke, Rolf Schubert and Werner Petasch on traffic offences[14] and the theoretical work on the application of mathematical methods in the investigation of traffic offences by Eckbert Klusener.[15] These attempts to work out or try out specific methods were followed by Gerhard Stiller's work[16] on methodological problems of criminology, which represented the conclusion of a further stage in the evolution of a socialist criminology in the GDR. An equally valuable contribution came from actual practice, where scientific methods had begun to be applied in analysis, and from the first symposium for the struggle against juvenile crime, organised in 1964 by the Institute for Criminal Law of the Humboldt University and in a number of contributions on methodological aspects.[17]

An additional factor was that sociology and psychology had made considerable progress in recent years and had provided valuable impulses for the development of a methodology of criminology.

Thus socialist criminology finds itself confronted with the question as to its subject and its objectives. The question is whether criminology is an independent science, and what its relationship is to criminal law study, to sociology, to forensic psychology and to psychiatry, and to other sciences concerned with man's social behaviour. These are not merely academic problems, to be answered one way or another without affecting the aims of research or its results. They are important questions for administrative practice, affecting the necessary scientific foundations of the conduct of the struggle against criminality and its causes, the composition and training of the necessary personnel, the organisation of scientific and practical investigations, etc.

The subject of criminology

Since criminology in the socialist countries has predominantly developed within the body of criminal law study, the first question one must ask is that of its relationship to criminal law study. Misgivings have been voiced about recognising criminology as an independent discipline because this might in a sense deprive criminal law study of the sociological foundation it had built up for itself in its first studies in the field of criminology, thus leaving criminal law study purely as a normative positivist concern. These misgivings are supported by the fact that a new line of study has been developing within criminal law study, namely the sociology of penal and educative measures, including the study of the application of penalties; thus another substantial portion would be removed from criminal law study.

These misgivings cannot be lightly dismissed; indeed they are lent weight by, for example, Szabó, who sees the essential distinction between criminal law study and criminology in the fact that the former is concerned with the criminal offence as 'a legal phenomenon' while criminology is concerned with criminality as 'a social phenomenon'.[18] This is reminiscent of the distinction made by bourgeois scholarship between 'descriptive sciences' and 'normative sciences'. Bourgeois science similarly holds that criminology looks upon criminality as a 'real' phenomenon while criminal law study sees it as a 'normative' or 'dogmatic' phenomenon. Criminal law study — according to Armand Mergen — is of a purely speculative nature whereas criminology is realistic, and quite the opposite of speculation.[19] This distinction and separation of juridical sciences from other sciences, among which criminology wishes to be included and, up to a point, has a right to be included — a distinction made by nearly all bourgeois scholars — is by no means a scientifically or logically indispensable sub-division of sciences but merely reflects the antagonism which rends bourgeois society. Criminology does not wish to be a 'humanity' but lays claim to the status of a natural science.

The reason for this is not that what are known as humanities or social sciences must necessarily be speculative, as Mergen assumes. In the course of development of bourgeois class society into capitalist and imperialist society the 'humanities' came under the dictatorship of the ruling capitalist class and developed into intellectual tools for the rule of this class. As the antagonism between the people and the bourgeoisie became exacerbated and the social basis of rule in capitalist society, by its development into imperialism, became increasingly narrowed down to monopoly capital and its militarist hangers-on, and the conflict between objective social necessity and imperialist rule became increasingly deep-seated, the so-called humanities became increasingly alienated from reality and increasingly ignored the exigencies of life. In the juridical field this was reflected by the conflict between law and life, which for juridical science in the service of the ruling class meant the transition to a crude positivism. Within such a juridical science the emergence of a scientific trend which wished to, or had to, regard criminality as a real-life phenomenon, was simply impossible. Any subjection of criminology to such a science of law was bound to lead to the end of criminology as a science. Mergen's opposition to such tendencies is therefore to be applauded. Nevertheless his distinctive criterion cannot be accepted because it is not based on a real scientific principle of differentiation between sciences but merely tries to make a virtue of a necessity inherent in bourgeois society. Anyone wishing to find a proper solution to the problem must refuse to be persuaded to accept criteria for the differentiation of sciences which spring from the antagonisms of bourgeois society – with all due respect for the honest endeavours of bourgeois criminologists. Otherwise he would unwittingly adopt the class-conditioned mental patterns of these bourgeois sciences.

Like criminology, the theory of criminal law also regards criminality and the criminal offence as a real social phenomenon. The major or minor criminal offence is to it not merely a normative affair but a reality of life. In this respect, therefore, Szabó's thesis that criminal law theory regards the criminal offence merely as a juridical phenomenon is not a real clue to a genuine delimitation criterion but a fallacy. As for criminology, it likewise regards criminality not just as a social phenomenon but also as a juridical phenomenon. The law is not some abstract norm existing somewhere and somehow, but an instrument for the shaping of the life processes of society and hence a necessary part and a necessary aspect of these social processes and phenomena themselves. A phenomenon in the life of society becomes 'criminal' to the extent that it is treated as such by socialist law. The concept of criminality necessarily contains legal aspects. Criminality does not appear in two separate forms – that of a criminal offence under the law and that of a social phenomenon.

Criminal law theory and criminology therefore share the same concept of criminality and criminal offence with sociology, psychology and psychiatry. The relationship of criminal law theory and criminology to the criminal offence itself is likewise the same. Thus the attempt to draw a line between criminology and criminal law theory – the one viewing criminality only as a social phenomenon and the other as a juridical phenomenon – falls flat.

Finally, criminal law theory and criminology are interdependent. Criminal law theory, for instance, has developed objective and subjective criteria of what is to be treated as a criminal offence or as criminal behaviour and what is covered by legislative practice; criminology accepts all this as

the tacit prerequisite of its own work. Criminal law theory, in turn, utilises the findings of criminology by developing them into new scientific
and legislative knowledge. Neither of the two disciplines is the prerequisite
of the other but they are interdependent and cross-fertilise one another.

Nor will the differences between criminal law theory and criminology
be found in the general tasks mapped out for them. Not only these two
disciplines but all sciences concerned with the social behaviour of man —
from philosophy through economics to the specialised separate disciplines
— have to make their contribution, in conjuction with social practice, to
the liquidation of criminality; each of them, however, must do this from
its own specific knowledge, from the observation and scientific analysis of
their common subject.

Again, the differences cannot be found in the assertion that criminology looks upon criminality as a social phenomenon generally while criminal law theory looks upon the individual act. Criminal law theory does not
examine only the individual act; in fact, it is its task to develop a whole
series of meaningful generalisations. To this end it must examine criminality both as a social phenomenon and as an individual act. On the other
hand, criminology cannot avoid investigating the criminal act because
otherwise it would not be in a position to judge the social phenomenon as
such.

Care will therefore have to be taken to avoid misleading boundary lines.
In order to draw the line between certain social sciences — and these
include both criminology and criminal law theory — it is necessary to
remember the general criteria which distinguish one social science from
another.

In the study of law it was customary at one time to see the principal
differentiation of the various fields of study in the fact that they would
regulate different social conditions. Although this is an aspect worth considering, it is not the sole criterion. Thus, constitutional law regulates
certain fundamental problems of criminal law while, on the other hand,
criminal law regulates certain definite constitutional relationships. Soviet
science has pointed out that there are delimitation criteria contained also
in the method of regulation of processes by the State. Eventually the
realisation prevailed that any delimitation within jurisprudence must take
account of the degree of generalisation of the different fields of study.
Thus the theory of law differs from the various specialised fields of study
not in that it deals with different relationships but in that it embodies
more general correlations or principles which underlie all relationships and
processes forming the subject of the theory of law. The common denomi-
nator of the social sciences is the fact that they are all concerned with the

laws of trends in human society and its structure, the distinction between the major disciplines resting in the fact that they are concerned with different forms or aspects of the movements in society.

One of the most recent findings of the socialist social sciences is that the management of society is part of their subject. Each discipline makes its own contribution to the management and regulation of social processes. In this sense it can be said that society in the social sciences is aware of the different forms of its movement and of the control of this movement, of its own life manifestations and functions. Another realisation is the fact that the manifestations of the life of society, as viewed by different disciplines, are inevitably of a complex nature so that the individual field of study — apart from Marxist philosophy and sociology — cannot always view the whole phenomenon but in principle always only one side of an integral process. The aspects for defining the subject of a science and its boundary lines with another are therefore of a multiple nature.

If one proceeds from these aspects one finds that the *subject of criminal law theory* is determined both by criminal law and its application to the individual case and also by the totality of State and social jurisdiction. The tasks of criminal law theory are mapped out by socialist criminal law and the practice of criminal law. Criminality as a social phenomenon and the criminal act as a concrete individual phenomenon thus become subjects of examination of criminal law theory. The principal objective of criminal law theory thus coincides with the objective of socialist criminal law as a specific instrument of the State for the liquidation of criminality. This principal aspect is characterised by the problem of responsibility and guilt under criminal law, its conditions, aspects and its realisation in the totality of legal practice just as in each individual decision. Criminal law theory is concerned with the tasks, the function and the limits of criminal law and the application of criminal law. The objective is the development of criminal law practice into an instrument for the guidance of human beings — of the punishable individual as much as the whole of society — towards a fully responsible attitude; this must be done by realising the individual criminal-law responsibility of the offender against the law and by the enlistment of social forces for the implementation of the socialist principles of law.

The theory of criminal law is concerned with criminality from the point of view of gaining a deeper understanding and increasing the effectiveness of socialist criminal law and the practice of law. Criminality is of interest, first of all, as the subject of criminal legislation generally. Proceeding from real-life phenomena, criminal law theory analyses the structure of criminal behaviour. It defines and categorises the various criminal phenomena according to their essential characteristics and necessarily develops this activity to the finest analysis in order to map out specific characteristics for the various groups of offences, for individual types and variants of these types, with a view to providing legal practice with scientifically founded criteria for the application of the criminal laws. Secondly, criminal law science examines criminality as a general phenomenon and as an individual act from the point of view of State or social measures involving individual responsibility; the aim here is to evolve the most purposeful and efficient system of measures and also of specific qualitative and quantitative assessment principles for the administration of justice in the individual case.

A whole number of further aspects could be listed to show that criminality is not viewed by criminal law theory (at least by socialist criminal law theory) as a positivist normative phenomenon, or exclusively in this light, but as a real social phenomenon. At the same time it is obvious — and this to us seems to be the real criterion of its subject in respect of criminality — that it must necessarily examine criminality from the point of view of the implementation of the tasks of socialist criminal law as an instrument for the development of the individual's socialist relations with the State, with society and with each other. These tasks extend just as far as the means available to criminal law. These are the measures of individual responsibility under criminal law.

In the investigation of criminal phenomena the main problem for criminal law theory is how to develop individual responsibility under criminal law into an optimally effective contribution, and how to check criminality, reduce it and finally liquidate it. This responsibility is by no means regarded by criminal law theory as a merely normative problem of constructing juridical concepts but as a social-psychological and sociological fact. We can therefore state that the theory of criminal law examines criminality as a social phenomenon and as an individual phenomenon with a view to the elaboration of scientific principles for the determination of the prerequisites, nature and extent of the individual's responsibility under criminal law. In doing so it pursues a scientific objective which can be tackled only by it and by its means, and in doing so it accepts from all other disciplines concerned with man's social behaviour those findings and results which are significant for the scientific determination of responsibility. It does not therefore exist in the kind of normative seclusion that is typical of bourgeois criminal law theory.

The same applies to the problem of the causes of criminality. It is by no means the case that the determination and examination of these causes are the exclusive preserve of criminology. However, criminal law theory is generally concerned with the causes of criminality only to the extent to which they are significant for the determination of responsibility on the legislative scale or on the scale applying to the administration of justice in the individual case. Criminal law theory cannot close its eyes to the problems of the causes of criminality, but it is chiefly interested in the conclusions drawn from these causes as they apply to the determination of responsibility and less in the causes as social phenomena.

The measures concerning criminal responsibility which are available to the judicial organs are capable only to a limited extent of removing the causes of criminality. But, even so, these measures contribute to their removal. A higher degree of people's personal responsibility, such as must be achieved by socialist legal practice, is apt to liquidate such remnants of isolation of people from each other as are reflected in criminal behaviour. But these survivals are only part of a system of conditions which we call the causes of criminality because somebody occupying an isolated position within society — whether through his own fault or not — is considerably more inclined to make a criminally wrong decision than anybody else. Unpunished criminality encourages other similar acts. The criminal responsibility of the individual counteracts this. It leads, eventually, to the liquidation of the causes of criminality by contributing towards the education of the offender and hence liquidating the causes of criminality within the offender's personality. These are three highly important aspects of the individual's criminal responsibility, aspects of importance in the struggle against the causes of criminality. However, they also mark the limits of the efficacy of criminal responsibility. Simultaneously they mark the boundaries of criminal law theory and its contribution towards the liquidation of the causes of criminality. This is not to say that present-day criminal law theory and criminal law practice have already reached their full effectiveness in the area here discussed. Indeed it should be pointed out, in line with the demands made by the State Council, that the execution of individual judicial actions might be more effective if all endeavours were consciously focused on working in this threefold way towards the liquidation of identified causes and conditions of criminal acts and thus turning these proceedings into a lesson for society.

If reference is made here to the limitations on the removal of the causes of criminality by way of the realisation of the individual's responsibility, this must not be confused with the tasks of the judicial organs in the liquidation of the causes of criminality. These go beyond the boundaries of the realisation of the individual's criminal responsibility and also beyond the findings which criminal law theory can provide.

Here then begins the practical field of activity of criminology. Criminology is the study of the causes of criminality and the laws underlying its operation in the sense of social (material and ideological) phenomena, as well as the contribution to the elaboration of principles designed to reduce and progressively liquidate criminality by means of comprehensive social and State measures necessary and feasible within the framework of the further systematic transformation of society in the direction of communism. The question arises in this context of whether the phenomenology — the structure and movement as well as the manifestations of the criminal offences — is not also the subject of criminology, especially as most studies described as criminological studies are predominantly phenomenological. Apart from a few fundamental theoretical statements on the causes of criminality we find valid statements at present chiefly in the phenomenological field. However, in our view, phenomenology does not represent the particular subject of criminology even though criminology must work in a phenomenological way. The phenomenology of criminality is the subject both of criminal law theory — which to date has accomplished the most important discoveries in this field — and of criminology; and yet it is not. The phenomenology of criminality is for both disciplines only a transitional stage in the acquisition of knowledge but not an independent subject. Hence the thesis that criminality as a social phenomenon is the subject of criminology does not contain the whole truth because it is open to a purely phenomenological interpretation. But that would be the end of criminology, its decline into purely empirical and relatively purposeless considerations.

Similarly we do not believe that Szabó correctly defined the task of criminology when he stated that the subject of socialist criminology was criminality as a *real phenomenon* whereas other disciplines regarded it as a socially *possible* form of deviant behaviour.[20] In so far as philosophy, sociology or psychology concern themselves with criminality they do so, within the scope of their particular tasks, both as a real and as a possible form of human behaviour, and the same is true of criminology. For it, too, criminality is at the same time reality and possibility — and there is no reason to think that anything is to be gained by making a distinction between criminality as a real and as a possible deviant behaviour pattern in order to define the boundary line between different disciplines. Certainly we have not so far found such a differentiation criterion to be of any real use. The problems of reality and possibility are problems which must necessarily concern any science aiming at discovering the laws of any trend. But they cannot divide one discipline from another because they do not in fact denote different subjects.

Nor can there be any appreciable fundamental difficulties of delimitation vis-à-vis the theory of criminal investigation. The theory of criminal investigation is likewise concerned with the causes of criminality. It has long moved beyond the view that its task is confined to the development of procedures and techniques for the elucidation of individual actions and for the discovery of the offender. In line with the goals of socialist criminal law practice it must endeavour to develop methods for the comprehensive elucidation of all criminal offences. This necessarily includes the determination of their causes and conditions. On this point criminal investigation theory differs from criminology in that it aims at developing procedures and techniques for the discovery of the causes and conditions of a criminal offence such as are to be applied in their specific criminal proceedings by investigatory and fact-finding organs, and which serve the realisation of its specific tasks and objectives. The subject and tasks of criminology, on the other hand, go beyond the boundaries set by the specific criminal proceedings. Criminology and criminal investigation theory are thus necessarily closely linked and must complement and fertilise each other.

As for the relationship of criminology vis-à-vis sociology, we do not believe that any serious delimitation difficulties are likely to arise here. Any sociology which makes criminality and its causes the object of its researches must inevitably become criminology and adopt the research methods of criminology, i.e. sociology must turn into criminology whenever it wishes seriously to conduct research into criminality.

Matters are similar with regard to social psychology, which is concerned chiefly with the principal psychological determinants of human behaviour within definite groups. So long as it concerns itself merely with the general determinants of socially negative behaviour there will be no delimitation problems since it will be considering such socially negative behaviour on a higher level of generalisation. As soon, however, as it turns to the subject of criminality from its specific point of view it becomes criminology and — as in the case of sociology — must apply the methods of criminology unless it wishes to forgo all hope of coming to grips with the real material of its researches.

Criminology, which must concern itself both with the social and with the psychological problems of criminality and its origin, is thus a specialised discipline of a particular type vis-à-vis the two above-named sciences. This is true both of the phenomenological and of the aetiological sides of its work. We believe therefore that there is no such thing as special criminal sociology or criminal psychology or criminal psychiatry alongside criminology. These concepts merely describe partial areas of a comprehensive criminology. All these various trends of examination are part and parcel of a true socialist criminology.

The phenomenology of criminal offences or of criminality is not, as we have observed, the main subject of criminology or of criminal law theory. The phenomenological investigations which both these disciplines have to pursue are merely intermediate stages on the way to the real subject. Criminology conducts this phenomenology — i.e. the investigation of manifestations, the distribution in time and space of criminal behaviour, and any changes both generally and within the boundaries of specific categories of offences — merely in order to derive from these manifestations the relevant questions concerning the causes of criminality. Although the phenomenology of criminality is by no means the real subject of criminology, it is nevertheless absolutely indispensable since without a knowledge of the effect one cannot get down to its cause.

By describing the causes of criminality as the subject of criminology we find ourselves again in opposition to the suggestion of Szabó who, in his otherwise rather interesting study, believes that criminology should elucidate 'the individual's development into a criminal'. His ideas are most clearly expressed in the following sentence: 'Examination of the individual's development into a criminal as an object of pragmatic criminological research means the discovery of socially determined behaviour dispositions, i.e. the description of a behaviour model capable of explaining how criminal behaviour, which is treated by sociology and psychology as a possibility, becomes genuine reality.' Szabó believes that this 'limitation' of the subject is necessary because — so he claims — socialist criminology is unable, through the limited state of basic sociological and psychological knowledge, to answer the question of 'how the existence of criminality in socialist society is to be explained' — although he claims to acknowledge that the phenomenon of criminality is socially determined. [21]

Szabó's concept of the subject of criminology springs from the belief that he is unable at present to answer the question of why criminality exists but at the same time he is unwilling to abandon the position of its being socially determined. It seems rather strange to adopt, on the one hand, a general determinism and on the other to regard the determined character of concrete criminal phenomena in the socialist society as inexplicable, or to represent all previous explanations as being more or less speculative. Szabó's premise that criminality in the socialist society is inexplicable as a phenomenon is mistaken. The fact that a considerable unexplored area still exists in the field of the causes of criminality is no sufficient reason for narrowing down its subject. Every science has a certain unexplored region in front of it, a region it tries to cast light on, and indeed this contradiction between knowledge already gained and the awareness of lack of knowledge is one of the mainsprings of its further development. Socialist criminology, compared with other sciences, certainly has no cause for putting on sackcloth and ashes. Man in his social and individual processes is surely without doubt the most complex subject a science could investigate. Even his readily observable normal behaviour and the determination of what is to be regarded as normal are quite difficult enough — how much more difficult then is a form of behaviour such as criminality, a behaviour ultimately directed not only against the existing society but against the acting individual himself. We believe that, while criminology must certainly adopt a self-critical attitude to its findings, in view of the practical and scientific successes of socialist society there is no justification for the kind of pessimism that is found in bourgeois criminology.

It is the task of criminology, by investigating the causes, to provide both a scientific explanation of the existence of the phenomenon of criminality as a social phenomenon and also to discover the laws reflected in a certain criminal behaviour. *Criminology, therefore is the study of the laws governing the causation of criminality as a general social phenomenon and also as a specific individual act.* However, we do not believe that it is the task of criminology to discover some miraculous 'causant of criminality' or to embark on a chase after some random constellation of circumstances which in an individual X with personality factors Y at a point in time Z — this point in turn being characterised by circumstances A to W — produced the decision to commit one specific act and not another, in one place and not in another, and at one time and not at another. Such a line of approach, which leads the undoubtedly meritorious American criminologists Sheldon and Eleanor Glueck to the attempt — if we may exaggerate a little — to draw up for each inhabitant of a country a prognosis of criminality or non-criminality, seems to us unpromising. Such an approach merely tempts one to pursue chance and to negate the creative factor in man.

Criminology — no matter how imperfect or perfect it is — can invariably only discover *tendencies* to criminality and no more.

For criminology, criminality is both a real event, i.e. the given reality of hundreds, thousands, or hundreds of thousands, of criminal actions in the past and the immediate present, and it is equally a possibility, i.e. the criminality to be expected in the immediate and more distant future. Criminology, in fact, is concerned with criminality and its causes not merely in order to find an explanation for actual events in the past but in order to create the foundation for a comprehensive preventive struggle against criminality by liquidating its causes. In this task the scientific explanation of past events is an essential and indispensable step; but sight must not be lost of the ultimate objective. Any real criminology must therefore concern itself with prognosis, although in socialist criminology this has a different trend from prognosis in bourgeois criminology. Socialist criminology must, by means of its prognosis, supported by and proceeding from the general prognosis of the development of socialist society, furnish society with soundly grounded indications of which definite social (material and ideological) conditions or circumstances must be liquidated in order to ensure that people who might be exposed to the determining effects of such conditions or circumstances do not decide in favour of criminal misbehaviour. This is the true, the essentially prognostic, task of criminology.

There is, however, yet another aspect to prognosis, one which plays a part particularly in jurisdiction and youth work. We refer to the prediction of the future social behaviour or the further personality development of an individual who has become punishable. Every sentence, every decision of a conflict commission, makes a prognosis to the effect that the chosen measure is apt to lead a certain individual towards responsible behaviour. As for the assessment and determination of the predicted positive effectiveness of penal or educational measures — and this is not possible without a thorough knowledge of the personality of the offender and the potential educative effect of the chosen measures upon a certain individual — such a prognosis is not the business of criminology but of the theory of criminal law or the study of the effectiveness of State-imposed educational measures.

In our view, therefore, the criminology of socialist States must aim at positive prognosis, and this it is able to do. The foundations of socialist society, the basic economic, political and moral-cultural relationships of the individual with society, with the State and with one another provide, in principle, every opportunity for a forward-looking change of all relationships and conditions, every opportunity for arriving at such a resolution of contradictions as would exclude conflict-causing situations or conflicts between the individual and the fundamental rules of social behaviour. However, this opportunity does not unfold automatically but only in the train of systematical and purposeful actions by State and society.

The new social-economic structure of society demands that criminology, like any other science concerned with conflicts between the individual and society or between individuals among themselves, should orientate itself towards such a forward-looking prognostic activity. In this way it can overcome the pessimistic stage of prognosis, as inevitably inherent in bourgeois criminology, and must indeed do so because otherwise it would get bogged down at a stage of little use to society, and its work would be incomplete, socially disorientating, confusing or doubt-producing. Naturally, every positive prognosis made by socialist criminology inevitably also contains the statement that unless the requisite and possible changes are made in the social circumstances or the condition of a person a decline in the given criminal phenomenon cannot be expected. Nevertheless it is exceedingly important to the development of society whether a science contents itself with registering negative features and demonstrating the laws governing their effects or whether it simultaneously points the way towards their liquidation.

It is clear, therefore, that the subject of socialist criminology — regardless of what its actual present performance may be, both qualitatively and quantitatively — goes a long way beyond the determination of 'the individual's development into a criminal', as formulated by Szabó. Criminology must investigate which determinants emerge from definite conditions and complexes of conditions to direct an individual towards possible criminality. The task of assessing how the intersecting and interacting determinants have, in a particular person, at a particular time and at a particular place, led to a specific criminal decision is not one for criminology but properly belongs to each individual specific criminal proceeding. Only an examination designed specifically in relation to an individual phenomenon can discover how exactly that individual phenomenon has been caused.

There are close reciprocal relations between such proceedings and criminology, resulting in cross-fertilisation. But no science, however efficient, can relieve criminal proceedings of the task of investigating in the individual instance the actual transition from possibility to reality. There can be directives for this but no precise formula. This must necessarily remain the creative accomplishment of individual criminal proceedings since it is clear that this transition, the decision to commit a criminal act, must be different in each individual case. This decision is the result of a combination of the most diverse, often very dissimilar, circumstances so that it would be quite pointless to look for one single key or crystallisation point. Man, for better or worse, is a creative being who — disregarding automatic or motor actions — personally processes all external and internal circumstances into an independent decision on each conscious action. Man's creativity vis-à-vis the given objective and subjective factors is shown not only in positive but also in negative attitudes and decisions. Any criminology disregarding this fact would be hopelessly condemned to mechanistic limitation. There simply is no single formula to which every actual individual decision could be reduced or which might serve as a substitute for this decision of the individual; there cannot be such a formula — unless one follows Sigmund Freud and Theodor Reik to the far-fetched speculation that man becomes a criminal through a general sense of guilt and a need for punishment, or unless one asserts with Paul Reiwald and Armand Mergen that society needs the criminal for a release of its own subconscious emotions. [22]

The tasks of criminology

Another problem closely connected with the definition of the subject of criminology is whether this subject also includes the elaboration of a comprehensive system of methods designed to liquidate criminality and its causes. The Soviet criminologist Aleksey A. Gertsenson believes that, alongside the investigation of criminality and its causes, it is the task of criminology to design measures for the prevention of crime, measures aimed at the complete liquidation of criminality. [23] Similar formulations of the tasks are found in the basic programme of the Research Group for Juvenile Criminology attached to the Department for Youth Problems and in the long-term programme of the Scientific Advisory Council for Criminality Research under the GDR Prosecutor General.

Clear though the definition of these tasks is, it is nonetheless necessary to determine exactly the part to be played by criminology as a scientific discipline in the discharge of this task.

Anyone investigating the causes of criminality discovers a very great variety of circumstances and conditions which have to be changed if their negative tendencies are to be eliminated. The conditions to be investigated — this much can be anticipated about the causes of criminality — are phenomena from all spheres of life. They have no separate existence, isolated from other phenomena, and cannot therefore simply be swept away as rubbish. Instead we frequently find that an empirical phenomenon contains in itself both negative and positive features, or that the old and the new are sometimes closely interwoven.

The progressive reduction and liquidation of such phenomena in society generally is primarily a question of deliberate control of the social transformation process in all fields of social life; the removal of those circumstances which have in the past caused criminality cannot be performed, as it were, casually but can only be performed deliberately and from accurate knowledge of the state of affairs. The first question here is what long-term action is needed in order to liquidate, deliberately and purposefully, the known causes of criminality in line with the further building and development of socialism. The second question is what social measures must be taken in the given situation, within the given realm of possibilities, in order to liquidate long overdue conditions and circumstances.

A study of the relevant resolutions of the Party Congresses or Plenary Meetings of the Socialist Unity Party (SED) shows that both in general and in particular terms the strategy has been worked out, for each stage in the development and also in the great long-term perspective of society, for preventing criminality by means of deliberate social change and qualified guidance of society. We also realise that this can in fact be accomplished only by the party of the working class. Such a comprehensive strategy which makes the struggle for the liquidation of criminality no longer the task of a government department but the task of the whole of society can be developed only within an organ such as the Party, an organ which helps society to become aware of its own road.

As for the details of this transformation within each sphere and the nature of the changes, criminology, having developed or still having to develop the specific methods for the discovery of the causes of criminality, must determine both the need for these changes and also the range of the circumstances to be changed. Moreover — proceeding from the fundamental knowledge derived from the Resolutions of the Party and from the social sciences generally — it must define the general direction of these changes.

But this solves only some of the questions which have to be tackled if the struggle for the reduction of criminality is to be purposefully and systematically conducted at all levels of State and social life. Discovery of the causes of criminality and determination of the direction of necessary changes are not enough. It is necessary to establish which real roads are to be followed, in view of the present state of economic, political, cultural and moral development, in order to reduce the incidence of each given criminal phenomenon and its causes in the given sphere of life. This cannot be accomplished by criminology alone.

Such roads and measures cannot simply be invented. They are not just a matter of a creative imagination which paints the ideal picture of a society free from the contradictions which lead to social or individual conflicts. Socialist criminology would remain stuck in the realm of speculation if it confined itself to this. On the other hand, its expertise and terms of reference are insufficient for it to work out these roads and measures alone. The elaboration of such real roads and measures becomes a problem of joint work by the leading State and social organs responsible for the social processes in each given field, the leading organs of the practice of socialist law, the socialist theory of criminal law and of criminal procedure, criminology, and all those disciplines which are concerned with man's social behaviour.

This is a complex task which can only be solved in a complex manner — by the concerted efforts of the different organs of the State and of society with the most varied scientific disciplines. It is a task which must be tackled both on the central and on the local planes. In this sense, therefore, no State or social control organ and no science concerned with man's behaviour is relieved of the duty of contributing to the elaboration of measures for the liquidation of criminality. This can be demonstrated by a number of examples.

Juvenile criminology states that one of the determinants of the criminal misbehaviour of juveniles is their lack of a fundamental political and ideological attitude. This in turn has a whole number of causes in the education and upbringing of juveniles and children by parents, school and social organisations, by groups in which juveniles live wholly or temporarily, the negative influences of the West, etc.

Other statements say that certain phenomena of juvenile criminality — apart from the effect of general determinants — are caused by the influence of quite definite groupings of juveniles.

Investigations have moreover shown that criminality among juveniles in the shape of rowdyism is not infrequently due to the fact that they are incapable of meaningful leisure activities satisfying their human needs or that they have failed to learn to develop an appropriate standard of needs and to satisfy them in harmony with society.

What remedies there are for this in the present conditions and within available possibilities, or how a universally positive political and ideological education can be guaranteed, or how certain groupings might be tackled even at the pre-criminal behaviour stage through the work of public organisations, or how a more cultured leisure life can be organised and shaped for juveniles — all these are questions which criminology alone cannot answer. Unless criminology is to remain stuck in dilettantism or to think up measures of which no one will take notice, it will have to embark on the road of joint work with State and social organisations and with other scientific disciplines.

On the other hand it must be emphasised that the State and social organs responsible for the control of specific processes of society's life must not treat criminality or its causes as something that is outside their concern. It is their duty, in turn, to apply the findings of criminological research and to work towards elaborating and applying measures for the progressive reduction of criminality and its causes. These organs, for their part, will have to co-operate with the judiciary organs, with criminology and with other sciences. Not until this has been achieved will the only promising link have been forged between the struggle against criminality and its causes and the building and development of new socialist social relations.

The first and quite significant steps in this direction have been taken by the GDR Prosecutor General's office in a number of regions and districts in the struggle against infringements of the labour protection law and against traffic offences as well as in the field of youth work. It is now necessary for these beginnings to be elevated into a system of co-operation between the most varied State and social organs and the most varied scientific disciplines. Only such a collaboration can produce truly effective and realisable measures — because no matter what question is asked about this or that cause of criminality it is invariably seen that it transcends the limit of criminology and spills over into the sphere of direct leadership of the social process and the subjects of other sciences.

The judiciary organs and criminology have an important part to play in the elaboration of such measures. Since they are practical and scientific institutions possessing an extensive expert knowledge of the trends of criminality and its causes, or else are concerned with their study, it is their task to develop this expertise in such a way that, in co-operation with other State and social organs and sciences, it can be transformed into State and social management practice. Law practice and criminology thus become an important source of information for State and society control generally. At the same time they have an important say in the determination of the appropriate measures because from their analysis of negative phenomena they are in a position to make conclusions as to what positive features have to be ensured in future.

Seen in this light, criminology has a critical function also in socialist society. But whereas criminology in bourgeois society, if it wants to remain faithful to its mission as a science, must ultimately arrive at the revolutionary negation of the bourgeois system of property and society, as Marxist criminology has done, socialist criminology stands in a different relationship to society. Its critique does not have to be directed against society and its social and economic foundations, and in fact must not be so directed unless it wants to violate the laws of science. By its criticism of material and ideological conditions, circumstances and phenomena which give rise to criminality, criminology supports the purposeful elimination of those phenomena which are alien to socialism itself, which are not in line with the new socialist economic and political structure of society, or which distort the nature of socialism. The function of socialist criminology, therefore, consists in making a contribution to the complete assertion of socialism in all spheres of material and ideological life and more particularly in everyday life.

Socialist criminology must not, therefore, confine itself to the mere registration of negative features and hence to passiveness towards criminality and its causes. It has a very weighty part to play in the elaboration of the system of measures for the progressive reduction of criminality and its causes. Its particular task is to establish in which spheres of life the causes of criminality are to be found and by whose work they can be removed, what sciences are to participate in the study of which problems, what information on the specific situation should be passed on to which State and social organisations or sciences, and what changes are to be aimed at in which spheres of life.

This requires, of course, that criminology must succeed in integrating itself into the management of society, that it must not be content to lead an existence aside from positive constructive work but see itself as an integral part of the management of society. It must supply the material and the expert knowledge required by the management organs in order, in the process of the general advance, to liquidate also the negative phenomena of our present reality.

This view of the rôle of criminology has been constitutionally endorsed by the decree of the GDR Council of Ministers of 7 August 1965, which makes it the duty of local administrative authorities to 'make use' of the findings of juvenile research and in particular of juvenile criminological research in the 'elaboration of measures for promoting the initiative of young people and in continuous work with young people'. It is the duty of criminology to integrate itself deliberately into this system of political and social leadership in order to ensure the optimum effectiveness of its work.

After this definition of the subject and tasks of socialist criminology the question arises of whether criminology is a juridical science or some other science. As was pointed out earlier, socialist criminology developed within the body of socialist criminal law theory. Moreover, medicine and psychology had begun to concern themselves more or less independently with criminality and its causes, and produced some very remarkable results. It is undisputed in all socialist countries that criminology is a social science just because its subject is the specific behaviour pattern of members of society.

At the same time, criminology is not one of the familiar traditional disciplines. Its subject, the causes of criminality, is by its nature a complex social phenomenon pervading, or embedded in, all spheres of the material and spiritual life of society and the individual.

The system of reference from which criminology has to proceed in order to have any prospect of success cannot be the automatic trend of criminality. In that case criminology would not get beyond mere empiricism or the bourgeois viewpoint. If criminality is accepted as an 'eternal' feature of human society, as a necessary correlation of responsible human social behaviour, or – as Hegel would have put it – as an organically linked aspect of liberty, property and law, while being the negation of all these, and hence one of the indispensable forms of existence of liberty, property and law, the system of reference of criminology would have to be sought in criminality itself and criminology would thus be a science contained, as it were, within itself. If, however, criminality is not endowed with this character, i.e. seen as the evil eternally associated with good, if instead it is understood – as it is by Marxism – merely as a primitive manifestation of human behaviour, with its social (material and ideological) roots in primitive social conditions and thought patterns, in conditions therefore which are not necessarily predetermined by man's eternal nature and character, then the scientific system of reference of criminality research cannot be contained in criminality itself.

Hence the system of reference and assessment of criminality can only be the general processes and the laws governing them, the laws determining the behaviour of the individual in society. In consequence, any scientific criminology must take account of all existing knowledge of man's social behaviour. It must similarly take over all methods of gaining knowledge which have already been developed by other existing scientific disciplines in order to discover the laws governing man's social behaviour. This means, of course, that criminology can exist only as a complex science into which are integrated all those sciences which can contribute to the discovery of the laws governing man's social behaviour. What distinguishes criminology from these sciences is the fact that, on the one hand, it is complex in a comprehensive sense, which endows it with a new quality and that, on the other, it has as its sole subject the causes of a definite form of negative social behaviour, i.e. criminality.

It is obvious that this subject, dependent as it is on criminality, also demands its own methods of research or information-gathering, methods which are no longer identical with the integrated scientific methods of other disciplines. It should be emphasised, however, that the research methods of criminology must necessarily derive from the research methods of other disciplines. No matter how much one must condemn criminal behaviour, it is nevertheless human behaviour which as such is investigated by the social sciences, by medicine and by the other sciences from their different points of view.

There is nevertheless a certain specific character about criminological research methods. Investigation of the causes of criminality depends on criminality itself, i.e. the commission of specific criminal offences. By his socially negative deed, which devalues him both legally and morally, the offender enters into a specific relationship with society, a relationship regulated by criminal law, judicial administration, criminal procedure and the criminal record rules. The need to discover criminality necessarily also entails that the offender's personality is respected in an entirely specific manner.

For its part criminology must respect the limitations deriving from the above and must appropriately adapt the knowledge-gathering procedures it has taken over from other scientific disciplines. There is a considerable difference between the investigation of socially valuable behaviour and its causes and the discovery of the causes of criminal behaviour. There is a difference between tracing the development of a socially respected personality through all its phases and that of a person who has depreciated himself by his behaviour. This particularity applies not only with regard to the offender but also with regard to all other persons who are responsible for the circumstances which have driven him to criminal action. What matters is not simply the purely subjective problem of possible dishonesty but the objective problems which demand that the investigation of negative behaviour and its causes must necessarily reveal differences compared with the investigation of positive or neutral modes of behaviour, and that all this must be further intensified when dealing with the most negative modes of behaviour, with criminal actions. Criminology, therefore, cannot simply adapt the methods of other scientific disciplines but must vary them according to the subject and, if necessary, develop methods of its own.

Criminology unites within itself the findings and investigation methods of the most varied scientific disciplines. These extend from Marxist philosophy and historical research through constitutional and legal theory, the theory of criminal law and other juridical disciplines, through economy and psychology and its branches, all the way to educational research and medicine. This complexity alone entails a new quality of the methods used. Each individual investigational procedure of criminology has to take account of philosophical, psychological, educational, penal, economic and other questions relating to society and the individual.

The problem of criminology in the socialist countries lies in the fact that its has developed from the theory of criminal law and that criminal law theoreticians still dominate it. They do not realise the complexity of criminology to anything like the necessary extent. Gertsenson, with whose basic concepts we largely agree, for instance believes that criminology must take account of the findings of other disciplines and put questions to those disciplines; however, he avoids the thesis that criminology is and at the same time is not a juridical, economic, psychological, educational and medical discipline just because it is a complex science or what is known as an interdisciplinary science. We, on the other hand, believe that any further progress depends on this very realisation of the character of criminology. [24]

Socialist criminology is an independent complex discipline of the social sciences, which both processes the findings of the various social and natural sciences, applying them to its particular subject, and also develops its own methods of research and specific findings. It follows that there can be no such thing as a criminologist per se who would be well grounded in all relevant areas. Only a scholar who is at the same time an expert in the field of one of the fundamental sciences, either a social or a natural science, can be a criminologist. This is not clearly understood by those working in the theory of criminal law, and even less so by those in other disciplines.

It further follows that criminology as a taught subject can exist only in the form of a special course based upon the fundamental scientific study particular specialised subject. The purpose of such a course is to equip the specialised student with the requisite supplementary knowledge. Such a specialised course must closely combine theoretical and methodological instruction with practical research work.

There are many experts in administrative and social bodies who are concerned with the fight against criminality. They may be judges, prosecutors, youth service helpers, members of local organisations, members of the People's Police, consultant psychologists, etc. All these must have some training in criminology.

Careful thought should therefore be given to how these persons are to be equipped with the basic criminological knowledge which would enable them satisfactorily to discharge their responsible and difficult tasks. The best solution − or at least the one most suitable at the present level of knowledge − would seem to be training courses for specific groups of persons. The principal subject of such training would have to be the practical application of the findings of the various disciplines to the liquidation of criminality, with considerable emphasis on the actual practice in State and society.

After the above considerations of the subject and the tasks of criminology it is now possible and necessary to determine the relationship between this specialised discipline and practice. Truly scientific criminology cannot be the work of the lone researcher nor can it be tackled by theory alone. Scientific criminology, as we understand it, is possible only if it is conducted jointly and according to a concerted plan and with unified methods by full-time scientists and State practice. Scientific criminology presupposes the collaboration of theory and State (including social) practice. Criminological research is always at the same time practical work, including in particular State control work. Theory and practice must fruitfully combine in criminological research if useful results are to be achieved. Scientific criminology is possible only as the joint effort and practical work for the liquidation of the causes of criminality.

In the GDR this realisation has gained acceptance in the work of the Department and of the Scientific Advisory Council for Criminality Research under the Prosecutor General, as well as in the Department for Youth Problems and its Scientific Advisory Council. What matters now is that the beginnings of a new scientific working style are further developed through the increasing enlistment of State and economic control organs as well as of other sciences, and through a greater and more purposeful concentration of effort in the planning of feasible measures for the reduction of criminality and its causes.

In contrast to the situation in the bourgeois capitalist countries, socialist society possesses all the necessary conditions for making this fruitful unity of theory and practice truly effective.

Notes

[1] J.D. Bernal, *Science in History*, London 1969.
[2] Cf. B.L. Schubert, *The Method of Investigating the Causes of Anti-Social Actions*, Moscow 1963.
[3] Cf. A. Mergen, *Die tatsächliche Situation der Kriminologie in Deutschland*, Hamburg, n.d., p. 3.
[4] Cf. R. Hartmann/J. Lekschas, *Zur Theorie der Ursachen, Bedingungen und Anlässe der Kriminalität in der DDR*, Berlin 1964 (Contributions to the First International Symposium 'Die Jugendkriminalität und ihre Bekämpfung in der sozialistischen Gesellschaft', published by the Faculty of Law of the Humboldt University, Berlin); also J. Lekschas/W. Loose/ J. Renneberg, *Verantwortung und Schuld im neuen Strafgesetzbuch*, Berlin 1964.

54

[5] Cf. K. Marx/F. Engels, *Werke*, vol. 2, pp. 225 ss.

[6] Cf. K. Marx/F. Engels, *The Communist Manifesto*, in: *Werke*, vol. 4, pp. 459 ss., cf. also F. Engels, loc.cit., pp. 430 ss.

[7] In his essay 'The Questions of Principle of Basic Criminological Researches' (*Acta Juridica*, Tom VII) (hereinafter called *Acta Juridica*), Budapest 1965 (in English), A. Szabó believes that socialist criminology lacks the 'basic sociological knowledge' for explaining deviant behaviour in socialist society. He believes that there is a total lack of theoretical foundations for any such explanation. But even Marx, Engels and Lenin made it quite clear that the socio-economic transformation of society into socialism cannot automatically or instantly accomplish a complete change of men whose features have been moulded by thousands of years of private ownership. The fundamental pattern of human social behaviour, as stemming from an outdated social structure, can only gradually be replaced and must for a considerable period of time harbour the danger of a clash with society's inevitable demands. With all the modesty due to a relatively young scientific discipline, criminology ought not to overlook the foundations provided by the universally known theses of Marxism—Leninism.

[8] Cf. J. Streit, *Klassenkampf und Strafrecht*, Berlin 1956, p. 105.

[9] Cf. also the Appendix.

[10] W. Orschechowski/K. Manecke/H. Sahre, *Formen, Umfang, Ursachen und Bekämpfung der Kriminalität im HO-Warenhaus Leipzig*, Berlin 1959.

[11] Cf. E. Buchholz, 'Der Diebstahl und seine Bekämpfung in der DDR', Habil. thesis, Berlin 1963, and G. Knobloch, 'Zur Persönlichkeit von Tätern gegen das sozialistische Eigentum in den VEB der sozialistischen Industrie der DDR', thesis, Berlin 1964.

[12] Cf. the critique practised by Hartmann and Lekschas against the various causal theories propounded by M. Benjamin, Böhme, Buchholz, Hinderer, Stiller and others (*Zur Theorie der Ursachen ...*, loc.cit., pp. 37 ss.), as well as their argument with A.B. Sakharov, who exerted a certain influence on literature and practice in the GDR for some time.

[13] H. Harrland, 'Die Bedeutung der Kriminalstatistik für die Leitung des Kampfes gegen die Kriminalität, ihre Funktionen, ihre Organisation und ihre Arbeitsweise', thesis, Halle 1963.

[14] A. Lutzke/W. Petasch/R. Schubert, 'Die Ursachen und Bedingungen der durch Übertretungen herbeigeführten Strassenverkehrsunfälle im Großstadtverkehr und ihre Bekämpfung aus polizeilicher Sicht', thesis, Potsdam-Babelsberg 1965.

[15] E. Klüsener, 'Zur Formalisierung des Ablaufs von Strassenverkehrsunfällen als Untersuchungshilfe', thesis, Berlin 1965.

[16] G. Stiller, 'Theoretische und methodologische Grundlagen der kriminologischen Forschungen in der DDR', Habil. thesis, Potsdam—Babelsberg 1965.

[17] Cf. *Jugendkriminalität und ihre Bekämpfung in der sozialistischen Gesellschaft*, Berlin 1965, especially the contributions by S. Walczak, pp. 50 ss., G.M. Minkowski, pp. 73 ss., A. Szabó, pp. 93 ss., Z. Svancar, pp. 106 ss., K. Vodopivec, pp. 115 ss., M. Vorwerg, pp. 119 ss., B. Skaberné, pp. 125 ss., M. Kadar, pp. 169 ss., W. Gutjahr, pp. 191 ss., H. Szewczyk, pp. 208 ss., J. Helm/E. Kasielski, pp. 220 ss., G. Göllnitz, pp. 227 ss., J. György, pp. 235 ss., G. Feix, pp. 246 ss., B. Redlich, pp. 254 ss.

[18] A. Szabó, *Acta Juridica*, loc.cit.

[19] Cf. A. Mergen, *Die tatsächliche Situation* ..., loc.cit., p. 5.

[20] Cf. A. Szabó, *Acta Juridica,* loc. cit., and A. Szabó, in: *Jugendkriminalität und ihre Bekämpfung* ..., loc.cit., pp. 101 ss.

[21] A. Szabó, loc.cit., p. 110.

[22] Cf. H.E. Göppinger, 'Die gegenwärtige Situation der Kriminologie', *Recht und Staat*, Tübingen, Issue 288/289, p. 30.

[23] A.A. Gertsenson, *Introduction to Soviet Criminology*, Moscow 1965 (in Russian).

[24] In their book *Verantwortung und Schuld im neuen Strafgesetzbuch*, Lekschas, Loose and Renneberg still assume that criminology is part of criminal law theory (loc.cit., p. 56). As the more recent evidence here adduced shows, this view is no longer tenable, as it entails the danger of criminology being excessively subordinated to criminal law aspects and thus needlessly circumscribed in its effectiveness.

2 Theory of the Causes of Criminality in Socialist Society

Dialectical determinism as the foundation of criminological research

Any science — including one concerned with examining certain empirically observed phenomena of life as to their essential inherent connections with other empirical phenomena — requires an unambiguous theoretical foundation. Without a theory in line with objective reality even an empirical science such as criminology would degenerate into purposeless empiricism. True, a number of bourgeois criminologists, in order to demonstrate their opposition to the speculative positions of other criminologists, have declared criminology to be a 'pure' empirical science, a science which lacks any specific theoretical foundations and which must not acknowledge any theoretical principle as the starting point for its researches. But even these criminologists do in fact adhere to certain theoretical positions. These are found, in particular, in their research methods and their attempts at interpretation. Even the neo-positivist statement that criminology can be a science only if it declares its statements to be 'falsifiable' and if it refuses to accept any kind of received truth, either cancels itself out by its own inherent logic or results in a rule of absolute doubt — something which Hegel rejected as philosophical nonsense — or else it is merely a piece of theoretical sleight of hand, designed to conceal its true theoretical starting point. Socialist criminology must not allow itself to be forced on to such a theoretically nihilistic course, even if the occasional bourgeois criminologist subscribing to philosophical neo-positivism may have succeeded, by his empirical researches, in discovering certain correlations. It is to be welcomed that the more recent bourgeois criminologists have rejected speculative views and ingrained bourgeois prejudices. But if that rejection goes too far, leading to the negation of all theoretical conclusions or starting points, then that is no reason for socialist criminology to follow the bourgeois criminologists into this nirvana of theory.

Discussions on criminological problems, both in the GDR and in other socialist countries, have revealed the existence of attitudes which might lead to just such a sliding into pure empiricism or into the transformation of hitherto reliable knowledge into 'hypotheses'. Thus we regard it as somewhat unhelpful to approach criminological research as though no kind of information were as yet available on the causes of criminality, as though we were still totally ignorant about all concatenations giving rise to decisions leading to criminal acts, as though criminology would have to start from scratch and would first have to 'verify' all past conclusions. To quote an example, psychologists, educationists and literary scholars have long reached the conclusion that trash and pornographic literature, as well as similar cinematographic and other would-be 'cultural' products, lead to the deformation of the moral make-up of people, and especially of children and juveniles. It has furthermore been known for a long time that morally disturbed individuals are more frequently and more readily apt to make criminally wrong decisions than those who are morally rooted. It was from this realisation that the ban on such products and the struggle for morally valuable literature and art have sprung. Socialist criminology could do no greater harm to itself or to society than to deny such elementary realisations of cause and effect.

The presentation of hypotheses which can be proved correct or wrong in the course of investigation is a useful, productive and necessary method whenever criminology is about to penetrate into hitherto unknown areas. It is a mistake, however, to make a fetish of hypothesis and to concede no more than hypothetical character to all past discoveries and conclusions. Hans-Jürgen Lander, for instance, claims that the statement that criminality is a phenomenon which can be progressively narrowed down under socialism and totally eliminated under communism is no more than a 'hypothesis'. In spite of its obvious 'heuristic' value it nevertheless required 'verification through the actual experience of society's life with its continually changing conditions in the further socio-historical and economic-technical development'.[1]

We do not wish to enter into an argument with Lander here, or to point out that this 'hypothesis' has been in existence for a very long time and can be found in the social analyses of Marx, Engels and Lenin. It is, moreover, one of the fundamental concepts upon which the GDR State Council, in 1961, began to reorientate the practice of socialist criminal law and which subsequently was the subject of the Resolutions of the Sixth Party Conference of the SED and the State Council's Decree concerning the further development of socialist jurisdiction. We do not expect Lander, simply because of our reference to Party Resolutions or statements by the Marxist—Leninist classics, to accept this fundamental starting point of socialist criminology as an 'article of faith'. That would be of no use to anyone. But we do believe that scientific knowledge can be gleaned not only from empirical observation but also from the theoretical analysis of essential correlations and determinants. This analysis is the outcome of more than a hundred years of scientific work by the theoreticians of Marxism—Leninism, work based on more comprehensive empirical and theoretical investigations than have gone into any other theory of society.

Criminality — whether theft, bodily injury, sexual offences or even homicide — is partly a human aberration, partly a piece of barbarism or even inhumanity. However, there is no perpetual reason and no immutable cause for man to err, to act in a barbarous or inhuman manner, when he has the opportunity of satisfying his genuine needs in a human way and when he has a chance of developing truly human needs.[2] The fact that deviations from the basic norms of social behaviour have existed in the past and still exist in the present, or that inhumanity and barbarism existed or still exist, does not mean that this must be so for all time to come.

By establishing a socialist society we have made a start on abolishing the barriers created against humanity in man-to-man relations by private ownership, so that individuals can now gradually lose the habit of unproductive, destructive conflict between themselves, as manifested in criminality.[3] The practical experience of the development of a socialist way of life over nearly half a century supplies us with a vast amount of evidence in support of this view.

It follows, therefore, that it is scientifically unsound to try to refute a statement proved by extensive theoretical findings and studies merely by putting forward contrary hypotheses or to try to reduce it to an ordinary hypothesis. The struggle of our society for socialist humanist relations between human beings therefore is not an experiment based on an unverified hypothesis. Any criminology basing its propositions and studies on such uncertain foundations would fail to meet its social responsibilities. The principle of scientific discussion that simple contradiction is not enough to deprive universally accepted and practically confirmed conclusions of their objective truth must apply to criminology as to any other discipline. A scientific argument is not just anything that is conceivable but only what can also be confirmed by objective reality.

The ideological basis from which any socialist theory of the causes of criminality in socialist society must proceed is Marxism—Leninism, more particularly dialectical and historical materialism. The theory of the causes of criminality in socialist society, however, must similarly contain the conclusions of all other disciplines of Marxist social sciences just as much as the findings of the natural sciences in so far as they are concerned with human action and the development of the human personality.

The theory of the causes of criminality must therefore be comprehensive. It must open up all roads towards a comprehensive examination of these causes and provide for the utilisation of all scientific findings that may be useful to its own inquiries – no matter from which specialised discipline they are received. Care must, however, be taken to see that, in the utilisation of the findings of other disciplines, these are not merely taken over and selectively compiled but that they are also applied, i.e. creatively processed in accordance with the subject under investigation.[4] Unless that is done there is a risk of 'psychologisation' or 'economism' or some other deformation of these studies and hence of misorientation.

Proceeding from the above-stated goals of the theory of the causes of criminality in socialist society, as they stem from the demands of the Sixth Party Congress, one arrives at the following clear conclusion: the theory of the causes is not concerned merely with the problem of 'causality', of a simple non-recurrent relation, with a 'specific time-determined direct objective correlation between two phenomena'[5] – known as a causal relationship – but with the application and evaluation of a dialectical determinism.

It seems to us that an exact theory of the causes of criminality definitely requires a distinction, in line with the findings of Marxist philosophy, between causality and dialectical determinism. This distinction, unfortunately, has not so far been made in theoretical discussions. GDR authors writing on questions of causality[6] or on the causes of criminality have more or less equated causality with determinism, with regularity of pattern, and with necessity. This has given rise not only to a great number of difficulties for the theory of the causes of criminality but also to the danger that it might slip into mechanistic or determinist ideas.

In his critique of these widely held theories Herbert Hörz points out that causality, the causal connection, should mean no more than the fundamental time-linked objective connection between two phenomena. He writes: 'It is more in line with scientific ideas if causality is understood as the direct specific interrelation between two processes, whereby the one produces changes in the other.'[7] No statement is therefore made about necessity or chance, nor about any inherent regularity of the process; a 'causal relationship exists both when we are dealing with an unambiguous co-ordination of cause and effect and also when that co-ordination is not unambiguous'.[8]

The law of causality states no more and no less than that all phenomena of objective reality are in a cause–effect relationship with other phenomena, whereby this relationship refers to the direct specific inter-relation. It therefore follows, as Hörz rightly emphasises, that the investigation of the connection between different phenomena must not be confined to a mere statement of their causal connection.

Since this establishes only the — however fundamental — essential connective link of one phenomenon with another, but not the specific nature or quality of this connection, it is necessary to look for other forms of such connections although, in that case, the boundaries of simple direct connections must be transgressed, and 'the inter-relations of a totality of causal relations' must be investigated:

> The emergence of necessity in chance, the realisation of possibilities — these are possible only on the basis of the objective existence of specific and direct relationships between material processes. The same is true for succession in time and for co-existence in space. This does not mean that co-existing phenomena or consecutive phenomena must causally condition one another. It only means that they exist on the basis of a totality of causal relations. Utilisation of objective causality makes it possible to discover natural laws. This is done by emphasising various facets of the totality of causal relations by formulating laws of spatial and temporal connections between phenomena, i.e. laws of structure and movement.[9]

Similarly, in the theory of the causes of criminality it is not enough to examine simple causal connections. It is necessary to discover the part played by the different objective and subjective phenomena in a multiplicity of causal relations referring to criminality as a phenomenon of society as a whole and to trace the regular patterns governing the trends of criminality. The mistake is frequently made of halting the examination of the causes of criminality once the simple direct connection, i.e. the specific causal connection, has been dealt with. In this way, however, one comes to a halt at the *next cause*, the decision to commit the deed and its emergence in the mind of the culprit; one therefore — deliberately or unwittingly — stops short of the investigation of further essential inherent connections. But these concern not only the simple direct connections between two phenomena but also the indirect connections of a totality of causal relations, i.e. entire processes. Yet this is precisely the task of the theory of the causes of criminality. Establishment of the simple causal connections is the objective factual foundation of the 'theory', just as the causal connection is the objective foundation of the laws of movement.

Anyone wishing to examine or *discover* the laws of movement, or trends, of criminality — and this is what really matters at the present stage of development of the theory of the causes of criminality in socialist society — must free himself from traditional mechanistic ideas concerning these regularities. The new philosophical insights provided by the development of contemporary natural sciences into the diverse nature of regularities and natural laws will have to be correctly absorbed. The ideas on the nature of these regularities, as found in criminal law theory, frequently still reflect uncertainty and a clinging to mechanistic and materialist concepts. In line with the idea of the natural law, as it is found in classical mechanics, this concept is understood as reflecting a simple direct necessity — in much the same way as the jurists of bourgeois enlightenment did. The application of such a concept of the natural law to movements in society, especially to criminality, led even the bourgeois enlighteners to a position of fatalism, and this result is still sometimes observed today. Alternatively it leads to ideas of spontaneity in the fight against criminality.

Hörz, working in the field of the natural sciences, showed that the concepts of the natural law as derived from classical mechanics are inadequate in explaining all the forms of natural movement. In this connection he distinguishes between dynamic and statistical laws:

> The fundamental difference between existing and future causal relations renders it impossible to make any statements concerning the future with the aid of the law of causality alone. The law of causality merely states *that* all phenomena in the future are causally determined. What we need, however, is statements showing *how* future events are determined. The laws of classical mechanics furnish us with statements to the effect that one state of a physical object necessarily follows its preceding state. This form of the law, making a statement about the direct dependence of a future state upon a present state, was described as a dynamic law. In modern physics this is distinguished, above all, from a statistical law according to which there is no longer a direct necessary connection of the future state of an individual object with its present state. [10]

Dialectical determinism correctly comprehends the relationship of causality and regularity and recognises more than *one* form of the law. It liberates the questions of possibility and reality, chance and necessity from their mechanistic limitations and that is why it must also be applied in the theory of the causes of criminality in socialist society. Particular note should be taken of the fact that only in the rarest cases do the laws governing human action denote simple direct necessity within the meaning of classical mechanics. Whereas the dynamic law of classical physics knows only one definite possibility of behaviour for a single object under given conditions, the statistical law — to quote Hörz — provides 'a possibility only for a totality of objects' from which there result 'probabilities for the individual objects, realised on a chance basis'. [11]

In another study Hörz has this to say on the problem:

> Statistical laws are laws governing totalities of objects. Each object is determined by the totality of the forms of connections and relations with its surroundings. Each individual object exists in a connection which leads to the totality. The connection of objects with one another makes it possible to discover general relationships which do not apply to each object in isolation but only describe the behaviour of the totality. The connection between the laws of the totality and the individual objects is manifested in the fact that from the behaviour of the totality conclusions may be drawn as to the behaviour of the individual object. But no absolutely exact prediction can be made for the behaviour of any individual object from the behaviour of the totality. [12]

Dialectical determinism therefore not only asks questions about the fact of causal connections but also about the nature of the connections between various phenomena. The same applies to the theory of the causes of criminality. If it confined itself to stating that the specific connections of cause and effect must be investigated for each separate criminal act, then it would be totally superfluous as a separate theory alongside the general theory of causality. A science is expected to furnish not only insights into the essential inherent connections of a trend but also predictions based upon these insights. This leads us to the problems of possibility and reality and necessitates the question of how to apply the general philosophical realisation that, given certain conditions within each set of causal relations, certain regularities — among which the dynamic and statistical laws have so far been identified — are valid and provide a basis for genuine predictions.

The investigation of causal connections which have led to a criminal action is invariably the investigation of *reality*, more particularly of a limited single phenomenon of reality. What is established is the fact that certain phenomena of reality have produced another phenomenon — the criminal act. If criminality is understood as the sum total of all criminal acts committed then it is necessary, first of all, to establish which of the many individual phenomena of reality has led to the given multiplicity of diverse criminal acts. This is still a case of discovering given specific individual — however numerous — causal relations. If theory were to stop at this point then it would do no more than register a great variety of processes none of which is repeated in the same way, and such a registration would be relatively useless without a further scientific penetration in depth — simply because these statements are statements of non-recurrent chance events. The objective, however, is the provision of a directive for the investigation of those *factors* of which it can be predicted that, whenever they are present, certain processes will repeat themselves; and it is on the strength of this knowledge that preventive measures can be applied.

In the field of criminal law theory Michael Benjamin, Buchholz, Stiller and others have recently pointed out, on the basis of the findings of Soviet science, that the criminal act as an individual phenomenon and criminality as a general phenomenon are always only a possible effect of certain other phenomena — the remnants of the old society. The phenomena identified as the cause of the individual act or of criminality generally — as emerges from the most diverse investigations — carry within themselves no more than the possibility of determining the individual to commit criminal acts. The criminal act may occur as the result but need not do so.

The concept of possibility thus understood covers a multiplicity of problems. The statement that criminality is no more than a possible effect of these causes does not, however, exclude the assumption of a dynamic connection between the causes of criminality and criminality itself; i.e. criminality, though only a possibility, should be seen also as the only possible effect of these causes. But even in such connections governed by dynamic laws the transformation of a possibility into reality can be prevented by the intervention of new conditions without in any way impairing the validity of the dynamic law governing the connection between these phenomena. Possibility and predictable regularity are not mutually exclusive concepts. The phenomena described as causes of criminality can, in socialist society, give rise to quite diverse effects. We can note two very different directions of effect. On the one hand, provided they have been identified as survivals of the old society they can result in purposeful work by the Party and society aiming at their liquidation; these endeavours will be joined by the overwhelming mass of the members of society.

On the other hand, a small portion of the members of society will continue to be subject to the destructive effects of these phenomena. But this does not mean that those who are exposed to the spontaneously destructive effect of such phenomena and succumb to it will necessarily commit criminal acts of any kind. The effects of such survivals on persons yielding to them can be of different kinds. Thus, the effect of bourgeois ideology on members of our society may lead them to display incomprehension vis-à-vis the fundamental questions of development, or to hold harmful views and theories on certain problems of life, or to remain inactive or indifferent to necessities demanding personal activity from them, etc. But they need not necessarily develop any anti-social activity. Only in a minute proportion of these people do these survivals, under the most diverse and continually changing conditions of social and individual life, in effect trigger criminal acts.

Even leaving aside the fact that under conditions of socialism the same phenomena produce the absolute opposite of criminality, i.e. a systematic and increasingly effective struggle for their liquidation, it should be remembered that in referring to the causes of criminality we invariably mean phenomena of which criminality is only one of several possible effects and indeed the most extreme possible negative effect. It is clear therefore that the connection between criminality and its causes is not a dynamic law in the sense of mechanics, i.e. no mechanistic-linear causality. Human beings — as Walter Ulbricht pointed out at the Second Bitterfeld Conference, speaking generally and not only of the survivals of the old [13] — are no longer at the mercy of the action of conflicts but, thanks to socialist relationships, are capable of mastering them and of more and more effectively solving them. It is necessary, therefore, to shed the bourgeois-mechanistic concepts of causality and inevitability concerning criminality trends when dealing with the examination of criminality in socialist society and the question of its determinism.

The question then arises of whether it is altogether proper to apply the concept of cause to such a phenomenon as criminality. From a philosophical point of view Hörz has registered his objections by arguing that the concept of cause can be applied only to specific causal relations, i.e. events which have already taken place. [14] From a philosophical point of view, he argues, the use of concepts such as cause and effect is justified only within such specific individual causal relationships where one phenomenon has been directly triggered by another. In consequence, he argues, a different conceptual notation is needed for the concept of the causes of criminality. Much as we agree with such an application of the concepts of cause and effect within the framework of a specific causal relationship, we would nevertheless point out that society cannot do without the concepts of cause and effect also within the framework of more extensive systems of reference. In our view it is necessary to apply these concepts not only to specific causal relationships but equally to entire social processes — and this is in fact what is happening in a great many ways in everyday social practice. Philosophy should therefore endeavour to bring the use of its concepts in line with such practice.

The theory of the causes of criminality proceeds from actually established causes of individual criminal acts just as much as of criminality generally. It finds that definite phenomena have time and again acted as causes but it also notes that these phenomena, isolated as they have been from their context, have not in every case operated as causes of criminality. They are nevertheless called causes of criminality because it has been established that, among the great multitude of changing general and individual conditions they were the motive force for the emergence of the decision to commit criminal acts.

From the fact that certain phenomena have been *proved* to have led to criminal acts in the past, theory makes conclusions, allowing for the rôle of varying conditions, as to the possible future criminal effect of such phenomena. It is bound to do so because the reality of each new criminal act proves that these possibilities (tendencies) are in fact transformed into reality so long as such phenomena exist. True enough, these are statements merely about the possible effect of certain real phenomena, i.e. about the causes of possible criminality. Their operation can only be prevented by the progressive liquidation from society of those phenomena which have been identified as the real causes in past causal connections. In such a drive it is totally irrelevant whether the specific phenomenon which is being liquidated — e.g. slovenly economic management in some particular enterprise — would in fact have led to cases of theft in the future or not. In mounting practical measures for the liquidation of the causes of criminality it is sufficient to know that such phenomena have, in a large number of cases in the past, acted as the causes of criminality.

There is no need, therefore, to abandon the concept of the causes of criminality merely because the investigation of individual acts is concerned with already accomplished cause—effect connections, whereas the general theory of the causes of criminality or of certain categories of offences makes statements about as yet unrealised and merely possible future connections. It should be remembered, however, that it is not the task of the general theory to formulate the connections of specific individual acts. That is the business of procedural investigation, fact-finding, elucidation and possible judgement or sentence. Theory is concerned, on the basis of knowledge gained from the investigation of facts, with the possible criminal effects of the totality of identified causes or of certain individual phenomena, with the objective of elaborating the specific conditions for the systematic elimination of such phenomena or the limitation, by legal measures, of their possible negative effects.

Such phenomena, therefore — even if we are concerned only with their possible effects — must be called causes of criminality, since any other name would be misleading and apt to weaken the struggle against them by

66

confining it to the elimination of such particular phenomena as have been the causes of criminal acts already commited. Any other nomenclature would needlessly impair the effectiveness of the struggle against all such survivals of the past.

This use of the concept of cause is shared not only by the theory of criminal law and criminology but by all other sciences as well. It follows the dialectics of possibility and reality and is in conformity with the tasks of science. If, for instance, medical science in conjunction with dietetics states that a certain excessive consumption of animal fats is the cause of certain nutritional troubles or even diseases, and therefore calls for a reduced intake in order to preserve the national health, it certainly does not mean that every individual consuming excessive amounts of such fats must necessarily become ill. Nevertheless, scientists do not shrink from using the causal concept in this connection since they have identified a definite possible effect on the human organism of an excessive consumption of animal fats.

The first important requirement is for causal-mechanistic ideas to be abandoned. Alongside causal-mechanistic or dynamically regular processes there are other processes in which a continuous change and a continuous diversity of specific conditions form part and parcel of the process itself and therefore are part of the phenomena whose changes are to be examined. Theory must accept this variation of conditions as a given fact, as part of the nature of the process itself, but must nevertheless seek the phenomena which are apt to cause certain variations.

It is this kind of process that we are dealing with when looking at either the individual criminal act or criminality generally. Every human being differs from every other. People vary in their personality make-up, and the conditions under which different individuals live differ. In searching for the causes of the behaviour of different people this specific variation must be taken account of from the very start. Otherwise one would be chasing after a chance combination of conditions. If, however, one accepts this diversity as a premise one finds that certain individual phenomena necessarily produce quite diverse effects from different individuals, so that one can eliminate from the outset any regular pattern of effect produced by individual phenomena upon a multiplicity of people. This follows not only from human nature and the variety of people's living conditions, but also from the nature of society itself, from the diversity exhibited by social relations in the specific behaviour of classes and strata of society and in the behaviour of individuals. The conditions prevailing in socialist industry differ from those in other spheres of production or life. There the socialist working morale emerges as the core of socialist morality altogether, which in turn is carried into the individual's everyday life under the leadership of the party of the working class. The likely effects of the survivals of the past — in interaction with the social relationships — must therefore show a great deal of diversity, the more so if one considers the individuals upon whom they act. Here an important part is played by accidental factors; nevertheless the effect of these survivals as a whole is not an accidental feature or one that must elude identification.

The significance of the law concept in criminological research

Having rightly excluded a dynamic-law type of regularity as determining the causes of criminality, one's next question must concern the nature of the causal connection between the causes of criminality and criminality itself — i.e. whether the concept of natural law or regularity can be applied at all to this connection. Before this point can be decided it is necessary to examine the problem of the laws or regularities of society and to ask whether the relationship between the causes of criminality and criminality itself, as the effect of these causes, deserves the status of social laws or regularities.

In order to find the correct methodological starting point for the examination of this problem one has to return to the findings of Marxist philosophy. The validity of a law of social dynamics — and this should be emphasised since mechanistic-deterministic concepts occasionally lead to considerable errors in this area — is neither absolute nor unlimited, nor free from the time and place co-ordinates of social conditions. Every regularity, which is only a particular kind of connection between causally linked phenomena, depends on the existence of certain conditions.

> Dialectical determinism [Hörz states] liberates the concepts of causality, determinism and law from their mechanistic limitations. It demonstrates that the classical concept of causality was one-sided, stressing as it did the necessary link between a certain cause and a certain effect and regarding the world as the sum-total of such causal relations. Determinism, in this context, means acceptance of the view that objects and phenomena are conditioned (causally dependent) and determined (structured) in their overall connections. A fundamental aspect of determinism is the acceptance of the basic form of objective connection, the causal connection. Since, however, each causal relationship is only one aspect of this connection, the actual emergence of each causal relationship is determined by the other

causal relationships connected with it. The totality of such relationships can be described as the conditions for the emergence of the one relationship.

Abstracting from inessential random connections, a law emphasises the substantive, necessary and general connections. It therefore reflects certain relationships out of a totality of causal relationships. These laws, which are likewise valid only under definite conditions, enable us to make predictions. Under the conditions essential for the validity of the law the connections about which the law makes a statement will occur also in the future. In making this statement the law comprises only the totality of necessarily realised possibilities. First, this regularity is realised in chance occurrences. Secondly, entirely new and previously unknown phenomena may emerge whose laws have yet to be discovered. Thirdly we have the realisation also of accidentally determined possibilities which are inessential or, if they become essential, fall under the above headings. [15]

The idea of immutable objective laws is thus seen as a crude oversimplification of the problem and must therefore be abandoned. The social laws are dependent for their existence on certain social conditions. If these conditions are changed the laws are changed with them. As the conditions of life in the socialist society are in a state of constant revolutionary change it follows that the inherent social laws of motion are likewise undergoing continuous change.

The laws of society relate to human actions. They embrace the essential necessary general connections between various forms of human behaviour, the forms of movement of man's social life. They are thus not something outside human behaviour but are immanent within it. Whether and how they manifest themselves in human action depends entirely on the character of the social order, on people's living conditions and on their actions. Under the leadership of the Party of the working class and on the basis of the new socialist production and living relations the people in a socialist society progressively learn to attain mastery not only over nature but also over their own social existence. They learn to control the laws of their own life and thereby — to quote Engels — accomplish the leap from the animal kingdom into the realm of freedom. It is a peculiarity of the laws governing the evolution of socialist society that they do not act spontaneously or independently of the will of the working classes and strata under the leadership of the Marxist-Leninist party. They require the deliberate and systematic activity of the working people. That is an essential condition for the validity of these laws. In the absence of such systematic activity it may happen, in some sphere or other, that these laws of socialist development do not come to fruition, or not wholly to fruition. Thus, so long as the GDR's frontier was open it was not possible to tackle certain tasks in the economic sphere, and this impaired the effectiveness of the economic lever of material incentives. Removal of these restrictive conditions and the systematic development of the new system of economic planning and management inevitably also made the levers of material incentives more effective.

Thus the deliberate and systematic activity of the people, guided by the Party, the social organisations and the State, is a necessary condition for the effective operation of the laws of social development in socialist society. They are not therefore natural laws operating regardless of man's deliberate and organised activity. At the same time, given this deliberate and organised activity of the people, these laws of social development operate with the same irresistible force as natural laws even though, in the absence of such activity, they do not operate at all. This point must never be lost sight of when reference is made to the laws of development of socialist society. The formulation of any specific law or regular pattern thus implicitly embraces the need for a definite social activity.

This applies also to the regularities marking the struggle against criminality. These have been scientifically developed and summarised in the programmes of the Communist Party of the Soviet Union and the Socialist Unity Party (SED) in the German Democratic Republic.

In the programme of the CPSU we read: 'Increasing prosperity, rising cultural standards and the awareness of the working people create all the prerequisites for the liquidation of criminality, eventually replacing penal measures under criminal law by social influence and education. Under the conditions of socialism any person who has slipped from the path of honest work can return to useful activity.' [16]

The programme of the Sixth Party Congress of the SED has this to say on the subject:

> Implementation of the tasks of the comprehensive building of socialism is the basis for the systematic struggle for the gradual elimination of criminality from the life of society. In the German Democratic Republic the relations of capitalist exploitation have been eliminated, and the social and economic roots of crime thus very largely removed. The transition from capitalism to socialism, however, is taking place amongst a multiplicity of conflicts and in struggle against stubborn survivals of capitalist living and thinking habits which, moreover, are continually being nourished anew by external

influences. This is reflected also in criminality. In order to make the norms of socialist law a solid foundation of man's activities this complex process, whereby people strip old habits, must always be borne in mind and actively promoted. The growing strength of our society provides all the prerequisites of a successful struggle against criminality and law infringement, a struggle to be conducted with extensive participation by the public. It is above all necessary to develop preventive activity. The causes and conditions which favour crimes and law infringements must be identified and removed. [17]

These statements, both in their theoretical and practical significance, are a reflection of the mastery of the processes of social life and development in a socialist society led by the revolutionary parties of the working people; this mastery will ultimately lead to the liquidation of criminality in the communist society.

This raises the question of whether criminality itself is an inevitable phenomenon in socialist society, i.e. whether it is governed by social laws. The above-quoted statements from the programmes of the CPSU and the SED point out that criminality is a necessity neither for a society building communism nor for a socialist society.

The laws of motion in society always relate to the connection between the nature of society and certain essential manifestations of it, a connection basically determined by the social and economic structure of society. In this sense all social laws are laws of historical movement, as formulated in the Declaration of Communist and Workers' Parties. Hence, as far as criminality is concerned, socialist society reflects the action of the law of deliberate and systematic struggle for the progressive reduction of criminality and its causes. As Marx and Engels pointed out in their analysis of the working-class movement, this law began to emerge simultaneously with the revolutionary working-class movement, so that — seen from the point of view of its nature and historical mission — the revolutionary movement may be said to have begun its liberation from criminality even at a time when society was still subject to the rule of capital.

The revolutionary establishment of a socialist society therefore represented also the revolutionary liquidation of the main social and economic causes of criminality. The law of deliberate and systematic struggle for the progressive reduction of criminality and its causes began to be valid at that point in time. Socialism, therefore, both in terms of its socio-economic structure and the humanist way of life it provides for man on this basis, also represents the progressive reduction and liquidation of the causes of criminality and their destructive effects on man. That is the social law governing criminality in a socialist society. That is why the GDR State Council has declared in several resolutions that in socialist society no one need become a criminal.

We can thus state that criminality is not a social-law-determined phenomenon of life in socialist society.

The fact that criminality does not have its roots in the laws of the development of socialism and is not itself an inevitable phenomenon of socialism does not, of course, mean that criminality in socialist society is totally unmotivated, that it appears without any social cause, as it were from the individual's sheer wickedness, or that between it and its causes there are no regular patterns of connections to be discovered. But we are no longer dealing here with the laws of society but with internal recurrent essential connections between certain phenomena which continue to exist but which neither determine the nature of movement of society nor stem from the nature of socialist society itself. Nevertheless, they are phenomena with which socialist society will have to cope by overcoming them in the process of building the new society. We must distinguish, therefore, between social laws determining the inherent movement of society and laws which exist within limited causal connections. It is the task of the theory of the causes of criminality to discover the internal connections between the causes of criminality and criminality itself in order to create a scientific basis for concrete preventive measures.

The statement that criminality is not a social phenomenon stemming from the basic social structure of socialism, i.e. not an inevitable social pattern, has run into opposition not only in the camp of bourgeois criminologists but also among certain criminologists in the socialist countries, and has given rise to counter-hypotheses. Bourgeois criminologists see it as a 'propaganda formula' or as an 'unverifiable article of faith'. They reject such proof as may be unambiguously obtained from an analysis of the nature of the social structure of society and make everything a question of 'ideology' in the worst sense of the word. Such arguments, springing as they do from the realm of the irrational, are not scientific arguments and there is no need to refute them; the 'belief' that the findings of Marxism—Leninism are simply 'matters of belief' will scarcely be susceptible to rational argument.

Lander, on the other hand, put forward a counter-hypothesis which, in a slightly different formulation, is essentially held also by the West German criminologist Stephan Quensel. He thinks the question 'worth raising whether such phenomena of social life as are subsumed under the concept of "criminal" do not perhaps arise from the fact of social contradictions or the "clash of opposites" as possible extreme variants, remaining as it were embedded in them, and under changed social conditions merely acquire a changed content and at the same time a changed yardstick of judgement with regard to the socially required norms of behaviour'. [18]

It is not quite clear what Lander means. If he is asking whether there will not now and again occur transgressions even in a communist society then there is no need for his counter-hypothesis. No one ever claimed that the communist society will be a society of 'angels' where flare-ups of temper may not here or there lead to conflicts between individuals, in the course of which the participants may occasionally also forget and violate the rules of mutual behaviour – quite apart from pathologically conditioned excesses about whose continued existence there is no dispute.

But these conflicts, even if they take the form of individual excesses, have nothing in common in their social character with the criminality with which we are dealing at present and which we have resolved to liquidate. These will be individual conflicts of limited scope and range, with which society will able to cope on its own without the need for coercive measures by the State such as are represented by criminal legislation or the State's judicial system.

Already criminality is beginning to lose its character as a social conflict. It is no longer an individual anarchist protest reaction by the alienated individual against the prevailing conditions, springing from antagonistic conflicts based on the socio-economic structure of society. It is no longer the extreme negative reflection of elementary social conflicts in the behaviour of the individual but only the echo of such (already abolished) antagonistic basic conflicts. Criminality in socialist society is no longer a product of objectively insoluble situations. Instead, it is an individual's specific conflict – conditioned by certain social and personal circumstances – with society, with the State, with minor collectives or with other individuals, a conflict in which the lawbreaker violates the elementary basic norms of social behaviour.

Criminality is thus no longer a phenomenon marking the explosive discharge, in the form of extreme negative behaviour patterns, of essentially social conflicts affecting not only the individual concerned but entire sections of society or society as a whole. Nevertheless, criminality as we have to observe it in socialist society today is still not a limited individual conflict which no longer touches upon or significantly affects social co-existence; it continues to be the expression of social and individual conditions or circumstances which, though not in line with the nature of socialist society, nevertheless exist in the practice of everyday life. But these are conditions and circumstances which are transient and can therefore themselves be eliminated.

A view similar to Lander's is supported by the Yugoslav criminologists Ljubo Bavcon, Bronislav Skaberné and Katja Vodopivec, who state that 'man nevertheless remains a "living" human being acting in specific conditions and whose actions depend, among other things, also on his moods, health, temporary psychological malaise, natural influences and certain other factors. For these reasons we cannot confidently expect that in a communist society the generally accepted elementary principles of social co-existence will never be infringed. We are not Utopians, Lenin said, and we must accept the possibility of individual excesses, regard them as inevitable, and therefore we cannot do without suppressing such excesses.'[19]

As we have said before, we do not ourselves believe that in a communist society there will not be some violations of norms, and in extreme cases also — for the reasons adduced by the authors and for others — possibly grave excesses by individuals. What measures society will take to deal with such infringements it is impossible to say as yet without indulging in speculation. The future will show. However, there is a very considerable difference, in terms of social character, between criminality as a mass phenomenon, as at present affecting the behaviour of a not inconsiderable percentage of the population, and some possible individual excesses in particular circumstances. What matters at the present is not the blueprint of a Utopian society in which even individual excesses would be unthinkable, but the creation of a social order which will exclude criminality as a mass phenomenon — and indeed, it is only as a mass phenomenon that criminality really is criminality.

Yet Lander goes considerably further than this in his hypothesis, developing the following argument: criminality is a conflict or a contradiction between the individual and society; there will always be individuals and there will always be society; according to the rules of dialectics there will also always be contradictions or conflicts between opposites — hence criminality will always exist even though names, yardsticks of assessment and counter-measures may change.

For one thing, it is probably wrong to equate criminality with the dialectical contradiction or the clash of opposites as the motive force in the development of history (developmental contradictions). Lander, almost without noticing it, has here shifted the level of the discussion. He uses the concept of contradiction, or of the unity and clash of opposites, in relation to the development of mankind generally. But in this system of reference not every conflict is a developmental conflict. Criminality, at most, is a conflict in such a system but never a contradiction determining the movement of society. 'Unity and the clash of opposites' do not mean that human beings are facing each other in pairs, fighting with each other, or that history is nothing but a picture of people in conflict with one another over some problem or other. Criminality is a *definite social phenomenon* in conflict with the rules of human co-existence. The fact that there will always be contradictions because they are at the heart of all movement, or that matter without motion cannot exist, does not imply that certain finite contradictions will always continue to exist.

From the fact that movement in human society is a movement governed by the unity and clash of opposites one must not conclude that certain specific contradictions must exist for ever. For in that case slavery, feudalism and capitalism would likewise have eternal existence. The eternal existence of a specific phenomenon can be proved only by proving the eternal duration of its specific conditions of existence. Lander's hypothesis, however, does not meet these requirements and is not therefore a verifiable scientific hypothesis.

Bavcon, Skaberné and Vodopivec endeavour to prove, by quoting specific phenomena, that criminality is not a phenomenon alien to socialism but is linked with it as a system, and that the occurrence of criminality is therefore itself governed by the social laws of the dynamics of socialism. Their view is endorsed in other socialist countries by those criminologists who see criminality as a negative manifestation of the achievement principle or as a reflection of the conflict between ever-growing requirements and ever-limited possibilities of satisfying those requirements, or else a time lag between individual awareness and social reality, etc. As for these last-listed arguments, we have shown them to be untenable in connection with Lander's hypothesis. We need therefore only discuss here the views of Bavcon, Skaberné and Vodopivec.

The differences between their positions and ours are clearly revealed in the following passage: 'Criminality, therefore, is an indispensable and inevitable phenomenon even under socialism, at the present stage of the evolution of society. It is the consequence and the by-product of an objective state of affairs and of a law operating regardless of human volition. Criminality, therefore, is not just a survival of the old within the consciousness of the people, but arises on our own soil, from our specific production relationships and from the resulting social conditions and their superstructure.' [20]

It is true that for a time socialist criminology maintained the thesis that criminality must be explained exclusively by rudimentary survivals in human nature, but this has since been unanimously rejected so that there is no need here to refute it. The rejection of such a thesis, however, does not mean that criminality itself may not, for one thing, be a 'birthmark' of the old society out of which socialism has developed as a revolutionary consequence. For another thing, it does not mean that criminality is not also caused by conditions or circumstances which for their part are 'birthmarks' or 'survivals of the old society' — and these, as everybody knows, cannot be removed at one fell swoop but only step by step and by prolonged systematic and purposeful work.

Bavcon, Skaberné and Vodopivec maintain that this is not the case but that 'the production relations can give rise to criminality'. They believe that the socialisation of production relations has 'by no means made man the free master of his fate in a social sense'. He has not yet, they maintain, 'developed into a social being in the true sense of the word'. Socialism, they say, neither guarantees man's full self-determination nor does socialisation of the means of production alter his specific relationship or attitude to the means of production. [21]

The idea that socialism has not made any real change in the specific position of the individual in production or towards the means of production seems to us to be the point at issue. Perhaps in Yugoslavia, a country which has to contend with particular difficulties, there has really been no marked change, at least in appearance, in the position of the working people — although this does not seem very convincing to us in view of all the reports about the social and economic achievements attained at great effort by the Yugoslav people. If our undoubtedly meritorious colleagues Bavcon, Skaberné and Vodopivec were concerned with specific Yugoslav conditions we would not presume to argue with them; but since they refer to socialism generally we must be permitted to dispute the theoretical position revealed in their work.

It is by no means a fact that the 'socialisation of the means of production' — which incidentally is not confined, as Bavcon, Skarberné and Vodopivec suggest, to the 'nationalisation of the means of production' but has likewise been realised in the establishment of co-operative property in the countryside, the establishment of production co-operatives of artisans, and in other forms [22] — has brought about no change in the position of the producer in the production process or in society. It is certainly correct that even the socialist producer cannot arbitrarily control the means of production. In any case such 'freedom' is neither desired by socialism nor desirable in any other objective sense. That would not be freedom but anarchy.

The socialist producer (with the exception of old-age pensioners, children and persons incapable of work, for whom other forms of the realisation of their right to socialist State property are available in the shape of various welfare schemes, realises his ownership of the means of production through participation, by the work he performs directly in the production process or at some other place of society in line with the necessary division of labour. But such work is no longer surrender of the merchandise 'labour' in an exploitative relationship but the realisation of proprietary rights in socialist property. And this in turn has resulted in a revolutionary change also of the specific relationships within the production process and indeed of all relationships within the specific labour relationship.

This is not the place to list these changes in detail. They are reflected in the rights of trades unions, in labour brigades, in collective contracts, in the system of economic planning and management, in the development of socialist democracy at the individual's place of work, in the State and in society, in mass participation in the regulation of all processes, including the administration of justice, etc., and they clearly reveal how man, on the basis of socialist production and living conditions, is increasingly becoming a social being and the master of his fate.

These changes have been made possible by the abolition of the exploitation of man by man; they are reflected by the progressive removal of the survivals of the old society in accordance with the present level of economic and political development, and of the development of human awareness. It seems to us therefore incomprehensible that these changes should be ignored and that man in a socialist society should be described as an unfree being at the mercy of alien powers and blind fate. Freedom is not arbitrariness. Freedom does not mean that every individual can decide all matters, even matters concerning himself, in accordance with his own ideas alone. Society is and always will be a highly complex organism and a highly organised system; the individual — no matter whether he occupies a decision-making or a more humble function in that system — will never be able to move quite as 'freely' as he would like but will have to fit himself into the system. It is not quite clear, therefore, what concept of freedom our Yugoslav friends have in mind when they assign to man in socialist society a 'subordinate position in the settlement of social affairs', a position determined by the limited state of development of production relations. The very abstraction of 'the individual' per se, as an agent confronted by forces impeding him in the settlement of social affairs, strikes us as a mistake of scientific method.

These and similar views, however, are not just superficial ideas but philosophically founded theoretical views which deserve serious discussion. The theoretical basis of these views no doubt is the philosophical concept of the continuation of 'man's alienation' under socialism, the view that this alienation is not just a survival of the old society but a genuine product also of socialist society.

The most explicit representative of such an alienation theory is the

Polish philosopher Adam Schaff, who has recently emphatically declared that the alienation of the individual must not be seen only as a feature of life in an exploitative society but also as an aspect of man's life in a socialist society. [23] We agree with Schaff that it would be a mistake to form an illusory picture of life in socialist society. Indeed, for criminology to try to gloss over these real problems of life would be tantamount to surrendering its scientific character. Nevertheless we cannot go along with Schaff's theory of alienation. It provides no genuine or useful solution for the development of society.

Engels called the transition from capitalism to communism man's leap from the animal kingdom into the realm of freedom. The historical period in which this 'leap' is performed is the period of socialism. In terms of the evolution of the human personality this is a period when, as a result of the transformation of all conditions — economic, political and moral — man also strips off all the residue of the old society and develops into a new free human being.

The criminal court judge, the criminal law researcher and the criminologist are very much aware of the extent of the deformation, degradation and crippling of man as a result of his alienation caused by exploitative conditions; they also realise that the socialist revolution does not simply produce the new man like a phoenix rising from the ashes. Added to this is the fact that, from the outset, socialism does not develop on its own foundations but that these new foundations of life must first be created as a result of socialist transformations proceeding over a number of decades. These transformations are linked with the scientific-technological revolution, in the course of which the new material and technological foundations of socialism are born and with them the new moral, cultural and educational foundations of life.

All this results not only in successes but also in difficulties, which are moreover complicated and multiplied by the fact that the products of the past alienation of man continue to be active in the individual's public and social life. Schaff calls these 'after-effects' of man's alienated position vis-à-vis his work, vis-à-vis himself and vis-à-vis society, a position which stemmed from exploitative relationships, an 'alienation' connected with socialism as such.

We cannot escape the impression that Schaff and certain other criminologists have here fallen into a trivial error. They observe these after-effects of alienation not only among clearly degenerate individuals but quite frequently also among respectable people who neither belonged to the former exploiting classes nor were directly influenced by them. They observe this alienation in individuals who, in some instances, did not even experience the old society with its disastrous contradictions. They record that the manifestation of this alienation at State level – an unimaginative soulless bureaucracy – which was part of the character of the State of the exploitative society can be observed also in the behaviour patterns of the new State.

Whereas we, on the basis of Lenin's teachings, regard all such phenomena as alien to socialism, as something which the masses of the people under the leadership of the Party and the State must strive in every possible way to overcome, Schaff describes them as an 'alienation' organically linked with socialism, something whose continuous existence we must accept.

It is not a fact – as Schaff suggests – that anyone not accepting his concepts is trying to design an illusionist, Utopian picture of life in socialist society, glossing over the contradictions, difficulties and frictions found in real life. The important thing is what one understands by socialism and what by alienation. It seems to us that Schaff is confusing cause and effect when he mistakes the stubborn survivals and after-effects of alienation for alienation itself. Schaff maintains that 'alienation' is brought about by the mere fact that man must objectivise his activity if he wants to live in a society. In consequence he is, as it were, automatically subjected to the power of the object which he cannot himself manage. [24] Under socialism the organ for the 'management of objects' is the State which, according to Schaff, confronts man almost like a 'Moloch'.

Schaff believes that he can base himself here on Lenin who, defining the function of suppression typical of the exploitative State, remarked that in the highly developed socialist State of the future only the function of 'management of objects' would remain. Although Lenin was intending to say that the State's typical power over people would wither away or be progressively abolished, Schaff interprets Lenin's dictum as though even a socialist State would have to practise that disastrous power of objects against man. [25]

As so often before, we observe in Schaff an almost imperceptible shift in his frame of reference. In Marxist–Leninist theory the concept of 'alienation' is used to characterise a particular social position of man, marked by antagonisms and representing, in the given social system, an insuperable barrier to the deployment of his human personality. The typical manifestation of this was the spontaneous, arbitrary power of the object produced by man himself, which under the given exploitative relations turns against its own creator. But no champion of Marxism ever intended to imply that the products of human activity, an activity which is bound to be 'objectivised' in products – though also in spiritual products — possessed any a priori fateful danger of man's own activity — or its objectivisation in the shape of products — turning against himself or against his life. The founders of Marxism—Leninism were far from attributing to human activity the odium of ancient Greek tragedy. It seems to us that Schaff has not entirely escaped the danger of representing man, as it were, in an existentialist manner, as his own enemy. This danger invariably arises when the same words are used in different systems of reference and account is not taken of the fact that as a result they are bound to change their meaning.

Any theory of alienation which, regardless of the nature of social conditions, construes for mankind an eternal danger of alienation and which fails to take account of the fact that the socialist State is anything but a Moloch [26] turning arbitrary power of objects against the people who have produced them, but rather 'guides and manages the people' towards the realisation of their most genuine living interests — any such theory of alienation is unfit to be the starting point either of a scientific management of society or of socialist criminology.

Our scientific analysis of the social structure of socialist society on the contrary demonstrates that this social structure — just because it has achieved the abolition of exploitative relations — contains within itself all potentialities and possibilities of a free development of the human personality, i.e. one that is based on the objective laws of social evolution — and that this is not just a possibility in the socialist countries but in fact a genuine, measurable and continually developing reality.

Such a fundamental position does not rest on the assumption that 'paradisial' conditions already exist in the socialist countries, or that the degree of socialisation achieved, and hence man's liberation, already represent perfection, or that there are no limits to the development of the human personality in the actual conditions of present-day life. Any such view would be Utopian and would lead to positivism, to the glorification of the status quo and hence to the denial of the need for further development. There is a difference, however, between seeing the limits of the present development in the structure of socialist production and living relations, i.e. in the system of socialism, and in seeing these limits in material and ideological conditions which prevent all the advantages and potentialities of the socialist system of society from coming to fruition.

A great deal of importance attaches to what we mean by socialism. If it is taken as the sum total of the empirical conditions still prevailing in the various socialist countries, as a mixture of old and new relationships, connections and conditions of a material or ideological nature, as a conglomeration of the most diverse behaviour patterns or behaviour rules, then one might easily come to regard it as a 'hardship' to be overcome as soon as possible, as a condition in which criminality is an inevitable feature under the laws of society. This would mean confusing the old and the new, mixing up the promise of the future with what is withering away, equating aspects determining future development with aspects impeding development, a failure to distinguish the essential from the inessential. That is the way in which Bavcon, Skaberné and Vodopivec use the concept of socialism. In this form we cannot accept it as a fundamental scientific concept of socialist criminology.

In referring to socialism as the 'transitional period' between capitalism and communism, in referring to socialism as still bearing the 'birthmarks' of the old society, the Marxist—Leninist classics did not mean to put forward a concept of socialism which would blur all distinctions between the various empirical phenomena. To the Marxist—Leninist classics socialism was the germinal form of the new communist society. Communism to them was not something different from socialism but merely the full development of all potentialities already inherent in the social structure of socialism. But these cannot assert themselves in a vacuum but only under the prevailing material and ideological conditions. It is the level of the development of productive forces, the political, cultural and moral level of social and individual life and of human consciousness which determine the extent to which the new features of socialism have already produced real changes and the extent to which they are still dormant as potentialities awaiting realisation. Between the new social structure and the new social and individual consciousness built upon it, a consciousness which in turn determines new behaviour patterns on the one hand, and the survivals of the old society on the other, there is no mechanical dependence but a reciprocal relationship tending towards a change in, or a liquidation of, the conditions and phenomena which impede socialist potentialities.

It is not the socialist production relations, nor 'the given state of development' of production relations, which impose on man limitations to the free development of his personality. These production relations, after all, contain within themselves a progressive tendency, a drive towards a further unfolding of their socialist and communist features. Such limitations as can still be found to the development of man's personality consist in just those conditions, phenomena and relationships of a material and spiritual nature as obstruct the free unfolding of socialist production and living relations and views.

The limitations found at present in the socialist countries to the development of socialist relations and of production and everyday life have their roots, therefore, not in the system of socialism but in the level of material and spiritual life found at the time of the revolution, a level which, after the ragings of fascism and the destructions of World War II was exceedingly low in every respect — economic, political, cultural and moral. Added to this is the fact that centuries of feudal and capitalist rule had moulded all social life and the social and individual consciousness to the behaviour patterns and way of life of the exploitative society.

The present-day socialist countries are not simply confronted, as Bavcon, Skaberné and Vodopivec believe, with 'a few insignificant survivals of the class society'[27] but with frequently considerable and persistent remnants of the old life, all the more resistant as they often present themselves as 'modern'. We consider it a mistake — a mistake which might seriously disorientate the public — to describe such old manifestations, behaviour patterns, relationships and modes of thinking as anything other than what they are — remnants of the capitalist society or of social systems preceding it, such as feudalism. And if we look beyond the frontiers of Europe we find to this day, in certain Asian countries, remnants of ways of life and behaviour patterns stemming from the period of slavery or, as for instance in West Irian, even earlier social systems. From what we know of the history of Yugoslavia, that country too is still burdened by a legacy not only of capitalism but also of feudalism.

We cannot therefore go along with Bavcon, Skaberné and Vodopivec when they maintain that such phenomena, 'e.g. various forms of discontent, hostility, a sense of injustice, envy of those better off',[28] are human experiences which can be described as reflecting the socialist production relations, i.e. which are caused by them. There is even less justification for the claim that the socialist production relations might give rise to a 'revolt against a society which tries to push the individual to the sidelines'. We do not deny that such phenomena do exist, but we object to their being described as intrinsic products of the basic social structure of socialist society.

It is obvious, therefore, that science cannot arbitrarily use the concept of socialism for an undifferentiated sum total of conditions, relations and circumstances to be found in the actual life of socialist countries without falling into error and causing pessimism. If, on the other hand, one sees socialism as a stage of the development which from within leads to communism, to the liquidation of all remnants of earlier social systems, then there is no cause for either illusions or pessimism. One cannot attribute to the nature of socialism something that socialism is about to eliminate. This approach is not based on any wishful thinking but on exact scientific reasoning.

It may be thought that this is a purely 'academic' argument about concepts, an argument of no practical use whatever, seeing that Bavcon, Skaberné and Vodopivec similarly maintain the view that one cannot just idly fold one's hands and wait 'for better days'. No doubt many lines of specific research in Yugoslavia will follow much the same lines as in the GDR. Nevertheless there is need for clarity about fundamental positions. For Marxism – as we have pointed out in connection with arguments about the material nature of criminal acts – concepts exist not for their own sake but as theoretical guiding lines for action in science and practice.

Most importantly, the criticised theoretical positions deny the existence of differences between exploitative conditions with their effects on human action, on the one hand, and socialism on the other. Unwittingly they thus find themselves in a position very close to bourgeois criminology. If socialist criminology were to accept this position it would run the risk of simultaneously accepting the fundamental thesis of bourgeois criminology about the perpetual existence of criminality and of uncritically adopting the bourgeois methods of criminological research; this would rob it of its forward-looking optimistic character.

Moreover, in mapping out specific lines of research it matters vitally whether this is done in a way favouring the advance and perfection of man's socialist relations with society, with the State, and with one another, or whether what is possible in our day and under our conditions is seen as something relatively useless since it continues to lead the individual into the same old hopeless contradictions and conflicts leading to criminality. In fact any unprejudiced examination of the development in the socialist countries will prove that the trends of social behaviour stemming from the new social structure have already eliminated a vast amount of conflict material and hopeless situations, so that people who have grown up in the new society now see a number of such situations, situations typical of bourgeois society, only as something from a dim and distant past or from stories and novels. Socialist society has long verified the hypothesis that criminality is not an inevitable regular aspect of its own evolution.

The concept of the causes of criminality

Having discussed the concept of law or regularity in dialectical determinism and examined its importance in a theory of the causes of criminality in socialist society, we must now consider the question of what phenomena of objective reality must be covered by and be reflected in the concept of cause.

The principal question is that of the connections between criminality and objective reality. Our subject therefore is criminality as a social phenomenon, on the one hand, and objective reality on the other. The aim of this examination is the isolation of whatever inherent connections exist within this totality of causal connections.

To achieve this we must first isolate from all causal connections those which are essential connections between phenomena. In objective reality, as we know, all phenomena are in an objective general relationship with each other and also in a universal interaction with 'causes and effects continually changing position ...'. [29]

The process of isolation leads us to the real essential connections. As Engels says: 'In order to comprehend the individual phenomena we must snatch them from their general connection, view them in isolation, and at once the changing movements will become visible, the one as cause and the other as effect'. [30]

Our problem, therefore, is not concerned with just any connections, since such connections must always exist on the basis of the universal interaction of all phenomena. Our problem is concerned with the regular, law-governed connections. This dialectical materialist starting point must not be lost sight of. Failure to grasp the question of the causes of criminality in any other sense must lead not to the understanding of the laws of motion but to a mere catalogue of accidental and random circumstances under the heading of causes.

Bourgeois imperialist criminology, *biologically* orientated as it is, for instance believes that the causes of criminality are to be found in nature itself, in man's biological make-up. Thus it quite seriously maintains that the cause of sexual offences is to be sought in man's sexuality. [31]

The same kind of attitude is also reflected in the views held by bourgeois imperialist criminology on the problem of the causes of criminality. Under American influence the term used nowadays is invariably 'relationship', i.e. a functional relation between criminality and certain phenomena of objective reality in exploitative systems, and the demand is therefore made that the research for the causes of criminality should be abandoned. [32]

This scientific failure has not only social but also philosophical roots. Bourgeois criminology can only interpret causality mechanically, which means that dialectical processes are not comprehended or understood. It is worth noting that the necessary critique of this philosophical starting point is now being practised with particular perseverance from 'the Right'. Thus Richard Lange seizes on this new situation in bourgeois criminology for conducting his campaign against all determinist views of man in the exploitative society and to use the phrase of man's allegedly indeterminist 'freedom' for covering up the repressive function, the class character, of imperialist criminal law. [33]

It seems to us therefore that it is an important task of socialist criminology to reveal the social and philosophical basis of this 'clash of opinion' within bourgeois criminology by elucidating the dialectical-determinist point of view on the problem of the causes of criminality. Such an elucidation might clear the path for those scholars who, from a critical position, endeavour to explore the causes of criminality in bourgeois society; it should help them understand the true social conditions of the existence of criminality and hence also to overcome the limitations of a mechanical —materialist way of looking upon them.

After this short discursion into bourgeois criminology we can return to our initial question. These are the things we must bear in mind:

The question about the inherent regular connection between criminality and certain aspects and phenomena of objective reality serves the endeavour to control this connection once it has been identified – i.e. to change the world and to contribute to the victory of socialism and communism. Any such connection can be revealed only if objective reality, the various aspects and phenomena of our life, are boldly faced, if they are not glossed over but laid bare as the first step towards their liquidation and towards the victory of socialism.

One of the principal theoretical conditions for the discharge of this task is clarity on the use of the concept of the causes of criminality. A large number of authors in the past – regardless of the fact that they have made some very significant discoveries of certain correlations – have failed to clarify what phenomena of social life they were labelling 'causes of criminality'.

There was the more or less widely held view that only the 'individualistic, anti-social attitude of the culprit', [34] the attitude which led him to commit his offence, should be understood as the cause of criminality. The very first specific criminological researches, however, showed that the real problem of the causes begins beyond, or rather 'on this side of', the 'individualistic attitude'. It is an over-simplification to describe the subjective causes of criminality in the offender's mind simply as 'individualism'. 'Individualism' explains only one of many possible manifestations of human consciousness.

Of course, the offender's decision to commit his deed, a decision which unites all other psychological processes such as his aims, further intentions, motives, hopes, emotions, needs, ideological views, etc. into a conflicting unity, is the nearest 'immediate' cause of his act, simply because any act has its origin in the mind of the agent, the individual. But this would turn the question of the causes of criminality into a question about the psychology of the action, whereas in fact we are after something different — the causes which make individuals living in a socialist society commit criminal acts. Here, as we have seen, the simple question of causality, which asks only about the 'immediate' causes, is no longer sufficient.

Whereas a court of law, examining a sequence of events in order to establish whether a definite consequence was the effect of a definite action, traces the causal chain back, link by link, from the consequences to the deed, in order to establish the strictly limited causal sequence for the purpose of evidence, the determination of the causes of criminality is a somewhat different process. Here, too, the causal connection from the offender's decision to the offence is traced back to its roots in objective reality — these include also ideological trends in society — but the connections which are here being established are not the same as those in the investigation of the external sequence of actions. We cannot content ourselves with the direct immediate connections of the causal chain. We must take into account also indirect connections, the interaction of various influences, probabilities and statistical laws. Thus, if trashy or pornographic literature is found among the possessions of a juvenile guilty of rowdyism, we must not — unless of course he directly admits to having imitated the acts of violence extolled in this literature — assume a direct connection between the decision leading to his offence and such trashy reading matter. Anything else would be a distortion of reality. At the same time it would be wrong to exclude this trash from the area under examination simply because it was not an 'immediate' cause. Modern psychology has shown that such products do indeed have an effect — except that such an effect is only in the rarest of instances as immediate as is often believed by simplifiers.

The question of the causes of criminality is thus certainly concerned with regular connections but not solely with 'immediate' or 'direct' ones; in the great majority of cases these will be indirect but nevertheless law-determined, 'regular' connections. Any simple determinism, therefore, is useless for the investigation of the causes of criminality. We have here further evidence that a strict scientific approach to the theory of the causes of criminality does not involve its limitation to causal-mechanical ideas which merely have an appearance of exactitude but in fact run counter to the dialectics of life.

The task of socialist criminology is not simply to remove the 'ideological' basis of criminality but any other basis as well. Besides, in principle no offence is due solely to ideological causes. Any such assumption would presuppose the idea that an ideology could exist on its own, without any real foundation. Any such belief would merely be a variant of the theory that the causes of criminality are to be sought in man's 'perpetual wickedness' and that criminality, therefore, is part of man's nature, an inhuman aspect of his unchangeable character.

With such a theoretical concept the task, mapped out by the Party and the State, of eliminating criminality and its causes from the life of society could never be discharged.

Any theory of the causes of criminality in socialist society which could serve as a directive for scientific and practical research and at the same time as a fundamental explanation of the continued survival of criminality requires clarity on the contents and function of the concept of 'causes of criminality'. It is therefore necessary to recapitulate a few general conclusions.

First, criminality is a social phenomenon. Although it is made up of numerous individual acts by individual offenders, as a social phenomenon, i.e. in relation to society as a whole and its material and spiritual life, it is more than the mere sum total of such individual actions. It is the totality of these actions or behaviour patterns. By totality we mean not only the sum total of such individual actions but also the totality of interrelations — effects or consequences — between these phenomena and their social environment, as well as the internal relations among these separate phenomena. This means, of course, that as a social phenomenon it must ultimately also have social causes. It is not, therefore, possible to explain even one criminal phenomenon solely from the individual characteristics of a human being. The causes of sexual offences thus do not lie in the mere biological sexuality of the individual but spring from social phenomena which have to be investigated. The personal characteristics of the individual certainly play a part in this, but they are not on their own decisive.

Second, as a definite social phenomenon criminality has a very definite characteristic aspect or quality. This aspect or quality must ultimately be shared also by the social cause whose effect or consequence criminality is. A socially indifferent phenomenon cannot therefore ever be a cause of criminality.

Third, criminality as a definite social phenomenon is alien to socialism, to the new human way of social life. It is not part of the character of this new form of social co-existence. In consequence, the cause producing this phenomenon cannot be part of the character of socialism either. It must spring from other phenomena which, though they exist in reality, are not part of the nature of socialism.

Thus bodily injury may have sprung from the offender's drunkenness. Drunkenness, admittedly, still exists as a social phenomenon; indeed it has definite objective and subjective conditions of existence — such as 'boozers', where consumption of alcohol is still the main purpose and where drinkers encourage one another to show who can 'take' most. This has nothing in common with the socialist way of life.

Fourth, an ever deeper insight into criminality — as scientifically worked out in the resolutions of the SED and the State Council — shows that criminality is not a uniform or homogeneous phenomenon. It is — in our present knowledge of the subject — differentiated and equally embraces petty theft, individual murder and even genocide. Hence the causes cannot be homogeneous either, and the differentiation of phenomena must be reflected in a differentiation of their causes.

Thus it is instantly obvious that crimes against the GDR — even if a 'non-political' asocial individual has allowed himself to be enlisted for espionage — must have causes of a totally different social quality from, for instance, some culpable infringement of a maintenance order.

Fifth, we must remember that each phenomenon in society is in a dialectical reciprocal relationship with numerous other phenomena. It follows, therefore, that criminality cannot be reduced to a mechanical-linear relation between one cause and one effect. Such a direct linear causal relation, as found for instance in the field of simple mechanics, cannot govern the complex social phenomena which make up criminality. We must therefore bear in mind that each cause is a whole complex of phenomena.

This becomes obvious if we remember how a man arrives at his decision to commit an act. The factors here are needs, emotions, hopes, motives, state of mind, ability to concentrate, perseverance, etc. It is from the presence or absence, the co-existence or clash, the mutual interaction of these diverse processes that man's decision springs. But each of these different psychological phenomena in turn has different objective causes which happened to be present at the moment of the criminal act or in the life of the individual. Any reasonably thorough investigation must show that these very diverse subjective factors, which may even include deep contradictions, cannot have sprung from a single cause but must be the result of the action of a multiplicity of phenomena.

Sixth, criminality is the action of individuals. It is manifested in certain forms of human behaviour. These actions by people endowed with reason and pursuing specific aims and objectives must likewise be borne in mind in examining the problem of the causes of criminality.

This means that the complex causes of criminality must be at once of objective and subjective character. Although man, in committing criminal acts, is determined by external circumstances – i.e. objective phenomena of his environment – this determinism is not therefore linear or mechanical. Man as a reasoning being is able to recognise objective necessity and to be guided by this realisation towards deciding in favour of a relevant social mode of behaviour. This ability or, in other words this real possibility, inherent in the nature of man's free will, means that a theory of the causes of criminality must not adopt a simply mechanical-materialist point of view, i.e. the idea that certain objective phenomena must necessarily, with absolute certainty, lead to a criminal act. Instead, a dialectical materialist attitude will remember that – as the Soviet psychologist S. L. Rubinstein has put it – the objective phenomena are 'refracted' in the mind of the individual.

It is a mistake, therefore, to try to identify factors or circumstances – a kind of criminality virus – which would inevitably give rise to criminality. The Czechoslovak scientist Schubert similarly opposes a mechanical oversimplification of the theory of the causes of criminality. He points out quite correctly that such a theory could not be universally valid, nor would it even offer an explanation of criminality under the conditions of capitalism: 'In spite of pinpointing the exploitative system as the main cause of criminality, the existence of the subjective factor in the emergence of criminality cannot be excluded. The subject cannot be exempted from active participation in the emergence of criminality even in the exploitative system – with the exception of specific critical cases touching on the defence of existence as such. To do so would mean to deny the individual's active participation in determining his mode of action ... Even under capitalism the subject has assessed his position and defined his attitude and the preservation of his interests. According to the degree to which prevailing conditions of social life affect him, according to the degree of his awareness of being able to preserve his interests, he chooses his behaviour.' [35]

Seventh, as we have said before, the essential task in the discovery of the causes of criminality is the identification of essential connections between phenomena. This means that from among all the correlations linking phenomena with one another those must be isolated which determine and produce the essence of the phenomenon of criminality. These then are the cause.

Eighth and finally, it is important to remember that criminality is action by individuals possessing the power of choice. Man lives in a definite society. For that reason the character of that society must always be borne in mind in determining the causes and their mode of operation. It is moreover obvious that the character of this social order also determines the extent, the nature and the manner of solving the contradictions within that order. Thus exploitation of man by man and the resulting consequences, such as hardship, misery, demoralisation, depair, fear for one's livelihood, antisocial attitudes, a ruthless pursuit of profit, fierce competition frequently developing into a struggle for social existence, etc. — these are the main social causes of criminality in the exploitative society. They are at the same time essential features of these social orders. Such contradictions cannot be resolved within these orders; the most that can be done is to mitigate their extreme effects. These phenomena, by way of contrast, are alien to socialism since in its nature socialism means the liquidation of exploitation. In so far as rudimentary traces of some of these phenomena continue to exist, they are merely survivals of the old society and easily overcome and eliminated. In examining the causes of criminality one must never, therefore, overlook the character of the social order under discussion. There are no causes of criminality which exist above the social orders or independently of their character.

We therefore understand the concept of the causes of criminality as a complex of social and individual phenomena of material, ideological and individual-personality character, a complex which, because of its nature and its inherent contradictions to the new humanist socialist relations between individual and State, society and his fellows, can spontaneously determine man to adopt a behaviour which is dangerous to socialist society, to its further evolution and its material or spiritual living processes, or which objectively and in an antisocial manner obstructs or damages certain aspects of these living processes, and which infringes the legal order. [36]

Another question, which must be clearly kept apart from the above-discussed problem of the laws of social development, is that of the internal determining effect of the causes listed. Between the causes of criminality and criminality itself there is an inherent regular connection. This must be revealed with the aid of the basic findings of Marxism—Leninism, political economy, Marxist social psychology, individual psychology, more particularly the psychology of action and of the development of the human personality, juvenile psychology, educational research, etc. Only thus can a starting point be found for the neutralisation of the effectiveness of those causes upon the individual's mind, quite apart from the fact that the causes as such must be liquidated. The question of whether there are discoverable internal regular connections between the causes of criminality and criminality itself is highly controversial. There is a widespread belief that although such connections must be investigated they are not governed by any law because this would be in contradiction with the above-mentioned regularity of a purposeful and systematic struggle for the progressive liquidation of criminality under the conditions of socialism.

It needs emphasising that a distinction must be made between the laws of the development of society, laws which govern the direction and nature of social-historical evolution and therefore belong to a different, greater, social system of reference, and the law-determined connections between certain limited social phenomena. This is not to deny that the laws of social development also permeate and modify such specific interrelations. Moreover, regularity, i.e. the operation of laws, must not be equated with some fateful inevitability. The fact that a phenomenon had a cause which produced a law-determined effect does not mean that the action of the individual in society is in any way predetermined.

One cannot warn often enough against this widespread idea of the inescapability and eternal validity of objective laws (both the laws of social development and the regularities existing between limited phenomena); such a concept frequently leads to resignation because it implies an inevitable operation of cause and effect.

Even the laws governing the development of society do not operate inevitably. The revolutionary development of human society shows that man, by changing the conditions of his social existence, also changes the operation of objective laws. Socialist society differs from exploitative systems also by the fact that such objective laws have been identified and brought under control. Thanks to the masses led by the Party, socialist society is capable — by action and not just by wishful thinking — of replacing the operating conditions of certain social laws and bringing new ones into operation. Socialism, therefore, is a period of extensive replacement of old regularities through the revolutionary transformation of the working and living conditions of human society. But it is, at the same time, a social order in which certain old phenomena either continue to be partially effective, or have been transformed, or entirely removed. To recognise this has nothing in common with fatalism.

If man in socialist society is able even to gain control of the laws of social evolution, of increasingly understanding and managing them — for example, the law stating that imperialism tends towards war is already being thwarted, even at a time when imperialism still exists, by a broadly based comprehensive struggle of the people — then it is obvious that there is no inevitable connection between individuals and the regular effects produced by certain conditions.

The internal structure of the causes of criminality and of the individual criminal offence

We have described the causes of criminality as a complex of phenomena, of material and spiritual, general and individual, psychological and ideological nature. The concept of the causes of criminality thus covers a multiplicity of phenomena which are interconnected and interdependent and which interact in their specific negative effect on the individual's decision to adopt a definite social behaviour. Any investigation of how the individual's decision has come about will show that a great number of separate phenomena are present in each case as effective conditions. It follows that there is no specific criminal act, let alone a category of criminal offence, that is 'caused' solely by a single phenomenon. The question therefore arises of whether an undifferentiated multiplicity of phenomena should be regarded as the cause of criminality or whether some differentiation and separation of emphasis is possible between the various effective phenomena. The question thus concerns the relationships between the separate elements within this complexity, the function of each individual phenomenon within the system of conditions, or − in other words − the internal structure of the causes of criminality.

Marxist philosophy and the consideration of individual acts suggested a differentiation of the phenomena effective in the emergence of an occurrence into causes and conditions. On this basis Hartmann and Lekschas have proposed a distinction between causes, conditions and occasions of criminality. [37] However, as the critique of Lutzke [38] and Manecke [39] and the study of Stiller [40] have shown, and as had been emphasised earlier by Horst Luther and Gerhard Feix, [41] this attempt must be regarded as a failure.

Hartmann and Lekschas saw the essential distinction between the causes of criminality and the conditions of criminality in that the causes, as complex phenomena of life, because of their inherent conflict with the social requirements of socialist society, are apt to determine individuals to adopt an anti-social or society-endangering behaviour. As for the conditions of criminality, on the other hand, they saw these in the fact that, in the area where the decision to commit criminal acts is made, the new socialist relationships have not yet been sufficiently developed to prevent the commission of the criminal act − i.e. in the lack of criminality-impeding factors.

However, social life is not so structured that wherever such criminality-impeding factors may be lacking there is a vacuum; in fact, other circumstances come to the fore in such conditions. Yet any investigation of such factors or circumstances shows — as the latest empirical studies and their analysis have demonstrated — that these are all conditions belonging to that complex of phenomena labelled the causes of criminality. The attempted distinction is therefore a fallacy.

The critical examination of these theses seems to have shown that it is not possible to apply the distinction of causes and conditions — the latter, moreover, being subdivided into 'indispensable', 'sufficient', 'favourable' or 'general' — to a totality of phenomena such as make up either criminality as a whole or certain categories of criminal offences. The distinction is useful only in the investigation of the conditions effective in the occurrence of a single specific event.

Hörz [42] has more recently made an interesting attempt to define these concepts. His view seems to us useful in differentiating between the rôle of various phenomena in accidents due to human carelessness. His principles for distinguishing between causes and conditions in a definite specific event, however, show that this fine differentiation can only be made with regard to the real function of a definite individual phenomenon and only with specific events which have already taken place. Hörz points out that the same phenomena could in another process easily exchange their functions. Thus a road in bad repair can be the 'condition' of a traffic accident in one case and the 'cause' of one in another. A badly maintained road is a 'condition' for an accident if it was properly marked as a dangerous stretch of road and the driver disregarded the warning. It becomes the 'cause' if there was no warning and if its danger was not readily obvious to a careful driver. It therefore decisively depends on the combination of circumstances in each definite process whether a phenomenon in a specific occurrence is a cause or a condition. Only from the constellation of circumstances — and not simply from the specific phenomenon itself — does the function emerge which the phenomenon in question has discharged.

We have already noted that criminology is concerned with criminality both as an analysis of criminal acts already committed and with a view to possible criminal acts. But if cause and effect can exchange places even in criminal acts already committed, then it would surely be mere speculation to label any phenomenon 'cause' or 'condition' with regard to any possible future effect. Criminology bases its findings both on the analysis of individual actions and on a totality of actions. It must therefore so formulate its concepts that they make allowance for the differences and variants existing in the real world. We believe, therefore, that criminology should distinguish between 'causes of criminality' and 'causes and conditions, including immediate occasions of criminal acts'. The former concept endeavours to explain criminality as a totality of phenomena occurring within a definite unit of time (month, quarter, year, five-year period or decade) or as an integral whole or a special category of offences (theft, bodily injury, sexual offences, etc.) from the essential conditions determining them, and to reveal the regular operation of such conditions.

Whereas we regard the differentiation into causes, conditions and immediate occasions as necessary in the investigation of the individual action, this is not possible for criminality as an all-embracing totality of criminal acts over a year or even longer periods of time, or for the totality of a category of offences over a certain period. The concept of the causes of criminality therefore covers all the above-named diverse phenomena which in specific individual instances have alternately discharged the functions of a cause or of a condition of the emergence of various decisions to commit various deeds. Any other understanding of the concept of the causes of criminality is impossible without running foul not only of facts but also of dialectics. This means that the concept of the causes of criminality is no more than a totality of interacting or mutually interlinked phenomena. This concept can embrace only such phenomena as conditions or elements of the complex of causes as have appeared, in changing correlations, with a certain regularity or with constant repetition. We must establish which phenomena, time and again, and while continually changing their functions, have been identified as the 'causes or conditions of individual actions'; in this way conclusions can be arrived at about the regularity of their mode of operation in the causing of criminal patterns of behaviour.

Unique phenomena or phenomena effective only under extreme conditions cannot therefore be acknowledged as causes of criminality, since the concept of the causes should cover only those phenomena which have been effective over long periods of time and in a large number of criminal acts.

To quote Szabó, [43] a great deal of 'selective' work remains to be done. In spite of the results already achieved, socialist criminology is still in its beginnings.

In this pursuit criminology cannot content itself with a mere compilation of external factors — e.g. too much or too little pocket money, or no pocket money at all, for juveniles; one of the parents dead, parents divorced, child living with mother or father, or with grandparents, etc. — but will have to proceed from quantitative analysis of factors and assessment of correlations to a qualitative analysis of the factors and their effect on the individual's inherent control system. At the same time criminality will have to endeavour to absorb and utilise the knowledge already gained by other scientific disciplines.

Criminology, therefore, will have to move from the recording of surface factors to the analysis of the internal contradiction of these factors, and in doing so assess the negative effectiveness of such factors or conditions upon the system of the individual's socialist relations with the State, with society and with his neighbours. To that extent we believe that factor analysis and correlation calculation, as well as other similar methods, certainly have their place in socialist criminology or will have to find such a place. At the same time — as we shall show in the next chapter — the manner of the application of such methods in bourgeois criminology will have to be critically examined to make sure an uncritical acceptance and application of such methods does not result also in an acceptance of the fundamental bourgeois concepts underlying these criminological investigation methods.

It is thus the task of criminology to develop methods of quantitative and qualitative analysis and, along the lines practised by Stiller,[44] scan the boundary disciplines for suitable methods of investigation, methods which might be applied, or modified, to its own subject.

Only then will it be possible to determine the order of magnitude of definite material or spiritual, or more generally social or individual phenomena within the system of conditions which makes up the causes of criminality. The conclusions arising from the theory of Marxism—Leninism and from past research regarding the classification of the various phenomena will be set out in Parts II and III of this book, when a rough system of categories will be seen to have been chosen for arranging the phenomena according to social conditions of criminality and the personality of the offender as representing relatively independent groups of phenomena within the complex of causes. Both groups are in close interrelation with one another, conditioning each other and becoming causes of criminality only through their joint action. They nevertheless possess a relative independence, and their investigation often requires such differentiated methods of research that their separation seems justified.

The establishment of the function or the order of magnitude of definite phenomena within the complex of the causes of criminality and the development of methods for their quantitative and qualitative analysis can only partially be accomplished by theoretical work. Direct empirical research is equally necessary and important. New methods cannot be worked out at the desk but must spring from theoretical considerations together with direct practical research into the solution of definite problems. We have here a continuous interaction of theoretical considerations and empirical research. The present state of development of criminology cannot yet be described as satisfactory in this field; there is need for much patient, persistent and laborious work. 'Inspired' attempts to cut through the Gordian knot rarely prove successful.

While we have rejected any internal differentiation within the complex of phenomena into those that are only causes and those that are only conditions, realising the interchangeability of these rôles under certain combinations of circumstances, matters are different when we investigate the individual act.

In each specific individual instance the separate conditions contributing to its occurrence always have their specific function in the course of action or occurrence, and it is therefore possible and necessary to determine which function they have discharged — whether that of 'cause' or that of 'condition' or merely that of 'immediate occasion'. We have already shown that Hörz [45] has made a useful contribution to exact investigation by developing these principles of differentiation. But there is one aspect which receives less than its due attention in his work.

In the case of specific occurrences, especially in criminal offences due to negligence, but also in so-called offences of omission, the differentiation between 'causes' and 'condition' of the act and its consequences relates not only to the way in which the decision to commit the offence was brought about but also to events subsequent upon this decision or the inception of the act. Criminology, however, invariably only examines the question of why people in our order of society decide to commit a criminal act. It therefore tries to discover the causes and conditions leading to the decision to commit the act, regardless of whether the act represents a deliberate or a clearly negligent action, an offence of omission or commission.

To keep to our example of an accident, what interests us therefore is no longer the causes and conditions leading to the occurrence of the accident, i.e. a preliminary examination of criminal responsibility, but the question, once criminal responsibility has been established, of how the offender came to take his negligent decision. There are, therefore, also in the investigation of individual instances, different systems of reference for using the concepts of cause and condition.

The concept of the 'causes and conditions of a criminal act' therefore comprises not just any causes and conditions encountered in connection with the criminal act, but only the causes and conditions of the criminal decision. An examination of such a specific single event will similarly reveal the complexity of the conditions encountered.

Marxism—Leninism, Marxist sociology, social psychology and individual psychology all show that man's decision to take an action is invariably governed by a multitude of conditions. No human mode of behaviour can be explained as the result of a single event. The mechanistic view is often encountered that all conditions with the exception of the one which one wishes to label the sole cause can be labelled 'invariables'. In consequence it is said: under the conditions $X_1 - X_n$, Y is the cause of Z. This looks logically very exact but is nevertheless incorrect: no such 'invariables' exist in human action since external conditions and specific personalities are never identical. This is not to deny the legitimacy of the method of calculating the effect of 'variables' in a psychological experiment – especially as this method stems from the dialectics and the interaction of various factors. But in contrast to the 'causes of criminality' the determination of the 'causes and conditions of the specific individual criminal act' requires the establishment of the precise order of magnitude, the actual function, of each condition established.

Thus, if it is found that in a particular case a certain offender has gone through a pronouncedly negative development of his personality, resulting in a hardened asocial attitude which virtually makes him seek an 'occasion' for committing his criminal act, then this personal development is the decisive factor in this case and hence the 'cause', whereby all the components which contributed to such a negative development of his personality make up the 'complex of causes of this criminal act'. In such a case, muddle and indiscipline in the area in which the act was committed may very well have played no more than the rôle of a condition and will have to be described as such.

In another case, by way of contrast, where we are dealing with a person with an entirely normal positive development of his personality, the distortions and aberrations in his mental world, which led him to make a decision out of character for him, may well have been caused by just such muddle and indiscipline, so that in this case they were effective as some of the conditions making up the complex of the causes of his offence. They will then have to be boldly described as its causes. The specific conclusions to be drawn from this realisation as to the nature and extent of the individual's criminal responsibility cannot be the subject of this theoretical study of criminology. Suffice it to say that the fact that in one specific incident a certain phenomenon was the 'cause' and in another the 'condition', that in one case the bulk of the causal conditions was to be found in the individual's personal development and in the other case in external conditions, may be of vital importance in the choice of legally available measures – such as long-term education while the punishment is served, or suspended sentence, or even trial by social-judicial organs. Needless to say, the multiplicity of other essential aspects precludes the application of any mechanical directives.

As far as the organisation of the struggle for the elimination of these causes and conditions is concerned, this distinction is of no importance. Proceeding from our general concept of the causes of criminality, we regard as the causes and conditions of a criminal act all those phenomena of life which must be seen as survivals of the old society and which carry within themselves the capability of leading the individual into conflict with the demands of socially adjusted behaviour. In this sense the survivals of the old society are not only its direct legacy in the shape of specific conditions, relationships, views and thought patterns but also such phenomena as take their origin from the material, psychological, ideological, educational-background, cultural and moral imperfections of the life which the old bourgeois society has bequeathed to us.

The concept of survivals includes not only phenomena which arose under conditions of capitalism but also those which have arisen more recently. But even these more recent backward features are not the expression of the new socialist relationships but the products of old inherited imperfections of life which survive not merely because old relationships continue to exist but which also give rise to new imperfections. One example is the inadequacy of young parents in bringing up their children; this springs partly from their acceptance, from their own parents, of traditional 'educational methods' and partly from the still limited facilities of our society to enable all parents to bring up their children correctly.

We agree with Manecke [46] when he says that bourgeois society has left us a multitude of unsolved problems and that it would be wrong to regard them as belonging to socialism itself, instead of being survivals of the old society, merely because we identify them as problems to be solved in the course of the building of socialism.

It is important that both the causes and the conditions of specific criminal acts are liquidated. The point of attack should not depend on whether a phenomenon acted as a cause or merely as a condition, but on which is the quickest and most effective way of liquidating such phenomena within the framework of the overall tasks of society. Thus, for instance, if certain disparities in the wages and salary system have led young people into negative behaviour patterns, and if these can only be eliminated in the course of development, there is then little point in lamenting about their negative effects. If these conditions are bound to continue for a finite period of time then their negative effects must be neutralised.

By 'the causes of a criminal act' we therefore understand such conditions in the personal development of the individual concerned and such actual conditions of his life, as have given rise to his negative ideas or to the specific system of negative attitudes from which the decision to commit his deed have sprung. This concept of the 'cause of the criminal act' never comprises only the most immediate condition in the offender's mind, the one which clearly triggered his decision to commit the act, because that would mean dealing only with a purely individual subjective component. The concept comprises a whole scale of causal chains whose origin lies ultimately outside the offender's mind, in the history of his personal development and in the actual external conditions of his life and environment. What matters is not the establishment of a single phenomenon as the cause of his act, but the identification of entire interconnected causal chains which have given rise to the subjective phenomena in the offender's mind, or to his attitude, driving him to his act or to the loss or temporary suppression of normally present inhibitions. Hence the investigation of the causes of a specific criminal act must necessarily go beyond the limits suggested by Hörz for the examination of the causes of traffic accidents or similar occurrences.

Such a determination of the causes begins methodically by tracing backwards, from the decision to commit the act — as the effect to be examined — those causal chains which have given rise to it. Here there are a few points of guidance. To start with, the relationship of the decision to commit the deed to the personality of the offender must be investigated in all its separate components in order to establish which aspects of the given personality are to be regarded as contributory causes of the decision to commit the act.

The next question to be investigated is which actual external circumstances have operated as causes of the emergence of the decision, always remembering that these external circumstances must have entered into the decision to commit the act in a subjectively processed form.

These two lines of investigation, although being closely linked — since ultimately they both lead to the statement that a particular personality component and certain external circumstances, interlinked with one another, have led to the decision to commit the act — are nevertheless relatively independent lines of investigation and should, for the sake of orderly investigation, be kept apart.

By way of contrast, the conditions of the criminal act are those phenomena which, while not having triggered the specific decision in the above-stated meaning, nevertheless facilitated the making of the decision or determined its nature. Thus the fact that parents pay no heed to a child's way of life or activities is not in itself the cause of that juvenile's decision to commit theft in self-service stores. But it facilitates such a decision because the juvenile believes that he will be able to hide his loot unnoticed by his parents. The decision itself may be triggered off by the parents' inability to control the juvenile's covetousness, by allowing un-justified expectations to grow up within him and, moreover, by his in-volvement with a group of juveniles priding themselves on a demonstrative contempt for the norms of social life.

The expert reader may have noticed that in dealing with the concept of the condition of a criminal act we have avoided the term 'favouring'. From a philosophical point of view any condition 'favours' an occurrence since otherwise it would not have any effectiveness with regard to that occurrence. Nothing is therefore gained by the use of this term.

The 'conditions' in turn have their own 'causes', as Hörz has correctly observed, and it is necessary to trace also these causal chains in order to conduct the social struggle for the elimination of such clearly identified conditions and in order to strike at the root of the evil. The causes of such conditions may often be found to lie in the apathy of parents to acquire the ability to bring up children, combined with inadequate activity by State and social organs in helping the parents towards a correct upbringing of their families, or in other phenomena.

The distinction between these concepts is necessary in order to get to the substance of the problem and to distinguish the 'causes' and 'condi-tions' from the mere occasions. Naturally, any action is occasioned by something or other, but the occasion is irrelevant. The reason why it should be identified is merely to avoid the superficial, the phenomenon, being mistaken for the cause or the condition and the true relations in effect becoming distorted. Thus the fact that a more or less drunk person who has an 'old' grudge towards the police feels 'affronted' by a People's policeman's demand to see his identity papers, detecting, as he believes, 'contempt' in the policeman's voice, is at best an occasion but neither the cause nor the condition of a criminal act; there is no need therefore to waste any more time on it beyond simply recording the fact.

Needless to say the occasions should also be removed or cleared away — but one must not expect their abolition to lead to the liquidation of criminality since the merest trifles may give occasion to criminal acts.

In dealing with the problem of the causes of a criminal act we men-tioned that by tracing the occurrences back we arrive at a whole network of causal chains the further we delve into the past. The same is true of the problem of conditions and may even be said of the occasions of a criminal act.

This raises the question of how far the investigation of an individual case should be pursued in order to gain an exact conspectus of the causes and conditions. A distinction will have to be made here between crimi-nological investigations of individual cases as supplementing mass investigations – which in turn, according to the criminological problem in hand, can be either longitudinal or cross-section investigations both of the offenders personality and of the actual circumstances – and the elucidation of the causes and conditions of the criminal act within the framework of a specific criminal proceeding.

We have said elsewhere that the nature and scope of the identification of causes and conditions in an individual instance must depend on the specific purpose pursued. [47] In criminal proceedings this purpose is defined by the criminal proceeding as an instrument for the determination of the individual's criminal responsibility. Certain legal provisions and State documents, however, refer to the 'comprehensive' elucidation of the causes and conditions of the criminal act, and this has been taken to apply to the legal proceedings themselves, with the result that judges, prosecutors and investigation personnel were expected to perform tasks which they simply could not cope with. Neither the time at their disposal (statutory investigation periods), nor their equipment (extensive criminal and forensic-psychological investigation methods combined with slight possibilities of using expert evidence), nor indeed their training could possibly enable them to uncover *all* cause–effect connections involved. That would require a more universal training than that of a jurist – a training, in fact, which no individual could have but which only a team of differently trained researchers could provide.

We believe therefore that – except in cases where the law requires analysis in depth, e.g. in cases where special expert opinion has to be obtained, or in juvenile proceedings – the judiciary organs have discharged their task in establishing the causes and conditions of the criminal act when they have identified the directly effective internal and external causes and conditions and the function and relative weight attaching to these phenomena in the specific case.

The directive issued by the Prosecutor General's office concerning the registration of circumstances for the purpose of statistical records of criminal acts has provided a first fruitful basis for the work of the judiciary organs. Obviously this work will be further improved as time goes on. It is the task of criminology, in co-operation with criminal law theory and the theory of criminal proceedings, to evolve further criteria for the determination of the causes and conditions in criminal proceedings. The present book must content itself with pointing out that it is a mistake to transfer automatically the demands we must make on the criminological examination of individual acts to the specific criminal proceedings. The demand for a comprehensive determination of causes and conditions, as found in various laws and documents, will have to be met by a division of labour between the investigations of the judiciary organs and criminological research.

We have made it clear that criminology as the science of the causes of criminality is not simply concerned with criminality as a comprehensive totality of phenomena, or with one limited to specific categories, but equally with the examination of individual occurrences. The difference between criminological research and the investigation of a criminal offence by specific proceedings does not mean that the proceedings are concerned only with the individual act and criminology only with the totality of acts and their causes, but that the objectives of the two procedures differ from each other. The criminal proceedings serve the establishment of individual criminal responsibility and the social objectives resulting therefrom. Criminological investigation of the individual act, on the other hand, presupposes the establishment of criminal culpability. It must proceed from this result — which can only be obtained in criminal proceedings and in no other way — because only after the conclusion of criminal proceedings can it be known for certain whether a criminal act has been committed or not.

Criminology, in order to arrive at valid statements, must endeavour to make certain questions, in so far as they are compatible with the tasks of criminal proceedings (which include the observance of statutory periods of time), part of its own methods. Again we see that the investigation of the individual act is part of the criminological investigation, and that criminology and State practice in the investigation and elucidation of criminal offences must be intimately linked in order to achieve the necessary results with a minimum of effort. To this end criminology must fit itself into the framework imposed on the criminal proceedings. Any attempt to transform criminal proceedings into a criminological research project must be rejected, since that would lead to a distortion of the tasks of court proceedings. On the other hand, the development of criminological research models makes it possible to achieve a certain synchronisation of fact-finding procedures for the court and of the collection of the data needed by criminology. Criminology and criminal proceedings can thus greatly assist each other.

Notes

[1] H.-J. Lander, 'Zur Psychologie der vorsätzlichen Handlung', in H.-D. Schmidt and E. Kasielke (ed.) *Psychologie und Rechtspraxis*, Berlin 1965, p. 124.

[2] Cf. A. Kurella, 'Der sozialistische Mensch in der technischen Revolution', *Neues Deutschland* of 16 March 1966, B edition, p. 4.

[3] W. Ulbricht, *Programmatische Erklärung des Vorsitzenden des Staatsrates vor der Volkskammer am 4. Oktober 1960,* Berlin 1960, pp. 69 ss. A similar fundamental view of the causes of criminality is held also by V.N. Kudryavtsev ('Die Kategorie der Kausalität in der sowjetischen Kriminologie'. résumé in *Staat und Recht*, 1966, no. 5, pp. 868 ss.); we basically agree with that view.

[4] H. Hörz, 'Zur Anwendung der marxistischen Kausalitätsauffassung in der Rechtspraxis', *Neue Justiz*, 1966, no. 5, pp. 137 ss.

[5] H. Hörz, 'Zum Verhältnis von Kausalität und Determinismus', *Deutsche Zeitschrift für Philosophie,* 1963, Issue 2, p. 166.

[6] Cf. J. Lekschas, *Die Kausalität bei der verbrecherischen Handlung*, Berlin 1952; also J. Renneberg, *Die objektive Seite des Verbrechens,* Berlin 1955.

[7] H. Hörz, 'Zum Verhältnis von Kausalität und Determinismus', loc. cit., p. 157.

[8] H. Hörz, loc. cit., p. 155.

[9] H. Hörz, loc. cit., p. 158.

[10] H. Hörz, loc. cit., p. 167.

[11] Ibid.

[12] H. Hörz, *Der dialektische Determinismus in Natur und Gesellschaft*, Berlin 1962, p. 126.

[13] W. Ulbricht, 'Uber die Entwicklung einer volksverbundenen sozialistischen Nationalkultur', *Neues Deutschland* of 28 April 1964, B edition, p. 3.

[14] Cf. H. Hörz, 'Zur Anwendung der marxistischen Kausalitätsauffassung ...', loc. cit., pp. 137 ss.

[15] H. Hörz, 'Zum Verhältnis von Kausalität und Determinismus', loc. cit., pp. 168 ss.

[16] *Programme and Statutes of the CPSU* (quoted from the German edition, Berlin 1961, pp. 100 ss.).

[17] W. Ulbricht, *Das Programm des Sozialismus und die geschichtliche Aufgabe der Sozialistischen Einheitspartei Deutschlands, Berlin* 1963, pp. 358 ss.

[18] H.-J. Lander, 'Zur Psychologie der vorsätzlichen Handlung', loc. cit., p. 124.

[19] L. Bavcon/B. Skaberné/K. Vodopivec, *The state of juvenile criminality and forms of the struggle against it in the Socialist Federal Republic of Yugoslavia*, Ljubljana 1964, p. 16 (unpublished conference paper for the First International Symposium 'Jugendkriminalität und ihre Bekämpfung'.

[20] L. Bavcon/B. Skaberné/K. Vodopivec, loc. cit., pp. 15 ss.

[21] L. Bavcon/B. Skaberné/K. Vodopivec, loc. cit., pp. 14 ss.

[22] Cf. also W. Ulbricht, 'Sozialismus bietet jedem Bürger eine Perspektive', *Neues Deutschland* of 19 March 1966, B edition, p. 3.

[23] Cf. A. Schaff, 'On Problems of Alienation', *Studia Sociologiczno*, 1964, no. 4, pp. 5 ss. (Polish); preliminary publication of a section of his essay *Marxism and the Individual*, published meanwhile.

[24] A. Schaff, loc. cit., p. 34.

[25] A. Schaff, loc. cit., pp. 27 ss.

[26] A. Schaff, loc. cit., p. 29.

[27] L. Bavcon/B. Skaberné/K. Vodopivec, loc. cit., p. 14.

[28] L. Bavcon/B. Skaberné/K. Vodopivec, loc. cit., p. 15.

[29] F. Engels, 'Herrn Eugen Dührings Umwälzung der Wissenschaft' ('Anti-Dühring'), in: K. Marx/F. Engels, *Werke*, vol. 20, Berlin 1962, p. 22.

[30] F. Engels, 'Dialektik der Natur', in K. Marx/F. Engels, *Werke*, vol. 20, loc. cit., p. 499.

[31] E.g. Villanowa, *Kriminalität und Sexualität*, Berlin 1928, p. 161, as quoted in G. Feix, *Die Bekämpfung von Sexualverbrechen an Kindern*, Berlin 1961, pp. 23 ss.

[32] W. Middendorf, *Soziologie des Verbrechens*, Köln-Düsseldorf 1959, p. 222; W. Middendorf, *Recht der Jugend*, 1961, Issue 4, p. 59; W. Middendorf, *Kriminalistik*, 1960, Issue 6, p. 271.

[33] R. Lange, 'Grundfragen der deutschen Strafrechtsreform', *Schweizer Zeitschrift für Strafrecht*, 1955, p. 373; also 'Wandlungen in den kriminologischen Grundlagen der Strafrechtsreform', in: *Hundert Jahre deutsches Rechtsleben*, Karlsruhe 1960, pp. 345 ss.

[34] Cf. the argument against such theoretical positions in R. Hartman/J. Lekschas, 'Zur Theorie der Ursachen ...', loc. cit., pp. 37 ss.

[35] L. Schubert, 'The Method of Investigating the Causes ...', loc. cit., pp. 82 ss.

[36] This concept of the causes of criminality, developed by R. Hartmann and J. Lekschas ('Zur Theorie der Ursachen ...', loc. cit., p. 53) has been generally accepted in GDR criminal law theory and criminology so that it

may be regarded as a recognised working concept, to be further refined by future criminological work.

[37] Cf. R. Hartmann/J. Lekschas, 'Zur Theorie der Ursachen ...', loc. cit., pp. 148 ss., pp. 154 ss.

[38] A. Lutzke, 'Theoretische und methodologische Aspekte der Untersuchung von Rechtsverletzungen im Strassenverkehr', *Staat und Recht*, 1965, no. 12, pp. 2007 ss.

[39] K. Manecke, 'Die Ursachen und begünstigenden Bedingungen der Straftaten in der DDR', *Das Strafrecht der DDR*, Allgemeiner Teil, Berlin 1965, Issue 1, pp. 52 ss.; ed. Extramural Department of the Humboldt University in Berlin.

[40] G. Stiller, *Theoretische und methodologische Grundlagen ...*, loc. cit.

[41] H. Luther/G. Feix, *Die Verhütung und Bekämpfung der Jugendkriminalität in der DDR*, Berlin 1963, pp. 63 ss.

[42] H. Hörz, 'Zur Anwendung der marxistischen Kausalitätsauffassung ...', loc. cit., pp. 137 ss.

[43] Cf. A. Szabó, *Jugendkriminalität und ihre Bekämpfung ...*, loc. cit.

[44] Cf. G. Stiller, *Theoretische und methodologische Grundlagen ...*, loc. cit.

[45] Cf. H. Hörz, ibid.

[46] Cf. K. Manecke, 'Zur Theorie der Ursachen der allgemeinen Kriminalität in der DDR', *Staat und Recht*, 1966, no. 3, pp. 417 ss.

[47] Cf. J. Lekschas, 'Zur Feststellung der Ursachen der Straftat durch die Gerichte', *Neue Justiz*, 1965, no. 15, pp. 478 ss.

3   Critique of Bourgeois Criminology

Preliminary observations on the purpose of a critique of bourgeois criminology

The theoretical position outlined in the preceding chapters provides us also with a starting point for a fruitful critique of bourgeois criminology. It is the task of such a critique to reveal the social function of bourgeois criminology and its basic positions, to evaluate the results it has achieved and to examine its research methods. Merely to assess the findings of bourgeois criminology as reactionary is not enough; this is not what is meant by critical examination. There is indeed a danger that bourgeois criminology, on the one hand, is rejected in this rather unconvincing manner without serious argument, with the result that aspects of the scientific character which it has adopted from the natural sciences are ignored, or, on the other hand, that socialist criminologists incapable of finding a scientific starting point for its critique will accept bourgeois criminology more or less uncritically.

The social basis of imperialism and militarism is increasingly narrowing down because of its anti-human policy. In consequence, and under the influence of the example of socialist society and its sciences, a new humanist trend can be observed to be developing in several areas of the bourgeois social sciences. Any black-and-white rejection of bourgeois criminology would therefore be detrimental to a true policy of alliance with those scientists. An uncritical adoration of bourgeois criminology and its research methods, on the other hand, would lead to the subjection of socialist criminology to bourgeois juridical thought, to a way of thought ingrained also in those bourgeois criminologists who otherwise approach the problems of criminality by no means as juridical apologists — such as psychiatrists, psychologists and sociologists.

The practice of such a critique requires a clear theoretical starting point. This cannot primarily depend on whether a bourgeois criminologist has succeeded in correctly understanding some criminal phenomenon and its immediate causes, on whether he can correctly assess the quantity and quality of offences by one method or another, because all this merely means that he accepts the reality of life or that he distorts it and doctors it from a certain political or other point of view. Our sole yardstick for judging bourgeois criminology must be the question of what attitude its scientific findings reveal to the laws of social evolution; what proposals and findings it is capable of submitting to human society for the solution of the conflicts revealed in criminality; and on whether it is prepared to draw the socially indispensable conclusions which follow from an in-depth understanding of criminality and its causes.

At the same time, the fact that one bourgeois criminologist or another is not prepared or is unable to draw all the consequences from his findings must not be the sole yardstick in judging him. What is important for the assessment of the achievements of bourgeois criminology is whether the contradictions which give rise to criminality have been identified without any attempt to gloss over them and whether humanist proposals have been developed for the solutions of the problems — even if these are not realisable in bourgeois society — or whether, on the other hand, reality has been distorted to serve reactionary political or social objectives. A critique of bourgeois criminology must therefore be capable of differentiation. This means that its approach must be both historical and philosophical in order to grasp the internal contradictions of bourgeois criminology itself and thus to reveal the tendencies dormant in it.

Bourgeois criminology has a relatively long history. In recent years, in particular, it has produced such a mass of literature that it would be impossible within the scope of this book to extend our critique down to its last ramifications. All we can do here is sketch the outlines of such a critique on the basis of a material revealing the typical trends in bourgeois criminology. In this sense such a critique must be seen also as a contribution to the raising of the scientific level of socialist criminology.

Finally, there is another important aspect of any examination of bourgeois criminology. A comparison of criminality and its trends and causes in different social systems is a matter of interest to the research worker in the field. Socialist criminology naturally depends here to a large extent on the findings of bourgeois criminology since obviously it cannot conduct its researches in the bourgeois countries. It must examine, therefore, which findings of bourgeois criminology are usable for such a comparison. The work of Soviet criminologists, in particular, shows the value of such comparative studies, providing as it does deep insights into such correlations as exploitative conditions and criminality, aggressive policy and criminality, State monopoly and criminality, moral decay of society and criminality, etc. The prerequisite of such comparative studies, of course, is a dialectical and historical—materialist approach to the findings and data of bourgeois criminology in order to avoid misjudgements or superficial interpretations.

The position of bourgeois criminology in bourgeois society

Bourgeois criminology can only be correctly understood as part and parcel of the bourgeois social consciousness. A brief outline of its development will elucidate its intellectual position and social function.

H. Ellenberger, Hans E. Göppinger and others are basically correct in regarding the studies of Cesare Beccaria and Karl Ferdinand Hommel, the case collections of Pitaval and Paul Johann Anselm Feuerbach and the statistical work of Lambert-Adolphe-Jacques Quetelet as the first major beginnings of criminological research.[1] But it was only towards the end of the last century that bourgeois criminology in the European countries began to develop into an independent science. The bourgeois theory of criminal law, which by then had long become positivist, was concerned with criminality only from the point of view of criminal law, engaging chiefly in the definition of concepts for judicial practice and, at most, discussing problems concerning the extent of punishment. The only discussions on crime as a real phenomenon took place in connection with the penal reform movement, but these too were concerned only with culpability and the definition of circumstances with a view to future legislation. This theory of criminal law was interested in the offender merely as a convict. As a person the individual was of interest only when it was a case of subjecting a political opponent to the power of the State. When no genuine culpability was found an attempt was made to turn him into a culprit by construing a harmful attitude which, it was claimed, was liable to turn all his actions into criminal ones. The theory of criminal law — anxious to serve the ruling legal system and hence the ruling powers — did not regard it as part of its duties to reflect about any problems beyond the mere application of the valid criminal law to criminal offences actually committed. It defined its own limits, and these limits consisted in the interpretation of the valid norms, in the maintenance of the status quo.

By way of contrast, bourgeois enlighteners did not shrink from describing crime not merely as a juridical fact but also as a reality, as a product of the contradictions in society. Indeed, without such an understanding it would not have been able to practise such an effective and humanistic critique of the feudal criminal law. However, Beccaria and Hommel still reveal a totally different attitude to reality. To them, realistic consideration of the crime and its causes are still issues of normative criminal law.

In Germany the distinction emerged only when the bourgeoisie began to participate in the exercise of State power, or at least when it was believed to be theoretically participating in power (e.g. in Feuerbach's writings; his doctrine of criminal law no longer concedes any place to the discussion of the crime as a real-life phenomenon). Thus this theory of criminal law — not only in Germany but in most countries — developed into a clearly normative discipline which did not consider it its task to 'delve into the origins' of criminal legislation.

Although the criminal law theory of the day tried to conceive the criminal act merely as a normative problem, this did not satisfy society in the long run. It was soon found, in the evolution of bourgeois society, that criminal law and its application were not a panacea for conquering crime. It was not, therefore, surprising that, alongside criminal law theory, other scientific disciplines should have begun to concern themselves with criminality. To them, criminality was not just a juridical phenomenon but one belonging to reality, to the practical life of society. This development was favoured by the trend of criminality itself. Bourgeois society, praised by the bourgeois philosophers such as Kant and Hegel as the best of all societies, proved totally unable to cope with crime. The earliest statistical observations, both in England[2] and in France[3] — i.e. in two almost entirely bourgeois countries — showed not a constant level of crime over the years but a marked increase. In Prussia[4], in spite of the tendentious interpretation of certain apologists — to the effect that war was a purifying cold bath also for a country's criminality — criminal statistics similarly showed criminality to be steadily increasing. Thus criminality became a phenomenon, even for bourgeois society and its ruling circles, which could no longer be tackled by the aloof concern of criminal law theory which was interested only in the law but not in reality. Bourgeois society was compelled to accept crime as a reality and it did so by producing, alongside criminal law theory, a field of scientific study of criminality, later to establish itself as criminology. This new trend in scientific investigation necessarily developed outside the sphere of positivist jurisprudence.

Historically criminology emerged as a scientific discipline filling the gap left by the bourgeois jurisprudence of the day. The new discipline was seeking to answer the question which the official criminal law theory either failed to pose or was reluctant to answer. Much as the ruling bourgeois circles were interested in defending their criminal law theory, the bourgeoisie nevertheless demanded a theory which it believed would explain criminality as a social phenomenon and propose more effective measures than those of criminal law, in the hope that it might thus successfully wage the social war between society and criminality.

Germany before the outbreak of World War II had a whole army of criminals, reflected in a figure of roughly 250,000 sentenced persons with a previous criminal record. Moreover, as capitalism moved into the stage of imperialism and increasingly became an instrument for the persecution and suppression of political opponents, criminal law acquired a marked reactionary political bias. The edge of the criminal law was aimed one-sidedly at a revolutionary working class movement and justice was transformed into a tool of political terror. By its submission to the political police, justice became a mainstay of imperialist tyranny. The more the contradictions of capitalist-imperialist society were exacerbated and the social basis of the rule of imperialism narrowed down to monopoly capital and militarism, the more clearly was this transformation seen and the more ruthlessly was the struggle against criminality pushed into the background in favour of an intensified political persecution. This change is reflected also in criminal statistics. Whereas in 1914 the number of persons sentenced for offences against the State, public order and religion amounted to roughly 94,000 and sentences for offences against the person and property to roughly 460,000, in 1940 there were roughly 178,000 sentences for offences against the State, etc. and roughly 415,000 sentences for major or minor offences against the person and property. Justice had become a weapon of German imperialism in its political struggle against the democratic movement among the people. While the politically reactionary activity of the judiciary was continually gaining ground, the incidence of criminal prosecutions steadily declined. Yet crime — as witnessed by the findings of bourgeois criminality researchers of the day and by other contemporary documents — went on increasing. Crime statistics less and less reflected the real trends in criminality. In the face of this development justice with its penal measures, extremely limited as they were in their social effect, proved totally powerless.

Bourgeois criminology was faced with a difficult task and soon found itself in a dilemma from which it has not emerged to this day. On the one hand it was to investigate criminality as a social phenomenon of life and therefore, if it was to achieve genuine scientific results, it had to approach its subject without bias. It would have had to uncover mercilessly all those conditions and personality factors which led to criminality. But this would have led it to a critique of society. Any such a critique — as Marx had shown as early as 1858 in his famous article on the death sentence, utilising early criminological observations of bourgeois scholars — could not have stopped half-way at an empirical description of deplorable conditions but, in line with the rules of scientific procedure, would have arrived at a fundamental critique of the basic social structure and the fundamental conditions of capitalist society.[5]

On the other hand, neither the bourgeois State nor the ruling classes were anxious to provoke or encourage any such social critique which was bound to lead to revolutionary demands for a transformation of society. That, of course, must never be the result of any criminality researches inspired by them. Thus a limit was set from the start to the discovery of truth by bourgeois criminology.

The theoretical reflection of this was a self-imposed limitation of criminology proceeding from the unproven axiom of the eternal nature of criminality. Fundamentally this had already been developed by Hegel, the great philosophical interpreter of bourgeois society. Bourgeois criminology was thus from the very outset in a straitjacket which precluded a crossing of the bounds of permissible social criticism in the direction of a revolutionary scientific analysis. This axiom was once more proclaimed — roughly about the turn of the century — to be the starting and finishing point of any consideration of criminality; this was done in particular by Franz von Liszt,[6] the leader of the politically reactionary sociological school in Germany. It was meant also as a deliberate differentiation from the demands of revolutionary social democracy. Proceeding from its scientific analysis of society, social democracy had put forward the well-founded thesis that it was possible to create a social order, of a socialist and communist humanist character, in which there would no longer be any internal need for criminal behaviour and which therefore would hold a real hope of banishing criminality from the life of society. The prerequisite of this would be the liquidation of the exploitation of man by man, which gives rise to the crudest selfishness as a behaviour pattern necessary for the individual's survival and which, in consequence, brings the individual into a disastrous antagonism to society and to his fellows.

Even such militantly democratic scholars as Adolf Merkel,[7] who opposed the transformation of criminal law into a reactionary political tool, clung to the belief in the eternal nature of criminality. It was partly due to these scholars that the thesis of the eternal nature of criminality, put forward in disregard of the findings about the laws of social revolution, was able to don the cloak of scientific objectivity. This pernicious thesis had become historically reactionary as conditions were ripening for a socialist social transformation which would bring with it also the progressive liquidation of criminality. The proven scientific socialist view which, on the basis of the identified laws of social development, proceeded from a new humanist model of the individual and did not therefore condemn man to eternal wickedness but granted him the opportunity of an evolution worthy of a human being, was labelled by bourgeois ideology as a mere Utopia or a philanthropical speculation.

Thus bourgeois criminology, even though in part it developed as an opposition to positivist criminal law theory, was beset by unfavourable conditions from the start. It was forced into a framework which prevented it from developing beyond a limited measure. This framework enabled the ruling forces of the State to misuse, for their various reactionary political purposes, the findings of bourgeois criminological research, since this declined to transgress the framework of the capitalist social order.

A contradiction therefore emerged between a predetermined system — i.e. the eternal nature of the society based upon private ownership and the resultant eternal nature of criminality — and a scientific research method which had to adapt itself to a subject understood as really existent — i.e. criminality, offenders, the causes of criminality and the development of an offender's personality. These methods, of necessity, had to be scientific and not speculative unless criminology was to get bogged down in an irrational position which was totally useless even to the bourgeoisie. As a result, bourgeois criminology has become marked by an insoluble conflict between system and method, a contradiction which does not make it easy for socialist criminology to make appropriate judgements on bourgeois criminology.

Bourgeois criminology cannot simply be dismissed as reactionary regardless of the research methods it has developed or the results it has achieved; nor, on the other hand, must it be declared as a progressive or class-neutral science just because of certain positive results and methods, regardless of its inherent scepticism due to the theoretical system it pursues. Yet both these judgements — inappropriate as we think they are — can be found in present-day socialist criminological literature. While the former view represents a sectarian attitude, the latter runs the risk of revisionist deviation and ideological coexistence; though it likes to describe itself as anti-dogmatic and open-minded it represents in fact an act of submission to bourgeois criminology.

All those who, openly or secretly, admire present-day bourgeois criminology for its extensive methodological apparatus should always remember that a methodology based upon a historically reactionary system as an unquestionable axiom is subject to limitations in its scientific character, limitations which, beyond a certain point, make it useless for any comprehensive scientific discoveries. Socialist criminology, therefore, must adopt the same approach to it as Marxist philosophy has adopted to Hegelian philosophy and its system and methods.

It would be a mistake to believe that one might simply cross out the system but adopt unchanged the method worked out within that system.

The system inevitably acts on its method, and any unmodified adoption of the method would inevitably mean that elements of the system were taken over with it. With all respect for the achievements of bourgeois criminologists in the development of research methods capable of elucidating the connections between certain social phenomena and personality development on the one hand and criminality on the other, we must never overlook the fact that the whole methodological apparatus is not designed to establish the correlations between the laws governing life in the capitalist social order and criminality. It must not be forgotten that its methods are suitable only for discovering the external connections between certain definite and limited empirical (social or psychological) phenomena and criminality. Any in-depth examination of scientific problems is thus excluded from the outset. Questions about the connections between social structure, the prevalent social behaviour patterns and criminal behaviour patterns have never been seriously raised by bourgeois criminology. Socialist criminology, however, cannot content itself with a methodology which excludes from its scope the fundamental question concerning the causation of crime.

Although in socialist society the principal social cause which in earlier social systems produced criminality has been eliminated, the transformation of the socio-economic structure has not been instantly followed by the disappearance of old social behaviour patterns produced by the liquidated exploitative social structure. Socialist criminology therefore needs a methodology which enables it to probe the very depths of social behaviour problems. Adoption of bourgeois criminological research methods would throw it back to a positivist position which could only lead to barren empiricism.

Conflicting trends in bourgeois criminology

The internal contradictions peculiar to bourgeois criminology, reflected on the theoretical level as a conflict between system and method, were reflected in practice by a conflict between subordination of the aims of criminological research to the objectives of the ruling powers in the State and the humanist aspirations of a number of criminologists who wished to control the material and spiritual misery of society which found its expression in criminality. The interest of the ruling circles in maintaining their political and economic power was found, in the long run, to be incompatible with any humanist proposals designed to check criminality. Thus bourgeois criminology from its very beginnings contained within itself a number of sharply clashing tendencies.

Socially reactionary and anti-human tendencies in bourgeois criminology

Wherever the historically reactionary system, and with it the submission of criminology to the interests of the ruling circles, predominated and progressively developed into imperialism, criminology was marked by politically reactionary and anti-human features. In the train of thus-orientated theories there followed a progressive loss of scientific approach, and irrationalism and speculation held the field in criminology. These tendencies can be traced even in its very beginnings. In Germany they took the form of the so-called anthropological (Lombrosian or neo-Lombrosian) school and the so-called sociological school[8] which opposed the growing criminality with extermination and terror, and which matched imperialism's call for violence and reaction by proposals aimed at a tightening of penal coercive measures. The same line was taken by the former Reichsgericht judge Otto Mittelstädt,[9] who from certain politically reactionary and half-digested criminological data drew the conclusion that society could master criminality only by means of the executioner's axe and the guillotine, by starvation and flogging, and generally by developing the terror aspect of punishment. Thus bourgeois criminology was discredited by reactionary tendencies at the very moment of its emergence. However much such tendencies conflicted with the views of humanist scholars among the bourgeois criminologists, they certainly were not a foreign body within bourgeois criminology but merely represented the full flower of the internal contradictions contained within bourgeois criminology itself.

This emerges with particular clarity from the development of criminology under the conditions of fascism. It was in the anti-human racialist and biological theories of fascist criminology that this internal contradiction found its most marked expression, becoming a horrifying criminal reality in the so-called 'criminal-political programme' of German fascism. With the support of such criminological doctrines fascism practised a penal terror directed, first of all, at the regime's political opponents within the country — primarily communists, social democrats and later anyone else disagreeing with the regime, and later still all suspected opponents.

In pursuance of the reactionary anti-human laws and the demagogy which marked the fascist regime this terror was presently extended, under racialist pretexts, to neutral sections of the population — principally Jews and gypsies — and finally also to criminals. The concept of the sub-human, to which criminology had made its contribution with its reactionary doctrines of types of offenders, was used as justification for any judicial or other official or semi-official terror. It was moreover misused for the purpose of a criminal precipitation and conduct of the war. Evidence of this are the sentences passed by special courts, the Reich Court and the People's Court, which held that a political opponent of the regime was *a priori* a criminal and traitor to his country. Further evidence is supplied by the Nuremberg race laws with their commentaries and the sentences passed by the courts on the basis of those laws, further the criminal law decree concerning Poles and Jews, and finally the amendments to the criminal law, including the 'sociological' school's proposals for preventive detention and the concept of the habitual criminal, as well as a variety of barbarous ordinances concerning the punishment of adult and juvenile so-called serious offenders.

The balance sheet of the victims of such a 'crime policy' in the political field, to which criminology made its contribution, is known to the world. Less well known — as Franz Exner [10] reported in 1947, not only without any compassion but indeed with macabre pride — is the fact that this reign of executioner's axe and guillotine, starvation and flogging had demanded roughly 10,000 victims since 1937 — so-called serious offenders rendered 'innocuous by preventive detention', in most cases 'transfer' to a concentration camp. The death sentences passed by so-called civil courts alone assumed mass character. According to the official criminal statistics, which do not include the sentences of special courts, a total of 1,146 death sentences were passed in 1941, a total of 3,393 in 1942, and a total of 2,693 during the first six months of 1943. One cannot judge the criminological doctrines under examination without bearing in mind these facts. We entirely agree with the retired President of the Danish Senate, Franz Marcus, [11] who said that in assessing criminality during the Nazi period, or in any historical contemplation of criminology and criminal law theory, these events cannot be ignored because otherwise one would inevitably arrive at distortions and at a glorification of Nazi fascism.

The real value or worthlessness of a theory — including criminological theories — cannot be measured by fine talk, by logical or biological hypotheses, or by the profession of 'good' intentions, but only by the effects which it produces or favours or supports in practical life. The practice of 'crime policy' is the crystallised reality of the system of ideological positions and of the methods produced by it. The practice of fascism has shown that an irrational and speculative criminology — no matter if it pretends to hold biological, depth-psychological, racial or any other positions — is inevitably reactionary and anti-human because it becomes a pseudo-scientific cloak for all kinds of politically reactionary and anti-human aspirations by the ruling imperialist circles.

It performs such a socially dangerous function even if it refrains from making any kind of dangerous crime policy proposals, leaving the development and application of such measures to the 'politicians'. In our day, and especially in Germany where the events of the Nazi period revealed the true criminal meaning of such methods, it is not enough to oppose reactionary programmes. It is necessary to fight against all irrational and speculative theories and methods themselves because they provide the intellectual basis and the theoretical cloak designed to conceal the true intentions. We therefore agree with Mergen, [12] who comes out against any kind of speculation and irrationalism in criminology and who demands that a scientific criminology should adopt an exact scientific position that is verifiable at any time. Any infiltration of irrational or speculative methods or attempted interpretation of empirical observations must lead to a loss by criminology of its scientific character and to its subjection to the aims of the ruling political circles. It is a well-known method of these circles to subject to themselves any science, in this particular case criminology, by forcing it on to a road of speculation and irrational argument. The career of a man like Exner should serve as a warning: beginning with exact researches into the criminality of World War I and achieving genuine results, he progressively surrendered to speculative and irrational arguments which led him to the slippery slope that ultimately made him an intellectual accomplice of fascist practices and, even after the collapse of fascism, clouded his view and prevented him from recognising the criminal character of fascist crime policy.

Social-critical trends in bourgeois criminology

It should be noted, however, that bourgeois criminology also contains within itself a number of realistic social-critical tendencies which emerged clearly in its development but are not receiving adequate attention by present-day bourgeois criminologists. It is the more regrettable that socialist criminology has so far failed to apply a differentiating yardstick which would clearly separate the different trends of bourgeois criminology from one another. [13]

This critical trend, whose method is empirical observation without any unverifiable interpretation attempts, first emerged in Quetelet's famous study and was found also in the work of German authors after the turn of the century. Special mention should be made of Karl Finkelnburg, who sharply opposed the inflationist trend in an increasingly imperialist German criminal law. He calculated that, because of the punishment mania of the German empire under Kaiser Wilhelm, one in every six living men born in 1910 had been condemned and sentenced by the German judiciary. [14]

He demonstrated that life in Germany had become a life in a jungle of criminal law articles. To what state, he asked with historical and political prescience, had the ruling circles and their obedient judiciary, including the jurisprudence of the day, brought such a hard-working and honest people as the Germans?

A similar humanist and critical note can be observed in early studies of prison methods and penal enforcement, which showed that the German prison system with its inhuman conditions provided breeding places of crime rather than institutions to educate the citizen. [15]

The most conspicuous upsurge of this school of thought within German criminology was observed after World War I. This war had led to the full flowering of all demoralising and socially disruptive tendencies of imperialism, now in its great crisis, and in consequence released a huge flood of criminality threatening the collapse of society into a chaos of individuals destroying each other. Exner was the first to refute the legend, fostered by Prussian imperialism and militarism, that the effect of war on criminality was that of a purifying cold bath. But whereas Exner gradually moved away from these social-critical reflections, Moritz Liepmann took up the problem in his *War and Criminality in Germany*, written for the Carnegie Fund for International Peace. [16] He demonstrated irrefutably that the imperialist predatory war — Liepmann himself did not realise this aspect of the war but simply referred to the war — and the tendencies triggered or caused or favoured by it, represented the direct cause of the growing wave of criminality which appeared towards the end of the war and after its conclusion swept over Germany. Liepmann put forward the thesis that post-war criminality was, in its essence, wartime criminality.

This socially critical attitude of bourgeois criminology was reflected also in a number of other studies, e.g. Werner Lorentz's work on homicidal offences. [17] Exner, Liepmann and others also discovered that since World War I there had been a kind of social structural shift among the exponents of criminality. Whereas in the past the main bulk of criminals had come from antisocial and other elements, the social stratum of the *Lumpenproletariat*, i.e. elements of all classes and strata of the population who, unable to stand up to the destructive social and moral conflicts of society had suffered shipwreck — it was now, as Liepmann put it, the 'intact sections' of the population or, as Exner formulated it, downright 'bourgeois circles' that were responsible for the bulk of criminal offences. [18] The close connection of exploitation and criminality, of private ownership and criminal acts, had suddenly become evident also in the shape of the middle-class offender.

It goes without saying that such a social-critical trend in bourgeois

118

criminology — a trend which was bound to emerge if bourgeois criminology wished to comprehend criminality as a real-life phenomenon and examine it with exact scientific methods — was not welcomed by the ruling circles.

The fascist seizure of power, in line with the official promotion of all reactionary trends in German criminology, also put an end to this socially critical school of thought. It is probably only an accident, or due to the inattention of the Nazi censorship, that a few studies maintaining this social-critical position continued to appear occasionally. It had become obvious that a further accumulation of such discoveries would have compelled bourgeois criminology to pose the question of the connection between criminality and the capitalist social structure. The ruling circles would have found themselves faced with the danger that criminological research financed by them, and originating from within the order they supported, would arrive, as a result of strict scientific work, at the same fundamental critique of society that had long been practised by the working class movement and moulded into a programme for the revolutionary transformation of society. The results of the researches of Liepmann and others have created a real opportunity for a social alliance between science and the working class movement — an alliance which scientists should have concluded from considerations of their national and scientific responsibilities.

Fascism, using its means of coercion and its social and ideological demagogy, succeeded for twelve years in halting this trend in Germany. However, it did not succeed in killing it because it sprang inevitably from the internal contradictions of bourgeois criminology itself. This is clearly proved by Karl Siegfried Bader's work on post-war criminality, [19] and by the studies of his disciples. These, and more particularly the studies of West German writers on juvenile criminology, continue the social-critical orientation set by Finkelnburg and Liepmann. [20]

It is interesting and at the same time regrettable to see these researchers, on the one hand, identifying phenomena belonging solely to the capitalist—imperialist way of life as the direct causes of criminality and, on the other, clinging to the taboo of the eternal existence of the bourgeois capitalist society and of criminality. They shrink from crossing the boundary line they have drawn for themselves and they dodge the question of the connection between the phenomena identified by them as causes of criminality and the capitalist—imperialist structure of society. Only sporadically, as in Mergen's collection of essays, [21] can a few albeit hesitant voices be heard demanding the liquidation of that taboo.

It is because of this social-critical trend that bourgeois criminology produces a whole series of valid conclusions which can be processed by socialist criminology and 'stored' at a new stage of development. Especially when he 'forgets' the limitations imposed on him by his 'system' and when he approaches the phenomena and correlations of life free from prejudice does the bourgeois criminologist arrive at conclusions which threaten to explode his system.

A typical representative of this trend is Hans von Hentig who has been concerned in particular with the phenomenon of American gangsterism and its manifestations and causes. Hentig displays a commendably dialectical approach, taking into consideration historical, economic, social-psychological, individual-psychological, law-enforcement and educational aspects. He then arrives at the conclusion — which he may not spell out so clearly but which is obvious to anyone studying society patterns from a scientific point of view — that gangsterism has its ultimate cause in the emergence of monopoly capitalism with its effect on the life of society, and that in consequence it is nothing more than the reflection of monopoly capitalism in the underworld. [22] Legal monopolism and gangsterism as an illegal manifestation of the same thing are so closely interlinked that they cannot be strictly separated either in the economic or the political sphere, and very frequently merge into one another. But although a consistent pursuit of his empirical studies and dialectical interpretation of his results should have led Hentig to proceed to a fundamental social critique of monopoly capitalism and State monopoly, he has not taken this step. In consequence he loses himself in mystical and fatalistic observations and thus devalues his scientific discoveries and conclusions, the best yet achieved by bourgeois criminology. His work more than any other reveals the limitations of the bourgeois system and thought pattern.

Much the same is true of the work of a number of American criminologists. Thus Edwin H. Sutherland developed Liepmann's first conclusions about the gradual 'bourgeoisation' of criminality in Germany and discovered in the life of capitalist—imperialist society a new social manifestation of criminality whose exponent is the capitalist business world or the 'entrepreneur class' — the so-called white-collar crime. [23] This social-critical school of thought also produced a number of discoveries in the field of research methodology and interpretations of correlations. Sutherland, for instance, found in his studies of juvenile criminality that this was 'learned' as a social behaviour pattern, albeit a socially negative one. [24] If he had extended this conclusion to the fundamental model of selfish individualist behaviour patterns, produced by the socio-economic structure of capitalist society as the so-called socially adequate form of behaviour, he would have arrived at even more far-reaching conclusions concerning juvenile criminality.

His pupil Albert K. Cohen [25] likewise arrives at useful results concerning gang crime. He finds that this develops chiefly in what we would call an asocial environment. The members of such juvenile gangs, Cohen explains, try to maintain themselves against the 'middle and upper classes', which look down on them, by developing a false assurance of their own worth. In this way they engage in a kind of social war against the official order. But Cohen does not ask himself the question of who actually produces this 'lower class', thereby giving rise to that pernicious gang phenomenon among certain sections of American youth. Equipped with a scientifically untenable set of ideas on the problems of class structure in a bourgeois imperialist society, which causes him to confuse the concept of 'class' with that of a demoralised stratum of society, he eventually drifts into downright speculation which ruins his originally positive approach to empirical observation. We shall have more to say about the dangers inherent in the methods of Cohen and other bourgeois criminologists, dangers to the scientific value of their results and interpretations.

Bourgeois criminology both in the past and in our own day thus comprises socially reactionary and anti-human tendencies together with markedly social-critical ones. Since both schools of thought accept the axiom of 'the eternal existence of criminality' or 'the eternal existence of the infringement of norms' — as Quensel formulated it in his latest work [26] — it often happens that diverse points of view appear in the work of different authors, sometimes confused to the point of totally blurring the concepts. It also appears that certain authors are by no means always clear about the social consequences or tendencies of their theories.

Indeed, in spite of the frequent acerbity of argument between various bourgeois criminological schools of thought, it is sometimes even doubtful whether bourgeois criminology is aware of the conflicting social trends existing within it. This awareness seems to us to be most highly developed among those criminologists who tend towards socially reactionary proposals. The social rôle of the powerful — whose favour they curry — and their social-political intentions — to which they wish to assimilate — are relatively unambiguous. After the experience of fascism in Germany there should be little room for any mistake about the terrorism of increased and intensified use of violence in the so-called crime policy of imperialist countries.

While the reactionary wing, whose fundamental theoretical concept is rooted in anti-communism, reveals a clear awareness of the socially reactionary function of its theoretical concept, the realisation that it must champion society's humanist interests against reactionary terror is less clearly developed among the exponents of the socially critical school of thought. In many cases their attitudes may also be governed by fear of being suspected of 'communist' ideas. We therefore find the reactionary wing displaying insolence and aggressiveness in debate with the opposite trend;[27] by contrast the socially critical trend is super-cautious and — even when outspoken in argument — still too reticent to name the socio-political cause of the dispute.

The conflict between system and method virtually fetters the socially critical trend in bourgeois criminology. Thus, while Mergen argues vigorously against the 'philosophical', i.e. irrational and speculative, school of thought within West German criminology, he still shrinks from stating that this so-called philosophical school is about to erect the 'criminological' sub-structure for the proposed arch-reactionary criminal law reform whose final result — in much the same way as under Nazi fascism — can only be a penal terror system running amok.

Among criminal law scholars in the Federal Republic of Germany Arthur Wegner openly warned against fascist dangers in penal policy and jurisdiction as early as 1951 and 1954. Certainly Wegner's own criticism of the reforms proposed by the ruling circles of the Federal Republic, as well as the criticism of Herbert Jäger and Jürgen Baumann, is marked by an impeccable understanding of the laws of movement in society, an understanding which it would be pleasing to see also among criminologists of the socially critical school of thought.

The variety of trends found in the work of individual criminologists makes it exceedingly difficult to determine which of the two camps they belong to. To make matters worse, a number of criminologists, in an attempt to dodge the argument, support so-called 'mixed' theories and points of view. Some of them even believe they must eliminate the 'one-sidedness' of the opposing theories or basic concepts and 'mediate' between them; but that makes confusion worse confounded. There can be no mediation between reaction and humanity. Such 'mediators' merely prove by their attempts that they are very far from having grasped the socio-political function of criminology.

Because of this confused picture of bourgeois criminology a number of socialist criminologists have thought that the only way out of the chaos of bourgeois views is a drastic cutting of the Gordian knot. Some of them, as for instance Gertsenson,[28] believe that bourgeois criminology is predominantly marked by powerful reactionary tendencies. Others, such as Szabó, acknowledge the very real methodological achievements of bourgeois criminologists and their politically humanist attitude, and therefore regard this as the essential trend. [29] We cannot follow either of these extreme judgements. The only possible way is that of dialectical-historical critique — a critique which, on the one hand, perceives the great danger of the reactionary school of thought and, on the other, points both to the positive aspects and the bourgeois limitations of the socially critical school. An exchange of ideas, in the scientific sense, i.e. with a view to the promotion of all positive beginnings and an overcoming of all socially negative limitations, is possible only with the socially critical school of thought. The intellectual ground for a dialogue between socialist and bourgeois criminologists can only be humanity — and this entails common rejection of inhuman theories.

The methods of bourgeois criminology

An examination of the socially critical school of thought in bourgeois criminology — pursued not with the aim of one-sided rejection but of defining the tasks of present-day criminological research — from a certain point onwards develops into a critique of the methods of bourgeois criminological research. Hartmann, [30] in particular, has laid some solid foundations for such an examination and has shown that bourgeois criminology, on the one hand, proceeds from an incorrect concept of society and, on the other, accepts a pessimistic image of the human being. In spite of all the emphasis on social 'circumstances' as the causes of criminality, criminality is ultimately still seen as being rooted in the eternal wickedness of the individual. This starting point characterises not only the system of bourgeois criminology but, to a greater or lesser extent, underlies its research methods and interpretations. The system, in a sense, is latent in the methods themselves.

In making this overall judgement of the methodological foundations of bourgeois criminology we do not overlook the fact that here and there attempts can be seen to depart from this unpromising methodological foundation. This seems to be true particularly of Horst Schüler-Springorum and Rudolf Sieverts, who observe that 'sociality and criminality are not identifiable "in themselves" — as for instance hereditary factors — but always only in the texture and context of the prevailing social order. The time-conditioned social order is not only the "background" of social misbehaviour, but the two condition each other reciprocally.' [31] They are sceptical about the thesis of the eternal existence of criminality without, however, going as far as to reject it. They are clear-sighted about the limitations of care for individuals who have become culpable in bourgeois society and warn against going to such extremes as the Utopian ideas of 'public help' for juvenile delinquents in Western Germany. 'The ideal solution,' they argue, 'i.e. help for *every person* at risk according to *his* needs, is at best imaginable only in a community whose sole function would be the practice of love of one's neighbour ...' [32]

Although we ourselves would not choose this definition for socialist society, we nevertheless believe that its present development in fact shows a society being built up in which all potentialities are created for genuinely 'helping every person at risk according to his needs'. Such a formula would not be a bad description at all for the objective of socialist judiciary practice.

The researches of Schüler-Springorum, Sieverts, Cohen and others reveal a method designed to comprehend criminality in its general fundamental social context; but we also find that the concepts used by them are not sufficiently qualified to enable them to reach satisfactory conclusions. Thus Schüler-Springorum and Sieverts refer to the social order and draw some very attractive conclusions. But these can only be really useful if the question about the determinants of a social order are asked – i.e. the fundamental structure of ownership and its effects on social behaviour.

Cohen and others use such concepts as class, stratum, etc. Clearly they feel that these concepts hold the key to a deeper understanding of the problems. However, they do not derive their 'class concept' from the socio-economic structure of society or from man's objective position within the given property relationships, but interpret it in a highly subjective or 'intuitive' manner. The findings which Cohen, for instance, arrives at for the 'lower class' or 'working class' are therefore scarcely acceptable and at times amount to a defamation of the working class.

Other bourgeois criminologists operate with the concept of 'culture' and in this connection refer to 'sub-cultures', etc. It is not clear, however, to what classes and strata this culture concept refers. Even less clear is the effect of the ownership structure upon the cultural life of the various classes and strata. Thus it does not emerge whether these concepts refer to the culture imposed upon society by the monopolies, with all its disruptive tendencies, or to the culture of the petty bourgeoisie, or to the cultural life of the working class, severely limited as that is by exploitation and oppression, or perhaps even to the 'culture' of asocial elements or the underworld. Much as we welcome the discovery of correlations between the multi-strata cultural life within society and criminality as a methodological advance in the research of bourgeois criminologists, and much as we look forward to having to verify their findings, we cannot accept the

124

framework of their method because it distorts the true relationships within society by the use of woolly concepts. Such a method can produce neither appropriate questions about the real structure of society nor the correct answers to them.

Much the same applies to the so-called control group investigations in bourgeois criminology. These proceed from an entirely acceptable starting point in that they set out to measure criminal behaviour not on its own but against the behaviour norms prevailing in the real life of society.

Sexologists, in particular, and other scientists have demonstrated that in bourgeois society there is a deep contradiction between the system of social behaviour norms predetermined by legal or moral norms, on the one hand, and the actual life of individuals on the other. But this method at once becomes suspect when, ignoring the real class stratification in society, it haphazardly compares groups of persons who have or have not behaved criminally. Such a method can be meaningful only if it conducts its comparisons with full consideration of the individuals' origins and roots in certain classes and strata of the population and the problems resulting therefrom for their social behaviour. Anything else would presuppose the existence of problems not affected by an individual's belonging to a particular class or stratum of the population. Any such control group investigation must presuppose clarity on class relationships and on the different position, the material and spiritual situation, of the classes in society and their relations to the given public order, as well as the laws governing their origins and evolution. If such problems remain outside the researcher's purview then the value of group investigations is reduced in the measure in which these problems have been neglected. The same applies whenever small social groups, such as the family, forms in school, etc., are investigated in connection with crime research. Such groupings are likewise greatly dependent in their behaviour, and indeed in their behaviour potential, on the class of their members.

A different problem is represented by the so-called prediction tables. The first ideas about the possibility of predicting criminal misbehaviour appeared as early as the twenties. Major work was subsequently done in this field by the American researchers Eleanor and Sheldon Glueck. They developed strictly empirical methods to establish correlations between definite factors of the social environment and the development of juvenile delinquent personalities on the one hand and the decision in favour of criminal behaviour on the other. In a lifetime's work they attempted to verify their results by the introduction of control group investigations and eventually developed prediction tables concerning the possible criminal behaviour of juveniles.

Ever since then the 'prediction of criminal behaviour' has been much talked about throughout bourgeois criminology, and indeed it is found also in the literature and the researches of socialist criminologists. Fritz Meyer in a recent study examines the present state of prediction research in Western Germany and in it presents an improved prediction table concerning recidivism. [33] This table comprises twenty-one points. Whenever only 0 to 2 points out of the total of 21 which make up the prediction of recidivism are present, the prediction is 'favourable' (i.e. recidivism is not likely); with 3 to 6 points the prediction is 'doubtful' either way; if on the other hand the table shows 7 or more points then the prediction is that the individual concerned will become a 'recidivist'. According to Meyer — if we may just list 7 of these points — a young person with a parent who has been punished once for a criminal offence, who has lived in the household of his divorced mother (provided she has not re-married), who has played truant at school or has had to repeat a form at least twice, who has subsequently on average changed his place of work every four months, who has spent more than six months in an 'approved school', who has run away from there and who before reaching the age of 21 has either committed 'fraud', 'professional immorality' or 'resistance to public authority', or who has engaged in 'begging', cannot escape the prediction of inevitable recidivism.

This kind of prediction table presents the given negative or unfavourable circumstances as immutable in their more or less destructive effect, so that a young person finding himself in such a situation has no other option than criminality. It may be perfectly true that under the conditions of bourgeois society these prediction points have a certain validity. But it is an appalling thought that even a criminologist proceeding with relatively exact methods such as Meyer, a man who rejects the speculative methods of 'intuitive' prediction because their validity is slight and the prediction arbitrary and not verifiable, gives no thought whatever to whether there do not perhaps exist some chances of eliminating the socially negative effect of the listed conditions.

The result of such a positivist approach is that Meyer subordinates his findings to the socially and politically reactionary intentions of the criminal law reformers when he declares in conclusion:

> When the criminal law reform is enacted and the new institution of educational detention is included in the list of penal measures, these findings should enable the judge to make the difficult prediction that 'an overall assessment of the offender and his actions reveals the danger that he may develop into a potential criminal'. This danger is

to be regarded as present not only when recidivism can be expected with 100% 'probability' but also whenever the probability of recidivism is 80%, since all that is required here is the danger of a development into a potential criminal and not that the defendant is a potential criminal already. [34]

The vicious circle in which bourgeois criminology finds itself trapped is thus alarmingly obvious. Approved school, sentence or 'educational detention' — all these measures conceived as weapons against criminality simultaneously become points on a prediction table which 'states' that a person who has undergone these measures must, with 100 per cent certainty, commit another criminal offence. These prediction tables, therefore, envisaging as they must further coercive measures against the individual, acquire a downright barbarous character. They become a predictive judgement on the necessity of lifelong incarceration of persons who are not even granted a logical opportunity of proving their fitness to live in society.

We believe, therefore, that the idea of prediction as such is not unfruitful, and indeed can be exceedingly valuable, provided one determines its social function. But so long as prediction means the expectation of possible negative modes of behaviour by a definite individual, as is done by bourgeois criminology, it leads the crime policy of bourgeois countries into the cul-de-sac of increased application of State coercion against individuals. For what other conclusion can one draw from the prediction that someone will commit another criminal offence with a certainty of 80 to 100 per cent — what other conclusion than that coercion must be applied against him? Surely such a negative prediction explicitly or tacitly assumes that the individual cannot be affected by any positive influences and that he lacks the strength to resist criminal temptations. Such a prediction — in terms of methodology — makes the individual the victim of destiny and, by excluding the question of abolishing the causes of criminality, merely diverts attention from the essence of the problem.

Because of its mistaken starting point this kind of prediction necessarily leads to pessimism, fatalism, scepticism and hence political reaction. A humanist prediction, therefore, can only be positive — i.e. it must show up the conditions and personal circumstances which have to be overcome in order to prevent criminality and recidivism. It must therefore aim in the opposite direction to the present prediction theories of bourgeois criminology. Since bourgeois criminology lacks the methodological equipment for such positive predictive work, its prediction tables are not only of no value but they are also downright misleading. Much as we acknowledge the praiseworthy personal endeavours of those engaged in prediction table research in bourgeois society, much as we are convinced that the original intentions of such researchers were humanist in character, and much as we sympathise with the Gluecks who objected to a pessimist interpretation of their prediction work, we nevertheless feel compelled to point to the inherent pattern of negative prognosis in bourgeois society because it leads science and society into a dangerous blind alley.

Bourgeois criminology at the crossroads

In view of the accumulation of a number of findings springing from empirical research, on the one hand, and in view of its experiences of fascism and the failure of all efforts so far to control criminality, present-day criminology finds itself in a real crisis. This is reflected in the growing number of contributions concerned with the 'situation' in criminology and seeking new roads.

Walter Reckless, a well-known American criminologist, trying to explain criminality by social circumstances and conditions, states:

> One gains the definite impression that major and minor crime in the developed countries of the world today is due to forces lying within the human personality, to disturbed relationships between individuals, and to social situations in which behaviour models and attitudes of an antisocial nature are propagated and adopted. In such countries ... it seems as if the economic factors do not directly act upon the emergence of major or minor crime... We have come through the industrial revolution and are in the middle of another 'revolution' — a revolution consisting of a deep-going transformation of our family system, neighbourhood life and corporate structures...
>
> I should like, if I may, first to consider the revolution in the individual ego in our society and its relationship to modern criminality. Owing to the effect of emancipation and the loss of family and corporate structures the individual child or young person becomes unable to rise like a balloon, to move outwards and upwards without stabilising ballast. He can strive for a position, for self-assertion, power, luxuries, excitement and love. He may now give expression to his lack of rights. He may develop a modest frustration. He may complain, he may protest. In consequence a major part of criminality nowadays represents a break-out by the individual from his constraining barriers, an attempt to magnify himself. It is a nuisance.

128

And it is serious. But it is also progress if placed beside the dependent, reverent, subjugated, restricted, inhibited, reserved and conservative self of the day before yesterday, dependent as it was on the social status of a person.[35]

Admittedly Reckless is unable to show any socially effective solutions since he, too, fails to break through the above-mentioned taboos of a bourgeois approach to the problem; but he and many others with him, such as the well-known British criminologist Hermann Mannheim,[36] have reached a point where the shedding of these taboos has become a question of preserving the scientific character of their researches.

Bourgeois criminology cannot endlessly repeat its empirical findings without one day going over to a genuine ruthless socially critical analysis and without tackling the root of the evil through radical proposals for a transformation of social conditions — proposals which will have to be based on the objective laws of social development. The accumulation of empirical data has in fact long refuted the thesis that criminality is eternal because it springs from man's eternal wickedness or sinfulness.

All the findings of bourgeois criminology — in so far as they have been arrived at without prejudice and not blended with speculative attempts at interpretation[37] — have not only proved the finite character of the causes of criminality but have also demonstrated that none of the circumstances which give rise to criminality is unchangeable. They have moreover shown that criminality is by no means rooted in the 'wickedness' of individuals but in contradictions which drive the individual into spontaneous anarchist socially blinded clashes with the official order of social life. Criminality therefore is, on the one hand, the discharge of a dull discontent of the individual with the existing bourgeois order and, on the other, a reflection of the demoralisation and degradation of man under bourgeois conditions. It is the release of the tension between juveniles and the public order, an ugly solution of the conflict between a two-faced hypocritical sexual morality and system of legal norms, on the one side, and the natural life of human beings suppressed by just this moral system on the other. A much-vaunted individualism and egotism finds its ruthless expression under the guise of alleged freedom; the greed for profits of big and small business reveals itself in a continuous transgression of the bounds of what is permissible; the brutality and cruelty practised by militarism and a police regime are transferred to the behaviour modes of individuals towards each other, a fear of existence engendered by clamour for war and nuclear war rubs off on the everyday life of the people — in short, the maxim that one only gets on by ruthlessly pursuing one's own interests and using one's elbows is triumphant.

Bourgeois criminology has amassed an immense amount of evidence. But what it has proved is not the eternal existence of criminality but the fact that criminal patterns of behaviour inescapably stem from the nature of bourgeois society itself, that they have been connected with it and will remain connected with it as long as it exists. The evidence does not allow of any other conclusion. Whenever bourgeois criminology tries to prove its thesis by reference to 'habitual' or 'professional criminals' or to the 'potential offender', it carefully ignores the fact that even these people act, or first acted, not from any delight in evil but because in their moral degradation they are nothing other than the quintessence of human beings without anchor of their own helplessly exposed to the destructive contradictions of their society. The mere existence of this army of asocial habitual and professional criminals, gangsters and potential offenders is the most striking evidence of the destructive effects of the conflicts rending bourgeois society.

Any criminology which, in this situation, proposes to concentrate solely on the individual and which only proposes ways of educating those who have fallen, or ways of 'protecting' society from them by long-term incarceration, ultimately misses its scientific purpose — no matter how humane its educational proposals may be.

The best representatives of present-day bourgeois criminology have long realised that present bourgeois crime policy is totally unable to solve the problem of criminality. Samuel Haig Jameson, for instance, points out that a public which proceeds from the principle of retribution is hardly likely to find the right measures to deal with criminal offenders.[38] Donald E.J. MacNamara found that the American prison system in its present form, far from providing help for those who have tripped up, represents a decisive obstacle to any effective reintegration.[39]

German bourgeois justice and the German bourgeois State have, throughout their development, followed different roads of crime policy, all of which have failed. The nineteenth century swore by prison sentences — as late as 1882 three-quarters of all sentences were for imprisonment — but criminality went on rising. From the turn of the century until the end of the twenties the emphasis shifted from imprisonment to fines — but throughout that period criminality continued to grow. The shift was no doubt partly due to the fact that the capacity of German prisons was no longer equal to the growing flood of convicted persons and partly also to an increasing realisation of the pointlessness of imprisonment. But this change in crime policy produced no success. Criminality scarcely reacted to the change in penal measures and continued to depend solely on its prime causes — and these, needless to say, were not tackled by the capitalist-imperialist State because this would have meant shaking its own foundations.

The Nazi State and its theoreticians among the jurists believed that persecution of persons for their beliefs, the deterrents of death sentence and long-term imprisonment in the shape of preventive detention, resulting in a vast number of people being detained in concentration camps, were suitable means of conquering criminality. But even this 'new crime policy', which itself had turned criminal, failed to produce results. It merely contributed towards a further rise in crime figures.

Quite apart from the fact that justice itself became criminal by its inhuman terror, general criminality can be seen, even from the distorted and doctored Nazi statistics, to have continued growing. Even the introduction of security measures in the shape of preventive detention, praised by the 'sociological' school as a panacea for criminality but in fact no more than a disguised indefinite term of incarceration for which the commission of a criminal offence was only a pretext but not the legal grounds, ultimately proved a total failure, as shown by Joachim Hellmer in a very impressive study. [40] Fascism and its crime policy produced not a drop but in fact an enormous increase in criminality, just because of its brutalisation and barbarisation of the whole life of society.

Thus, at the end of nearly two centuries of bourgeois crime policy, bourgeois criminology is no nearer a solution of its problem than at its beginning. It is extremely interesting that those bourgeois criminologists who preserve their scientific character, i.e. those who refuse to give up their socially critical attitude, have remembered the fundamental thoughts of bourgeois enlightenment and have rediscovered Beccaria. Once more they are searching for a humane solution of the problem and, as all previous attempts have failed, they are now compelled to ask themselves whether their former road has proved the right one. One gets the impression — for instance from Gustav Nass's opening address at a Beccaria celebration [41] — that present-day bourgeois criminology has reached a crossroads similar to that reached by bourgeois enlightenment 200 years ago. Nass is right to point out that bourgeois enlightenment accomplished its achievements when it realised that, in order to attain its humanist ideals, it must ally itself with the revolutionary forces of its day.

While this rediscovery of Beccaria or Hommel is to be welcomed, it must be remembered that every period demands its own solutions. By all means let the socially critical school of thought in bourgeois criminology regard Beccaria as an example — but the value of this example does not lie in imitation or repetition of his views or theses.

131

By pointing the way towards socialism our age has at the same time shown the road away from criminality. If bourgeois criminology wishes to draft a genuinely new crime policy it will have to learn from Beccaria and from other criminal law enlighteners, and in particular from the great philosophers Kant, Fichte and Hegel, that it must pose the questions of so-called crime policy in a much more fundamental way. The failure of bourgeois penal coercive measures should have taught them that criminality cannot be abolished without fundamental social transformations.

The demands of the West German Criminological Society:

> Creation of a unified system in the social struggle against crime, abolition of the monopoly of the dogmatic sciences in the assessment of criminality, of circumstances of crime and of anti-social behaviour, consideration of the essential findings of the empirical sciences in the reform of the criminal law, direct application of criminological experience to crime prevention, education of the society, the treatment of offenders and their social rehabilitation ... transformation of a retributive justice into a clinical justice concerned more with the offender than the offence [42]

are bound, under the system of imperialist militarist tyranny, to become not the democratic and humanist reforms envisaged by the authors of such proposals but merely consolidate the power of State-monopoly bureaucrats over individuals.

Humanist solutions require a society in which selfishness and individualism are not behaviour principles vital to survival but where mutual help, respect and recognition are directives also for personally successful behaviour, in which collective work is not self-sacrificing altruism but the prerequisite of the well-being of each individual. Bourgeois criminology has developed a large number of proposals and programmes whose central idea is the abolition of the causes of criminality and educational help as the only promising means of reducing criminality.

Such a programme was recently proclaimed at the 11th Juvenile Court Convention in Münster by Hans Peters. However, the mere proclamation of such a humanist programme is not enough. What is needed now is a struggle for the transformation of social conditions so that this programme may be realised. Bourgeois criminology will have to draw its own conclusions from the fact that in Germany peaks of aggressivity by the ruling circles have invariably been accompanied by a rise in criminality or that such peaks were followed by a powerful eruption of criminality.

Aggressivity does not mean only external aggressiveness and war preparations but it also means the progressive abolition of internal democracy,

132

the spiritual preparation of the people for aggression through the liquidation of humanitarian values, the stimulation of primitive greed, the militarisation of public life, the diminution of society's ability to manage its own affairs, etc. A struggle against war and the preparation of aggression and for the restitution, strengthening and further development of democracy also means the awakening, consolidation and strengthening of the society's and the individual's ability of self-government in a socially useful manner. [43]

The theoretical and practical programme of a bourgeois-humanist criminology must seek co-operation with those forces in society which are in a position to realise such a social policy. The socially critical and humanist programme of a criminology striving to work for the benefit of mankind must stand or fall on the question of which forces in society it bases itself upon. That is the decision bourgeois criminology must face. Unless it does so there is a serious risk that all the findings and humanist proposals of criminology will be transformed by the ruling forces into reactionary reforms. The West German criminal law reform, which has drawn from all criminological research only the conclusion to intensify and multiply the application of criminal law coercion against a real or predictively putative offender, must be seen as a warning.

There is no doubt, moreover, that political and scientific reaction have joined battle with the socially critical school of thought in criminology, in the hope of subjecting it to a speculative, irrational, philosophical kind of criminology characterised not by scientifically verifiable statements but by an 'avowal' in favour of the State-monopoly crime policy. Mergen is resisting this tendency by claiming for criminology the status of a natural science. We believe, however, that criminology in the bourgeois countries cannot be helped so much by its attempt to gain recognition as a natural science, which of course it is not and never can be, as by a deliberate struggle against politically reactionary tendencies, a struggle for the preservation or restitution of democracy in criminal law and by a long-term support for fundamental democratic transformations in society. Only thus can it justify and realise its humanist aspirations.

Notes

¹ Cf. H. Ellenberger in A. Mergen, *Kriminologie heute*, Kriminologische Schriftenreihe, vol. 2, Hamburg 1961, pp. 43 ss., and H.E. Göppinger, 'Die gegenwärtige Situation der Kriminologie', loc. cit., pp. 3 ss.

² Cf. F. Engels, 'Die Lage der arbeitenden Klasse in England', in: K. Marx/F. Engels, *Werke*, vol. 2, pp. 225 ss.

³ Cf. L.A.J. Quetelet, *Soziale Physik oder Abhandlung über die Entwicklung der Fähigkeiten des Menschen*, Jena 1914—21.

⁴ W. Starke, *Verbrechen und Verbrecher in Preussen, 1854 bis 1878, eine kulturgeschichtliche Studie*, Berlin 1884.

⁵ K. Marx, 'Die Todesstrafe — Herrn Cobdens Pamphlet — Anordnungen der Bank von England', in: K. Marx/F. Engels, *Werke*, vol. 8, pp. 506 ss.

⁶ Cf. J. Renneberg, *Die kriminalsoziologischen und kriminalbiologischen Lehren und Strafrechtsreformvorschläge Liszts und die Zerstörung der Gesetzlichkeit im bürgerlichen Strafrecht*, Berlin 1956.

⁷ Cf. A. Markel, *Gesammelte Abhandlungen aus dem Gebiet der allgemeinen Rechtslehre und des Strafrechts*, Strasbourg 1899, pp. 830 ss., especially p. 844.

⁸ Cf. C. Lombroso, *Der Verbrecher in anthropologischer, ärztlicher und juristischer Beziehung*, Hamburg 1877; see also J. Renneberg, *Die kriminalsoziologischen und kriminalbiologischen Lehren ...*, loc. cit.

⁹ Cf. also O. Mittelstädt, *Gegen die Freiheitsstrafen, Ein Beitrag zur Kritik des heutigen Strafensystems*, 2nd ed., Leipzig 1879.

¹⁰ Cf. F. Exner, *Kriminologie*, 3rd ed., Berlin—Göttingen—Heidelberg 1949.

¹¹ F. Marcus, 'Erheblicher Rückgang der Jugendkriminalität vor dem zweiten Weltkriege', *Monatsschrift für Kriminologie und Strafrechtsreform*, 1965, Issue 6, pp. 298 ss.

¹² A. Mergen, *Die tatsächliche Situation ...*, loc. cit., pp. 8 ss.

¹³ Beginnings of a differentiated consideration are found in J. Lekschas, *Studien zur Jugendkriminalität*, Berlin 1965, p. 23, and at the First International Symposium, 'Die Jugendkriminalität und ihre Bekämpfung in der sozialistischen Gesellschaft', loc. cit., as also in the post-doctoral theses of R. Hartmann and G. Stiller.

¹⁴ K. Finkelnburg, *Die Bestraften in Deutschland — Ein Ermittlungsversuch, wie viele Millionen der deutschen Reichsbevölkerung (Reichsvolkszählungstag vom 1.12.1910) wegen Verbrechen oder Vergehen gegen Reichsgesetze bestraft sind*, Berlin 1912, p. 33.

¹⁵ Cf. in particular E. Wulffen, *Kriminalpsychologie*, Berlin 1926.

[16] Cf. M. Liepmann, *Krieg und Kriminalität in Deutschland*, Stuttgart—Berlin—Leipzig 1930.

[17] W. Lorenz, *Die Totschläger*, Kriminalistische Abhandlungen, Leipzig 1932, Issue XVIII; F. Exner, *Krieg und Kriminalität*, Kriminalistische Abhandlungen, Leipzig 1926, Issue I.

[18] Cf. M. Liepmann, *Krieg und Kriminalität ...*, loc. cit.; F. Exner, *Krieg und Kriminalität*, loc. cit.

[19] K.S. Bader, *Soziologie der Nachkriegskriminalität*, Tübingen 1949.

[20] Cf., as one example of many, H. v. Hentig, *Das Verbrechen*, vols. I and II, Berlin—Göttingen—Heidelberg 1961, 1962; also H. Schüler-Springorum/R. Sieverts, *Sozial auffällige Jugendliche*, Munich 1964.

[21] Cf. A. Mergen, *Kriminologie heute*, loc. cit.

[22] H. v. Hentig, *Der Gangster*, Berlin—Göttingen—Heidelberg 1959.

[23] E.H. Sutherland, in: *The Sutherland Papers*, Bloomington 1956, ed. A.K. Cohen/A. Lindesmith and others, pp. 46 ss. (in English).

[24] E.H. Sutherland, loc. cit., pp. 7 ss.

[25] A.K. Cohen, *Delinquent Boys*, Glencoe 1955 (in English).

[26] S. Quensel, *Sozialpsychologische Aspekte der Kriminologie — Handlung, Situation und Persönlichkeit*, Stuttgart 1964, pp. 9, 114.

[27] Cf. for instance H.J. Schneider's critique of S. Quensel, *Sozialpsychologische Aspekte der Kriminologie — Handlung, Situation und Persönlichkeit*, Stuttgart 1964, reviewed in: *Goltdammers Archiv für Strafrecht*, 1965, pp. 350 ss.

[28] Cf. A.A. Gertsenson, *Introduction to Soviet Criminology*, loc. cit.

[29] Cf. A. Szabó, *Acta Juridica*, loc. cit., pp. 65 ss.

[30] Cf. above all: 'Persönlichkeit und Schuld jugendlicher Straftäter', Habil. thesis, Berlin 1965.

[31] Cf. H. Schüler-Springorum/R. Sieverts, *Sozial auffällige Jugendliche*, loc. cit., p. 64.

[32] Cf. H. Schüler-Springorum/R. Sieverts, loc. cit., p. 61.

[33] F. Meyer, 'Der gegenwärtige Stand der Prognoseforschung in Deutschland', *Monatsschrift für Kriminologie und Strafrechtsreform*, 1965, Issue 5, pp. 243 ss.

[34] F. Meyer, loc. cit., p. 246.

[35] W.C. Reckless, *The Crime Problem*, New York 1955, pp. 109 ss. (in English).

[36] H. Mannheim, *Criminal Justice and Social Reconstruction*, London 1949 (in English).

[37] S. Quensel, *Sozialpsychologische Aspekte ...*, loc. cit., p. 114. To Quensel, criminality is neither 'sickness' nor 'sin'. To him, crime as a 'norm infringement' is 'an inevitable consequence of human structure'. He

thus labels something old with a new, socio-psychologically accented name. Quensel's logic is as simple as it is erroneous. To start with, he drains the problem of its real content by equating the most serious crimes to just any infringement of the norms (i.e. murder = violation of some disciplinary rule). He next proceeds from the (entirely correct but in the given context meaningless) premise that human society will always need a certain regulation of its vital processes, and hence also norms of behaviour. He then seizes on the common experience that, given the complexity of social existence and the infinity of individual human aspirations, there will always be deviations of specific individual behaviour from the general norm; from this he concludes that, since norms are eternal, their infringements must also be eternal, and since crimes are infringements of norms crimes, too, must be eternal. They belong, he claims, to man's 'structure'. What Quensel overlooks is the fact that there are qualitative differences between crimes and other norm infringements. As he fails to prove that this difference is immaterial, his entire theoretical position collapses.

[38] Cf. *Crime in America*, ed. H.A. Bloch, New York 1961, pp. 32 ss. (in English).

[39] Cf. *Crime in America*, loc. cit., pp. 61 ss.

[40] J. Hellmer, *Der Gewohnheitsverbrecher und die Sicherungsverwahrung 1934 bis 1945*, Berlin 1961.

[41] A. Mergen, *Zweihundert Jahre später*, Hamburg 1965, pp. 7 ss.

[42] A. Mergen, *Zweihundert Jahre später*, loc. cit., p. 19.

[43] Cf. J. Lekschas, *Studien zur Jugendkriminalität*, loc. cit., pp. 10 ss.

PART II

The Social Conditions of Criminality in the German Democratic Republic

Preliminary Note

The fact that criminality continues to exist in the GDR — as it does in other socialist countries — as a social phenomenon on a socially relevant scale demands an explanation. Such an explanation must be on a social — and not a biological or some other meta-social let alone metaphysical — basis; it must, moreover, cover the specific social conditioning of criminality in the GDR. Such an explanation is possible on the basis of Marxist—Leninist theory — and only on that basis. The following chapter will attempt to outline such an explanation, both as a point of reference and a mapping out of future tasks for criminological research.

4 Criminality as a Socially Conditioned Phenomenon in Capitalism and Socialism

Each criminal offence, and criminality as a whole, represents a specific form — a socially negative and destructive form — of social behaviour by individuals and as such is subject to the general laws and conditions of social behaviour. In emphasising the general laws of social behaviour we do not wish to deny the existence of specific individual-psychological or biological aspects of human behaviour. But these are not subjects of this investigation.

In order to comprehend criminality in its social determination one has to start from the social determination of social behaviour generally. Diverse, contradictory and haphazard as the individual's actions and behaviour may be, and much as individual peculiarities play a part in the occurrence of individual actions, ultimately these are governed by socially deeper-lying regularities which impress a direction and content on the seeming chaos of diverse human action.

Engels was the first to prove that 'the course of history is determined by internal general laws...And wherever chance operates on the surface it is invariably governed by hidden inner laws, and it is these laws which have to be discovered.'[1]

It is the historic achievement of dialectical and historical materialism, founded by Marx and Engels, to have discovered these internal kinetic laws of human society and of the dominant social behaviour of its members as being founded in the dialectics of productive forces and production relations — and thus ultimately in the socio-economic or property ownership structure.

This conditioned interaction of productive forces and production relations demands and produces in each social grouping a specific fundamental type of social behaviour. This specific fundamental pattern of social behaviour is reasonably well known from accurate and detailed descriptions, even pre-dating Marxist philosophy, and from literature and art. One need only remember the models of Hellenism, the early Middle Ages, the rise of the bourgeoisie, or — as a particularly extreme pattern at the other end of the scale — of fascism. Each period develops its own particular basic form of social behaviour, reflected sometimes in ideals, philosophical attitudes or even in proverbs and popular sayings. We find them in Plato, Thomas Aquinas, Kant, Fichte, Hegel, etc. Prior to Marx, however, the socio-economic determination of these human aspects and behaviour patterns remained undiscovered; instead they were regarded as absolute, eternal and universally valid.[2] This theoretical separation and isolation of behaviour patterns from their economic basis also pursued an objective purpose — in addition to the overtly or secretly pursued aim of guiding the behaviour patterns of the exploited and oppressed classes and strata by models propagated by the ideologists of the ruling classes. This objective purpose was the establishment of some relatively independent existence for these 'internal models'. This explains the continuous existence of such behaviour patterns even when their economic foundation has changed or disappeared. This relative independence is also the philosophical basis of the various idealistic 'theories' which regard such behaviour patterns as given to man once and for all, i.e. as 'purely anthropological'.

Methodologically the concept of the basic pattern of social behaviour (in ordinary language known as the way of life) is of particular importance because it represents the *necessary link* between the socio-economic structure of a given society and the many thousands of accidental forms of social behaviour by its individuals. It makes it possible to classify such individual behaviour and relate it to the typical behaviour of an epoch, a form of behaviour objectively rooted in and founded on the socio-economic structure. It is this objective socio-economic reference frame of behaviour patterns that distinguishes us from idealist behaviourism, which examines the categories of behaviour solely in themselves and unhistorically.

The question as to the social determination of criminality can therefore be defined as that of the relationship of criminality to the basic pattern of social behaviour in the social system under review: is it adequate to it or inadequate?

The basic pattern of social behaviour in capitalism, the last social order producing goods on the basis of the private ownership of the means of production, is individualism and selfishness, the isolation and alienation of the individual, the conflict between individual and society. Private ownership of the means of production, forced into a position of antagonism by the conditions of production and exchange, forces the private owner — and in exploitative systems only the private owner counts as an individual — as the representative and exponent of the kinetic laws and objective interests of private ownership into objectively inescapable behaviour patterns which are directed both against the interests of other private owners and against those of society as a whole.

This pattern of social behaviour, developed and refined over hundred and thousands of years, has become deeply ingrained in social awareness and is reflected in such sayings as 'Charity begins at home', 'Blood is thicker than water', etc. Contrary to widespread belief it should be emphasised that this basic pattern of behaviour and thought is not merely an ideological phenomenon but a form of social behaviour and hence a real subjective and objective phenomenon.[3]

Acceptance of such a basic pattern for a certain order of society must not be taken to mean that in such a society there are only such modes of behaviour. The infinite multiplicity of human reactions and behaviour cannot be totally encompassed by the basic pattern in question; in every society there are countless actions which are inadequate to that pattern or even directly opposed to it. Its social function consists in the control of the basic social behaviour of people in line with social production and living conditions, in identifying a typical mode of reaction of individuals among thousands of chance factors, in such a way that these reactions of the individual can be seen as good, reasonable and normal.

The conflict between separate individuals and between the individual and society as a whole, a conflict typical of social systems based on the private ownership of the means of production and governing social behaviour in such systems, inevitably results in a large number of individual actions which deny or violate the interests of others, or of the community. It therefore makes it necessary — with the help of the State — to create a matrix, a system of rules, chiefly of legal norms, designed to reduce to a justifiable minimum such natural, inevitable and inherent infringements of other individuals or of society as a whole.

This is clearly illustrated in Article 903 of the German Civil Code which (a) sanctions the basic pattern of social behaviour of the private owner — to dispose over his property as he chooses — as an essential social fact, yet (b) finds itself compelled, at the same time, in the interests of other, or all, private owners to set down a *de jure* limitation — the law, or the rights of third parties.

Needless to say, the real social conflict and the prevailing behaviour pattern of a war of all against all cannot be solved or abolished by any legal regulations, however prettily worded. To try to use moral or legal norms with a human façade, but springing from a social order based on the private ownership of the means of production, in order to oppose the vital interests of private ownership and the actions and subjective aspirations springing from it is like trying to plug a bursting dyke with one's bare hands. In social systems based upon the private ownership of the means of production ruthless selfishness and individualism are ever-present forms of social behaviour.

Certain particularly far-reaching violations of the interests of other individuals or of the community are highlighted as criminal acts and defined as criminal offences by appropriate criminal laws. This means that the criminal law of exploitative systems penalises actions (behaviour patterns) which in their social essence are in line with the basic pattern of social behaviour in those societies but in their form have transgressed a (basically variable) limit. The criminal law of exploitative States − disregarding for the moment its openly reactionary rôle in illegally persecuting socially progressive forces, and its resistance to the course of history − is aimed, paradoxically enough, at the products, consequences and indeed excrescences of its own social soil. This social soil, full of contradictions as it is, and the basic pattern of social behaviour adequate to it, inevitably and ceaselessly produce and reproduce their own victims. The bourgeois 'theory' of the offender's *need* for punishment may well be an unconscious ideological reflection of this state of affairs.

In other words, criminality in capitalism − and in all other social systems based on the private ownership of the means of production − is adequate to the fundamental type and basic pattern of social behaviour of this society, because of the society's socio-economic structure; criminality in capitalism inescapably springs from this socio-economic basic structure and cannot be liquidated so long as this society continues to exist.

An effective and radical struggle against criminality under capitalism therefore requires, as an indispensable condition, the abolition of its own socio-economic structure with which criminality is indissolubly bound up. As is well known, this is the road shown by Marx and Engels, who were therefore a thousand times more far-sighted than all those earlier and present-day bourgeois criminologists whose subtle researches into causes and predictions can ultimately produce nothing but fatalist impotence and disappointment so long as the capitalist order itself is preserved.

Matters are totally different under socialism, and therefore a different explanation and interpretation of criminality is needed. The fundamental difference between capitalism and socialism, which must be our methodological starting point, lies in their totally different socio-economic basic structures.

Under socialism the private ownership of the means of production has been abolished and overcome; production takes place in conditions of common ownership (national or co-operative ownership of the means of production). The new position of ownership is realised — and can only be realised — by active participation in social production, in work. Under such conditions the social basis of a behaviour pattern characterised by individualism and selfishness has been removed; the new socio-economic basic structure demands and produces a new pattern of social behaviour — that of collectivism, of the 'We' replacing the 'I' in thought and action, of comradely co-operation and mutual help.

The essential features of this behaviour pattern of the new man have been clearly outlined and formulated in the ten commandments of socialist morality proclaimed at the Fifth Congress of the SED and in the programmes of the Communist Party of the Soviet Union and the SED, as well as in the Moscow Declaration of 1960.

However, there is no simple mechanical relationship, no instantaneous reflection of the new socialist socio-economic basic structure in the new socialist behaviour pattern, or the features of the new man with his higher socialist awareness and ethos.

On the one hand, socialist thought and action, though confined to the proletariat as the social vanguard, began to form, in bud as it were, even under capitalism, as the product of the inner contradictions of that social order. The reality of capitalist exploitation and class struggle gave rise, among the proletariat, to thought and behaviour patterns of solidarity, of conscious discipline and of an aware co-operation. With the establishment of socialism, especially of its socio-economic foundations, this basic pattern of social behaviour was both developed and transferred, as a new generally valid behaviour pattern, from the leading social forces, the party of the working class, to the rest of society. Its power as a determinant of social behaviour increases to the extent to which the political and moral unity of the people is established and consolidated.

On the other hand, this new basic pattern of social behaviour does not suddenly, with the victory of socialist production relations, become absolute or solely dominant. The old, entirely opposite, behaviour of private ownership, which over hundreds and thousands of years has struck deep roots in man's thinking and action and, in consequence, has achieved a high degree of relatively independent existence, cannot be expunged overnight. Instead, a great deal of painstaking work, under the leadership of the Marxist—Leninist party, is necessary to transform *all* social (material and ideological) circumstances and conditions so that a new behaviour pattern can be developed and implanted. This requires time — years and even decades — and cannot be accomplished in a single generation. In his 'revelations about the communist trial in Cologne' Marx referred to the historical order of magnitude and the social scope of such transformations when he said to the workers: 'You will have to go through fifteen, twenty, fifty years of civil wars and popular struggles not only to transform conditions but to transform yourselves and fit yourselves for political rule...'[4]

Under our particular conditions this process of invalidation of the old behaviour pattern and evolution of a new one, a process which, psychologically speaking, is probably subject to similar laws as conditioned reflexes or any other process of re-adaptation, is being impeded in particular by two external social circumstances:

1   the action of socio-economic remnants[5] of private ownership which – in particular in the spheres of everyday life and of human, in particular intimate, relations – provide conditions for a confirmation, re-invigoration or consolidation of the old behaviour pattern;
2   the existence of capitalist countries, more particularly imperialist Western Germany. We are not thinking only of deliberately hostile or ideologically harmful influences such as television, radio, etc. Equally effective are a variety of spontaneous influences of the old behaviour pattern prevailing in Western Germany and in other Western countries with or without decadent distortions and modifications, which largely also form part of the arsenal of ideological subversion. Account must be taken in this connection not only of ideological seduction but also of the spontaneous effect of false ideals, tempting glossy façades, etc., and the large number of personal contacts and private channels of information.

We therefore have to record the fact that the new socialist behaviour pattern, in line with the socio-economic structure of socialism, is already well defined, that it is being increasingly developed in everyday life, that it is in fact by now the dominant pattern and increasingly gaining in strength; on the other hand, however, and on a socially still relevant scale, we observe the effects of the outdated behaviour pattern which still produces certain individual actions of the old type. This old behaviour pattern has come to us in its capitalist or late-bourgeois or even fascist form. However, it is based on and rooted in thousands of years of private ownership, which is why it has appeared to be the eternal human behaviour pattern. Hence two totally opposite behaviour patterns are existent and effective in socialist society, each tending to determine individual actions of fundamentally different character.

This reflection, incidentally, reveals the methodological importance of the more or less independent concept of 'behaviour pattern'. It enables us to provide a social and materialist explanation of relevant individual actions, e.g. a criminal offence, without having to refer it directly to material conditions which no longer exist in present-day reality, such as the socio-economic structure of capitalism. The behaviour pattern, as we have said before, is thus not merely an intellectual or ideological phenomenon but may be seen as an objective and subjective phenomenon of virtually a material nature.

We therefore have in socialism a behaviour pattern — the socialist pattern which dominates and is rooted in the socio-economic structure of socialism — which, on the basis of its social and collective orientation towards the interests of the community, towards harmony between the individual and society, towards the attuning of the interests of the individual and of society, does not give rise to any socially disturbing, destructive or other modes of behaviour liable to infringe the interests of the individual or of society, and hence also criminal modes of behaviour.

This socialist behaviour pattern excludes criminality in its essence. From its dominant position it follows that criminality in a socialist society is no longer an inevitable attribute or inescapable social phenomenon, but that it is alien to society and that there no longer exists any inherent social need for the commission of criminal acts. This idea was expressed in the well-known formula of the Decree of the State Council of 30 January 1961: 'In a socialist society no person need become a criminal.'

Convincing as this argument is, it must not be made a fetish. The progressive abolition if criminality is not just a matter of statistical figures; these are merely its more or less adequate and accidental reflection. What matters is the progressive removal of the conditions which give rise to criminal acts. In other words, even a partial or temporary increase in certain criminal statistics would not invalidate the objective validity of the systematic and purposeful reduction of criminality as outlined above.

The old behaviour pattern, which still persists, continues to tend to give rise to actions which violate the interests of other individuals or of society as a whole and which, under certain objective and subjective conditions, may themselves acquire criminal character. This old behaviour pattern — with all its manifestations, including such criminality as still exists — is totally alien to the character of socialism, i.e. its socio-economic structure and the ideas and way of life stemming from it.

The socialist epoch is thus characterised by two totally opposing tendencies — for and against criminality — and of these it is the tendency of systematic struggle for the reduction of criminality that is the dominant and victorious one.

Needless to say, the distribution and dominance of the two opposed behaviour patterns is not tied to individuals in the sense that some would behave in a capitalist and others in a socialist manner. In fact, these behaviour patterns cut right through our actual society, clashing and inter-mingling. The result is that, sometimes triggered accidentally, persons with a predominantly socialist way of life and thought may occasionally go off the rails — in extreme cases in a criminal way — and that individuals with marked attitudes of the old type may perform socially adequate actions and perhaps never commit criminal acts at all; should they, however, commit criminal acts then these are adequate to their personality and the behaviour pattern dominating it.

Criminality under socialism is therefore not determined by its socio-economic structure. Criminality in the German Democratic Republic — disregarding offences against the State which are rooted in the existence of imperialism in Western Germany and the fundamental antagonism be-tween the two Germanys — is thus not determined by ownership or class relationships, i.e. the deeper social structures. It is not therefore — as it is is in capitalism — inherent or indissolubly linked with the fundamental structure of society. Under the conditions in the GDR it is a relatively 'superficial' phenomenon which is totally alien to the core or the inner nature of our society.

The statement of the SED Party Programme that the socio-economic roots of criminality have largely been abolished in the German Democratic Republic does not mean that there are no social causes of criminality left and that the only existing causes, or the essential ones, are merely ideo-logical in character. The scope of social relationships is much wider and much richer than that of the fundamental social structure and embraces diverse and conflicting phenomena. Among these are inherited old behav-iour patterns whose independence and resilience can still give rise to criminal acts. As Marx proved in his critique of the Gotha Programme, socialist society *'develops* not on its own foundations' but *'emerges* from capitalist society'; it is thus inevitably 'still marked in every respect — economic, moral, spiritual...with the birthmarks of the old society from whose womb it has sprung'.[6]

Marx's exposition clearly outlines the dialectics between being and thinking, between what exists objectively and what subjectively, and leav-es no room for any one-sided ideological interpretation of the causes of criminality. Heinz Kallabis is therefore quite correct when he states:

> Matters are often represented as though the relationship between the new socialist reality and the social awareness of individuals was no more than a contradiction between the advanced objective living conditions of a socialist society and a backward awareness, i.e. peo-ple's views and habits inherited from the old capitalist society. If that

were the case one would merely have to raise the individual's social awareness to the level of the new material living conditions. This no doubt is a vital aspect of the dialectics between social reality and social awareness under socialism, but it is not the whole dialectics.

The fact is

that certain bourgeois factors in the individual's way of thinking are not simply ideological survivals from the old capitalist society, but in a sense reflections of the state of economic development of the socialist society. If one wishes to judge and control these ideological processes realistically then one must take account of these objective conditions of contradictions in the development of the social awareness of individuals, conditions which spring directly from the material circumstances of socialist society.[7]

Ladislav Schubert similarly opposes an idealistic interpretation of the causes of criminality:

A concept which wishes to serve as a methodological directive for the investigation of antisocial actions must regard the concept 'survivals of the past' as comprising everything that socialist society is compelled to fight against as a pernicious heritage. Not only the subjective factors (survivals in the consciousness of individuals) should be emphasised but also such factors as are present in the economic and cultural spheres. Any one-sided emphasis on the subjective component would run counter to scientific truth because the relationship between the individual and society is one that is reciprocally conditioned, marked by the reciprocal effects and the active participation of the subject in the transformation of objective reality and, at the same time, of himself. A concept thus confined can then serve as a directive for determining the method of investigating antisocial actions, as it thus excludes the risk of a one-sided consideration of the phenomenon.[8]

It is important that these factors and conditions are not seen as static but as continually engaged in interaction. Erich Schüler reminds us that criminality cannot be explained 'solely as the effect of so-called negative factors but from the relationship between the old and the new, the power and effectiveness of the one as against the other, both in the individual instance and, under somewhat changed aspects, in general.[9]

In other words, criminality does not simply spring from non-socialist phenomena. It also springs from shortcomings in the building of socialism,

147

e.g. from inadequate guidance, from mistakes in socialist education or work with people, from weaknesses in the application of the economic laws of socialism. What matters is the specific interplay without which, for instance, we should be unable to explain why two — admittedly different — individuals, under identical conditions of upbringing and guidance behave and develop differently from each other or why two individuals, roughly equal in their moral maturity, may at times adopt totally different attitudes when confronted with divergent, unevenly developed socialist conditions.

In other words, our specific analysis of causes must not be confined to a mere enumeration or summation of the factors effective in one instance, let alone of only the negative factors, but it must set these in relation to the still ineffective positive factors and generally attempt to comprehend the reciprocal and contradictory dependence and determination of the factors, i.e. their overall structure.

In consequence, none of these circumstances, whether 'bad' home, or political propaganda 'over their heads', or lack of control and organisation, or alcoholism, etc., can simply be labelled a cause of criminality. However, it should be understood that such failings are detrimental to society not only on general grounds but also because, in certain combinations, they may contribute to the emergence of criminality.

A specific socially related crime analysis might, therefore, reveal which of the measures and innovations designed to prevent criminal acts should be introduced at once and which at a later date, i.e. at a higher stage of social development, or following appropriate preparation, or given appropriate resources, etc. Such measures could be material and organisational, or spiritual and cultural, or moral-educational. The last category is of particular importance because it endows the individual with a greater degree of insight and moral stability, and therefore helps him to stand up to avoidable but nevertheless existing and sometimes as yet insoluble shortcomings and contradictions, or at least prevents him from giving way to some spontaneous anarchist anti-social reaction. This is further proof of the overwhelming importance of the subjective factor, of working with people, and of the need for effective guidance.

An important part in this overall complex of objective and subjective survivals is played also by the productive forces whose development had been impeded under capitalism and which thus found themselves on a relatively low level. In this respect the socialist phase of development, according to Marx, has the historic task of bringing about, 'hand in hand with the comprehensive development of the individuals, also a flowering of their productive forces', attaining, by the time the communist phase is

148

reached, such a degree that 'all mainsprings of communal wealth will flow more amply', enabling 'society to write upon its banners: from each according to his abilities, to each according to his needs! ' [10]

The backwardness and limitation of productive forces [11] — made worse in the German Democratic Republic by the consequences of the war and the imbalance resulting from the division of Germany — represents a further specific contradiction with substantial effect upon human modes of behaviour.

The reality of a typical social behaviour pattern, its dominance and effectiveness, largely depends on objective prerequisites. The private ownership of the means of production enabled the private owner — given adequate ruthlessness, business acumen and skill — to gain advantages for himself at the expense of others. The behaviour pattern of selfishness proved successful and paid off. That is why it became so deeply rooted.

A totally opposite behaviour pattern proved its worth for the proletariat struggling for its rights and for political power — the behaviour patterns of proletarian militant unity and solidarity, based on the realisation that only if the united working class makes common cause with all democratic forces can social progress be achieved, wage struggles successfully conducted, and democracy and peace secured.

Under socialism, following the establishment of the political power of the working class, once the question of 'Who whom?' had been decided and social production relations established in town and countryside, i.e. in the specific conditions of economic development, matters became much more complicated.

The new social behaviour pattern asserts itself and proves itself in practice to the extent to which the individual — or a specific grouping — directly experiences that what benefits society also benefits the particular enterprise or individual. As is well known, the new economic system of planning and management is fundamentally designed to ensure such a harmony of individual, group and society-wide interests through the system of economic levers, of material and spiritual incentives. In other words, this harmony of interests is the main driving force of our development, but it is not yet a universally present or automatic reality. Instead there are various conflicts: a plant may find it economically sound and profitable to adopt a particular line of production which may be undesirable from the national economic point of view; individual interests (such as qualifications, practice of one occupation or transfer to different work) may clash with the demand of the plant or the national economy. Moreover, for a variety of reasons, such as utilisation of certain bottleneck situations, a number of possibilities still exist — some legitimate, others

149

illegal or even criminal — of gaining personal advantage at the expense of others or of the community.

Other contradictions, naturally enough, spring from the distribution of reward in accordance with performance — a pattern adequate to socialism and aimed at the establishment of harmony between individual and social interests and to be replaced only at a higher stage of productivity by a higher pattern of distribution — to each according to his needs. Although everyone may be working to the best of his strength and abilities he will still only be rewarded in accordance with the social effect of his work, an effect which not only may vary because of the individual's subjective effort or his personal conditions, but will frequently also depended on a number of accidental factors, such as a person's parental background, state of health, local or family circumstances, etc.

To avoid misunderstanding: this is not to associate shortages with socialism. Socialism does not demand that anyone should forgo the satisfaction of his most basic needs, such as food, clothing, housing, culture, etc. The common social consumption pool assures everyone, whether young, old or sick, of an existence worthy of a human being, even if he is incapable of work. This pool ensures the satisfaction of a vast number of intellectual and cultural needs and the provision of public health and personal medical services. The principle of performance orientates the individual towards an ever-improved solution of the conflict between his needs and their satisfaction, between productive forces and production relations. Admittedly, the state of productive forces does not yet permit us to live in luxury. The only way of achieving that is the full assertion of the socialist method of production. This assures the individual not only of a better life at some remote future date but already ensures a steady improvement in his material standards of living and provides the opportunity for an ever fuller satisfaction of his needs. People learn through their own daily experience that the realisation of socialist principles at the same time means the fulfilment of their own personal interest, and that a true and satisfying solution of the problems lies just in this and not in some selfish or individualistic mode of action of the old style. They increasingly realise that the contradiction between their personal material needs and the available chances of satisfying them can be resolved only by the full realisation of the principle of distribution according to performance. Its realisation thus becomes the personal interest of the individual. With this principle , with its recognition and realisation by each individual, socialism provides a genuine and universally acceptable alternative to criminality, for instance to theft. This means that the individual must develop those needs whose satisfaction is possible for him by his own performance.

If therefore individuals have to set aside certain requirements for the time being, this does not mean that they have got into some existential crisis; it is merely an adjustment of continually developing diverse human needs to existing possibilities, and it is this that creates the conditions for a higher standard of living. Certainly this requires social awareness, but it does not mean a spartan attitude. The necessary renunciation of certain wishes is not a sacrifice but is possible without detriment to the individual's real interests.

In effect, however, some people do not resolve this conflict in a socially adequate manner but instead opt for a selfish, individualistic road which leads to only a seeming and temporary solution and in fact creates conflicts. The objective reason for this is the fact that the conflict is distorted into a negative pattern by various modes of behaviour and consequently produces destructive effects. We believe that the principal reason for this lies in the fact that a truly socialist relationship to this fundamental problem of social development does not yet exist everywhere or in every respect.

It is not only that persons who commit enrichment offences are still trapped in ideologically backward views on the issue of property but rather that outdated attitudes to property, in particular to socialist property, continue to exist, with the result that the above-mentioned conflict is bent into a negative feature. We are thinking of specific practical relations to socialist property: these include inappropriate or bad management of such property, its disregard as the property of society, allowing products to deteriorate, tolerating damage to the means of production, violations of the principle of material incentives, wrong application of the socialist principles of distribution, and similar modes of behaviour which, as it were, overlie the new socialist behaviour maxims, hiding them or blurring them, so that the individual may well believe that the old selfish property relations continue to exist and the first thing therefore is to think of oneself and of one's needs or desires.

This includes also the over-stimulation of demand by the faulty upbringing of children and juveniles; this gives rise to excessive expectations which are not justified by the individual's own performance and which spring from an idea that demands may be made on society without giving it much in return. This, too, is not just a subjective factor, but a wrong way of life, a bad example set by parents and educators who often discover too late that they have allowed utterly selfish ideas of life to develop in the children and juveniles entrusted to their guidance.

These then are specific real phenomena which should be identified as old survivals and deliberately eliminated. These attitudes and behaviour patterns, whatever form they take, are reflections or imprints of the ideology of the private-property-owning society: over decades and centuries they have assumed an objective existence in relationships, attitudes and modes of behaviour so that the individual now scarcely realises their origin or ideological content. He accepts them spontaneously as a tradition or even a 'philosophy of life', he practises them unthinkingly and thus carries them over to the new socialist relations with the result that conflicts are created. These modes of behaviour are thus in a sense an objectivised form of the old ideology. It was a mistake in the past to have failed to realise these peculiarities, to have failed to identify the objective existence of these ideological roots, and to have thus allowed the mistaken conclusion to be drawn that crimes of theft, for instance, are determined solely by the subjective attitude of the offender. Yet it is important — especially in investigating enrichment offences — that these surviving outdated modes of behaviour which contradict the socialist development should be identified because they are reponsible for the distortion and destructive effect of a conflict between the available possibilities of satisfying requirements and the individual's actual requirements, a conflict which does not in itself lead to criminality in a socialist society.

While this is not the place to go into the details of the relationship between the production of merchandise, the value law and the performance principle, it should be pointed out that the performance principle and likewise

> production of merchandise and the law of value... are genuine economic phenomena and laws of socialism and not survivals of capitalism, because their origins and mainsprings lie not in the past but in the socialist order itself...It follows from the nature of socialist society, both from the stage and the character of the productive forces and from the socialist production relations, that the relationships between socialist enterprises are in principle merchandise relations which must be realised by way of the market and by application of the law of value. [12]

The problems and contradictions between a correct attitude and mode of behaviour on the one hand and the really existing possibilities at the present stage of productive forces on the other, are particularly evident in such fields as education, the status of women, the upbringing of the younger generation, housing, etc., where we can do no more than realise step by step the objectives we have adopted.

It requires no proof — because it is universally known — that in terms of social and political-cultural achievements the German Democratic Republic belongs to the leading countries in the world. This does not mean that we are satisfied. But the present material level, including our manpower situation, still does not permit us to make even greater investments, desirable and important though this would be. In consequence we still have, at our present level of development, a number of objective contradictions (e.g. in spite of all our efforts we still have a shortage of places in crèches, facilities for young people, housing, etc.) which act as a brake on the development of a socialist awareness and on the growth and consolidation of a socialist behaviour pattern.

These objectively determined contradictions are bound to face the individual, in certain situations, with considerable moral or ethical challenges requiring him to hold down spontaneous individualist modes of behaviour which might temporarily seem agreeable and advantageous in favour of a socially adequate mode of action.

On balance we therefore find the following picture: socialist society, in our day and under present conditions, confronts the individual with a multitude of still-existing conflicts, contradictions and problems. It is not yet possible to banish such conflict matter from the life of the present generation. Nevertheless, from the point of view of its social structure, its dominant ideology and the behaviour patterns based on it, socialist society enables the individual who is affected by such contradictions to solve them in a way acceptable to him without feeling condemned to a hopeless life with no worthwhile future. Socialism, therefore, abolishes not every possible objective source of conflict — under the conditions of a private ownership society these would inescapably lead to criminality — and it would therefore be an illusion to try to base a theory of the causes criminality upon the assumption of the absence of conflict in a socialist society. However, because of its humanist fundamental structure, socialism offers ways of solving such problems, ways which may be chosen by the individual and which will lead immediately, or very shortly, to a satisfying settlement of the conflict. It is therefore important to teach people to tackle the conflicts facing them in a human and socially adequate manner. The purposeful and systematic struggle for the progressive reduction of criminality has thus two aspects — the liquidation of identified objective conflict matter and the education of the individual towards socially adequate solutions of such conflicts.

Under these conditions the subjective factor, the individual's attitude to society, to its problems and to behaviour within the society, gains increasing importance. To put it in a somewhat simplified form, the way in which the solution of a contradiction or conflict is approached – and that, to us, means also the commission or non-commission of a criminal act – depends very largely on the attitude and awareness of the individual faced with that decision. Accepting that conflicts or contradictions – whether real or imagined – have become soluble in a socially and individually satisfactory way, the centre of gravity of a criminal decision increasingly moves into the subjective sphere, into the sphere of the individual. In consequence, the individual's education is becomming increasingly important for crime prevention, just because such an education can effectively teach the individual to solve his problems in a manner worthy of a human being. This is not to say that one can deny the existence of objective causes of conflict, which indeed must be urgently eliminated. Socialist society is not a society of the well-fed who sit in judgement mercilessly and uncomprehendingly over the starving. Under socialism a criminal act is no longer, as it is under capitalism, a spontaneous anarchist revolt of the alienated individual against the prevailing social conditions which prevent him from living in a way appropriate to human dignity. We are no longer dealing with a conflict springing from the nature of society itself and rending it from within, a conflict without solution. Under socialism a criminal act is the expression of the conflict between the individual's limited insight, which prevents him from solving individual problems – a limitation which in turn has social roots – and the existing possibility of solving these conflicts in the interests of society and the individual himself. Because society itself is vitally interested in solving all genuine contradictions and conflicts in a way which would serve the individual as well as the community, the offender, in a sense, finds himself driven by his criminal act into conflict with his own objective interests – provided these are worthy of a human being – and hence with himself. A conflict arises between the individual's development potential as offered him by society and the behaviour patterns expected of him, on the one hand, and a criminal activity, a contradiction between genuine freedom and the non-freedom of the behaviour displayed by him, on the other.

A criminal act, therefore, reflects both objective conflict situations, existing independently of the awareness and type of behaviour of the individual offender, and also personal, individual conflicts or inadequacies.

A general social problem can be countered by general measures, more particularly measures of social transformation, of changing social conditions. But the more this problem detaches itself from fundamental causes, the more important it becomes to take account of the specific individual, objective and subjective, material and psychological causes of a criminal act (e.g. in assessing punishment) and to eliminate these factors (e.g. by special educational efforts, the solution of the individual's social problems, vocational promotion, etc.). It is less and less permissible to treat all offenders by the same yardstick in assessing the criminal character of their acts and determining appropriate penalties. In line with the Decree of the State Council of 30 January 1961 the personality of the offender, his characteristics as an individual, are being increasingly taken into account. This explains why Marxist criminology at present focuses its attention on the study of the offender's personality, without of course disregarding the social determination of criminality.

For the same reason also the socialist education of the individual plays an overriding part. By providing the individual with insight into the objective course of social processes it enables him to find the socially appropriate option of action in difficult situations. Since, at the moment, we are still unable to overcome certain objective discrepancies in our state of productive forces, socialist education performs an important social function by helping to a large extent to bridge these objective discrepancies or contradictions and by mobilising the individual for even more purposeful participation in the creation of the objective prerequisites of socialism.

Socialist education thus becomes a key question. Small wonder that, in his interview to *Einheit*, Walter Ulbricht re-emphasised this point: 'To build socialism means first of all to educate the people, to lead them forward along the road of deliberate struggle, and in this process to unfold their creative social forces.' [13]

Needless to say, the fostering of a socialist awareness must not be seen as a kind of moralising or sermonising. Socialist awareness is 'reality turned into consciousness', i.e. the reflection of the laws of social evolution as discovered and developed by Marxism—Leninism. [14]

> The idea of education [Karl Polak points out] is deeply rooted in the nature of our State and hence also our law. It reflects the power, inherent in our law, to transform society, positively to shape society, i.e. actively to mould a social awareness and hence eliminate all asocial or antisocial human behaviour. Our law, after all, is the expression of the historical mission of the dictatorship of the proletariat which includes the mission of helping society, establishing an organised and disciplined social pattern, and thereby liberating society from all conditions which impede its free and comprehensive development.It is only natural and inevitable that the idea of education should occupy an increasingly important place...If, therefore, we speak of education, of the moulding of consciousness, of the devel-

opment of the people's political and moral forces, of the development of labour discipline, social and State discipline, we do not mean some subjective instruction of the individual, let alone any guardianship by means of rules and regulations, but the assertion of an objective historical evolutionary process, the process of the revolutionary transformation of human life, led by the Party and the State, the harmonisation of the individual's actions with society itself, the individual's conscious identification with society.[15]

Education, to Marxism—Leninism, does not mean simply the conveying of definite items of knowledge; it means continuous practical work, designed to activate and mobilise the individual. The objective problems referred to above, in particular those stemming from the present state of the productive forces, can be solved only by human action. This means that socialist education, in line with socialist norms of morality – must be oriented towards the development, consolidation and assertion of socialist behaviour patterns which in turn will contribute to a further development of productive forces and production relations.

The above reflections do not represent any new discoveries. The social determination of criminality was revealed by Marx and Engels. The effect of old traditions under socialism, traditions which may manifest themselves in a criminal way, was first revealed by Lenin, and these conclusions have already been applied to conditions in the German Democratic Republic by the enactments of the SED and the State Council.

We are concerned with fruitfully applying these fundamental Marxist-Leninist realisations to criminological research. This must proceed from firm ideological and methodological foundations, from the basic Marxist knowledge of the social determination of criminality – even under socialism – if it is to discover and explain the complex social relationships which give rise to present-day criminality.

To avoid serious mistakes and erroneous speculations complete clarity is needed about the fundamental relationship between the basic concepts of Marxist criminology – as set out above – and specific detailed criminological researches. The Marxist criminological conclusions outlined above are to us fundamental truths which, because of their universal character, are statements of far deeper and far greater theoretical value than anything that can be produced by detailed specific research. These fundamental truths have been sufficiently proved in practice and by history.

However, upon this basis and within its framework, there is a rich field for specific criminological research, a field not only of theoretical interest but also of practical significance. Within this field the precise 'value' of

156

some relationship or other, of some circumstance or other, may be discovered or defined by further detailed investigation or by scholarly argument; this hypothesis or that may be verified or falsified, thousands of specific theoretical and practical questions may be answered or solved. It is within this framework that we must develop our own Marxist research methods. At the same time we must not expect that any such detailed research can question our fundamental theses.

Notes

[1] F. Engels, 'Ludwig Feuerbach und der Ausgang der klassischen deutschen Philosophie', in: K. Marx/F. Engels, *Werke*, vol. 21, Berlin 1962, pp. 296 ss.

[2] The changeability and transience of certain behaviour patterns has also been repeatedly proved by bourgeois scientists, some of whom − such as Margaret Mead, *Coming of Age in Samoa*, London 1949, quoting the example of the Samoan Islands, − go so far as to state that the observed behaviour patterns are not 'eternal' but depend on the social structure concerned.

[3] Cf. also H. Hiebsch/M. Vorwerg, *Sozialpsychologie im Sozialismus*, Berlin 1965, pp. 10 ss.

[4] K. Marx, 'Enthüllungen über den Kommunisten-Prozess zu Köln', in: K. Marx/F. Engels, *Werke*, vol. 8, Berlin 1960, p. 412.

[5] The party programme of the SED takes care to state that the socio-economic roots of criminality have been essentially, i.e. not yet entirely, liquidated.

[6] K. Marx, 'Kritik des Gothaer Programms', in: K. Marx/F. Engels, *Werke*, vol. 19, p. 20.

[7] H. Kallabis, 'Zur Dialektik der sozialistischen Bewusstseinsbildung und Problemen der Forschung', *Deutsche Zeitschrift für Philosophie*, 1963, no. 1, pp. 45 ss., 50.

[8] L. Schubert, *The Method of Investigating the Causes of Anti-Social Actions*, Moscow 1963, pp. 38 ss. (in Russian); German reprint in Aktuelle Beiträge zur Staats- und Rechtswissenschaft aus den sozialistischen Bruderländern, 1963, Issue 4, pp. 84 ss.

[9] E. Schüler, Review of 'Kriminalitätsursachen und ihre Überwindung, in *Staat und Recht*, 1965, Issue 11, p. 1926.

[10] K. Marx, 'Kritik des Gothaer Programms', loc. cit., p. 21.

[11] The state of productive forces includes not only technology but also the work force, in particular the workers' skills.

[12]   O. Reinhold, 'Die politische Ökonomie in unserer Zeit', *Einheit*, 1966, Issue 2, pp. 174 ss.

[13]   W. Ulbricht, interview in *Einheit*, 1966, Issue 2, p. 164.

[14]   Cf. K. Polak, *Zur Dialektik in der Staatslehre,* Berlin 1963, p. 362.

[15]   K. Polak, 'Die Rolle der Arbeiter- und Bauern-Macht und ihrer Justiz bei der Verwirklichung des Siebenjahresplanes', *Beiträge zum Strafrecht*, 1960, Issue 4, pp. 13, 15.

5   Some Specific Social Conditions of Criminality in the GDR

An attempt was made in the preceding chapter to set out a few more general correlations between criminality and the social conditions under socialism. However, for the practical struggle against crime, for the practical work of the State and social bodies concerned, for the practical actions of the popular masses, and for the development and introduction of appropriate measures for the further reduction of criminality, it is no less important to investigate the specific conditions of criminality at the present state of development of our country.

We shall be dealing here with very varied and differentiated social phenomena because criminality as a social phenomenon between individuals touches upon all spheres of social life and draws on the most varied laws, relationships and impulses. It is clear that certain areas or planes play a dominant part in definite types of offences — e.g. offences against the State are conditioned by imperialism in West Germany, sexual offences are conditioned by sexual relationships, etc.

There is, however, no evidence yet from past research of any absolutely clear-cut correlation between certain factors and certain offences. No such offence-specific causes of criminality have yet been discovered, i.e. causes which would not also have played a part in the commission of other types of offences. It follows, therefore, that the struggle against crime cannot — at least for the time being — be conducted on an offence-specific basis.

Our present knowledge thus compels us to pursue the struggle against criminality in a complex manner, which of course does not exclude specific measures aimed at specific offences (e.g. protection of property, stock control and stocktaking, guidance on sexual morality, etc.); such measures will in turn contribute to the emergence of an awareness of justice and of judicial discipline, and restrict infringement of the law generally. All we can do within the framework of this book is analyse a few significant social conditions for some large areas of general criminality, excluding offences against the State and offences against peace and humanity, since the causes of these have been adequately elucidated in the literature.

The importance of the individual's basic ideological attitude

Criminality, as much as the individual criminal offence, invariably touches on social relationships and hence on the offender's attitude to other members of society, to society as a whole and to its interests. But these are ultimately political and ideological questions whose connection with criminality cannot be denied; otherwise it would not be a social phenomenon.

This does not, of course, mean that an individual's ideological position can be judged from an isolated criminal act, let alone that one can draw from such an act the conclusion that the individual rejects a socialist ideology. That would be totally wrong, if only because an individual's attitude must be assessed from the totality of his relations and modes of behaviour, and not from an isolated action.

The fundamental political and ideological attitude of a person, which is more or less adequately reflected in his overall behaviour, is nevertheless of considerable importance in connection with any possible criminal behaviour on his part. Our criminological experience teaches us that the more clearly, the more firmly and the more sincerely a person is linked with socialist society, the less the likelihood of his committing a criminal action.

A criminal act is therefore not just some peripheral aspect of an individual's behaviour but − in so far as we are speaking about genuine criminal activity − invariably part of his personality and therefore connected with his basic political and ideological attitude. Naturally, this link with his political and ideological position varies for different offences. It is more clearly obvious in the case of offences against the State or criminal acts against the activity of State organs[1] than in some other offences.

In any event the development of a staunch political and ideological attitude represents a large measure of insurance of socially useful non-criminal behaviour. In this sense the question of an individual's basic ideological attitude may be seen as an overriding factor in the elimination of criminality-favouring relations. That is why we place this aspect at the head of our reflections.

Certainly the basic moral and political attitude of a citizen of our country is revealed in the part he plays in social practice, more particularly in his production performance. At the same time, our social practice greatly exceeds the area of confrontation with nature and includes certain social confrontations, a share in social thinking, a share in socialist democracy. It is only through comprehensive all-embracing participation in the building of socialism that the individual can truly and fully associate himself with society, integrate himself with it, and attain its degree of awareness and freedom.

In those areas where there are still shortcomings in this respect the inherited isolation of the individual persists and the conflict between individual and society is preserved as the most general latent condition for a variety of asocial and antisocial forms of activity, including criminal ones. Criminological experience also shows that offenders are predominantly people who still have a rather formal relationship with society and are not greatly involved in society's deliberate political actions (e.g. only formal membership in trade unions).

To avoid misunderstandings: we are not concerned here with political attitudes and beliefs but solely with the real objective relations between individual and society, even though these, of course, have a basis in people's attitudes.

There is no need to emphasise the responsibility which parents, schools, industrial enterprises and social organisations, in particular the German Youth, bear for the ideological education of the younger generation. A number of shortcomings in this respect may easily be reflected in criminal offences committed by persons without adequate political or moral anchor.

So long as the inherited isolation of the individual is not sufficiently overcome by our everyday social practice, so long as an individual has to plough his own furrow and remain isolated from society, then so long a general chance of antisocial behaviour continues to exist. For this reason we believe that the struggle against criminality must not be seen as a non-political, 'de-ideologised' or 'purely sociological' task but that it must be firmly embedded in the overall social and ideological education of the people.

The role of negative social group relations or the lack of social supervision

Man as a social being does not live directly within the total community of his society. He always, to a greater or lesser extent, lives in specific groups or group relationships through which he is linked to his overall social community — the family, the kindergarten group, the form at school, the team in the industrial enterprise, etc. Social relations therefore unroll not just generally but essentially 'in specific living groups, principally those of the production process...' as Hans Hiebsch[2] has formulated it. These specific group relationships, whose rôle and effect was for a long time misunderstood — resulting in a failure to comprehend certain types of individual behaviour — are of considerable importance for the moulding of the individual's personality and hence for the emergence of the individual's specific social behaviour, including criminality.

(a) The developing individual receives the attitudes and dominant behaviour patterns prevailing in his society chiefly through the mediation of his actual social environment, his own social group; i.e. he receives these views and attitudes in the subjective transformation, distortion or modulation existing among the individuals, more specifically the leading individuals, of his group. In his confrontation with his social environment the individual similarly confronts his own social group. That group, in a sense, is to him society as such. This is particularly true if he develops no other, or few other, social relationships or uses few other sources of general social information (e.g. press or radio). It is a well-known fact that in criminal persons direct relationships with society as a whole are frequently underdeveloped.

(b) This mediation by the individual's actual group is of major importance for his mode of behaviour not only because it influences the development of his personality, because it moulds the general behaviour pattern which will underlie his various modes of behaviour, but also because it directly affects the kind of action he opts for.

As a social being man depends on society, on his actual group, not only materially (in terms of production, food, drink, etc.) and culturally or intellectually (exchange of ideas through speech, music, art) but also in a moral or ethical sense. As an individual and as a member of society he needs society's recognition and acknowledgement, the satisfaction of his socially determined sense of worth, and clear conscience.[3] A positive assessment of his actions, his attitudes, etc., on the part of society, on the part of his own group, is of decisive importance to the individual's development as a person, to the unfolding of his potentialities and powers, to a productive balanced frame of mind, and indeed also as an important stimulus to his entire work. A positive assessment of his person is associated with an expectation of further good deeds, and this — since the individual does not wish to disappoint this expectation or lose the respect he enjoys — acts as a positive incentive.

The individual's experience teaches him how different modes of behaviour are assessed by society as a whole or by his specific group. On the strength of this knowledge — since as a rule he will not wish to lose the positive assessment he enjoys — he arranges his further behaviour. The overwhelming majority of individuals, therefore,will strive to avoid reprehensible, blameworthy and especially criminal modes of behaviour. Public opinion and social judgement are thus a tremendous — but hitherto in-

162

sufficiently mobilised — force in fighting criminality.

(c) In this social assessment of the individual's behaviour allowance must be made for a number of further relations and circumstances:

First, the official and general social assessment (and at times punishment) does not always agree with that of the specific group; they may diverge or even contradict each other (e.g. in certain sexual offences).

Second, the individual frequently lives in several specific social groups simultaneously, both official and unofficial ones (family, work team, private friends), and their modes of assessment may vary amongst each other or contradict each other.

Third, in the event of a clash of assessments by different social groups or at different levels, the individual invariably orientates himself by the one which agrees most closely with his own scale of values, the grouping to which he therefore has the strongest inner bonds and which, in consequence, has the strongest influence on him. But that is not always the socially most positive one. In such a case this influence may even directly promote criminality (e.g. in certain cliques of young people).

Fourth, the social assessment of an action presupposes that it becomes known to society or to the social group concerned; indeed that is the prerequisite of any kind of social supervision and reaction. This again can vary from one social group to another, especially if only a dubious circle of friends knows about the criminal act, but not the offender's family or work team.

The quality and internal stability of the social texture, the specific social relationships, are therefore of vital importance in the occurrence or prevention of criminal acts. Criminality occurs wherever and whenever the new socialist relationships between individuals and social supervision are as yet inadequately developed, where spontaneous anarchist socially aloof or inherited social relations set the tone.

> Wherever the struggle for the socialist forms of social co-existence and social joint work is waged — the struggle to make the individual fit himself firmly into the group — crime has no soil to spring from. Wherever these matters are in a bad way, wherever the political-morality factor is ignored, violations of the law are much more frequent. Anyone not going along with our socialist order, anyone closing his eyes to our social obligations and our social morality, anyone clinging to the old morality, runs the danger of moral decay and of drifting into law infringement and crime.[4]

This basic thesis, however, is not always directly or simply confirmed in practice — in the sense that there is a low degree of criminality in an enterprise with a good socialist working atmosphere, orderliness and good management, and a higher degree of criminality in enterprises with unfavourable social composition, a high degree of labour turnover, ineffective management. etc. — and indeed we even find evidence which contradicts, or seems to contradict, this thesis. Thus, generally speaking, criminality in villages and small country towns is considerably less than in big cities although the latter are as a rule more advanced in social, economic and cultural development.

Criminality is found in a particularly concentrated form at certain centres of reconstruction and at certain large-scale projects of socialism (e.g. the iron and steel centre of Eisenhüttenstadt and the oil industry centre of Schwedt),[5] in centres, therefore, where the new society is being built. But this observation seems puzzling or paradoxical only so long as one considers merely the external facts — the most modern technology accompanied by high crime figures — without also considering the underlying social relationships. The new technology demands new social relations and new people,[6] but these are not automatically available with the erection and installation of new plant. A combination of various circumstances can even give rise to considerable discrepancies between new technology and social relations. This contradiction is particularly marked in the capitalist countries, where the machine, because of these antagonistic conflicts, has become for man a downright hostile power. Bourgeois criminologists have established that the industrial revolution, which exacerbates man's alienation to an almost intolerable degree, also increases the trend towards criminality. In socialist society this contradiction cannot reach the degree of man's alienation. The scientific-technological revolution, therefore, will not in our society promote criminal tendencies but on the contrary increase our society's ability to overcome the survivals of the old society. The new socialist production relations, under which this scientific-technological transformation is taking place, ensure that this transformation will benefit both society and the individual.

Man's social behaviour cannot be explained exclusively or directly from the state of technology and the productive forces,[7] even though, of course, there are certain connections. It can be explained only on the basis of the totality of productive forces, production relations and social awareness, from the action of general and specific social relationships.

In this respect there is an important difference between small communities, on the one hand, and big cities and giant building sites or centres of socialist reconstruction, on the other. In small communities the traditional and organically grown social relations and ties are ubiquitous. Everybody knows everybody else, everyone knows what anyone else does professionally or privately, there is no great difference between an 'official' and 'unofficial' group. Anything unusual, any deviation from the norm, is instantly known, noted and produces appropriate reactions. In such a social sphere no individual can seriously escape supervision, and this therefore exerts an effective, restrictive function with regard to law infringement, or else tolerates only such infringements as it regards as excusable or legitimate, as for instance the taking of produce from the fields.

In the big cities, on the other hand, and frequently even more so at certain large-scale construction sites, the individual can often hide under a general anonymity, or else — which comes to the same thing — he divides his personality among different social spheres (work, family, private friends, leisure activities) in such a way that each of these is separate from the others and no circle knows of the other. Thus, for instance, it may remain unknown to an individual's team mates what he does in his free time, or how he behaves towards his family and vice versa, so that, from a political and moral point of view, he may be leading a double (or even multiple) life.

Conditions are particularly favourable for such a split or partial anonymity where individuals — snatched from their past social ties and perhaps only for a short period, or for a limited purpose, which therefore permits the emergence of only limited social relations — are thrown together at some place where social organisation and social supervision are non-existent or poorly developed, as has occasionally been the case at certain large-scale construction sites. This has its effect especially on young people.[8] The question here does not concern the efficiency or otherwise of the organisation of production since the relatively high criminality at such places is connected not so much with production as with living conditions and the inadequate nature of social relations outside working hours.

This is not only an East German problem. Stanislav Walczak, examining the situation in certain western areas of Poland and at such giant projects of socialism as Nowa Huta, Komin and the Rubnice industrial area, has concluded that 'among the most favourable consequences of the social processes' (the building of socialism, unlimited opportunity for social enhancement, material independence, etc.) there has emerged at the same time 'a negative phenomenon in the shape of weakened social supervision of young people, the destruction of a social relationship which is an indispensable condition for such supervision'. He further mentions — also in connection with the effect of the war — 'the weakening and at times total disappearance of traditional social relationships' and, as a peculiarity,

165

'in works' hostels the removal of supervision by the family'.[9] Thus socially negative groupings and social relations occasionally develop, stimulating or systematically promoting antisocial modes of behaviour, including criminal ones.

It is clearly necessary, therefore, systematically and deliberately to organise new socialist social relations and forms of social supervision, hand in hand with the planning and management of production, and to instil into everybody the ideal of 'Work, learn and live in a socialist manner' in order to stimulate positive social behaviour, establish and consolidate appropriate positive behaviour patterns, and thus very largely close the door to criminal deviations of the individual.

The criminality-restricting function of order [10]

A vital part in developing and shaping social behaviour and an internalised behaviour pattern is played by the creation of a solid order in line with objective social requirements. Regularly recurrent behaviour modes and situations lead to the development of certain social habits, of social automatisms, which facilitate or even abolish the need for the decision which normally precedes each action. Thus the external order is internalised and helped to evolve an appropriate behaviour pattern. Needless to say this is not a passive or mechanical process; the internalisation of the external order depends largely also on the individual's readiness. But the overriding importance of this relationship between external and internal order is not in doubt. The development of positive and socially useful habits — like regular and conscientious work, study, the acquisition of further knowledge, cultural activities — and of an appropriate behaviour pattern very largely determines the individual's specific behaviour and leaves little room for deviant, socially inappropriate or criminal modes of action.

The more clearly and firmly such positive social habits have become established the less probable are criminal deviations. It is therefore no accident that criminal actions are found more frequently with individuals who have no or only inadequate positive social habits (e.g. regular work) but who have acquired negative habits (frequenting of objectionable places of amusement, excessive consumption of alcohol, hanging about 'hippie-fashion', etc.).

Nor is it an accident that a casual attitude to work or a frequent change of the place of work occurs more frequently with young people, who have not yet fully absorbed the requisite social habits, such as regular work, than among older people, and that in consequence criminal deviations are more frequent. In other words, the ontogenetically conditioned fact that social habits are not yet sufficiently deep-seated among young people is a further reason why criminal offences show a relatively higher incidence in that age group. Positive social habits impress their mark on a personality — in its essential social manifestations — and at the same time provide a large measure of protection against the individual's going off the rails. Needless to say, even positive social habits are no absolute guarantee since any habit can be overridden, at least once, by an act of will which in turn may be triggered by a variety of impulses.

The development and consolidation of habits — or any necessary re-adjustment — are a complicated psychosocial process. It requires continuity, persistence, regularity, example, consistency and willingness on the part of the individual. Least of all can it be achieved by mere words. The most important prerequisite for it is a firm routine, or order, evolved from daily social practice and continually reasserted.

Such a routine or order, springing as a system of realisable norms from the objective tasks of social practice, determines the individual living in that system and governs his social behaviour. It becomes fixed in him as an internalised behaviour model. The compelling effect of a firm order, of a solid structure of norms, of a sure rhythm of life is so massive that the individual living under such conditions will as a rule accept all these for himself as a matter of course. Problems arise only where ruptures and contradictions occur, e.g. between an order as proclaimed and as in fact practised — a conflict therefore between word and deed. This is a problem familiar chiefly in connection with juvenile criminality.

The order determining the individual's personality and social behaviour is shaped by society, by human beings and their organs (officials) to the best of their ability; in consequence, it is only more or less perfect and therefore only more or less effective. As an order established by humans and by society it realises the unity of objective and subjective aspects, of idea, aim, will and practice, of the world as it is and the world as it should be. In other words, the order has systematising and normative character [11] — implying regular, obligatory and unfailing validity, etc. — and requires continuous realisation and confirmation in day-to-day practice.

This element of order extends over all spheres of social life, production, training and education, family and diverse human relationships. It comprises what we call the rhythm and flow of production, what we call industrial and labour organisation. The element of order covers essential aspects of the atmosphere at the place of work, the style of management, and the provision of safety measures and rules; it reaches as far as the norms of distribution (the principle of performance) and of professional and social advancement. We are not, of course, thinking of some self-sufficient rigid *a priori* order; the framework of order is invariably determined by the State and the objective demands of the life of society and must organically grow as these grow.

Human and social life needs the element of order, including those internalised rules derived from external rules. It supplies the individual, the team, and society as a whole with security, stability and an outlook for the future, and a solid basis for day-to-day practice, and thus serves the full development of the individual's creative forces and activities which are channelled by the element of order into a socially useful direction.

A firm internal and external order is a powerful bulwark against an essentially anti-orderly and antisocial spontaneous and anarchist criminality. This point is still often being ignored in everyday work. The strengthening of the element of order in all spheres of social life, starting with the family, is an important and still inadequately utilised reserve in the struggle for the reduction of criminality.

The rôle of cultural standards [12]

Experience shows that criminal acts are committed frequently by persons of a low cultural level. By culture or cultural level we do not simply mean a person's intelligence, his abilities or state of education, nor even exclusively his cultural background, breadth of reading or general education, but the totality of the material and spiritual values produced by the people and cultivated by the people as worth handing on. We include in the term a person's life-style, the nature of his relations with other people, as crystallised in manners and customs. The culture of a nation in this way reflects its attitude to the individual and to society.

Seen in this light criminality appears as the absolute opposite to culture because any criminality demonstrates disregard or negation of the individual, of society and all its affairs, whereas culture reflects esteem and respect for the individual and for society. Criminality and culture are thus mutually exclusive. The development of a nation's cultural standards and of a cultured personality is therefore — as correctly formulated in the programme of the Communist Party of the Soviet Union — an essential contribution to the reduction and abolition of criminality.

A number of difficulties and obstacles, both of an external material and an internal spiritual and ideological kind, remain to be overcome.

A cultured life and a cultured personality presuppose cultural material conditions at a person's place of work, in his education, leisure-time activities, etc. Many of our workshops, homes, cultural facilities and catering establishments — quite apart from their state of repair, due to the war and post-war conditions — have been inherited by us from capitalism which, as a matter of principle, had excluded the popular masses from enjoyment of the cultural values created by them. Capitalist tenement blocks and unsavoury bars in the big cities, and village taverns as the 'cultural centres' in the villages testify, as physical survivals, to this contempt for the working people. The systematic — even though costly and time-consuming — demolition of these old facilities and the erection of new, modern, more cultured homes and leisure activities thus deprive any survivals of uncultured life of their material basis and therefore narrow it down. As a result, not only the social structure of such urban areas is changed but, at the same time, the centres of criminality are physically removed; this is reflected in the territorial distribution of criminality according to new and old residential districts or certain parts of cities.

One of the most important measures designed to raise the cultural standards of the people and hence to reduce criminality even further is the law on unified education and the measures for the acquisition of vocational qualifications. However, objective possibilities, the limitation on material resources and the numbers and quality of available personnel still impose certain restrictions on these developments, in spite of the progress made so far.

A closely connected question is that of material and spiritual incentives offered by society for the attainment of a higher cultural standard. The capitalist view that a worker needs no culture because he is 'no more than the biological carrier of labour' (Alfred Kurella) has long ceased to be valid in our society. But the subjective striving for participation in cultural values (theatres, museums, literature, etc.) continues to be socially differentiated and is imparted to the younger generation by parents and schools to a greatly differing extent. The cultured individual and the striving for higher cultural standards still do not everywhere receive the acknowledgement due to them. This is reflected also in the way earnings are spent. These earnings — even though conditions are incomparably more favourable than in the past — are still spent only to a very limited extent on cultural activities while a far from inconsiderable part of them is frequently spent on alcohol.

Kurella very rightly points out that the 'accursed undemandingness' of the worker, systematically developed under capitalism where the reproduction of his labour (seen as merchandise) is confined to physiological reproduction — is a survival of the past which still burdens our present. Moreover, the bourgeoisie had exploited the cultural undemandingness of broad sections of the public for profitable purposes (the entertainment industry) and in this way achieved both the exploitation and the ideological fettering of the working people. This lack of cultural demands is also still found in our society and is being systematically nurtured by Western Germany. Kurella therefore urges that new demands should be stimulated and a new system of 'cultural services' developed which would simultaneously provide a dam against the penetration of Western non-culture and thus contribute to the further reduction of criminality.

Frequently material incentives are adequate to stimulate an individual's cultural development, more particularly his vocational qualifications. While some unskilled work continues to be more highly paid than skilled work, while higher education or vocational qualification does not appear to the individual to have any material rewards, while in fact it may even mean a material sacrifice, the ultimate aim of abolishing unskilled work completely must encounter massive obstacles.

The acquisition of qualifications — as indeed any cultural life generally — invariably demands the overcoming of a certain 'inner inertia', especially until appropriate social habits and requirements are firmly established; it invariably requires an effort of will-power and intellect. This cannot be achieved on a mass scale without some inner or external motivation. That is why, in the present economic situation, young people will frequently discontinue training courses or apprenticeships and, short-sighted as this decision may be, opt for the easier and seemingly more attractive road of higher-paid unskilled work, even though this may hold fewer prospects for the future. A solution of this problem of qualifications is possible only if this special effort, which after all benefits society as a whole, receives a much more conspicuous material and moral recognition.

The objective demand for higher qualifications does not just mean that a skilled worker produces more, or more valuable, work for society in economic terms. Vocational skill is invariably also linked with positive aspects of character and personality (development of certain socially useful characteristics such as will-power, perseverance, readiness to learn, etc., and of appropriate positive social habits); Kurella calls these the cultural component of work.

The acquisition of qualifications, in consequence, generally performs a criminality-reducing function; this is reflected in the statistical fact that criminality generally shows a considerably higher incidence among unskilled persons than among skilled. The lower incidence of criminal offences among persons with qualifications is due not to their expert knowledge or specialised training but to the fact that, together with their

170

qualifications, they have developed higher cultural and moral standards — in other words, that qualification has embraced their whole personality.

The raising of cultural standards is obstructed not only by material problems but also by various spiritual and ideological obstacles. The inherited capitalist view that culture is not something for the people has already been listed as such an obstacle. Under our particular conditions, i.e. the rule of imperialism in the western part of Germany, both the systematically organised and the spontaneous individual infiltration of non-culture and decadence from Western Germany and West Berlin makes it difficult for us to raise our own cultural standards. The danger of this influence is not only in its hostile ideological substance, in the deliberate ideological subversion and softening up, but also — and this is often overlooked — in the imperceptible way in which the influence works. To raise cultural standards mean to make demands both on the purveyor and on the receiver of culture, to make a deliberate intellectual effort. The easy, shallow, superficial pseudo-culture of the West, which often springs from and appeals to the lowest instincts, is more easily absorbed, seems more agreeable, and is therefore still often preferred. With the help of such 'cultural' offerings it becomes easier to make people accessible also to other far less harmless ideas, to attract them, to influence them in a harmful or even hostile manner, and to misuse them.

In the face of these dangers our cultural policy and our cultural workers are faced with the demanding task of supplying cultural performances — differentiated according to social groups, age and in other ways — which will 'appeal' to and develop the individual's taste in such a way that he recognises the Western products for the trash they are. In this way they can raise the cultural standards and contribute to the socialist education of the people, especially the young generation. The difficulties involved and the backlog to be made up are well known. The Eleventh Plenary Session of the SED Central Committee had occasion to criticise this backlog. The objective effect of this situation is that a number of people, in particular young people, are still addicted to Western non-culture, are obstructing their own cultural development and the unfolding of their own personalities, and may even, because of the harmful Western influence, allow antisocial character traits and behaviour patterns to grow up in them which in certain circumstances may lead them to criminality.

The raising of the cultural level and the development of a cultural personality — as a contribution to the further reduction of criminality — are closely connected with the difficult problem of leisure activities [13], as the major part of an individual's independent life is his free time. The experience of judiciary organs shows that the great majority of criminal .

offences are committed during free time or, at least, are connected with activities during free time, e.g. the theft of national property during working time for the purpose of 'black work' during free time or for parties, orgies, etc. This relative concentration of criminality is due not to the availability of free time as such but to the individual's inability to shape his free time in a meaningful, cultural and socially adequate manner, in a manner serving the development of his own personality, instead of misusing it for antisocial behaviour.

The fundamental social function of leisure time is the reproduction of the working potential, both in the biophysical, physiological and psychological and also in the specifically moral-human and intellectual-cultural sense. This question, too, can only be tackled from its social aspect. This means that the relationship between work and free time (the concept of 'free time' is meaningful only in juxtaposition to the concept of work) depends on the prevailing social order and its state of development, on production relations and the state of the productive forces, and the individual's awareness.

So long as work was uncongenial to the worker, so long as he was alienated from it, and so long as he still feels it to be alien — even though, under socialism, this feeling may by now be running to the objective situation — it is only natural that he should try to shape his leisure time, the time when he can feel 'at home', to be as different from work as possible. But the more his work becomes a vital need, the more he is absorbed in it and feels at home in it, the more this wish to shape his leisure time in a totally different manner will disappear. The two spheres of life will increasingly blend, the difference between them will be increasingly confined to purely external aspects (time and place, form, persons involved, clothes, kind of activity, intellectual or physical peculiarities,, etc.) and the individual will find his life fulfilled equally during working time and leisure time. Naturally, in shaping his leisure he will have to allow time for certain vital activities, such as the running of a home, etc.

What matters therefore is the nature of work. In this connection one must not overlook the technical aspect of an individual's work and its effects on the shaping of his leisure time. Work in our country is still highly differentiated — it can be physically hard work, mentally exhausting, monotonous, or physically and intellectually stimulating, etc. Since the alternation of exertion and relaxation, of stimulation and repression is the physiological basis of the reproductive function of leisure time (of recreation), this will take the form of diametrically opposed activities (compensatory activity, compensatory sport). Up to a point this is entirely normal and natural. However, in the case of excessive or one-sided stresses, still conditioned by the present state of the productive forces — requiring, during free time, an excess of physical and psychological regeneration, or forms of recreation involving total seclusion from society or recourse to alcohol — this contradiction can only be solved as our technological revolution progresses. The fact that the various contradictions occasionally combine — the lack of cultural demands combined with physical exhaustion frequently leads to drink — is a reflection of the present state of development and of the struggle between the old and the new.

We are faced here with a complex and protracted process of social and individual development. In social terms, admittedly, the basis for the conflict between work and leisure time has disappeared but, at least in certain areas, it continues to exist and is felt to exist by broad sections of the public. Individually the magnitude of this conflict depends on the individual's personality, his vocational activity and qualifications, his attitude to work and to his job, his intellectual and cultural level and his sense of social responsibility. Criminological investigations show that the majority of offenders practise a relatively primitive and one-sided form of leisure activity (taverns, shallow films, hanging about street corners, etc.) i.e. mostly passive and undemanding forms which basically are nothing other than a specific after-effect of the 'alienation of labour' under capitalism.

The more clearly the individual, especially the juvenile, is subjectively aware of such a conflict — which suggests omissions in management and education work — the stronger as a rule is his need and desire to display in his free time a totally different behaviour from the one he is compelled to display at work.

This means in the individual case that, according to the degree of influence exerted by decadent imperialist non-culture or influences, especially the formation of groups, an antisocial spontaneously anarchist undisciplined and irresponsible behaviour may result, including at times criminal behaviour. This means that the contradiction between work and leisure time may, according to the social framework and the specific conditions and personality factors, closely interacting with other social factors, perform a criminogenic function.

From the point of view of the social conditions of criminality, the problem of leisure activity is consequential and subordinate to the development of the individual's personality and his education, more particularly the raising of his cultural standards. Nevertheless the guidance of the younger generation towards meaningful and cultural leisure activities is of considerable importance because it concerns the utilisation of the potential of the young people's leisure time. This is a specific aspect of personality development and represents an important task for parents, adults generally and various organisations, a task whose solution should contribute to the reduction of criminality.

Objective contradictions in the economy and the criminality-restricting rôle of the economic system of socialism

The creation of the developed social system of socialism and of its nucleus, the economic system, entails the more comprehensive and more complete implementation of the economic laws of socialism, especially the relations between economic plan and law of value. A number of contradictions, in particular also between plan and law of value, between centralised management and greater independence of economic units, are solved on a higher plane. The economic foundations are thus laid for an even closer harmonisation of the interests of the individual and society as a whole. All these undoubtedly are processes which serve the liquidation of such social contradictions as may favour criminality.

These processes, however, unroll under technological conditions which differ from one economic sector to another because of differing production conditions, personnel, traditions, etc., and may indeed give rise to new disproportions. Above all, the problem of developing uniform principles of economic assessment, in line with economic requirements and valid for a prolonged period of time (e.g. quality norms, prices, interests, wages, production costs, depreciation rates, etc.,), also entail some undesirable objective possibilities. Thus, certain areas or individuals may utilise certain economic disproportions (shortages of material, inadequate production capacity, shortage of labour) or certain virtual 'monopoly positions' for operating the economic levers to their advantage and obtaining for themselves economically unjustified material advantages with the result that new discrepancies or negative consequences are produced, not only of an economic but also of a social, political and moral-ideological character.

So long as prevailing conditions do not exclude the possibility of gaining economically unjustified material advantages by legal, or at least not patently illegal, methods, so long will the intellectual reflection of this, in the form of selfishness, self-interest or the desire to enrich oneself at the expense of others, continue to exist. These are the motives underlying the overwhelming majority of offences against property and other economic offences, and these motives, if they are strong enough and the offender is lacking in appropriate moral fibre, may erupt in openly illegal, i.e. criminal, forms.

So long as the production of merchandise with its categories of value, exchange, markets, price, money, etc., exists, so long must the objective possibility exist for infringement of the equivalence principle, at least temporarily or partially, or at least as a subjective feeling of being privileged or underprivileged. In consequence, self-interest, the seeking of advantage and similar psychological reflexes — much as they are being narrowed down and reduced by a growing socialist awareness — will continue to have some scope, and criminal acts cannot therefore be totally excluded.

Mention must also be made in this connection of the principle of distribution according to performance — and not yet according to need, as under communism. This question concerns us here not from its purely economic aspect of the distribution of created values but in its reflection in the individual's mind and in its social aspect.

As is well known, the collective owner of social property effectively realises his position as owner by strictly organised collective participation in production (i.e. utilisation of the property), and public property, as a social relationship, in turn exists only as the joint work of all with its material conditions of production — whereby each individual co-operates according to his ability. This aspect is the same under socialism and under communism. What is different is the material reward of the individual — in socialism his reward is according to his effective contribution, i.e. differentiated, whereas under communism his reward is whatever he reasonably needs.

Compared with the conditions of capitalist exploitation the socialist principle of distribution is incomparably more just because it is based on the real equality of all individuals. All are owners and producers; 'no one can give anything ... except his work and ... nothing can pass into the ownership of the individual ... except individual means of consumption'. [14]

In his own mind, however, the individual merely registers the — usually still unequal — distribution in its outward manifestation and, as the objective necessity for such a distribution is not invariably understood or acknowledged, he occasionally feels it to be unjust. In his mind he then contrasts what, again subjectively, appears to be a very similar contributions — 'after all, don't we all work?' — with what are frequently very different individual shares in the overall social product. And as everybody lives only once he, naturally enough, wants to enjoy his life also in a material respect. Such views about unjust distribution are moreover supported by the fact that the principle of performance never exists in a pure or ideal form, i.e. that various economic requirements or external conditions (manpower situation) demand certain modifications, and that there are indeed also genuine discrepancies or infringements, some of them possibly well-

175

intentioned. It thus becomes exceedingly difficult for the individual at times to be sure where the principle ends and the modification begins, or indeed the infringement begins — quite apart from illegal incomes. Considering that life for an individual often seems to be governed by chance — in the way in which he has landed a skilled job with its reward, or in the way he can participate in the earnings of a spouse, or parents, or children, etc. — the frequently considerable and patent disproportion between incomes makes serious moral demands especially on the less well paid members of society and requires a high awareness on their part if they are to meet the daily demands and norms of social coexistence.

This objectively determined aspect of social awareness, with its possible criminal consequences, should not be entirely ignored even though it hardly ever figures prominently in criminal motivation. Now and again, however, considerations of this kind may play the part of self-justification in the individual's motivation process.

Among the objective and material social conditions of criminality — especially crimes with an economic aspect to them — mention must finally be made of those phenomena which are summed up under the heading of mismanagement and waste. Walter Ulbricht was the first to observe at the Eleventh Plenary Meeting of the SED Central Committee: 'The material products laboriously created by the working people were positively squandered.'[15] Experience of 'generous' and uneconomical handling of public property by managerial staff hardly helps to increase the working people's respect for socialist property. On the contrary, bad examples may provide negative stimuli and create indifference or even a readiness to satisfy one's own requirements at the expense of public property which will otherwise only be left to deteriorate.

These examples once more emphasise the rôle of the subjective factor, of ideological and moral educational work. Naturally, such work cannot charm away the objective conditions but it can help the individual to understand them and to face the resulting demands morally armed instead of being helplessly at their mercy.

As in every other sphere, here too education and explanation must be supported by deeds and facts which meet the objective interests of the individual and of society. The basic facts involved are the economic laws of socialism. They make it possible, on the basis of socialist production relations — in accordance with the state of social development — for an optimum of harmonisation to be achieved between individual and collective interests, an optimum of allowing for the individual's personal interests, and hence, eventually, the avoidance of such acute contradictions between individual and society as might result in criminality. But these objective economic laws of socialism are not spontaneously realised but only through the deliberate action of human beings, by purposeful guidance and management.

The development of the economic system of socialism and the steps and stages of its accomplishment represent the foremost theoretical and practical contribution to the solution of this task. This task is the adequate form of management of the economic laws of socialism at our present stage of development, in the phase of the comprehensive building of socialism, and the best way of solving the objective contradictions arising at this stage, including those which interest us as possible contributory causes of criminality. It follows that, regardless of the objective economic problems and difficulties mentioned above — difficulties which do not as yet enable us to tackle the liquidation of criminality — the concentration of all forces on the comprehensive and consistent accomplishment and execution of the economic system of socialism (in all spheres of society) is the principal road towards the further reduction of criminality.

The more the measures and instruments of the economic system of socialism are understood and applied, not only as purely economic mechanisms and levers but in their universal (political, economic, ideological) rôle as determinants of society and personality, the more they aim at enabling the individual to master the life of society and their own lives in line with objective requirements, i.e. to act freely, the more harmonic the unity of politics, economics and ideology becomes, the more successfully will criminality be reduced — and not only the crimes involving economic aspects.

Special problems and conflicts in the sphere of sexual norms

While we may know a few facts about the social conditions of criminal offences against property or of economic offences, our factual knowledge is 'highly problematical ... in the sphere of sexual crimes because in that sphere even the pattern of normal life is scarcely known, let alone that of criminal sexual life'.[16] In consequence, only a few observations can be made on this subject, and these do not apply to patently brutal and violent sexual criminal offences, such as clear-cut cases of rape. Human sex life, as it manifests itself in society and not on a purely biological basis, differs from the urge-controlled sex life of animals in that it represents a form of norm-governed social behaviour, i.e. that it is 'learnable', that it can be moulded by the internalisation of behaviour norms. It is therefore governed by the general principles of the evolution of social behaviour, of a definite behaviour pattern. The forms and norms of sexual behaviour, being a special variant of social behaviour, therefore depend on the same fundamental characteristics, which is why the general changes in human social behaviour throughout history are reflected in the area of sexual behaviour.

An important peculiarity of sexual behaviour lies in the fact that, being less rational and more strongly emotional, and probably not entirely free from primitive urges, it is much more difficult to control by rational norms than other forms of social behaviour, and that the stimuli and urges springing from natural biophysical causes frequently confront the individual with special moral and character demands.

Above all, the implantation of certain norms, which subsequently continue to live in customs and usages, and in tradition — even when these are clearly and unambiguously defined — is a process taking several generations. Special problems and difficulties naturally arise wherever old systems of norms are replaced by new ones, where a temporary hiatus arises, where the validity or obligatory nature of the norms is uncertain or where the norms are not universally acknowledged.

Finally, the norms of sexual behaviour must take account not only of changed social requirements but also of — possibly likewise changed — biological processes and facts.

We are at present living in a period of sexual revolution in two respects:

First, we are about to replace the basically medieval-Catholic concept of false and unrealistic norms of exclusively marital sexual life — which served male predominance and the protection of private property, and which were inevitably accompanied by all shades of prostitution — by the principle of deep mutual love as the basis of sexual relations between man and woman. This process of the emancipation of both sexes actually began under capitalism. But there the negation of the old norm is frequently manifested as a negation of all norms and principles — as free love, as sexual anarchy below the level of animal sex life, as decadent sex, as sex as an aim in itself. Especially in the USA and in Western Germany this negation, though it increasingly produces disastrous results by degrading the individual, is sometimes actually celebrated as a symbol of 'freedom'.

Second, we are faced with increasingly early sexual maturity, a process connected with the whole problem of acceleration. This early maturity conflicts with social and personal interests, and particularly with the legal norms concerning marriage — in so far as these are regarded as conditions of sexual intercourse.

178

Both these real processes raise questions which our society has not yet solved either in theory or practice. The general precept of socialist morality: 'You shall live cleanly and decently and respect your family',[17] while incontestably valid, requires some more precise interpretation. These are questions which the individual – especially the young unmarried person who cannot simply be condemned to celibacy or chastity, must somehow decide for himself and which are in fact independently decided by millions of people every day.

It must be emphasised that these real questions cannot be effectively answered with prohibitions such as 'Thou shalt not commit adultery', i.e. in a negative way, a way typical of the past and in particular of the moral teachings of the Church. Man requires a socially grounded positive orientation of his behaviour, an orientation taking account of his interests; he needs a positive universally recognised model of behaviour, a positive behaviour pattern. Our unambiguous and fundamental theorem of sexual relations on the basis of deep mutual love between man and woman is not enough. The individual wants a clear answer to how he should behave in specific situations.

On the other hand, especially among the working class under capitalism, certain new, healthy norms of sexual behaviour have developed more or less spontaneously on the basis of mutual love and esteem which are already being practised on a broad basis, in a differentiated manner, also in the German Democratic Republic but which have not so far been accurately defined or recognised as a socialist sexual ethic. Such a situation, remaining undefined but challenging every day in a variety of ways, is bound to result in a great many conflicts. It is also responsible for a certain fluctuation in the assessment of moral offences by the judiciary. It is likewise not surprising that an unclarified and undefined system of norms provides an inadequate counterpoise to decadent, imperialist or otherwise degrading and often urge-governed tendencies. Although the present unsatisfactory norms – unsatisfactory because they leave the finding of the correct solution to the individual but subsequently blame him for failing to find it – cannot be regarded as a source or starting point of sexual crime, it nevertheless represents a very relevant social factor in its mechanism of operation.

Nor should we overlook the fact that an inadequate solution of sexual conflicts combined with indifference towards the social norms, with their open rejection, or with a sense of doing something not officially acknowledged, is likely to result in further complications and psychological and moral stresses on the individual, and hence possibly even in criminal acts of a different kind (outbreaks of aggression). The conflicts in the area of sexual norms are therefore by no means confined, in their effects, to this specific category of offences.

All this shows the need for a scientifically founded socialist sexual ethic which would take account of the biological data, social requirements and individual interests and which, also by means of juridical norms, would act upon social life by way of popular-scientific propaganda. This would at the same time erect a powerful internal dam against imperialist immorality and immunise our people, especially our young people, from within. We are again faced with the realisation that in the absence of objective regular patterns and appropriate guidance blind elemental forces will spontaneously and anarchistically erupt.

A sensible solution could be found, from the point of view of criminal law, for the special case of homosexuality. Penalisation of simple homosexuality in the traditional manner of the criminal law has no basis either in biological or in social reality and has been handed down to us merely as a tradition from the Catholic-dominated Middle Ages. Simple homosexuality is of no social relevance, but its criminal prosecution – quite apart from an unnecessary load on the judiciary – entails conflicts disadvantageous to society, such as unenforceability of the law, concealed high statistics, the creation of conflicts between an otherwise respected person and the criminal law, encouragement of blackmail, etc. Besides, the criminal prosecution of a sexually stabilised homosexual brings no advantage whatever.[18] Impunity for the practice of simple homosexuality, as proposed in the draft of the new criminal code, would help to eliminate many a conflict. It is also much more important to help the younger generation by well-reasoned, meaningful and realistic positive norms in the sexual sphere and to shield them at an early age from abnormal practices. [19]

Conclusions

Our discussion of certain specific social conditions of criminality in the German Democratic Republic has made it clear that, under our social conditions in which, together with the abolition of capitalist exploitative relations the socio-economic roots of criminality have also been largely eliminated, criminality is neither immanent in the nature of our order nor does it consist of special features existing outside the social relations. Instead we have found it to be the specific manifestation of developmental contradictions associated with the transition from capitalism to socialism, contradictions in the material and spiritual—ideological spheres,

180

of specific forms of the confrontation with stubbornly surviving old thinking and living habits which are continually being nourished by hostile influences from abroad. In consequence, the struggle against criminality and the gradual liquidation of the social conditions giving rise to it is not the task of some specialised department or authority but one which can only be solved as part and parcel of the building of socialism generally and by society as a whole, by all State, economic and social institutions and functionaries.

It is on the strength of this scientific insight that the basic directive for the struggle against criminality is enshrined in the programme of the SED: 'The implementation of the tasks of the comprehensive building of socialism is the foundation of the systematic struggle for the gradual elimination of criminality from the life of society.'[20]

Our entire empirical criminological research again and again leads us to one conclusion — the answer to the question of how this liquidation of criminality is to be accomplished in its specific manifestations in the various social spheres is invariably by the systematic and purposeful development of a socialist society, as provided for in the resolutions of the Marxist—Leninist Party. The specific task of socialist criminology consists of identifying the criminal manifestations of the old order, in which the socialist elements have not yet been able to assert themselves, and to contribute, together with social practice — not necessarily confined to judiciary practice — to the assertion and promotion of the socialist evolutionary processes and, with the further progress of this positive development, gradually to deprive criminality of the soil it springs from. There is therefore no need for any special models for the struggle against criminality; all that matters is the complex realisation of the entire development in line with the directives of the Party and hence the progressive liquidation of criminality from the life of society, together with the social conditions which give rise to it.

Notes

[1] Cf. E. Buchholz, 'Der Diebstahl und seine Bekämpfung in der DDR', Habil. thesis, Berlin 1963.

[2] H. Hiebsch, 'Die Sozialpsychologie und ihre Bedeutung für die sozialistische Praxis', *Soziologische und psychologische Erfahrungen aus Forschungen und Praxis*, 1965, Issue 9, p. 192; cf. also pp. 189 ss.

[3] P.B. Schulz, 'Zur Dialektik des moralischen Werturteils', thesis., Berlin 1963.

[4] K. Polak, 'Die Rolle der Arbeiter-und-Bauern-Macht ... ' loc. cit. p. 21.

[5] H. Kuschel, 'Besondere Entstehungsbedingungen der Eigentums-kriminalität in Eisenhüttenstadt und Schwedt (Oder) und Schlussfolgerungen für die Bekämpfung und Verhütung der Kriminalität', thesis, Berlin 1966.

[6] Cf. G. Heyden, 'Die marxistisch—leninistische Philosophie und die technische Revolution' (theses), *Deutsche Zeitschrift für Philosophie*, 1965, Special issue, esp. pp. 29 ss., and J. Schmollack, 'Sozialistisches Menschenbild und technische Revolution', loc. cit., pp. 168 ss.

[7] It is in such a vulgar materialist over-simplification — as well, of course, as in the apologia — that the basic error of the 'theories' about 'affluent crime' lies.

[8] Cf. H. Kuschel, Besondere Entstehungsbedingungen der Eigentums-kriminalität ..., loc. cit.

[9] S. Walczak, 'Erscheinungsformen und Ursachen der Kriminalität Minderjähriger — methodologische Fragen ihrer Erforschung', in: *Jugend-kriminalität und ihre Bekämpfung in der sozialistischen Gesellschaft*, Berlin 1965, pp. 52, 62 ss.

[10] Cf. E. Buchholz, 'Der Diebstahl...', loc. cit.

[11] Partly in legal terms, including various detailed regulations, internal ordinances and statutes, and partly in moral terms.

[12] Cf. also, on this whole section, A. Kurella, 'Der sozialistische Mensch in der technischen Revolution', *Neues Deutschland* of 16 March 1966, B edition, p. 4.

[13] Cf. 'Die marxistisch—leninistische Philosophie ... ', loc. cit., esp. pp. 22 and 26; also B. Bittighöfer's special contribution 'Technische Revolution und Freizeit', loc. cit., pp. 218 ss.

[14] K. Marx, 'Kritik des Gothaer Programms', loc. cit., p. 20, where the reference is to accomplished socialist conditions.

[15] W. Ulbricht, *Probleme des Perspektivplanes bis 1970*, 11th meeting of the SED Central Committee, Berlin 1966, p. 24.

[16] J. Lekschas, 'Zur Feststellung der Ursachen der Straftat durch die Gerichte', *Neue Justiz*, 1965, no. 15, p. 479.

[17] W. Ulbricht, *Der Kampf um den Frieden, für den Sieg des Sozialismus, für die nationale Wiedergeburt Deutschlands als friedliebender, demokratischer Staat* (Report and winding-up speech at the Fifth Party Congress of the SED), Berlin 1958, p. 121.

[18] The GDR Criminal Code of 12 January 1968 no longer makes simple homosexuality a criminal offence. On the other hand, the need for making socially-disruptive modified forms punishable — as for instance under

Art. 175a of the old Criminal Code — seems to be undisputed.

[19] Cf. Arts. 122 and 151 of the GDR Criminal Code of 12 January 1968.

[20] W. Ulbricht, *Das Programm des Sozialismus* ..., loc. cit., p. 358.

The Personality of the Offender as an Independent Variable Among the Complex Causes of Crime and the Tasks of Criminology

In the earlier Parts we proceeded from the fact that criminality as a general social phenomenon arises from the dialectical interaction of external (objective) and internal (subjective) conditions. Within these dialectical and complex interrelations the personality of the offender is a very important variable.

The problems which may arise in connection with the investigation and assessment of the offender's personality therefore gain in importance as subjects of criminological concern. Both in mapping out research tasks and in empirical investigations they must receive the attention due to them.

These problems, meanwhile, have also become increasingly important to socialist criminal justice. This emerges clearly from the nucleus of socialist criminal law — the criminal responsibility of the individual. The limits and the contents of criminal responsibility in a developing socialist society, as well as the legal means, methods and ways of realising this responsibility, can be correctly assessed only if — as the State Council had demanded — the offender's personality, the state of his awareness, his motivation and his behaviour before and after the deed are considered. The criminal law invariably deals with a specific real human being.

These considerations alone make it clear that the question of the relationship between the complex causes of criminality as a general social phenomenon and as an individual act, on the one side, and the individual's criminal responsibility on the other is of great practical importance. It is the question of the individual's real responsibility for his actions and hence the question of the social need for criminal law. Criminology cannot avoid asking this question. The answer to it is one of the theoretical foundations of socialist criminology, for it defines the boundary where criminology and criminal law theory meet and dovetail. The problem was already touched upon in general terms in the first chapter of Part I.

In this part of the book we shall try to set out the theoretical and conceptual ideas for the solution of these problems and at the same time discover the specific questions to be posed by personality research in socialist criminology. We shall start with a chapter on the dialectical process of personality development. We are doing so deliberately because this will enable us to outline our ideological foundations and develop the image of the individual by which personality research will be guided and carried. This personality image is not some abstract construction remote from real life. The human model from which criminological research proceeds — either consciously or unconsciously — embraces within itself all major social, philosophical and ideological ideas essential to the formulation of theories and to empirical factual research, for the mapping out of such research, for the attainment of results and for the intellectual processing of the results. We will illustrate this by two questions which — though admittedly in extreme form — contain the possible, though diametrically opposed, ideas.

First: Is the development of the offender's personality, which forms the subject of criminological investigation, a dialectical interaction process between external and internal conditions in which society, as the relevant external system of reference, plays the principal part; or is the development of the personality — as stated or implied by bourgeois criminologists — merely a spontaneous development, or a mechanical growth of factors and data present in the individual's biological make-up and structure?

Second: Is this personality identifiable as such and, more importantly, can it be changed? Are we able, therefore, to develop it, educate it and change it intellectually, culturally and morally in the train of the general social development of the technological revolution upon which we have embarked in socialist conditions? Or is it — as stated or implied by certain bourgeois criminologists — helplessly at the mercy of unmanageable forces, condemned to boundless self-alienation, to isolation, to a meaningless senseless existence, and hence also to proneness to criminal actions?

These questions, though formulated in extreme terms, show clearly that the discovery of the answers will lead us straight to the centre of the great debate of our age.

6 The Dialectical Process of Personality Development - The Foundations of Personality Research

Bourgeois criminology, general speaking, is characterised by the idea that the human personality (P) is the product of disposition (D) and environment (E): $(P = D \times E)$.

The idea of such a model, which also underlies a so-called criminological formula,[1] separates the individual from society although he is invariably part of that society. It robs the concept of society of its specific historical content by introducing the pseudo-neutral concept of 'environment'. It reduces the development of the individual in society to the evolution of something that is already present within him in germ form, to the development of something already dormant in him through the stimuli of an objectivistically conceived environment. His development, therefore, is a simple evolution, or unfolding, or maturing, of what is already present. It basically reflects purely quantitative changes. The 'environment' supplies the stimuli and its only function is the triggering of something already latent in the individual's biological make-up, something passed on ontogenetically by way of inheritance.

Such a concept or model underlies not only the theoretical studies of the causation of criminality. It is found also in studies concerned with the education of the offender. Thus Joachim Hellmer states that education means 'the formation of the personality by bringing out what is already present in germ form in the individual's make-up'.[2] Such ideas ultimately also reflect a certain fatalist concept: in a sense man will always basically remain the 'old Adam' and his social fate, too, is predetermined. This fatalist aspect, which can be observed even in the original formula of man as the product of disposion and environment − is reflected also in the prediction theories discussed in the third chapter of Part I.

This mistaken methodological starting point, i.e. the attempt to proceed not from the society and the analysis of its laws, but from the individual, from the human being in isolation from society, is bound to lead into mistaken concepts and methods. The social problem of criminality, both as a general phenomenon and as an individual act under the conditions of an exploitative society, is transformed into a biological or individual-psychological problem.

Only by applying dialectical and historical materialism can the process of personality development be correctly grasped both by criminological and by criminal law theory research. The concept of dialectical materialism is concisely formulated in Marx's theses on Feuerbach, written in 1845. In his well-known sixth thesis Marx points out that man's human nature is not some abstract concept immanent in the individual but 'the ensemble of social relations'.[3] This means that man is not an isolated being determined solely by biological laws in the process of his individual development. He is, on the contrary, a social being. Marx's theses moreover contain the realisation that man as a social being is largely conditioned by the specific historical circumstances and relations under which the real process of his life and hence also the development of his individuality take place. Man's nature is therefore decisively moulded by society. This realisation means a rejection of all purely biological concepts. Inherited preconditions are thus no more than possibilities of personality development — not predetermined or ready-made embryonic psychological characteristics, The decisive conditions determining the development of an individual's personality are society, the essential characteristics determining it, and the general and specific laws governing it. The individual, as a member of society, is invariably the result, the product, of society.

Society, its nature and character, its prevailing practices and behaviour rules, and other similar forms and aspects of the life of individuals therefore decisively determine the human personality. By society we do not mean simply the sum total of isolated individuals — a view of society held by bourgeois criminologists who in this way conceal the specific historical character of society and postulate the eternal existence of criminality. Society, on the contrary, is the totality of relations and relationships and of the life processes taking place in them. It is the 'product of the interaction of human beings'.[4] It is created by man, just as man is created and determined by it; it is the 'sum total of relations, relationships ... of these individuals with each other'.[5]

Understood in this way, society is the essential determinant influencing the development of the human personality. It represents the essential external (objective) system of reference. The processes of the moulding of the personality, the growth of consciousness, must be seen and investigated from this point of view. These processes are therefore functions of the shaping of man's social and collective life. In its totality society thus provides the 'parameters' by which the personality and its development, also in a criminological respect, must be measured. Owing to its specific historical nature and through the mediation of social consciousness in all its forms, it presupposes modes of social behaviour and simultaneously creates patterns of behaviour (behaviour stereotypes) in line with its specific historical character. In other words, a society whose prime characteristic is the separation of the producer from the means of production, and hence the existence of exploitation, because of the production relations underlying such a society and the mode of production and lifestyle based upon it, presupposes and produces modes and patterns of behaviour in line with this character. These include the isolation of man from his fellows, business rivalry, mutual antagonisms, struggle for personal power or so-called social prestige. To the bourgeois ideologist 'all human life ... is pervaded by power and rivalry relationships'.[6]

These basic demands on man's social behaviour, springing as they do from the character of such a social order, are reflected in his personality and consolidated into definite characteristics. They achieve independent existence. Their real material basis is not always instantly obvious, so that bourgeois ideologists are able to declare them to be downright 'natural' human characteristics, Since the internal, relatively stable and essential connections, the laws between the nature of society and social behaviour, are not patent, the typical modes of behaviour can be idealised and ideologically justified as natural patterns of life inherent in the human make-up. Selfishness, boundless individualism, the egotist or manager type, are reflected and justified by the bourgeois social consciousness as natural or indeed as a model worth emulating.

To quote just one example: Eduard Spranger, referring to the type of the exploiter with an eye to his own main chance and to the social behaviour pattern stemming from a situation of exploitation, characterises it with the words: 'Indeed, the striving for personal advantage is something not merely approved of by the ruling morality but indeed demanded by it ... Only in a society of recluses, mendicant monks and ascetics would the moral judgement read differently. Economic selfishness, therefore, may be a positive ethical value.'[7] The relatively independent existence of these attitudes is one of the reasons for the stubborn survival of such social behaviour modes even after their essential material conditions have ceased to exist.

Socialist society is distinguished by the fact that — both as a precondition and as the result — it postulates modes of social behaviour in line with the nature of the fundamental socialist relations, i.e. stemming from comradely co-existence, co-operation and mutual help, from collaboration, collective effort and mutual respect. The reason — as Hans Hiebsch stated in justification — is quite simply 'that these social and economically rooted relations are lived, and must be lived, also within specific groupings especially those of the production process'.[8]

The law concerning the development of a socialist personality operates principally in the realm of production. That is its starting point and its basis, as clearly demonstrated by the history of the activists' movement down to the brigades and teams of socialist labour in our own day. At the same time, the scope of this law is widening all the time, encompassing all spheres of life and all relationships, and is thus closely connected with the purposeful and systematic struggle against criminality as a specific antisocial or socially dangerous social attitude. It must be remembered, however, that the law concerning the development of a socialist personality — as indeed any other law operating within the sphere of socialist society — does not act automatically. In socialist society it is realised only as the result of deliberate co-operative action by millions of people led by the party of the working class and acting on the basis of a clear objective from a sense of social responsibility towards the State, towards society and towards each other — i.e. from being creatively active for socialism.

The knowledge and complete command of the essential connections between the nature of socialist production relations and the social behaviour of the members of society are of great importance to criminology. It is the task of personality research to provide deeper insights into the operation of these laws because it is on such knowledge and mastery that the efficacy of all State and social measures against criminal social behaviour depends. Crime prevention and the struggle against criminality — i.e. the struggle against social modes of action opposed to the totality of these laws — must be seen in this light, from the point of view of producing, stabilising and guiding such modes of behaviour by means of the law, its development, realisation and application.

It is clear, therefore, that the subjective factor — the socialist consciousness which absorbs into itself and then reflects this law governing the development of personality — increasingly gains a measure of independence in this overall process. As Walter Ulbricht has pointed out, socialist awareness arises

> not automatically with the change of the individual's material conditions of life but has to be carried into the masses by the party of the working class on the basis of, and with the application of, Marxist—Leninist theory, of dialectical and historical materia-

lism... On the basis of socialist production relations, under the leadership of the party of the working class and supported by the worker-peasant power as well as by social organisations, there are formed the new socialist ideas, the new norms and rules of personal and social life.[9]

The determination process which we are considering here from the point of view of personality development, is thus dependent, both in its social character and in its contents, on the character of the prevailing external (objective) system of reference − the society − under whose conditions it is taking place. This very general statement, however, is not enough for the full comprehension of the dialectical process of personality development. It highlights only one side of it, albeit a very important one − the social and historical aspect, i.e. the social content, of this process. Another important aspect is the fact that the general social determination does not take place directly, i.e. under mechanical linear causal laws. Social influences do not run straight through the individual and hence do not produce any direct linear effects. Instead, they are mediated. This mediation takes place in two ways: on the one hand − under the aspect of personality − it takes place through the processing of all external (objective) impressions or influences within the consciousness of the individual. On the other hand − under the aspect of society − it takes place through the mediation of all its effects and influences, through certain groups and group relationships into which the individual is integrated, as well as through a variety of other forms of communication.

These two fundamental aspects, needless to say, are in dialectical relationship with each other and closely linked with the aspect mentioned before. Their examination opens up deeper insights into the overall dialectical process of personality development.

As a social and historical being man is distinguished by the possession of consciousness. The human attitude to nature and to society is largely determined by consciousness as a unity of thinking and feeling. Knowledge and skills are not passed on in humans − as they are in some other creatures − by genetic means. Each newly born human being inherits from past generations neither the results of material or spiritual work, nor the psychological or social qualities developed in the life process. All it receives genetically are certain anatomical and physiological conditions 'bearing within themselves the potential for the development of those processes'. [10]

All the prerequisites of social behaviour, of successful existence within society, are acquired and passed on by man through his social upbringing and education in the broadest sense. In this way the experience, the knowledge and skills, cultural values of past or present generations are transmitted to each individual. Whereas animals can as a rule acquire experience only for themselves, and that to a limited degree, in the course of each individual's life, so that species-specific information can only be transmitted to the next generation genetically, man is able to acquire, process, store and directly pass on to others the accumulated knowledge of the past. [11] The development of consciousness as a *conflicting unity of thinking and feeling* thus makes man a 'child of his time'. It enables him to assimilate to his environment (society and nature), and not only in the passive sense of submitting to it, of being at its mercy, but in the comprehensive meaning of mastering his environment, of being able to change it by his actions and, in turn, enriching his knowledge and experience, i.e. his consciousness, by these actions.

In this sense the human consciousness, or awareness, is one of the essential internal (subjective) conditions of the individual. All influences of the external (objective) system of references are refracted through his consciousness. Any forces acting upon the individual thus invariably act through these internal conditions which are, for the most part, characterised by his consciousness. It is thus again seen that the development of the individual's personality cannot be comprehended by mechanical ideas, by reference to linear cause—effect relations. Every material system — and man is such a system — possesses, as Georg Klaus has put it, 'system-specific internal conditions, and the result of an external influence upon such a system is invariably obtained through the interaction of these system-specific conditions and the external influence'. [12]

All the data reaching the individual from outside are processed in his consciousness and condensed into decisions resulting in acts (actions or omissions). We may state therefore that consciousness is the core of personality.

This core is not in itself a static magnitude. It develops and is moulded in the process of the individual's social and biological development (ontogenesis). In this process the external social determinants, from which we have proceeded as the primary factors, operate chiefly through upbringing and education. It is through this main channel that society continually confronts the individual with certain social demands upon his thinking, feeling and actions. The scale of these demands is socially oriented and naturally also depends on the individual's biological potential — i.e. the demands made on a small child will differ from those made on a juvenile and again from those made on an adult. Man is compelled to come to terms, actively, with these demands of his environment, demands made on him by teachers, educators, parents or other people, and indeed by certain situations in life.

In this reciprocal process his consciousness matures through his own activity — his intellectual processing *and* his actions. The process of consciousness formation is thus an essential part of personality development. In this reciprocal process between the demands made on the individual by society or its groupings, or demands arising from direct situations, on the one hand, and his active processing of them, on the other, man learns to control and govern himself. He develops his ability of self-determination, of social foresight of his actions, of orienting his own decisions by social norms and values. In this reciprocal process his 'internal (subjective) system of reference' grows and matures as a totality of experiences, knowledge, abilities and emotional foundation.

Consciousness, therefore, discharges the very essential functions of judgement, control and determination of social behaviour. That is why it deserves closer inspection in any examination of the causes of criminality. We shall have more to say on this point later. For the moment we merely wish to observe that the fact that subjective (consciousness) processes are basically determined by external determinants does not mean — as S.L. Rubinstein points out — 'that anything can be unequivocally derived from causes acting as external stimuli, independently of internal characteristics or of the interrelations of phenomena'. [13]

We have already hinted at a second aspect: the interaction between personality and society occurs principally through group relationships, through live communication. [14] In the course of his development the individual always passes through several groups. He grows up in his family, attends pre-school, educational and training institutions. He is employed at a place of work, he is a member of certain social organisations, and even in his spare time, to a greater or lesser degree, he belongs to a variety of groups, some of them spontaneously generated. He not only passes through several groupings consecutively but always belongs to several groupings simultaneously. It is there that he receives stimuli and frequently also undergoes very important consciousness-moulding experiences.

The individual is thus in a state of live reciprocal communication with the objects, processes, phenomena and above all the people of his environment. This means that the social, external determinants, with which we are here concerned with a view to the development of the personality of an offender, are invariably operative through certain social groupings and are mediated through such relations. In this process of mediation they are themselves 'refracted' or, to use a different analogy, 'filtered' through the

195

views prevailing in the group, even though these may be full of contradictions. It is by way of these group relations that the individual is linked to society.

Because they offer a 'direct physical demonstration of the social life' which is manifested in them, such groups, into which the individual is integrated, have a considerable determining effect. This is proved, in particular, by juvenile delinquency research. Erich Hahn rightly points out that 'the problem of the group is gaining in interest to historical materialism in the sense that under socialism, antagonistic class conflicts cease to be the determining motive force of social development and the essential content of the social structure'. [15]

Personality research must therefore take account of, or discover, whatever facts can throw light on the group environment and its importance to the individual's personality. The group environment, as the totality of the most important behaviour-determining conditions, comprises the material conditions of existence, i.e. the material circumstances of life, work and leisure; and the ideological and moral conditions, i.e. political, ideological and moral attitudes, rules and practices prevailing in the group relations; attitudes towards other groups and contact relationships springing from these. [16]

Such group relations represent an important force of social determination, vitally conditioning the social value and social significance, as well as the social content, of the overall process of personality development. Experimental investigations by Marxist social and individual psychologists have demonstrated the great influence which such group relationships exert on the social behaviour of the individual. They have confirmed the historical conclusions drawn by dialectical and historical materialism in respect of large-scale processes and major groups in history, such as classes, nations, etc.; they have once again proved that modes of social behaviour are the result of social conditions and relations. [17]

The personality research conducted by criminology must therefore concern itself with his aspects of group relations. Results obtained so far, in particular in the field of juvenile offenders, certainly show that such relations are frequently responsible for the 'handing down' of outdated thought and life habits in the form of certain social behaviour patterns or behaviour stereotypes. This happens in spite of the fact that the objective social position occupied by such social structures within the overall system of socialist social relations not only no longer promotes such thought and life patterns or habits but indeed has long given rise to new and higher forms of social co-existence. After the disappearance or abolition of the material basis of these outdated habits it is quite simply no longer necessary to practise maxims which were once demanded and produced by life in an exploitative order. Such an 'infection',which may also give rise to criminal social behaviour, may occur on entirely diverse levels of live social communication. It is therefore, in our opinion, the specific task of criminological personality research to analyse the group relationships in order: first, to discover the material and ideological (spiritual and moral) conditions which have had or may have such criminogenic effects; second, to explore the internal essential connections between such complexes of conditions and criminal social behaviour, together with its specific character which basically reflects such communicatively experienced conditions in an objective manner; and third, to determine the weighting or the order of magnitude, i.e. the social relevance, of such complexes of conditions as material or spiritual (political, ideological and moral) manifestations of old and outdated ideas, in order to mobilise those social forces which might, either instantly or in the long run, eliminate such potential threats and any possible negative social effects.

This theoretical outline of criminological personality research, however, must not overlook the fact that, alongside and simultaneously with the above-mentioned personality-relevant communication through definite social groupings into which the individual is integrated, there is also invariably some direct contact with other people; such contact, being a 'special social communication', can be directly 'experience-relevant', i.e. it may leave traces in the individual's thinking and feeling and determine his social behaviour. [18] The plane of this 'empirical communication', which may thus lie alongside or outside the plane of relatively firm group relations, must not be disregarded in an analysis of the case history of criminal offenders. The investigation programme, therefore, must take this line of inquiry into account. Nor must it be overlooked that the individual is, moreover, conditioned and moulded by direct society-wide information as dispensed by present-day news media and cultural channels. The arts, literature, the press, television and radio are the most important main sources of society-wide information, and it is through them that each member of society is directly linked with the life of society as a whole.

Under the conditions of a socialist society the individual receives, on this plane of society-wide communication, such information as will not obscure the true state of affairs but reveal the objective pattern of historical or contemporary events, thus helping each member of society and every social group (family, work team, etc.) to become aware of its responsibility, its position and its tasks in a socialist society. This communicative directness, however, bursts the bounds of personality-oriented group relations. It enables the individual to share in the life of other

197

groups and to acquaint himself with values, views and ideas which either go along with those of his personal reference group or which, at times, may diverge from them.[19]

An analysis of this society-wide communication and information plane is indispensable. It must be an integral part of the general analysis of external determinants. In the examination of criminal social behaviour and in the investigation of the personal case history of the offender it must always be remembered that two social systems, two orders of society, confront one another on German soil and, in line with their respective characters, radiate divergent determinants. This means that the process of consciousness formation may, in the course of the personality's development, be directly influenced and conditioned by the kind of information dispensed by the mass media, including works of culture and the arts. This process — as is shown by the findings of criminological and criminal law theory research on the personality of offenders — may produce socially negative consciousness factors. This happens more particularly when the individual takes his bearing from information put out by the imperialist social system and disseminated, in the form of psychological warfare, by West German mass media in the most varied disguises and in diverse forms against socialism, especially against socialist ideology, or when the individual is exposed to, or left at the mercy of, such information. In view of the severity of the class conflict in the world, and particularly on German soil, it is important that this aspect of personality development through direct social information is always taken into account by research. What we have just said about personality also, of course, applies to social groups.

We may therefore sum up the conclusions of this chapter as follows.

In the development of his personality, more particularly the development of his consciousness as a source of responsible social behaviour, the individual is socially determined. The social external determinant moulds the the consciousness of the personality in continually reproduced active interaction between society and the individual.

Consciousness enables the individual to realise, develop and promote social relations by his own activity. Being a unity of thinking and feeling, it is itself transformed in this interaction.

The determinant springing from society is refracted in the individual's consciousness and, more importantly, mediated by specific group relations into which the individual is actively integrated.

The development of the individual's personality, however, is influenced not only by experiences and actions mediated through specific group relations or directly by 'empirical' communication with the environment. It is determined also by direct social influences, impressions and experiences transmitted by direct society-wide information, especially works of culture or the press, radio, etc., so that, under the historical conditions of the class struggle on German soil, effects may be produced on the individual's consciousness contrary to the views, ideas and social demands of socialist society.

Notes

[1] W. Middendorf, for instance, describes man as a 'sum of disposition and environment' (*Jugendkriminologie – Studien und Erfahrungen*, Ratingen 1956, p. 79). E. Mezger has developed a 'fundamental criminological formula' – $krT = aeP \times ptU$, where the offence (krT) is the product of personality (P) and environment (U). Personality in its turn is the product of disposition (a) and development (e); environment is the product of personality-shaping (p) and deed-shaping (t) factors (*Kriminologie*, 1949, p. 5); cf. also E. Seelig, *Lehrbuch der Kriminologie*, 3rd ed., Darmstadt 1963, pp. 20 ss.

[2] J. Hellmer, *Erziehung und Strafe*, Berlin 1961, p. 41.

[3] K. Marx, 'Thesen zu Feuerbach', in: K. Marx/F. Engels, *Werke*, vol. 3, Berlin 1958, p. 534.

[4] K. Marx, 'Brief an W.P. Annenkow', in: K. Marx/F. Engels, *Werke*, vol. 4, Berlin 1959, pp. 548.

[5] K. Marx, *Grundrisse der Kritik der politischen Ökonomie*, Berlin 1963, p. 176.

[6] E. Spranger, *Lebensreformen*, Halle 1927, p. 213.

[7] E. Spranger, loc. cit., p. 229. The discovery of the inner connections or regular correlations through further research is of particular importance to criminological research because it will lead to a clearer exposition and interpretation of criminality trends in the exploitative society.

[8] H. Hiebsch, 'Die Sozialpsychologie und ihre Bedeutung für die sozialistische Praxis', in: *Soziologische und psychologische Erfahrungen aus Forschung und Praxis*, Berlin 1965, pp. 189 ss., esp. p. 192.

[9] W. Ulbricht, 'Des deutschen Volkes Weg und Ziel', *Einheit*, 1959, Issue 9, p. 1228.

[10] Cf. G.S. Kostyuk, 'Probleme der Persönlichkeitsbildung beim Kinde', in: *Beiträge aus der Sowjetpsychologie*, Berlin 1951, p. 87.

[11] Cf. also R. Löther, 'Moderne Genetik und wissenschaftliches Menschenbild', *Deutsche Zeitschrift für Philosophie*, 1965, Special isssue, pp. 182 ss., esp. p. 185.

[12] G. Klaus, *Jesuiten–Gott–Materie*, Berlin 1957, p. 333.

[13] S.L. Rubinstein, *Prinzipien und Wege der Entwicklung der Psychologie*, Berlin 1963, p. 5.

[14] We are guided in these arguments by the findings about the personality of offenders in whose case history the personality-shaping and consciousness-shaping rôle of group relations involving the individual emerges clearly. As for the more general theoretical questions and problems – e.g. how the society–group relationship must be mirrored in theory as an intellectual prerequisite of empirical research – these are discussed in E. Hahn's valuable study 'Bürgerliche und marxistische Gruppensoziologie', *Deutsche Zeitschrift für Philosophie*, 1965, Issue 4, and the same author's *Soziale Wirklichkeit und soziologische Erkenntnis,* Berlin 1965.

[15] E. Hahn, 'Bürgerliche und marxistische Gruppensoziologie', loc. cit., p. 406.

[16] We here base ourselves on the research results of W. Friedrich, 'Zum Problem der Verhaltensdetermination im Jugendalter', Habil. thesis part II, Leipzig 1965.

[17] Cf. for instance I. Koch, 'Untersuchung über die Wirkung des Trainings sozialer Verhaltensweisen im Kindergartenalter', thesis, Leipzig 1963; H. Hiebsch, 'Die Socialpsychologie ...', loc. cit., p. 193.

[18] Cf. H.G. Meyer, 'Technische Revolution, Soziologie und Kommunikationsforschung', *Deutsche Zeitschrift für Philosophie*, 1965, Special issue, pp. 358 ss., esp. p. 361. The hints contained in this article about theoretical work on the problem of social communication are, in our view, of considerable importance also for the further theoretical founding of criminology and for the the programming of empirical researches.

[19] Attention to this has been drawn especially by W. Friedrich, 'Zum Problem der Verhaltensdetermination im Jugendalter', loc. cit.

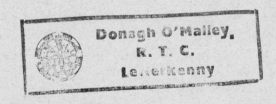

7   Freedom - Responsibility - Accountability - Their Significance in Criminology

The scientific category of freedom and responsibility — its significance in criminology

In the preceding chapter we described consciousness, representing the unity of thinking and feeling, as the core of the human personality. 'Anything that sets men in motion must go through their heads ...', Engels said.[1] In the individual's consciousness all external (objective) influences are processed in the broadest sense or — as Rubinstein calls it — 'refracted'. It is upon this state of affairs that the statement is based that personality is a relatively independent variable within the framework of the complex causes of a crime. Criminal law theory and criminology are here on common ground. Criminology, too, must take account of the fact that the 'cause' of a definite instance of criminal social behaviour (a criminal offence) is the individual himself to the extent that his action originated in his head. But whereas the theory of criminal law pursues questions of individual criminal responsibility and under this aspect — as discussed in the first chapter of Part I — develops the specific social and judicial means and methods for establishing responsibility in respect of both the offender and society, criminology examines the same state of affairs from a different point of view — that of the dialectical interrelations between objective and subjective factors — in order to attack the social problem of prevention of criminality as a social phenomenon. In this specific light it investigates the possibilities of prevention existing in socialist society and thereby makes its contribution to their utilisation and purposeful development.

The fact that man is, in a sense, the 'cause' of his actions immediately raises the question of the reality of the individual's freedom of action, of man's real responsibility for co-shaping society's life processes by his actions, of his accountability and hence of the real extent to which the individual is answerable to society for his actions. These are fundamental questions which primarily fall within the competence of criminal law theory from the point of view of the application of specific penal means

201

and methods. In reality, however, criminology must likewise concern itself with them because on the answers to them must depend the planning and execution of its empirical investigations and indeed also the social conclusions to which its findings will lead. And these answers can only be obtained if the position of mechanical materialism is finally abandoned and the materialist dialectics between objective and subjective factors are taken as the theoretical basis of criminological work.

An important part is played in this connection by the question as to the nature of the freedom of the individual. We have already touched on this in the preceding chapter in connection with the dialectical processes of personality development. Here we are concerned with the question of the extent to which the individual, whom we know to be fundamentally determined by external social determinants, is in a position, i.e. possesses the freedom, of himself deciding on his social course of action. In order to answer this question we must first proceed from the fact that man as a social being is raised by his consciousness above other living creatures and distinguished from them.

Because of this consciousness the individual is not helplessly at the mercy of the influences — the stimuli — of nature or society. They do not run through him and therefore do not produce any effects according to some causal-linear laws of mechanics. Thanks to his consciousness the individual is in a position to take into account the possible consequences of the actions which he decides to take, i.e. which he himself decides. He is able, in meeting his requirements in the broadest sense, to choose between objectively possible modes of behaviour and to perform his actions in line with knowledge and conclusions comprehended by his consciousness. This ability to determine his actions (to perform them or to omit performing them) was acquired by him through his evolution, in the process of his becoming a human being (his phylogenesis). In this sense man is 'free'. This kind of freedom to determine his behaviour in accordance with the general state of knowledge and to opt between alternative possible actions is entirely in agreement with the dialectical-materialist thesis on man's fundamental determination.

Rubinstein has described the stimuli and control of actions, as well as the part played in the entire action process by consciousness in the shape of subject-related and society-related considerations, as follows:

Man must detach himself from nature and confront the material world. He must attain freedom with regard to the immediate circumstances in order to possess the possibility of changing them. Freedom of his act of volition means that the behaviour of the individual is not directly determined by his immediate environment. But it does not, of course, mean that it is not determined at all. Acts of volition are no less determined and governed by laws than involuntary — i.e. impulsive, instinctive and reflex — movements. Their laws and determination are merely of a different kind. A direct determination has become an indirect one. The act of volition is mediated by the individual's consciousness.[2]

Consciousness therefore performs essential functions of mediation, both with regard to the psychological processing of environmental influences and the realisation and control of actions originating from the individual. Disturbances of these functions exclude or reduce the individual's responsibility. The problems and detailed questions arising under this heading for the individual's criminal responsibility and culpability under the socialist criminal law would go beyond the scope of this book. They are part of the subject of criminal law theory which must base itself, and indeed does base itself, on the findings of psychiatry and psychology.[3] Suffice it to state here that mankind, through its entire evolutionary process of humanisation (phylogenesis), has acquired these functions which are linked with consciousness as the dialectical unity of thinking and feeling, and that each individual acquires them anew as part of his own development (his ontogenesis).

The functions of consciousness are closely connected with the problem of so-called free will, i.e. with the question of whether man, being fundamentally determined from outside, is at all able to act 'freely' or not, or whether he does not merely react to external stimuli like a machine. From the position of dialectical determinism we are able to state that through his consciousness and its functions the individual is in a position, and has the subjective possibility, in the awareness of real options, of deciding for himself in favour of a certain course of action, i.e. on the basis of his consciousness the individual has the freedom of choice, of decision and of action. There is no such thing as absolute freedom of will, independent of any objective conditions, since man — see our quotation from Rubinstein above — is universally determined. But he has the freedom of choice, decision and action. We agree with Wolfgang Loose that it would be terminologically more useful and more exact to refer not to 'freedom of will' but to freedom of choice and decision, with which freedom of action is closely connected as a further criterion. Loose rightly points out that this concept of free will 'was used for centuries by idealist philosophers in the sense of an indeterminism of will and still produces in many people associations on those lines. Moreover, the term freedom of choice and

203

decision describes the state of affairs more accurately.'[4]

The scope and substance of alternative decisions thus available to the individual in his relations with nature and society are indissolubly linked with the social nature of the individual. Engels formulated this state of affairs as follows:

> Freedom consists not in some dreamed-of independence of the laws of nature but in the comprehension of these laws and, in consequence, in the possibility of making them work systematically for definite purposes. This applies both to the laws of external nature and to those which govern man's physical and psychological existence itself — two classes of laws which we may at best separate in our concepts but never in reality. Freedom of will therefore means nothing else than *the ability to take decisions with knowledge of the facts* [the present authors' italics]. The freer therefore an individual's judgement is in respect of a certain question, the greater the necessity for the contents of this judgement to be determined ... Freedom therefore consists in our control over ourselves and over external nature, based upon a realisation of natural necessities; it is thus inevitably a product of historical development.[5]

It is from this general concept of freedom, reflecting as it does the reality of life, that we must proceed both in scientific work and in practice. It illustrates clearly the problems of the individual's responsibility for his actions, which are in the truest sense of the word his 'own' and originate from him. It helps us realise why he is accountable for his own actions.

The freedom of choice, decision and action granted to the individual together with his consciousness is specifically historical and, being ontogenetically acquired and implemented, depends on the character and nature of the social order.[6] As Engels and Rubinstein have shown in their arguments, the whole of human history participates in that freedom. The principle of the social determination of personality development which, in the scientific investigation of criminality goes beyond the narrow scope of 'the subjects of the criminal offence', must be seen from the point of view of the freedom given to and acquired by the individual. This freedom is an integral constituent of the human personality because it is on its basis that the individual originates his actions, controls them, and therefore also is accountable for them. 'Such an action is, in the word's most genuine sense, a deed in which the individual emerges and by which he establishes his attitude to other individuals.'[7]

The realisation or the statement that, in a manner of speaking, the whole of human history participates in the individual's freedom of choice, decision and action, acquired by him together with his consciousness, is incomplete in this form. On this plane of reference the real social nature of this freedom and its social significance to the problems of responsibility and individual accountability cannot be comprehended. Their true social content is characterised instead by the social relations and relationships under which this freedom is actually realised. Their specific historical content — the ability to opt between decisions — depends on the prevailing social order and hence on the general and particular conditions of life and existence under which this human freedom is in fact realised. This has been convincingly proved by John Lekschas, Wolfgang Loose and Joachim Renneberg.[8] From the nature of the social order there emerge the individual's possible behaviour options — options both objectively and subjectively available.

Under the conditions of capitalist exploitation the individual's freedom becomes *genuine* freedom only when the individual is able to align himself with the kinetic laws of social development to opt for modes of action which are relevant for the assertion of these social kinetic laws, and to make an informed free choice among the available behaviour options on the strength of his knowledge and understanding. The above-mentioned freedom therefore only becomes a true human freedom, i.e. one appropriate to the social character of the personality, if the individual, in making his choice and decision, can acquire such informed knowledge and if, on the strength of such actions or deeds, he accepts necessity and serves it. The proletarian class consciousness which — shaped by a revolutionary working class party — has codified this knowledge of social kinetic laws into findings confirming the ways, means and methods applied by the popular masses in their daily work, shows the extent to which the general form of freedom, received together with consciousness, has, even under exploitative conditions, raised itself to the status of social decision. Such a consciousness under the conditions of exploitation is an expression of the true use of the freedom achieved by man in the historical process.

If this freedom is not utilised under the objective conditions of capitalism, it is vitally affected in its social core and content. The subjectively comprehended options of behaviour and social action are decisively narrowed down in important respects and reduced to a minimum in their historical-social effect. By his 'freedom of decision' and his 'freedom of action' the individual only reproduces the conditions under whose consciousness-determining overall influence he enjoys and practises his freedom of choice and decision.

From this point of view the relationship between criminality as an overall social phenomenon and the social order based on the producer's separation from the means of production and hence also from the results of social work must also be seen in criminological terms. Criminal social behaviour – e.g. robbery, extortion or theft – is based also upon a 'free decision' of the individual; seen socially, however, this 'freedom' in its real social content is generally man's intellectual and moral non-freedom, his intellectual and moral submission to the material and cultural power of social relationships. The limitation, by the individual's consciousness, of his freedom of choice, decision and action to modes of behaviour in line with the social conditions from which they have sprung, and which provide the social soil for such criminal social behaviour, therefore applies also when the individual resorts to this kind of solution of the conflicts experienced by him. We are entitled, therefore, to assess a criminal mode of behaviour as a manifestation entirely in line with this order, because it follows the social character of the order which alienates man from man in a great many ways and in *all* spheres of life, and which produces selfishness and blinkered individualism as a receipe for action and a behaviour stereotype.

To that extent, therefore, we also agree with the statements of bourgeois criminology which claim that criminal social behaviour is a phenomenon immanent in society and indissolubly linked with it.[9] The essential difference, however, consists in the fact that we isolate criminality in its internal stable, i.e. law-governed, connection with the social order based on exploitation, its specific historical socio-economic structure, and the social relations and relationships between individuals which arise from it; in this way we adopt the point of view of specific historical social analysis and critique.

It is true to say that in bourgeois criminology, in so far as it accepts the individual's freedom of choice, decision and action also in respect of his social behaviour, the formal aspect of this freedom is absolutised. But such an absolutisation means, in effect, transferring the investigation of the reason for criminal activity in a conflict-rent class society into the 'consciousness' of the individual offender. It presents the process of an individual becoming a criminal as a subjective problem of learning or adaptation. It diverts attention from the question of society's responsibility as a very real determinant and system of reference for individual social behaviour. In consequence, deliberately or unconsciously, the problem of criminality is stripped of its social aspect and of its social content. The problem of the individual's freedom of choice, decision and action is drained of its meaning by the formalisation of the consciousness functions, and indeterminism is revived in the new garb of so-called 'final over-determination'. [10]

Inasmuch as bourgeois criminology is based on a materialist environmental concept, proceeding therefore from the great importance attaching to the 'environment' in the emergence of criminal behaviour, it is unable to solve the seeming contradiction between social determination and the individual's 'free will'. This, incidentally, provides the theoretical starting point for those ideologists who argue altogether against *any* determinist view of the emergence of criminal decisions. Even though the various determinist concepts in bourgeois criminology — as analysed in Part I of this book — may be faulty or even unscientific in their theses, their starting positions and subsequently their results, and even though their practical conclusions may be illusory, they nevertheless reveal a more or less perceptible tendency to look for the causes of criminal behaviour not exclusively in the subjective sphere but outside the individual, in the 'environment'. Yet this tendency, however imperfect, represents such a danger to the maintenance of the fiction of an allegedly socially neutral and class-independent bourgeois-imperialist criminal justice that the reactionary forces find it necessary to polemise against any determinist traits in criminological cause research. One of the fiercest critics from the Right, Richard Lange, actually invokes the latest discoveries of the natural sciences. Thus he sharply attacks Fritz Bauer, who proceeds from a determinist concept, and remarks:

> Quite apart from the paradoxical nature of a world which grants to the atom and to the falling stone a measure of freedom from causality, but not to man, this objection [i.e. that man is basically causally determined — the authors] overlooks the fact that, in the history of philosophy, absolute determinism was justified in terms of the natural sciences and not from human nature ... [12]

The aim of this kind of statement is first quietly to confuse or to identify the problems of mechanical determinism with the problems and conclusions of dialectical determinism, and secondly to use such an identification for saving the indeterminist position of bourgeois-imperialist criminal law to maintain the fiction that, under the prevailing conditions, each criminal action is nothing but 'a failure' of the individual. [13]

Lange reveals the true socio-political reason for such attacks on the determinist concepts of bourgeois ideologists. The findings of bourgeois criminology, based on such concepts, seem to him dangerous because 'by this deliberate destruction of an institution [criminal justice — the authors] deeply rooted in the people they promote a disastrous draining of concepts, both in the general consciousness and in that of the offender.'[14] The illusion of the justice of bourgeois-imperialist criminal law can only be maintained, in his opinion, if any analysis of determinant environmental conditions is avoided. Just because Lange considers it dangerous to inform the popular masses about the real social reasons for criminality — in order to avoid public disillusionment — he regards the thesis 'that the criminal is only a sick person, a victim, a scapegoat or a martyr of society and that society is the real culprit ... as no longer a matter only for researchers or even for intellectuals talking amongst each other'.[15]

In view of this reactionary concept, which is the outcome of the 'clash of opinion' between bourgeois criminologists on the one hand and criminal justice ideologists on the other, or — in bourgeois terminology — between 'descriptive and prescriptive science',[16] the scientific solution of the problem under discussion is of practical importance not only for our own researches. It will also help the honest bourgeois criminological researchers in their arguments with particularly reactionary imperialist views and distortions.

We have already observed that the problem can be solved only if the formal aspect of the freedom of choice, decision and action, which develops with consciousness in the human evolutionary process, is not seen as an absolute. That is why Rubinstein emphasises that the dialectical view of determinism; by which we have been guided in comprehending the nature of freedom, is also at the same time a historical view.[17] This means that the nature of freedom can be understood, and the problem of freedom solved, only if a specific historical analysis isolates the real objective conditions existing for the individual, the conditions from which he can take his bearing in making use of this freedom. This means further that such freedom, available to him through his consciousness, can be applied correctly, in its social significance and in a manner appropriate to the social character and dignity of man if the objective and subjective conditions of man's fundamental social existence continually reopen to him real possibilities of orienting his decisions by what is socially useful and significant.

This means, finally, that there are social systems of reference which determine the conscious process of decision as models and ideals, bringing about a correct decision which takes account of what is objectively necessary both to society and to the individual. The social nature of such freedom cannot therefore be understood by the absolutisation of just one essential aspect but is indissolubly linked with the question of material, social and hence also spiritual freedom.

We see, therefore, that even under the conditions of exploitation, which

mean a social limitation of 'free will' without abolishing it 'in itself' —
disregarding the numerous instances of existential hardship and suffering
which may act as direct or indirect determinants — the process of liberation from criminality begins as a genuine utilisation of human ability: the
proletariat organises itself as a class and, with the help of a revolutionary
working class party, rids itself of the spiritual and moral fetters of exploitation. [18]

It is thus clear that the concept of freedom from which we proceeded
possesses a greater degree of determination under the heading of the individual's personality — i.e. as an increasing self-determination stemming
from man's own nature in harmony with social conditions. Freedom thus
understood is not to be confined to 'realisation of necessity' if by necessity we mean only the external conditions which the individual must identify in order to adjust himself or in order to change them and, in consequence, himself. [19] It also embraces an increased degree of self-determination. [20] Criminological research must take note of this intensified process
which was referred to also at the Eleventh Plenary Meeting of the SED.
This transcends the extension of the economic system of planning and
management beyond the sphere of economics so that, by its application in
all spheres of life, what is objectively necessary should also become subjectively desired. As early as in 1963 Walter Ulbricht, dealing with the guidance of people, raised the demand 'that what is correct, what is necessary
and what is feasible should also be done from understanding, from realisation of its necessity. Whatever has to be done should be done gladly. That
is part and parcel of human dignity and freedom and leads to deeper work
satisfaction.' [21]

All guidance and management efforts under socialist conditions — seen
from the point of view of the overall concept of freedom — aim at developing a greater degree of self-determination, both of social groupings and
of the individual. This means that criminal justice with the problem of
accountability inherent in it also serves this social process. The way and
forms in which criminal responsibility is achieved are therefore specific
measures serving the promotion of the self-determination of social groupings and of individuals who may be held accountable.

Socialist society on an ever-increasing scale enables all its members to
opt in favour of such actions as are in line with human dignity and
correspond to the particular state of the satisfaction of appropriate human
requirements. It thus represents the external (objective) system from
which the individual, through social consciousness, receives the data he
needs for practising his options of decision. Socialist society gives the
individual the freedom of recognising what is necessary in respect of

society and of his own social existence and, on this basis, of acting accordingly, both as the condition and the result of the existence and further development of that basis.

The fundamental relationship between society and individual is covered by the concept of responsibility. It expresses the fundamental social relation between society and its members and groupings. It is thus a category connected with the individual's relationships or actions in society. At the same time responsibility is a social problem, always reflected anew in an individual's consciousness process. It embraces this reciprocal relationship and its effect upon consciousness. It is the responsibility of society to see that all its members receive the information, and hence possess the maturity of consciousness required for an appropriate decision — i.e. a free decision — concerning specific problems of life. The individual member of society, on his part, has a general responsibility to acquire the information necessary for an appropriate decisions, to take his bearing from what is socially significant and useful, and to accept as the directive for his actions the social demands reflected in the social consciousness.[22] In other words, as a fundamental relation in socialist social conditions, responsibility is always positively aligned towards the reciprocal stimulation and promotion of all human qualities. It is aimed at attaining what specific historical freedom can be attained at each stage, the freedom which serves social progress, since socialist society endeavours to produce a personality very different from the soulless and unmotivated 'adaptation artist' invariably produced by capitalist society. [23] What it vitally needs is responsible and creative personalities . Responsibility, therefore, is continually reproduced, developed and realised as a fundamental relationship by the general historical dynamics of socialist society.

The new position of the human being in the general system of socialist relationships is the objective basis of the relation of responsibility which is reflected and assessed by the social consciousness through legal norms, social and moral rules, and ideas of morality. It is also the objective basis for real guilt, for personal culpability whenever acts (major or minor offences) are committed. The abolition of the essential socio-economic roots of selfish and narrow-minded social behaviour, and also of criminality as a social phenomenon, means that, with the victory of socialist production relations, the objective foundations have been laid for the individual's full responsibility. [24]

Just as the rôle and relative independence of the subjective factor — the socialist social consciousness guided by the Party as a history-moulding force embracing the popular masses — increases continually as part of the advancement of socialist society, so also increases the rôle and importance attaching to each individual member of society and his individual consciousness. That is the qualitatively new feature in the dialectics of object and subject.

As a result of this overall process the human personality — more particularly its nucleus, the individual consciousness — represents a relatively independent variable within the framework of the complex causes and conditions governing criminality both as a general social phenomenon and as a specific individual action during the transitional period from capitalism to socialism.

This relative independence has nothing in common with the outdated thesis that the 'cause' of criminality is 'merely' the individual's 'faulty consciousness'. Instead, as we have seen, it is based on the fact that socialism, as a new human order, has created and is developing real possibilities for each member of society, provided his brain is normally structured and functions normally, to choose socially adequate individual decisions and solutions concerning personally experienced conflicts without moving into conflict with the general social process or infringing the criminal laws. This independence is further founded upon the fact that, in the train of the general cultural and educational revolution, human abilities are growing and ripening, making it possible for the individual to attain and personally to utilise the freedom objectively attained by society as a whole, to recognise, as a member of a socialist community, what is personally necessary and to act on the strength of this realisation. With the growing part played by the socialist social consciousness as a history-shaping force the individual consciousness is supplied and enriched with the data it needs for identifying the tasks, duties, responsibility and position of the individual in a socialist community. The social conditions of socialist society give the individual the possibility of deciding in favour of what is right and socially significant. He is in a position to acquire the necessary knowledge and make it the basis of his actions. He thus bears responsibility for himself. All measures taken by the socialist State in the economic, political and cultural spheres are aimed at this social content of the individual consciousness process. They are designed to help every member of society to recognise and creatively realise his responsibility. With their blend of material and moral stimuli these measures, in harmony with the development of society, make increasingly high demands on each member of society, on all social groupings, so that their realisation simultaneously implements the law of the further development of socialist society. Seen in this light and understood as part of the overall historical process, we may say that social responsibility — including that of the individual member of society — is increasing, just as is the relatively independent rôle of consciousness.

This realisation of the increasing relative independence of consciousness does not mean that individual criminal responsibility is also increasing or that it must increase. Observance of individual criminal responsibility in socialist criminal law is a specific way, within the scope of the law, of solving those conflicts into which individual members of society have got towards society and its social demands through their own culpable actions. The strategy and tactics of the employment of criminal law as such a specific means depends, in our view, on the social character of these conflicts, on the social effects produced by an individual spontaneous-anarchist solution, and on the state of development of socialist society, the potentialities and possibilities of social reaction. Any absolutisation or one-sided hasty application of conclusions about the growing importance of human consciousness in the historical process of socialist society may lead to grave errors and is incompatible with the real efforts of socialist society to solve such conflicts. This realisation must therefore not be absolutised either in criminal law research or in legal practice, nor must conclusions for criminal justice be directly derived from it.

The value of such a statement lies in the emphasis placed on the specific nature of socialist educational work, which consists in promoting the process of socialist consciousness formation by guiding the individual's activity and influencing his ideological, intellectual, cultural and political—moral attitudes. The statement thus emphasises the importance of an all-round development of the characteristics of a socialist personality and at the same time confirms that a member of socialist society possesses a real chance and the moral obligation to work on himself in a political—ideological, intellectual—cultural and political—moral respect. The individual is not at the mercy of all surviving outdated views and beliefs but he is called upon to free himself of them. His responsibility extends to himself, to the development of all his abilities and creative faculties, i.e. he must himself contribute towards the continuous responsible realisation of the unity of social and personal interests. In short, our conclusion emphasises the individual's responsibility for himself.

Contents and forms of the offender's consciousness as internal conditions of criminal social behaviour

Under the leadership of the party of the working class socialist society has realised and continues to realise those historical tasks which Marx and Engels outlined in one of their early writings in order to characterise the progressive tendencies of the French materialists: namely, 'so to organise the empirical world that man in it experiences what is truly human, that he gets used to experiencing himself as a human being'. The new order provides, in the general process of history, 'for each individual the social scope for developing his own essential life manifestations'.[25]

A member of socialist society bears a real responsibility actively and creatively to shape all social fundamental relationships himself and to develop his capabilities for so doing. The objective foundations of socialist relations justify socialist society to expect and demand that its members should participate in the shaping of these relationships. If the individual does not come up to these expectations, and if in choosing his social options of action he takes his bearings not from a mode of behaviour possible for him but instead chooses an antisocial or even a society-endangering social behaviour, then, on the basis of his general responsibility, there arises an individual criminal accountability and personal culpability. This culpability is characterised in its social content by this objectively irresponsible decision, which fails to observe or even deliberately disregards the basic demands of society, by a social behaviour dangerous or hostile to essential aspects of the life of society; at the same time it also infringes the criminal law.[26] Culpability is a subjective expression of a faulty consciousness attitude on the part of the offender, in the sense that he attempts, in a socially blind, spontaneously anarchist, selfish or individualist, or even ruthless manner, to solve subjectively experienced contradictions, conflicts or difficulties, or to satisfy genuine or spurious requirements by that kind of social behaviour. It shows the offender being determined in his individual consciousness, as a unity of thinking and feeling, by outdated ideas and practices. Such an individual consciousness reflects faulty or inadequate social behaviour maxims, not in line with the nature of the new order. It is still based on patterns or concepts of thinking, feeling and action which are not socialist and basically spring from an outdated social order. Such consciousness contents may be of diverse nature. Their nucleus, without any doubt, is the bourgeois ideology as a system of ideas, theories and views reflecting the class attitude of the bourgeoisie and — through the society-wide information channels discussed in the preceding chapter — capable of influencing individual thinking, feeling and action. All consciousness data underlying criminal actions are undoubtedly conditioned by that ideology of the old society, or by certain aspects of it, or distorted or influenced by them. It is therefore entirely correct and necessary to regard the struggle against criminality, in its general social effect, also as a blow at bourgeois ideology and, accordingly, to mould it into a kind of political and ideological debate which will enable the individual to penetrate to fundamental ideological problems, in particular the individual's responsibility in our epoch. On the other hand, of course, it would be a crude over-simplification to equate all consciousness contents encountered in criminality research with bourgeois ideology or to label them as expressions of bourgeois ideology. Such an over-simplification would blur the complex processes of individual consciousness formation and yield no useful conclusions concerning political or ideological educational work. It would mean equating ideology with consciousness, whereas in fact ideology, or certain ideological positions, are only contributory factors in the much more complex social and individual consciousness even though, as we have pointed out, they can have a very important determining effect on it.[27]

The pursuit of this intellectual debate with each criminal offence, all the way back to its ideological nucleus, is necessary not only because bourgeois ideology represents the only survival in the individual's consciousness and the social consciousness factor behind each criminal offence, and that in consequence bourgeois ideology represents the only subjective force ('subjective cause'). The ideological debate is necessary because a deeper insight into the objective relationships which are socially relevant and individually relevant in determining the individual's socially appropriate behaviour can ultimately be attained only by such a debate. Only by clearing away, piece by piece, the consciousness data underlying a criminal offence — and these data include the survivals of bourgeois ideas — can the necessary consciousness-moulding and personality-determining educational work be done. What matters therefore is that the dialectics are understood, rather than that all consciousness data discovered in criminal offences should be immediately characterised as expressions of bourgeois ideology.

In addition — though occasionally linked with such ideological survivals through a whole series of stages and intermediary factors — there are also other consciousness data which have to be taken into account and liquidated. They include, for instance, habits of life and thought which came into being under the conditions of an antagonistic class society and which, having taken firm root in the individual's consciousness, continue to influence his decisions as 'internal models'. These include relatively consolidated qualities or intellectual and moral patterns and concepts of which the individual himself is frequently unaware. Such data in the individual consciousness, which govern and guide his thinking, feeling and action and which take their origin from the conditions prevailing in the old society but which have since established themselves in the individual's consciousness, are able to be passed on and, as it were, 'inherited' through direct person-to-person contact or 'empirical' communication. In analysing them it must be remembered that their social roots are deeper than a first glance will reveal. Such consciousness data are able, as an 'internal system of reference' or as an 'internal model' to determine an individual's attitude to the State, to the social order and security, to his fellows, etc. Their detailed criminological investigation and also their identification in each individual case are of the greatest importance to the liquidation of the causes of criminality. Even their characterisation as a relatively independent 'subjective cause of criminality' seems to us to be a first step towards prevention and towards the mapping out of systematic educational and instructional efforts.

An important part both in theoretical work and in practice is played by problems of everyday consciousness. To regard this as the reflection of the survivals of bourgeois ideology would be an over-simplification. What we mean by this term is a simplified and limited reflection of external conditions impinging directly on the individual's senses, more particularly on a relatively low level of ability of generalisation and frequently on a very low level of education and culture, resulting in an inability to understand essential objective connections and in allowing for them in the making of decisions.[28] Fritz Drewitz and Peter Hinze point out that this everyday consciousness consists of specific consciousness data 'comprising the empirical experience and knowledge acquired over generations of man's immediate working life and the moral norms which have developed from specific relations of individuals with each other and with their work, as well as accepted usages and naive ideas about ambient nature (e.g. naive realism) and about their own social situation'.[29] At the same time they point out that socialist production relations mould a socialist everyday consciousness and give rise to an accelerating mutual rapprochement of everyday consciousness and theoretical–scientific consciousness. It is clearly necessary to investigate this problem of everyday consciousness in greater detail, in particular to isolate its specific social content. Our present state of knowledge certainly suggests, at least in the field of petty criminality, that the kind of everyday consciousness we have described, unless it is changed and enriched by systematic political and ideological work, contains, or may contain, a tendency to misinterpret the direct sensual perceptions of life and to react to subjectively experienced contradictions, conflicts or situations by a spontaneous infringement of the norms and rules of social coexistence.

The realisation of these and similar consciousness data and their closer investigation seems to us important because only thus can social and individual educational measures, i.e. general preventive measures transcending the specific offence, be developed and introduced. This is a task to whose solution criminological research must make its contribution. Criminological personality research — which we shall examine in the next chapter — must, more particularly, discover and differentiate the social character of the consciousness data underlying specific offences or categories of offences. In this connection it is therefore also necessary to investigate in greater detail all the other characteristics marking the human personality, such as willpower, character qualities, etc.

Such specific characteristics must be considered if the offender's personality is to be assessed in all its aspects in the analysis of the complex causes of the crime and if his accountability is to be defined. In this vast field of criminological research philosophers, psychologists and psychiatrists will have to work alongside one another. Their starting point must be — as the Soviet psychologist Rubinstein has pointed out — that the human personality is neither a 'neutral' object nor a purely intellectual structure. In fact it is 'the unity and the real exponent of social relations', in other words the 'ensemble of social relationships'. [30] That is why criminological research, especially when applying the points of view of psychology and psychiatry, must not separate the offender's personality from the social conditions of its existence. The individual characteristics or peculiarities under examination may, in specific instances, have the weight of the essential factor — we need only mention the legal problems of impaired responsibility on grounds of insanity or the age of responsibility in juvenile crime. Criminology, however — because of the social problems it deals with — must invariably examine these problems from their *social aspect* and establish whether and to what extent they must also be judged as the effects of definite social circumstances acting upon the individual. We have already said that dialectical determinism is always at the same time a historical approach. This means 'that the effect of each actual factor also depends on what other factors an organism was previously exposed to, i.e. on the total history of the individual and its species'. [31]

It must therefore be remembered that the qualities characterising an offender's personality may often be the remote or belated effects of circumstances and conditions no longer existing in the immediate environment of the individual concerned. We must agree with V. N. Kudryavtsev who has pointed to this 'time lag' between certain environmental conditions and their processing in the consciousness and their effect in the mind of an offender. [32] Certain qualities characterising the offender's personality may have formed gradually through a variety of intermediate stages in the life process of the offender's personality. They have grown into characteristics and have only then attained their relative independence. Any analysis of individual evolution must therefore take note of these dialectical interactions if the mistakes of a mechanical concept of causality are to be avoided and the best possible lessons learned for the control of social processes.

If, therefore, in criminological personality research we emphasise the investigation of the determining effects of the system of real relations into which the individual is integrated, then this does not mean that we do not call for a detailed study of the 'internal conditions' of the offender's personality. Quite the contrary. The view expounded by us is the general scientific and theoretical platform from which research into the 'internal conditions' must proceed. Combined with the study of the individual consciousness is that of nervous and brain processes, conditions and peculiarities. Gerhard Göllnitz, for instance, has pointed to connections between such defects in brain processes, particularly belatedly diagnosed brain damage, and failures in the social sphere. [33] To dispute such findings would mean to weaken the struggle against crime. Criminological personality research — by the concerted efforts of psychiatrists, social health experts and psychologists — must investigate what internal connections exist between individual peculiarities characterising personally linked internal conditions and the brain, its neuro-physiological and neurodynamic processes, and certain criminal offences or groups of offences. We have already mentioned this problem in connection with juvenile criminality. [34]

Special mention must be made in this connection of Göllnitz and Hans Szewczyk [35] who have drawn attention to the importance of such specific criminological research into the interactions between the material substratum of the individual consciousness and social behaviour. The value of such an approach is:

First, that it draws attention to the connections between social adaptation difficulties, manifested in resistance to educational efforts or otherwise, or even in criminal activity, and such processes which need not always be pathological but which nevertheless condition or alter the individual's personality structure.

Second, that it provides socialist society and its management with hints and suggestions on how to diagnose such connections in good time and make appropriate provision within the framework of what is biologically possible and available at the present state of scientific knowledge, and in terms of optimal educational and living conditions for that kind of personality. These findings, therefore, must be taken into account in the mapping out of the programme of criminological personality research.

Notes

¹ K. Marx/F. Engels, *Werke*, vol. 21, Berlin 1962, p. 268.

² S.L. Rubinstein, *Grundlagen der allgemeinen Psychologie*, Berlin 1960, p. 628.

³ Cf. Bericht über ein Symposion an der Humboldt-Universität, 'Zur gesetzlichen Regelung der Zurechnungsfähigkeit und der Schuld', *Neue Justiz*, 1964, no. 5, pp. 144 ss.

⁴ W. Loose, 'Philosophische Probleme der individuellen strafrechtlichen Verantwortlichkeit und Schuld', Habil. thesis, Potsdam—Babelsberg 1965, footnote 164.

⁵ F. Engels, 'Dialektik der Natur', in: K. Marx/F. Engels, *Werke*, vol. 20, Berlin 1962, p. 106.

⁶ We are here making use of the study by R. Hartmann, 'Verantwortlichkeit und Schuld des jugendlichen Straftäters (Beitrag zur Theorie von der Täterpersönlichkeit)', Habil. thesis, Berlin 1965, as well as of the above-listed thesis by W. Loose.

⁷ S.L. Rubinstein, *Grundlagen der allgemeinen Psychologie*, loc. cit., p. 628.

⁸ J. Lekschas/W. Loose/J. Renneberg, *Verantwortung und Schuld im neuen Strafgesetzbuch*, Berlin 1964, chapter 2.

⁹ Cf. p. 156 of R. Hartmann, 'Verantwortlichkeit und Schuld ...', loc. cit., pp. 1 ss., 172 ss.

¹⁰ Cf. R. Lange, 'Grundfragen der deutschen Strafrechtsreform', *Schweizerische Zeitschrift für Strafrecht*, vol. 70, p. 390.

¹¹ F. Bauer, *Das Verbrechen und die Gesellschaft*, Munich—Basel 1957, pp. 19 ss.

¹² Cf. R. Lange, *Wandlungen in den kriminologischen Grundlagen*, Karlsruhe 1960, p. 366.

¹³ Cf. J. Hellmer, *Erziehung und Strafe*, loc. cit., p. 79; cf. also R. Hartmann, 'Die Wissenschaft vom Jugendstrafrecht unter dem Aspeckt des Nationalen Dokuments', *Wissenschaftliche Zeitschrift der Humboldt-Universität, Ges. wiss. Reihe,* Berlin 1962, Issue 6, pp. 829 ss.

¹⁴ Cf. R. Lange, *Wandlungen...*, loc. cit., p. 374.

¹⁵ R. Lange, *Wandlungen...*, loc. cit., p. 378.

¹⁶ This is the separation, based on Kant's philosophy, between the 'world of appearances', for which the laws of causality are claimed to be valid and which is the subject of the natural or 'real' sciences, and the 'world of the thing in itself', the intelligible world to which man belongs as a 'free' creature and within which the the laws of causality are said not

to be operative and which, in consequence, is the subject of the 'prescriptive sciences', such as jurisprudence.

[17] S.L. Rubinstein, *Sein und Bewusstsein,* Berlin 1962, p. 163; cf. also H. Hiebsch, 'Uber das Grundgesetz der Persönlichkeitsforschung', Gesellschaftswissenschaftliche Beiträge, *Wissenschaftliche Zeitschrift der Friedrich-Schiller-Universität Jena,* 1964, Issue 2; W. Friedrich, 'Einige Aspekte der Verhaltensdetermination', *Deutsche Zeitschrift für Philosophie,* 1966, Issue 1, p. 45.

[18] Cf. also the relevant section of this book.

[19] Cf. the interesting article by K. Fuchs, drawing attention to this problem, 'Moderne Physik und marxistisch–leninistische Philosophie', *Deutsche Zeitschriftt für Philosophie,* 1965, Special issue, pp. 67 ss.

[20] Cf. also S.L. Rubinstein, who points to the development of the will as a reflection of a growing competence for self-determination (*Grundlagen ...,* loc. cit., pp. 630 ss.)'

[21] W. Ulbricht, *Das neue ökonomische System der Planung und Leitung der Volkswirtschaft in der Praxis,* Berlin, 1963, p. 125.

[22] Cf. also R. Miller, 'Zu einigen Problemen der Ethik', and H. Kulak, 'Zum Problem des sittlichen Wertes', *Deutsche Zeitschrift für Philosophie,* 1965, Special issue, pp. 187 ss.

[23] Cf. p. 170.

[24] The objective basis of responsibility has been developed for criminal law in particular by J. Lekschas/W. Loose/J. Renneberg, *Verantwortung und Schuld ...,* loc. cit. Wolfgang Weiler further developed the philosophical aspects of the category of 'responsibility'; this is a most useful discussion, from the philosophical point of view, of the views put forward by Lekschas, Loose and Renneberg in their study on guilt referred to above. To W. Weiler, responsibility is a philosophical, in particular ethical, category, reflecting a certain relation between the subject and social values. He writes: 'It is the general expression of the ethical aspect of social relations, in which a behaviour subject necessarily influences objective social values in their emergence or development and in which that subject has ethical demands made on it, and is assessed in his attitude to these values in accordance to their weight compared with corresponding values.' W. Weiler, 'Zur Kategorie Verantwortung', *Deutsche Zeitschrift für Philosophie,* 1965, Issue 8, pp. 989 ss. (p.993).

[25] F. Engels/K. Marx, 'Die Heilige Familie', in: K. Marx/F. Engels, *Werke,* vol. 2, Berlin 1957, pp. 138 ss.

[26] On the concept of guilt cf. J. Lekschas,/W. Loose/J. Renneberg, *Verantwortung und Schuld...,* loc. cit.

[27] 'In ideology — as a system of social ideas, theories and views — we find reflected, from the point of view of society as a whole or from that of a class (in class society), the general connections and correlations governing social existence or separate aspects of it.' It becomes 'possible for the class to comprehend its social position and tasks, to recognise its social interests, and to formulate and comprehend its objectives arising therefrom' (W. Loose, *Philosophische Probleme der individuellen...*, loc. cit., p. 104). This general characterisation is the essential basis from which the specific contents of each consciousness involved in criminal phenomena have to be explored.

[28] Cf. W. Loose, Ausführungen auf einem Symposion der Humboldt-Universität in 'Zur gesetzlichen Regelung der Zurechnungsfähigkeit und des Vorsatzes', *Neue Justiz*, 1964, Issue 5, p. 144 ss.; by the same author: *Philosophische Probleme der individuellen...*, loc. cit.; cf. also J. Lekschas/W. Loose/J. Renneberg, *Verantwortung und Schuld...*, loc. cit., pp. 64 ss.; cf. also K. Marx/F. Engels, 'Die deutsche Ideologie', in: K. Marx/F. Engels, *Werke*, vol. 3, Berlin 1958, p. 26. They here describe 'everyday consciousness' as the consciousness composed of impressions and directly received sensual perceptions, experiences, etc., and 'directly .... interwoven with man's material activity and material intercourse', and hence a 'direct outcome of their material behaviour'.

[29] F. Drewitz/P. Hinze, 'Zum Begriff des gesellschaftlichen Bewusstseins und zum Verhältnis des individuellen zum gesellschaftlichen Bewusstsein', *Deutsche Zeitschrift für Philosophie*, 1965, Issue 9, pp. 1045 ss. (p. 1047); for the discussion see the sources listed here in footnote 2.

[30] S.L. Rubinstein, 'Theoretische Fragen der Persönlichkeit und das Persönlichkeitsproblem', in: *Beiträge zur Theorie der Persönlichkeit*, Berlin 1952, pp. 7 ss.

[31] S.L. Rubinstein, *Sein und Bewusstsein*, loc. cit., p. 163.

[32] V. N. Kudryavtsev, 'The Category of Causality in Soviet Criminology', *Sovetskoye gosudarstvo i pravo*, 1965, Issue 11, p. 85 (in Russian).

[33] Cf. G. Göllnitz, 'Milieuschäden und körperliche Defekte in ihrem Verhältnis zur Straffälligkeit', in: *Jugendkriminalität und ihre Bekämpfung in der sozialistischen Gesellschaft*, Berlin 1965, pp. 227 ss.

[34] Cf. R. Hartmann, 'Möglichkeit und Notwendigkeit der Gemeinschaftsarbeit bei der Erforschung der Jugendkriminalität', in: *Die Gerichtspsychiatrie in der neuen Rechtspflege, Med.-juristische Grenzfragen*, Issue 7, ed. H. Szewczyk, pp. 127 ss.

[35] From a wealth of literature we will quote only a few representative examples: G. Göllnitz, 'Über die Milieuanfälligkeit des hirngeschädigten Kindes', in: *Das milieugeschädigte Kind*, Jena 1961, pp. 40 ss.; H. Szew-

czyk, 'Fahrlässige Tötung im Verkehr — Die Grenzen psychischer Leistungsfähigkeit', *Psychiatrie, Neurologie und medizinische Psychologie*, 1964, Issues 10 and 11; by the same author: 'Der Persönlichkeitswandel im Alter', *Das Deutsche Gesundheitswesen*, 1965, Issue 36, p. 1665.

8 Criminological Personality Research and the Personality Analysis in Criminal Proceedings

One of the main tasks of socialist criminology is the study of the offender's personality. We shall call that study criminological personality research. Its task is (a) to investigate the social properties which characterise the personality and largely determine its thinking, feeling and action in the social sphere; (b) in this connection to discover and examine also the individual peculiarities of the personality and to find out whether and to what extent essential internal connections exist between such peculiarities and certain phenomena of criminality; and (c) above all to discover the complexes of social conditions which have vitally influenced the development of the offender's personality and thus to develop the specific laws of the social evolution of the offender's personality, both in its positive and negative aspects.

The findings of criminological personality research are important not only to legislation and jurisdiction, i.e. to the entire process of the practical application of the law. Their practical effectiveness transcends this juridical sphere and embraces the social problems of deliberate socialist personality shaping. The principal sources of criminological personality research, naturally, are criminal proceedings including hearings by social tribunals.

Any criminal proceedings must, in accordance with the valid legal provisions and the decrees and resolutions of the State Council, investigate the personality of the offender. This investigation of the offender's personality in the criminal proceedings is called personality analysis.

Such a terminological differentiation between criminological personality research and the personality analysis in criminal proceedings seems to us necessary in order to emphasise the differences existing between them in spite of the many aspects they have in common and in order to avoid any identification that might subconsciously arise from the use of the same concepts. The main purpose of criminal proceedings — the exhaustive examination of the whole problem of the accountability of the accused to establish his guilt or innocence — at the same time defines the functional limitation of the scope of personality analysis. The scope and the real possibilities of the investigation of the offender's personality, to be performed by the specific criminal proceedings, are laid down by law.

It would be unrealistic and asking too much of the juridical organs to expect that the demands of criminological personality research should be met by specific criminal proceedings. Criminology utilises the findings provided by criminal proceedings from the point of view of the individual's criminal responsibility. It generalises these in its theoretical reflections by referring to the findings and discoveries made in connection with the personality image of socialist man by sociology, psychology, educational science and last but not least philosophy. Within certain limits it also performs its own investigations which go beyond what is possible within the framework of a specific criminal case or what would indeed be necessary for answering the fundamental question of the accused's innocence or guilt. The distinction between these two activities will be promoted by a terminological differentiation.

Since, however, the criminal proceedings in a specific case continue to be the main source of information also for criminological personality research we shall deal with this matter in the last section of this chapter in order to stimulate the debate about the contents and limits of the personality analysis necessary in criminal proceedings and to provide a theoretical directive — albeit a tentative and general one — for such an analysis conducted by criminal proceedings.

Criminological personality research and its system

The first question which arises for socialist criminology in connection with the personality problem is whether and to what extent it should concern itself with identifying certain 'types of offenders' or adopt such 'types' or 'type characteristics' from bourgeois criminology. Bourgeois criminology has always been particularly concerned, in line with its social task and function, with defining such 'offender types' through empirical investigation and through generalisation on the basis of 'scientific empiricism'.[1] Although this method is in itself based on an error, the findings arrived at are frequently associated with models taken from medical or psychological personality theory.[2] This is partly due to the fact that bourgeois criminology — as mentioned in the first and third chapters of Part I — has historically developed from such disiplines as medicine (psychiatry) or psychology. They are the well-known 'offender types'

224

which Cesare Lombroso claimed to have discovered, such as the born criminal, the insane criminal, the criminal from passion and the occasional criminal. The biological basis of this type theory is obvious. Similarly the attempt to divide the personality of criminal offenders — on the grounds of the model of man as the product of disposition and environment — into endogenous criminals, i.e. those whose criminality stems from inborn dispositions, and exogenous criminals, for whom the 'environment' is said to have criminogenic importance, are ultimately based on biological views because even in the latter type the 'environment' merely acts as a trigger. The same tendency can be shown to exist in the writings of authors who, to a greater or lesser extent, follow the personality theories of Ernst Kretschmer, Karl Jung and Erich Jaensch.[3] All these have in common a more or less pronounced tendency to derive typological peculiarities of the personality's psychological structure direct from the individual's physical constitution, from constitutional peculiarities of the personality, and to ascribe ideological attitudes to man's 'nature', to his natural biological existence.

The social function of these and similar type theories is objectively characterised in two ways.

First, by the fact that a social problem — the question of the social conditions giving rise to and favouring criminality — is made into an edogenous biological or a subjective psychogenic problem. In their investigations these authors proceed from the isolated individual offender without examining the moulding of his personality by social determinants, by the large number of factors stemming from the social system. They view the individual exclusively in a one-sided absolutised manner, from biological or psychological points of view, in isolation from social factors. Attempts to distinguish between so-called environment offenders, latent offenders and offenders from inclination[4] spring from such foundations. All this is not to say that in a specific case it may not be necessary to take account of psychological or perhaps even biological peculiarities or special features of the offender's personality; these may indeed play a part, often a very important part, and their understanding can contribute to the explanation of the individual criminal decision. Indeed, any expert opinion called for by the judiciary on such questions as accountability (Article 51 of the Criminal Law) or the psychological age of responsibility or culpability of juveniles (Article 4 of the Juvenile Law)[5] is bound to refer to such peculiarities in order to explain the social emergence of the specific offender's personality and his social behaviour. But neither this realisation nor the specific research methods of forensic psychiatry or psychology are in a position to explain the social phenomenon of criminality, nor are they able to provide models to serve as 'standard types' of the personality of criminal offenders, mainly because in their very method they proceed from erroneous premises.

Secondly, the objective social foundation of such criminological type theories becomes obvious from the practical results they produce. In the course of the so-called great criminal law reform in West Germany the criminal types developed by such theories have, in the 1962 draft, become normative types such as 'latent offenders', 'habitual criminals' or 'conditional criminals'. Even though these conceptual categories of imperialist criminal justice are meeting with opposition among scholars in the Federal Republic,[6] it is nevertheless clear that the offender types developed by criminology and the appropriate doctrines are providing a theoretical and, in view of alleged empirical findings, also a 'factual basis' for a cloak of legality under which the increasingly oppressive function of criminal justice can be practised in the form of 'security detention' or 'preventive detention'.[7] Joachim Renneberg's profound study on the subject of criminal—sociological and criminal—biological theories continues to be both valuable and topical.[8]

The type theories produced, and still being continuously produced, by bourgeois criminology are therefore useless and unacceptable to socialist criminology.[9] It does, however, need a certain system for its empirical investigations of the offender's personality.[10] It should be possible to discover certain common factors, both of a social and psychological—ideological nature, among certain offender personalities, and these could be of the greatest practical value in planning the education or re-education of such personalities. There is, moreover, the chance that such a system of personality research may identify the common features hidden behind the accidental factors of the individual case history, so that constructive measures may be taken to change certain personality-relevant conditions and in this way facilitate, or indeed make possible, preventive efforts on a society-wide basis.

Socialist criminology, therefore, is concerned not so much with defining the 'types' of offender personalities as with systematising personality research with a view to an effective and purposeful application of research efforts. In this way it becomes possible to identify major essential and relatively constant common features underlying entire groups or classes of criminal offenders. We are referring not to basic or ideal types, such as those proposed by bourgeois criminology, but to common features in the individual consciousness of offender personalities, to common factors in the internal and external conditions moulding this consciousness. These factors should be identified and controlled.

226

There are, in principle, two ways of systematising criminological personality research: first, personality research from the point of view of the offender's age, and second, from the point of view of the offender's overall social behaviour or, in other words, his proving himself in society.

Naturally, these two basic approaches cannot be sharply differentiated because in real life they intermingle and interlock. Nevertheless, they seem to us to offer a useful principle of differentiation in the investigation of specific personality problems. They provide general directives and clear focal points for such personality research.

From the point of view of the offender's age criminological personality research embraces the specific problems of a young person's integration into socialist society, the process of the growth of ideological, political and moral knowledge, of understanding and abilities, the ripening of a socialist sense of responsibility. In this light the following specific trends may be distinguished: the problems of criminality of minors and the problems of criminality of young people. The need for such a differentiation is laid down by the normative rule of the Juvenile Court Law and the Juvenile Law. The legal distinction made here is generally based on social experience which we must respect even though it cannot form a rigid dogma or represent rigid boundaries; in many individual cases these general boundary lines do not conform with the reality of life or do not necessarily conform with it, as in fact is proved by the Juvenile Court Law with its rigid dividing line (Article 1 of the Juvenile Court Law, Juveniles Within the Meaning of the Law). [11] The need for such a systematic distinction according to age lies in the fact that it takes account of the social and biological process of personality formation, a process which at the same time is one of integration into social responsibility. This process takes place, at that age more than at any other, under strong direct social and State influences. The investigations carried out by juvenile criminology under the heading of age, therefore, lead to important problems of State and society-guided and controlled education and upbringing of young people.

Under the heading of age there is also another, relatively independent, complex of personality research which concerns crime by old or ageing people.

The age limit of such criminological personality research cannot be laid down as easily as for the earlier age groups. But we need only think of certain phenomena of sexual crime to realise the kind of problem we are faced with. According to Gerhard Feix, for instance, who investigated nearly 830 cases of sexual offences against children during the period from 1946 to 1958, the percentage of offenders over 50 years old was 33·8. Feix even speaks of a trend for this age limit to shift upwards. [12] We therefore consider it necessary for criminological personality research to provide also for a specific study of the problems of an age-conditioned disintegration of personality and its connection with certain criminal phenomena.

The second fundamental aspect — proving himself in society — seems to us particularly fruitful for a system of criminological personality research. From the outset it takes as its main bearing the relationship of the offender's personality to society. It thus takes for its starting point the decisive basic relation underlying the evolution of personality. Among the work that has been done in this field the following research trends emerge.

First of all there are the problems of the recidivist offender. He belongs to a group of offenders who have previously and repeatedly been held responsible for infringements of the social and legal rules and demands, and who, in their relations with society, have committed criminal actions more or less frequently over a relatively short space of time. This problem is well known from criminal statistics. [13] The most recent researches reveal the significance of and the need for such a relatively independent trend in criminological personality research. [14]

A closely related problem is that of the asocial nature of some recidivists. Lekschas and Renneberg drew attention to this problem in 1962. [15] Socialist criminology cannot avoid concerning itself with this problem of asocial behaviour. It cannot close its eyes to the fact that, especially among recidivists, asocial personality features can frequently be observed. Thus Rudi Frenzel in his investigations of persons guilty of culpable infringements of educational obligations pointed to the fact that in a large number of the 100 persons investigated by him alcoholism, uncontrolled sexual behaviour and a particularly marked work-shyness a part and were bracketed with such subjective qualities as cruelty, brutality, laziness, indolence and insensitivity. [16] Harry Mettin and Rolf Rabe in an analytical study of recidivist criminality in the sphere of theft classified the offender personalities under three groups. [17] The common feature of the first group, which embraced nearly one-third of the total, consisted in pronounced traits of asocial parasitical life. The characteristic of that group was an income springing from certain obscure sources, not connected with work, in particular from criminal acts. These offenders were positively afraid of work, they had got accustomed to an effortless 'income' without productive labour, and in their personality displayed a marked weakness of will, a deeply ingrained instability, pronounced emotional coldness and insensitivity. [18]

228

Another highly important direction of personality research is the investigation of the personality of first offenders. This research should be conducted principally as comparative research in parallel with recidivist offenders, as this approach might supply useful conclusions about possible differences in the personality make-up and chiefly in developmental and living conditions, and might thus enable appropriate conclusions to be drawn for administrative and social preventive endeavours.

The system here proposed marks no more than some general directives for criminological personality research. It is not intended to be either exhaustive or restrictive. The aspects mentioned above also make it possible to conduct and organise researches according to offences or groups of offences, or areas of life and production, or even according to types of culpability if we think of the specific problems of the offender through negligence.

Personality analysis in criminal proceedings

(i) Mention has already been made of the fact that, on the basis of socialist social relations the essence of responsibility under criminal law consists in leading the offender, by means of a just application of criminal law, to a responsible attitude towards the social rules and norms of socialist society.

This general and deeply humanist objective is realised through a comprehensive analysis of the offender's personality in order to take its findings into account in making a social, legal and moral judgement of his action, in determining the legal means of realising his individual responsibility, and in establishing the legal measures called for by a criminal offence.

Personality analysis in criminal proceedings is circumscribed above all by the fact that a citizen has to answer for a certain action (of commission or omission), an action which, as a completed process in the past, represents an independent unity of objective and subjective factors, an action which has violated the criminal law and produced society-endangering or anti-social effects. As such a unity the action is both the starting and the finishing point of personality analysis. Through this action the personality has up to a point objectivised itself. To that extent and in that respect the personality stands revealed before our eyes. Personality analysis, therefore, is always deed-related. In this deed-related character it has the general task, as Hans Hinderer has pointed out, of elucidating the criminal act in its social connections and in its individual determination.[19] Under the heading of cause research Lekschas similarly showed that the concern of the criminal courts must be deed-related. He believes that it is of prime importance to the courts to discover the objective and subjective determinants which have led to the offender's decision.[20]

From the point of view of individual criminal responsibility the task of personality analysis can therefore be characterised in two respects:

1   It must help to answer the question of the extent to which the action was in line with the given circumstances. This includes the degree, the form and the scope of personal culpability as the core of individual responsibility under criminal law.

2   Its findings must next help to determine the legal means and the legal consequences (punishment or educational measures) which, in view of the factual scope of the offence and of its real or potential consequences are necessary in order to abolish, in the truest sense of the word, the consciousness causes which underlay or determined the subjective decision, i.e. in order to bring about, guide, organise and control a change towards positive social behaviour.

Such a personality analysis is performed with the relatively independent objectives listed below, objectives which for reasons of clarity we list separately although, of course, there are natural internal links among them:

First, the subjective side of the integral complex of causes must be investigated. In this connection the dialectical interaction of social external determinants and internal conditions is identified. The interaction of these is analysed under the aspect of the subjective 'cause'. As a result of this specific analysis, based on the individual case history, the state of the individual consciousness must be established as the source of responsible action by the offender.

Second, the personality-related side of the social conflict must be identified — the conflict into which the offender has placed himself by his action, by his criminal offence, vis-à-vis society. In this connection the relation between the offender's personality and society, as mediated by his action (of commission or omission) stands at the centre of analytical considerations. Above all, the subjective (ideological and moral) contents, the degree and the scope of personal culpability are elucidated as a specific deed-related consciousness content.

Third, the specific social nature of the offender's personality must be explored. This means that the offender's social behaviour must be investigated in various essential social areas of life. In other words, his behaviour before and after the deed is established and thus, on the basis of the facts discovered, the question is answered of whether and to what extent the offence with which the offender is charged is in line with the specific social nature of his personality or else diverges from it.

Fourth, a specific course of education has to be prescribed for the offender's personality as a particular unity of social goal and legal measures and forms. In this respect it is necessary not only to discover the ideological and moral shortcomings and weakness of the offender's personality — those which have directly entered into the criminal action and have thereby become objectivised and materialised. It is also necessary to identify the starting points for a positive development of the personality so that, by means of and within the framework of the legal consequences decided upon (punishment or educational measures), the offender's social integration into socialist society can be set in motion, developed, guided and realised.

These four points between them characterise the overall and essential contents of personality analysis in criminal proceedings. They simultaneously define the functional limits of such an analysis. This analysis takes place throughout the criminal proceedings; it is not assigned to any particular section of them, even though the necessary data will have been discovered in the preliminary investigations and the intellectual processing of the findings reaches its highest legal form in the court's verdict. Personality analysis is thus the task of all judiciary organs at all stages of the proceedings, since they are all concerned with individual aspects or relatively independent objectives of a single unified process — to examine the offender's personality in its social and individual peculiarities and hence to understand it in its specific social character.

(ii)   The analysis of the offender's personality is based on the principle of deed-relatedness and universality. This means that it must not content itself with the statement that a certain personality has committed a criminal offence. The old doctrine of the 'subject of the criminal act or offence' is no longer adequate to comprehending the problems raised or promoting a solution of the resulting questions and problems. [21]

The principle of deed-relatedness and universality means that the main social characteristics of the accused's personality must be discovered since these mark his thinking, feeling and action and since the individual's relations with socialist society in general or with particular aspects are, as it were, objectivised by his criminal offence. Personality analysis therefore comprises the offender's personality — in Rubinstein's words — as 'an integrated totality of internal conditions through which all external influences are refracted'. [22] It concentrates on examining the state of development of the individual consciousness as the core of the offender's personality, since this is the motive force behind the individual's conscious society-related actions.

We have repeatedly pointed out that consciousness is the subjective basis of man's individual purpose-oriented action, i.e. of the principal form in which his social relations and relationships are realised and objectivised. Engels observes that all that sets man in motion must go through his head (his consciousness). He also says that the form which it takes there depends 'greatly on circumstances'. [23] These circumstances do not include only the external (objective) influences of society and nature, i.e. chiefly the strength, intensity and social character of society's influences in the broadest sense; they also include the state of the individual's consciousness. The offender's ideological, intellectual and moral position, his interests, opinions, convictions, ideals, etc., all belong to these 'circumstances'. They moreover include the structure of his brain, the dynamics of his higher nervous processes, as reflected in his temperament, and other processes. In short, the 'circumstances' cover the totality of present, acquired and internalized conditions. They include typical and general features which individuals living under identical or similar conditions have in common. But they also include unique, individual and unrepeatable features. It is in such internal conditions — above all in the individual consciousness — that the deeper reason lies which — as we have pointed out in another context — justifies us in speaking of the relative independence of personality as a 'cause' within the framework of the complex causes of criminal social behaviour. Here also lies the reason for the possible broad spectrum of motivations and hopes which mark and accompany the psychological processes of a particular social behaviour. Here also we discover why, under identical external conditions or influences, individuals may react either similarly or differently. These facts must be taken into account in an analysis of the offender's personality.

(iii)   The exploration of the personality is made basically by an analysis of the actions emanating from it. They are the principal source of knowledge enabling us to penetrate to the core of the personality, its state of consciousness. This main methodological road to knowledge was first marked out and emphasised by Lenin. Asked by what criteria we should judge the 'real' 'thoughts and intentions' 'of real personalities', he answered: 'There can, of course, only be one such criterion — the actions of these personalities. And since we are talking about social "thoughts and intentions" we must add: the social actions of the personalities, i.e. *social facts*'. [24]   In criminal proceedings the question about a citizen's individual responsibility is similarly concerned with such 'social facts' as documented in his actions.

Man's consciousness and the social and individual qualities which compose it are formed in his everyday life, from his social actions. On the other hand, they are also objectivised in man's activity, both in his actions and in his verbal utterances. [25] By an analysis of social behaviour we are able to establish the state of individual consciousness. Similarly, because of the interaction from outside and within, and because of the dialectical unity and interaction of man's consciousness and activity, [26] we have a real chance, by *deliberate guidance* of his activities, of cultivating in the individual certain socially desirable characteristics and weaning him from other, undesirable ones. By 'activities' we mean here the individual's confrontation with the conditions of his life, i.e. the unity of psychological (mental) processes with activity in the external world, in the shape of active social behaviour and action (of commission or omission).

Individual consciousness, as the unity of thinking and feeling, comprises the individual reflection of environmental influences, processed by man's higher nervous activity, and hence subjectively filtered, assessed and transformed. It is thus accessible only to the subject, to the agent himself. To third parties it is revealed only in the utterances, the behaviour or the actions of the individual. In this respect considerable difficulties are sometimes encountered. Certain occurrences − for instance a homicidal crime − may leave us stunned and we may then speak of the 'inexplicable nature' of such an action merely because we are not yet able to discover or judge the consciousness-related (rational or emotional) reasons or backgrounds either in their social or in their individual aspect. But such instances, in so far as they occur, do not in themselves prove that there is no 'explanation' from the offender's consciousness. All it means is that either science has not yet evolved a method of investigation or that in the individual instance the investigator still lacks the necessary skill or fails to apply available procedures for discovering the consciousness data and their social and individual background and foundations underlying such an occurrence. Such individual instances show clearly that the further development and practical application of personality analysis in criminal proceedings as well as the theoretical processing of practical findings are a genuine task of scientific endeavour, which must not therefore confine itself to the problems, no matter how important, of accountability or non-accountability on grounds of mental health, maturity, etc.

The difficulties of penetrating to the core of the offender's personality − its individual state of consciousness − by an analysis of his actions can only be overcome by the method outlined above. At our present state of knowledge these difficulties may be reduced, without prejudice to further research, provided the following methodological points are accepted as directives for personality analysis.

We start from the fact that the criminal proceedings, in examining responsibility, are basically concerned with establishing the state of the offender's consciousness. Without overlooking the fact that personality development is a process in time, we are nevertheless under an obligation of taking, as it were, a snapshot of the personality at a socially most significant moment (that of the criminal act). From this point of view, which also defines our limitations, we are dealing therefore with a critical analysis of the state of personality development attained; it is this analysis that the judiciary organs have to perform. In this they proceed from the act itself. This is the result of a definite subjective process of decision which unrolls within the psychological structures covered by criminal law theory under the concepts of premeditation or negligence. If one wants to penetrate to the core of the personality one must not stop at the registration of a definite external form of behaviour, of a definite action. It is necessary to proceed from outside inwards, from the external form of action to the underlying consciousness, to its political, ideological and moral state of development. Actions, as we all know, can greatly resemble one another in their outward form. This is the first set of problems to be solved within the framework of personality analysis, because the direct perceptual manifestation of an action may, under certain circumstances, be susceptible of several different interpretations. In its social value or negative value, and in its legal meaning, an action can be unequivocally identified and judged only when the subjective ideas, the subjectively pursued aims and objectives of the agent, are known. In order, therefore, to proceed, in connection with a definite external action, from possible ambiguity with its various legal and moral conclusions to an unambiguous view as to the nature of such an action, we must answer the question of what subjective causes, considerations, hopes and ideas have led the offender to commit his action. We are thus concerned with the question of the motive of a specific action.

Motivation is the subjective cause of a criminal offence or − in other words − the subjective internal reason with which the offender 'justifies' his action, his social behaviour, to himself. Such an internal 'justification' − for example, for having knocked down a citizen because he had 'dared' to call the offender to order − is basically the immediate trigger of his action. It is linked with the individual consciousness to the extent that it provides the key for discovering and judging that state of development of the consciousness as well as the deed-related value ideas and scale of values of the offender. As such it is grounded and anchored in the personality, in the thinking and feeling of the personality. To that extent also we are faced with a unity of deed-triggering subjective processes and the offender's personality. This unity determines the criminal action. In the majority of cases the questions raised by this can be satisfactorily answered. [27] The main sources of these answers are the offender's interrogations and statements, which we must analyse critically; further statements by witnesses with an assessment of the nature of the means and methods used by the offender; and an analysis of the entire commission of the act with allowance for relevant conditions of time and place, etc. The motives thus established can then be examined for their social significance and appropriately assessed. The analysis of these internal processes, which have entered into the objective aspect of the action, thus provides the key for judging the personality. The revealed social attitude which underlies the specific action which is the subject of the proceedings therefore may characterise the offender's personality in its direct deed-relatedness but need not necessarily do so. This is obvious, in particular, in offences from negligence — though not only in these — when a (perhaps very momentary) dereliction of duty by the offender may have resulted in serious consequences although in his normal social behaviour he may act in a thoroughly conscientious manner. Thus, as this example shows, a second set of problems of personality analysis is marked by the question of whether the deed-triggering factor and the social attitude manifested in its deed-relatedness have sprung from a fundamental motivation or fundamental attitude which normally guide the personality in its social behaviour or whether such a deed-related attitude here runs counter to them.

This second set of problems means that, while we proceed from the unity between the deed-triggering subjective elements and the personality of the offender, we must not stop there but examine whether and to what degree this unity conceals a deep internal contradiction. In other words, we must discover whether and to what extent the social behaviour objectivised in a definite individual action has sprung from a durable, relatively constant social attitude or quality of the offender, i.e. his overall personality, or whether it runs counter to it. To solve this problem the personality analysis must be extended beyond its direct deed-related aspects. Such an analysis must be comprehensive, in the sense that it examines the offender's behaviour in society before and after his deed. In this comprehensive analysis we proceed from the statement arrived at in connection with the offender's deed-related social attitude or qualities. In judging his overall personality we must remember that any such judgement remains a kind of hypothesis, a kind of scientific assumption which is not yet sufficiently tested. At this stage of our knowledge we cannot yet state with the necessary certainty that the social (ideological, intellectual and moral) attitude manifested in the offence the offender is charged with actually characterises his entire personality. In respect of the assessment of the offender's overall personality the deed-related statement has merely the value of a hypothesis.

In the course of further investigations it is then necessary to test this 'hypothesis' against other social modes of behaviour or actions previously practised by the offender in similar situations under generally similar conditions in certain social spheres or relationships. In this retrospective survey of the offender's past social behaviour or actions – a survey peculiar to criminal proceedings – such further actions, as it were, represent objective control data against which we test our deed-related 'hypothesis' to discover whether and to what extent the consciousness content identified for the specific deed is found also in the offender's social behaviour on other occasions and in other respects.

The line of personality assessment thus runs from the external aspect of a certain action to the discovery of the offender's deed-related social attitudes or qualities, and from such deed-related attitudes or qualities along further chains of relevant modes of his social behaviour and actions in various social spheres.

This method enables us to verify, by means of objective control data, whether our view of the offender's attitude as objectivised in his offence is confirmed or not, or modified, by the rest of his social behaviour. If, for instance, we discover that the conscious (ideological and moral) attitude reflected in his offence is manifested also in various other actions or modes of behaviour, and if we can establish that these underlie his behaviour and action in the truest sense of the word, then we may say that the deed-related attitude is genuinely typical of his overall personality. The findings of such an analysis then show that such a genuinely typical attitude – e.g. one which brutally, selfishly and narrow-mindedly pursues nothing but the individual's own advantage and disregards the rules of co-existence – is at the same time the logical explanation of the individual's actions under various conditions, i.e. that the offender – to keep to our example – invariably tries to solve personal conflicts regardless of the interests of other citizens and even by physical force. In that case the offence in our example – knocking down another citizen – would be merely one link in the chain of the offender's modes of social behaviour. The conflict manifested in his offence will then be partially conditioned, in its social character, its degree and its importance, by this character trait of the offender. The procedure described above presupposes that the following are included in the analytical examination of the offender: first, the objective material and psychological conditions under which he lives and works; second, his actual social behaviour within spheres of life of especial relevance to the development of his personality; third, his remarks, views and opinions about himself and his behaviour.

In this procedure we allow for the great importance attaching to objective facts. These we glean from interrogation, from statements by the offender, and finally also from assessments obtained from individuals or from social groups concerning the offender's social behaviour. The interpretation of these data provides a comprehensive insight into the individual consciousness, into the value concepts and opinions prevailing in it. We thus proceed 'from the facts, which admittedly always include a measure of theoretical interpretation, to their interpretation proper, in order to test this interpretation against new facts'. [28]

(iv) We have so far concentrated mainly on methodological problems emerging in personality analysis under the heading of deed-relatedness and comprehensiveness. But it is also necessary to look more closely at the questions of substance to be answered by the method outlined. As we have said before, we still lack detailed models or programmes for examining the questions of substance which have to be established with regard to the offender's personality in individual criminal offences or groups of offences. Nevertheless, existing studies by criminal law theorists – both the mass observation of entire groups of offences over certain periods of time or within certain spheres of life, and analysis of representative individual cases – make it possible to derive certain general theoretical principles which may be taken as the basis of practical personality analysis. This does not, of course, mean that a number of problems do not remain to be solved by further scientific work.

It is a fact that all criminal proceedings are basically concerned with finding the answers to three problems or groups of problems. These have been developed in Rubinstein's theoretical work. [29] In their breadth and complexity, as well as in the high degree of their generalisation, they characterise the essence of the personality analysis to be specifically performed in criminal proceedings. They also contain a great variety of problems which remain to be solved by scientific work on the personality problem, on the offender's personality. They are:

What does the personality want?
This question comprises not only the deed-related and deed-realising objective and purpose, in a sense therefore the actual deed-related 'disposition' and hence the question as to the individual consciousness reasons which led the offender to commit his deed; it also embraces the general basic orientation of the personality, its general needs, interests and aspirations.

237

What is the personality?
This question embraces the durable and relatively constant fundamental qualities determining social behaviour from within and generally characterising the personality. It therefore also includes the question of the intellectual, moral and ideological position from which the offender moulds his relationship with society and with social groups or groupings in relevant spheres of life. It also includes the question of the character of the personality, i.e. the relatively consolidated system of intellectual and emotional characteristics, and their individual features or peculiarities, such as temperament.

What is the personality capable of?
This question embraces the area of the more or less crystallised knowledge, abilities and skills of the personality. These therefore represent the starting points for any future educational work and hence for a positive development of the personality. They must, in consequence, be utilised especially in the educational programme designed for the personality of a specific offender.

The above questions in their universality and totality characterise the contents of personality analysis. They comprise the social dimension of the offender's personality in three fundamental directions — its relations with society, its relations with other individuals, and its relations with itself. This multi-dimensional approach leads us , by its results, to further conclusions concerning the social character of the specific offender's personality.

Of particular importance in any personality analysis are the offender's relations with society. These are reflected, above all, in his work, i.e. in his responsible, creatively active participation in the processes of the production of material or spiritual values. With young people the personality is still predominantly marked and determined by learning. A person's inner attitude or approach to work and learning is therefore an important criterion in judging the offender's personality. It shows how the offender reacts with his consciousness to the fundamental social demands of socialist society. It therefore also marks a fundamental ideological, intellectual and moral position and characterises the 'internal model' on the basis of which the offender realises the demands made on a member of socialist society and hence also the decisive relations of his own social being. Attitude towards work, and with young people also their attitude towards study, thus reflects the moral features of the personality. On the other hand, work and study are a most important source of identifying and studying the offender's essential personality-relevant way of life.

The discovery of a person's attitude to work enables us to draw valid conclusions about those personality characteristics which are of essential social significance. We can make statements on whether and to what extent the offender is aware of his own responsibility or of his position in socialist society; whether and to what extent he realises the objective and direct connections mediated by a certain sense of duty and responsibility. The facts discovered in this connection concerning the individual's attitude to work or study enable us to see whether and to what extent the offender possesses conscientiousness, initiative, enthusiasm, discipline, the ability to work efficiently, perseverance and single-mindedness. Naturally we must remember in this connection the interactions we mentioned earlier in respect of the whole problem of the causes of crime. In the discovery, judgement and assessment of possible shortcomings, weaknesses or strengths displayed by the personality in this social sphere of its life we must also remember the determinant effect which the specific living and working conditions and the relations realised by them as ideals and models either have or may have on the individual. That is why the facts investigated by us concerning the individual's attitude to work or study must also be analysed with an eye to such possible interactions. These interactions have been referred to by Loose and K. Dzykonski in their investigation of the rôle of ideology and social psychology in the assessment of the personality. [30]

Generally speaking, however, it can be stated that the personality's fundamental relations with society, as objectivised in a person's attitude to work, and hence to the social demands made on present-day man by socialist society, greatly influence and determine the overall assessment of the offender's personality, within the framework of the fundamental objective social significance attaching to his criminal offence. This fundamental relationship, reflected in work, must be taken account of in determining the legal consequences and in the shaping of the social personality-related contents of such legal consequences. The measures of State and society, provided for in the legal forms, must therefore be aimed at shaping, developing and consolidating this fundamental relationship between offender and society in order to condense his external experience of work under socialist conditions into an internal experience from which direct internal impulses stem for a social behaviour in line with the dignity of socialist man.

Personality analysis is further aimed at investigating the offender's fundamental attitude to other people. This covers the basic manner in which the offender shapes his relations with other individuals. These are highly significant personality-relevant social relations, realised predominantly in groups or groupings into which the offender is more or less firmly integrated and by which his feelings are frequently shaped and conditioned. They are realised in all spheres of life — within the family, at work and in his free time. The facts which we gain or refer to under the heading of social behaviour with other individuals enable us to draw conclusions about the fundamental ideological and moral attitude from which the offender himself subjectively shapes his relations with others. We thus obtain a valuable insight into the conditions which may have shaped the offender's personality and led it towards established habits of life and thought which act as 'internal models' or behaviour patterns. We are able to discover whether and to what extent he shapes these relations upon an honest, helpful and comradely basis, with love and respect for his fellow beings, and whether and to what extent this ideological and moral basis is overgrown or distorted by personality traits such as secretiveness, hypocrisy, mistrust, rudeness, etc.

Personality analysis must finally investigate the relationship which the offender maintains with himself, with his own outlook on life, with his objective position and with his responsibilities in socialist society and for his own development.

This specific trend of investigation finally raises all the fundamental questions of individual responsibility. But personality analysis must also extend to such problems as how the offender uses the possibilities objectively available to him and given to him by socialist society for his own improvement, for the development of the intellectual and moral abilities he is endowed with, and how he realises the harmonisation of personal and social interests in his relationship with himself. These, of course, are the problems which we have already encountered under the heading of socialist man's increasing self-determination and freedom. [31] This specific trend of personality analysis is concerned with such questions as whether and to what extent the offender possesses personality traits like confidence, a positive or a sceptical attitude towards life, indifference or boastfulness, self-effacement, self-discipline, self-control, patience, perseverance, resilience, etc. Of particular importance also is the question of whether and to what extent the offender is capable of critically judging himself and his social behaviour, both generally and in respect of the offence he is charged with, because such a social ability or characteristic provides particularly valuable starting points for personality development.

The above-listed specific directions of personality analysis are of course separable from each other only in a theoretical discussion. In the real life of an offender they are invariably interwined and shade into one another. Collectively they provide us with an insight into the state of the offender's consciousness and thus into the state of personality development. Collectively they enable us to perform a comprehensive assessment of the overall personality.

Such a multi-dimensional consideration and investigation method seems to us to be basically necessary in all criminal proceedings. But it also provides the foundation in criminological personality research for an emphasis on those facts which in empirical investigations result in an appreciation and assessment of the offender's personality.

Within the framework of the personality analysis performed as part of the criminal proceedings the centre of gravity will necessarily, up to a point, be determined by the fundamental character of the offence with which the offender is charged and hence by the kind of social relation he has violated. For instance, with offences directed against the person, against a human being, the most important aspect will be an analysis of the fundamental position from which the offender shapes his personal relations, although the other dimensions of personality relations, as described above, his relations with society, must not be neglected. With offences against the activity of official bodies the centre of gravity will probably shift towards the political, ideological and moral position from which the offender shapes his relations with the State, with the organs of socialist State power, with State or social institutions or authorities, i.e. his social activity, etc. With offences against property, finally, the centre of gravity will almost certainly lie in the area of how the offender works. His attitude towards work and learning is of very considerable importance in actions of this kind.

We can therefore state that the more objectively serious to socialist society is the offence with which the accused is charged, to its relations, life processes or the rights of its citizens, the more thoroughly and comprehensively must the personality analysis be conducted.

In the case of juvenile offenders a comprehensive personality analysis is desirable in every case. With juveniles the individual case history is relatively easy to trace. Although in such cases the immediate purpose of personality analysis is the establishment of the offender's accountability or culpability in terms of maturity, [32] analysis must not confine itself to this aspect. Especially with juveniles its findings are used for the best possible programming of judicial measures (educational measures or punishments) which serve the comprehensive development of the personality by arousing, strengthening and stabilising the offender's sense of responsibility.

Personality analysis in criminal proceedings is an organic part of the entire investigatory process whose main objective is the question of a

241

citizen's guilt or innocence. Its scope and contents are determined by the limits stemming from the question of individual criminal responsibility. That is why only such data are subjects of personality analysis as are in an essential internal relationship with the problem of individual criminal responsibility. The 'weight' of personality analysis is prescribed by these considerations. It is greatly determined by the objective character of the social relations violated or attacked by the offender.

Notes

[1] Cf. the scientific empiricism of R. Hartmann, *Verantwortlichkeit und Schuld...*, loc. cit., pp. 55 ss.

[2] Cf. E. Seelig, *Lehrbuch der Kriminologie*, loc. cit.

[3] Cf. E. Seelig, loc. cit., pp. 65 ss.

[4] Cf. O. Brückner, *Die Jugendkriminalität*, Hamburg, n.d., pp. 217 ss.; also K. Grathenauer, 'Die Ursachen und Bedingungen der Eigentumskriminalität Jugendlicher in der DDR', thesis, Halle 1962, pp. 21 ss.

[5] Cf. the new regulation of accountability and diminished accountability in Arts. 15, 16 and of the culpability of juveniles in Art. 66 of the GDR Criminal Code of 12 January 1968.

[6] Thus A. Wegner characterised and judged such normative typecasting attempts with the observation: 'The individual ceases to be the subject of the law. He becomes an object and a means to an end. That is the meaning of those theories about the offender, of that 'offender criminal law', which we have to oppose' (*Strafrecht* – Allgemeiner Teil, Göttingen 1951, p. 90). With equal justification the 'Denkschrift über die Reform des Jugendgerichtsgesetzes im Rahmen der grossen Strafrechtsreform' opposes any so-called 'preventive detention' of juvenile 'latent offenders' (cf. H. Schüler-Springorum in *Monatsschrift für Kriminologie und Strafrechtsreform*, 1964, Issue 1, pp. 1 ss.

[7] Cf. Konferenz der Juristischen Fakultät der Humboldt-Universität zu Berlin zur Bonner Strafrechtsreform in *Wissenschaftliche Zeitschrift der Humboldt-Universität, Ges.wiss. Reihe*, Berlin 1963, Issue 2.

[8] J. Renneberg, *Die kriminalsoziologischen und kriminalbiologischen Lehren und Strafrechtsreformvorschläge*, Berlin 1963, Issue 2.

[9] It is not yet possible to state for certain to what extent specific procedures or individual methods applied in personality research can be adopted by us. Here too it would be wise to adopt a fundamentally critical attitude.

[10] This point is also made by Soviet researchers; cf. M.I. Kovalev,

'Soviet Criminology and its Position in the System of Jurisprudence', Reports of the Universities, Leningrad 1965, Issue 1, p. 136 (in Russian). We do not, however, share Kovalev's view that criminology is a branch of criminal law theory but regard it as a scientific discipline in its own right.

[11] The GDR Criminal Code of 12 January 1968 has integrated juvenile criminal law into general criminal law; see Arts. 65 ss. of the Criminal Code. A juvenile in the meaning of the criminal law is a person over 14 but under 18.

[12] G. Feix, *Die Bekämpfung von Sexualverbrechen an Kindern*, Berlin 1961, pp. 11 ss. Forensic psychiatry also draws attention to these problems which are related to the age-conditioned degeneration of the personality; cf. H. Szewczyk, 'Der Persönlichkeitswandel im Alter', loc. cit., pp. 1665 ss.

[13] Cf. H. Harrland, 'Die Kriminalität in der DDR und in Westdeutschland im Jahre 1961', *Neue Justiz*, 1962, no. 23, p. 732; the same author in: *Schriftenreihe der DVP*, 1963, pp. 147 ss.; cf. also H. Weber, 'Zum Begriff der Straftat im künftigen Strafgesetzbuch', *Staat und Recht*, 1963, Issue 10, p. 1621.

[14] Cf. especially H. Mettin/R. Rabe, 'Der soziale Charakter des Rückfalldiebstahls und seine Täter', thesis, Berlin 1966.

[15] J. Lekschas/J. Renneberg, 'Lehren des XXII. Parteitages der KPdSU für die Entwicklung des sozialistischen Strafrechts der DDR', *Neue Justiz*, 1962 no. 3, esp. pp. 81·3.

[16] R. Frenzel, 'Die strafrechtliche Verantwortlichkeit bei Erziehungspflichtverletzungen — de lege ferenda — zugleich eine kriminologische Untersuchung', thesis, Jena 1964; by the same author 'Ursachen und begünstigende Bedingungen der Erziehungspflichtverletzungen', *Neue Justiz*, 1964, p. 4, no. 4, p. 110, no. 5, p. 141.

[17] H. Mettin/R. Rabe, 'Der soziale Charakter...', loc. cit.

[18] E. Buchholz ('Der Diebstahl und seine Bekämpfung in der DDR', Habil. thesis, Berlin 1963) and G. Knobloch ('Zur Persönlichkeit von Tätern gegen das sozialistische Eigentum in den VEB der sozialistischen Industrie der DDR', thesis., Berlin 1964) also draw attention in their investigations to the problem of asociality in obdurate law breakers.

[19] H. Hinderer, 'Die Persönlichkeit des Rechtbrechers im Strafverfahren der DDR', *Staat-Recht-Wirtschaft, Wissenschaftliche Zeitschrift der Martin-Luther-Universität*, Halle-Wittenberg 1964, Special issue, pp. 176 ss., esp. p. 178.

[20] J. Leschas, 'Zur Feststellung der Ursachen der Straftät durch die Gerichte', *Neue Justiz*, 1965, no. 15, pp 479 ss., esp. p. 480.

[21] Cf. H. Weber, 'Für die Überwindung des Dogmatismus in der Straf-

rechtswissenschaft!', *Neue Justiz*, 1962, no. 12, pp. 379 ss.

²² S.L. Rubinstein, *Sein und Bewusstsein*, loc. cit., p. 280.

²³ K. Marx/F. Engels, *Werke*, vol. 21, loc. cit., p. 268.

²⁴ V.I. Lenin, Werke (German edn.), vol. 1, Berlin 1961, p. 419.

²⁵ Cf. also U. Köhler, 'Einige methodologische Fragen der vollständigen Erfassung des menschlichen Verhaltens', *Probleme und Ergebnisse der Psychologie*, Berlin 1962, Issue V.

²⁶ Cf. S.L. Rubinstein, *Grundlagen der allgemeinen Psychologie*, loc. cit., pp. 28 ss.

²⁷ Even though we do not ignore the difficulties which will or may arises (cf. the articles by H.D. Schmidt in: *Psychologie und Rechtspraxis*, Berlin 1965), this vast field of theoretical work can only be tackled jointly by philosophers, psychologists and criminal law theoreticians. Here, too, models must be developed in the same way as for the study of the causes of crime.

²⁸ S. Rubinstein, *Prinzipien und Wege der Entwicklung der Psychologie*, loc. cit., p. 152.

²⁹ Cf. S.L. Rubinstein, *Grundlagen der allgemeinen Psychologie*, loc. cit., pp. 762 ss.

³⁰ W. Loose/K. Dzykonski, 'Zur Rolle von Ideologie und gesellschaftlicher Psychologie bei der umfassenden Beurteilung einer Persönlichkeit', *Neue Justiz*, 1963, no. 20, pp. 643 ss.

³¹ Cf. chapter 7 of the present book, especially, pp. 211-12.

³² Cf. R. Hartmann, 'Prüfung der strafrechtlichen Verantwortlichkeit Jugendlicher — untrennbärer Bestandteil der allseitigen Persönlichkeitserforschung', *Neue Justiz*, 1965, no. 15, pp. 476 ss.; cf. also the resolutions of the plenary meeting of the Supreme Court on the work of the courts in the further struggle against juvenile criminality of 7 July 1965, *Neue Justiz*, 1965, Issue 15, pp. 465 ss., and on the uniform application of Art. 4 of the Juvenile Court Law by the courts of 13 October 1965, *Neue Justiz*, 1965, no. 22, pp. 711 ss.

Part IV

Technique and Methodology of Criminological Research

9　Theoretical Problems of Criminality Research

The preceding discussions of the theory of socialist criminology would be incomplete without an exposition of its methodological foundations and techniques. Its methodological apparatus is of great importance for a science and its social effectiveness. From the methodological statements of a science it is in turn possible to draw valuable conclusions about its theoretical foundations, its scientific statements and its possible results. The connection between bourgeois theory and its method has already been shown in the third chapter of Part I with the example of the prediction tables of future criminal behaviour, as developed by bourgeois criminologists.

By deepening the conclusions reached so far and by generalising the experiences gained in the methodological field it is possible to make a contribution to the solution of still unsolved problems, to the deepening of the scientific character of research into the causes of crime, to ensuring a concerted procedure in questions of method, to the comparability of results and to the qualification of the efforts made by the numerous forces participating, each in its own way, in the struggle against criminality.

This part of the book describes various methods with their field of application and their limitations. An attempt is made to assign to each its place in the system of research methods. Psychologists and sociologists, above all, have achieved valuable results in their fields, and these have also been processed. Their findings and explanations have been partly adopted since criminology as yet lacks experiences of its own. At the same time the authors are anxious to make their own contribution to the foundations of a comprehensive system of methods for investigating criminality.

An important task of criminality research is the correct utilisation of the system of procedures developed for the research tasks in hand. Unhelpful as it is to underrate the psychological processes involved in the occurrence of criminal offences and thus to dispense with appropriate investigations, it would be equally pointless to apply methods of correlation computation when the objectivity and reliability of the investigations or the exactitude and certainty of the underlying concepts is not ensured.

All procedures must be comprehended within their own systems. The ability to comprehend their interlocking, their mutual dependence, very largely determines the standard of criminality research. Mathematical and cybernetic methods and their applicability to criminality research have remained disregarded by us. This is a task for specialists. Problems of data processing in criminality research have similarly been disregarded since, in our opinion, past experience is not yet sufficient to allow of generalisation. Specialised methods for the establishment of physiological or biological connections, e.g. psycho-diagnostic procedures, are likewise not discussed in this book. For them we must refer the reader to the medical and specialised literature.

Our understanding of the connection between the methods, the research subject and the views on the research subject — views gained on the basis of Marxist—Leninist theory — renders it necessary to treat also of such theoretical questions as the definition of the place of various procedures in a system as well as their practical application. Theoretical and methodological problems will be discussed here through examples of criminological research, in particular the investigation of criminality within the nationally owned area of the construction industry.

The unity of theoretical knowledge on criminality and the methods of criminality research

The study of criminality requires a comprehensive methodological basis, *a system of rules which determines the manner of proceeding towards the gaining of new knowledge*. It depends largely on the method whether the complicated processes underlying criminality can be comprehended in the way in which they develop in reality. In that sense the research method reflects the state of knowledge about the subject of research. This is ultimately due to the fact that all knowledge, by its nature, is reflection and is for the most part mediated by research methods.

This correlation between knowledge and research method is even more patent in the natural sciences. Thus it is obvious that the discovery of a virus will largely depend on whether the scientific discipline concerned is able to make the virus identifiable in its natural environment, in other words on whether a method of preparation has been found. Without such a method the existence of the virus cannot be proved and it will then scarcely be possible to render it harmless. Criminality, of course, is not caused by some crime virus but is the result of very complex and complicated phenomena of a social and individual kind, phenomena which

248

mutually condition one another and interact with one another.[1] It must nevertheless be stated that, analogously, our knowledge about criminality is largely determined by the standard of our research method and the degree of our mastery of it.[2]

A number of ideas — of no great interest in the present context — are associated with the concept of criminality.[3] We may proceed from the view that criminality represents the totality of modes of behaviour which, under our socialist criminal law, are characterised as antisocial or even society-endangering actions and which entail responsibility under the criminal law.[4] But this statement does not touch on the question of whether the discovered criminality coincides with real criminality, and whether the knowledge acquired so far about the causes of criminality is based on the examination of *all* modes of behaviour counter to criminal law.

Criminality research must proceed from those offences which have been discovered and whose authors have been identified. But these are not identical with total criminality. For one thing the number of discovered offences is smaller, and, for another, the offender is not always discovered even when the offence is known. There is no doubt that the number of offences really committed is greater than the number discovered, whereby the undetected 'dark area' varies a good deal according to different types of offences but will eventually be all but eliminated by the increasing social efficiency of the struggle against crime.[5]

The fact that the number of discovered offences must not be equated with total criminality raises certain problems for research. It is necessary to include a possible existing 'dark area' in one's considerations and conclusions. It must not be assumed that the discovered offences are necessarily representative of criminality as a whole — even though this may be approximately true for certain groups of offences. It is not intended to pursue this problem any further — but it is important to realise that criminality research can proceed only from discovered offences even though it must take into account the existence of a 'dark area'.

Another problem arises from the fact that in the present book criminality research is treated as part of criminology. This raises the question of whether criminality research is the task of criminology alone or whether criminal law theory must also concern itself with similar researches. There is agreement nowadays on the point that socialist criminal law theory, like any other sociological discipline, conducts precise researches and uses appropriate methods for so doing. One such example is the extensive study conducted by criminal lawyers on behalf of a commission appointed by the GDR State Council for developing a new socialist criminal code.

Criminal law theory must investigate criminality in the light of its own research subject and must develop its own method. Criminology for its part must develop the methods and the theoretical problems of crime research methods in line with its own tasks.

Discussion of the relations between criminality research and the various scientific disciplines is necessary because it entails, for instance, demands as to the depth of cause research, and these demands in turn require appropriate methods. The still very common limitation of criminality research to the data obtained by investigation in the criminal proceedings results in an as yet inadequate depth and validity of analyses, with the result that the development of a system of crime prevention is impaired. Clarification of the demands made by criminology on cause research will lead to progress in research and to the evolution of new methods.

The investigation of criminality or, as formulated above, the discovery of its trends of development and of the causes of criminality is not identical with the subject of criminology as a special scientific discipline. This point has been made before. However, the question acquires a particular significance from the point of view of method. It is the task of criminological research to establish laws and regular patterns. It is not enough — as might be assumed — to collect and process empirical material. The laws to be discovered might be formulated as follows.

1 Regular correlations between criminality and the conditions for its existence in social reality and in the offender's individual sphere. These phenomena in their complexity represent conditions for an objective, real chance that criminal acts might occur.
2 Regularities governing the incidence and development of criminality and connected with the conditions for the existence of criminality. These regularities are manifest in their tendency; they are independent of the effectiveness of the struggle for the systematic reduction of criminality.

The core of criminological research is the investigation of the causes of criminality. Discovery of regular laws enables effective means and measures to be worked out by which the socialist State, and increasingly also the whole of society, may overcome the phenomena identified as causes of criminality. Wherever the historical prerequisites of this are still lacking there at least the negative effects should be paralysed.

To state that criminality follows certain laws does not mean that it is an inevitable phenomenon or that it will be automatically defeated. Similarly, the fact that the process of the struggle against criminality and its systematic overthrow is taking place in line with a social law through the deployment of the forces of socialist society must not be taken to mean

250

that with the further building of socialism criminality will disappear of its own volition without any special efforts or measures being necessary.[6] It is important to realise that under socialist conditions the relationship between objective social laws and deliberate social activity has undergone a change. To socialist society, whose objective requirements are being deliberately implemented by the work of the popular masses, under the guidance of State and social management organs, the development of specific means and methods of the struggle against criminality and for its systematic elimination has become an immediate vital need. In the solution of this task criminology in the GDR endeavours to achieve the greatest possible harmony between the objective laws and the subjective work of each member of society in the struggle against crime.

The principal aspect of the investigation of the operation of the laws determining criminality is not therefore — as is sometimes thought — simply the statistical trend of criminality but the relation between objective social law in a socialist society and deliberate social activity. Useful conclusions must therefore be derived not so much from the external aspect of the development of criminality, its statistical trends and external structure, but from the emerging connection between the inevitable building of a socialist society and the restriction of the causes of criminality through the deliberate activity of the population.[7]

This also reveals the second reason why criminality research focused on the discovery of laws, as outlined above, is not identical with the subject of criminology. Criminology instead must, by more extensive researches and theoretical generalisations, make its own contribution to crime prevention.[8]

This more comprehensive definition of its tasks in turn reveals the inportance of criminality research. The standard of its results is bound to affect the quality of the work for the development of a comprehensive system of crime prevention.

The methods to be applied in criminality research can first be divided, according to their nature, into methods capable of comprehending criminality phenomena, the factors underlying them, their incidence and the closeness of the connections, and methods based upon the above serving the discovery of regular correlations from the process data. This distinction at the same time reveals the relationship between the subject of research, the views on this subject and the method of its investigation.

The unity of the research method is illustrated also by a retrospective look at the development of the theory of causes in the GDR and the methods applied at each stage to this research. While the whole of criminality and the individual offence were still regarded as an expression of the class struggle the problem of the causes was relatively simple to define; there was no need for extensive empirical investigations of the phenomena which in our socialist society contribute to the occurence of criminality. All fundamental questions were essentially solved by the deductive method. The exact investigations carried out at that time were therefore confined to a structural analysis of the phenomena. Criminal law research did not sufficiently concern itself with the frequency of factors relating to offenders or to their development and way of life in order to draw definite criminal law conclusions from such data.

Only when such an over-simplification was set aside and the thesis which had prevented an effective struggle against crime was overcome, did specific scientific criminality research, in particular cause research, move into the foreground, allowing the deeper roots of criminality to be investigated by a variety of methods in their total complexity, in their social connections and interactions. Special methods were developed, such as criminological fact finding. Moreover, methods familiar from sociology and psychology were suitably modified to fit the special subject of criminology and were thus turned into criminological research methods.

This now almost historical illustration of the connection between subject and method takes us to the present-day view that the causes of criminality are a complex of very diverse phenomena of both a social and an individual nature.[9]

If the offence is generally seen as the result of disturbed relations between the person concerned and society then it becomes obvious that all the aspects of an individual, social as well as natural ones, may play a part. The offence is conditioned in a multiple and complex manner. It follows, therefore, that criminality must be the subject of all scientific disciplines which study man in his social rôle and function as well as the natural relationships entailed. This requires a great variety of procedures. Criminology, as a complex science, likewise needs an appropriate method, which means that further demands must be made on the system of procedures to be created. However, this particular scientific disipline is still in its infancy and it is not therefore possible as yet to present its entire system of procedures.

We have already characterised the importance which the research method has for the state of knowledge of criminology; we have now tried to show that each research subject and the views held on it in turn determine the research procedures and their systematisation. Summing up, we can therefore state that the methods follow the progress that is being made in understanding criminality and its causes, and that theory occupies the decisive place as against method.[10] A further reflection which follows from the above is that criminality is not a homogeneous entity. It is differentiated according to the nature of the different groups of offences. We need only refer to the fundamental differences between offences against the State and so-called general crime. These must be taken into account in the further development, choice and systematisation of research procedures. Thus the decisive social causes of offences against the State — causes essentially located outside the GDR — must be investigated by different methods from those applied to the social roots of, for instance, offences against socialist property. In consequence, different specialised investigations are needed for crimes against the State — even on the part of economists and sociologists — from those concerned with offences against property.

Finally, the demands made on methods and the methods themselves must change as the character of criminality itself changes. The overwhelming majority of all offences has changed in character with the abolition of the essential socio-economic foundations of criminality inside the GDR. This necessitated the development of appropriate procedures, or else their adaptation to the subject under research and the changes it had undergone. The methods, therefore, must follow the objective movements of the subject itself, or be so developed and adapted that the subject is comprehended in its evolution.

Philosophical premises of exact criminality research

Application of a system of procedures as the premise of the discovery of internal laws

The typical feature of criminality research in the GDR is its orientation towards society and its requirements. Increasing emphasis is placed on the investigation of the social determination of criminality and the struggle against its roots is increasingly linked with the social development in our Republic. This is in line with the basic teachings and conclusions of the classical authors of Marxism—Leninism about the social and individual processes underlying social misbehaviour and about their liquidation in the course of the building of socialism — and subsequently of communism — and also with the findings of various sociological disciplines. [11] To discharge its social mission, criminality research must reveal the connections existing between criminality and other phenomena in the social and individual circumstances as well as in the offender's person. 'The first and most basic rule of scientific research generally and of Marxist dialectics in particular demands the investigation ... of the connection.'[12]

This rule applies both to the investigation of the individual infringe-ments of criminal law and to the analysis of a totality of phenomena, as represented by criminality as a whole or by various crime categories. It is, moreover, essential to discover those correlations which possess the char-acter of laws and to determine why criminal offences are still being com-mitted under our social conditions, and what laws govern the trends in criminality. Only when these laws have been discovered can criminology proceed beyond the mere collection of empirical data, as still frequently found in analyses, and organise effective methods of crime prevention. [13]

The literature of cause theory contains convincing proof that a limita-tion of criminological research to the discovery of causal connections fails to meet the requirements for the discovery of internal laws. [14] The causal connection, i.e. the direct linking of one phenomenon to another, [15] is not the same as the law governing such connections. The causal connection contains no information on the quality of the connection. [16] Both neces-sary and accidental phenomena alike are causally determined. [17] To dis-cover the laws governing these connections one must go beyond the mere statement of causal relations. On the other hand, the discovery of the internal laws governing these connections is possible only if the causal law is taken into account. It is necessary to apply the Marxist—Leninist doc-trine about the various forms of the relations comprehensively and, pro-ceeding from the determined nature of all phenomena and processes (determinism), to extract the law-determined connections. [18] The concept of law-determined connections is applied here in the sense of internal, essential, necessary and stable (general) connections. [19]

The identification of internal relations between two or more phenom-ena necessarily requires a well-founded theoretical position. This founda-tion is Marxism—Leninism, the scientific generalisation of the practical experiences gained in the building of socialism in the GDR, as enshrined primarily in the documents of the Socialist Unity Party of Germany (SED), and finally, proceeding from this basis, the scientific doctrine of the causes of criminality. The system of procedures, moreover, is deter-mined also by the character of the relations to be investigated. Mechanical concepts of the laws governing criminality have already been criticised and refuted in criminological literature.[20] The view is now generally held that criminality, in its incidence and in its dynamics, is governed by laws of statistical character, unlike the dynamic laws of classical physics. [21]

Only a large number of criminal offences — each individual offence being accidental — makes it possible to discover the laws underlying them. As Klaus puts it:

Statistical laws make no statement about separate individuals or individual events. They are statements about classes of individuals or events. The law of the declining profit rate in capitalism, discovered by Marx, is such a statistical law. It does not state anything about the actual decline of the profit rate in a particular capitalist country at a particular moment. Indeed, in certain cases the profit rate may even temporarily rise. The law merely states that, from an overall view, there is a tendency for the profit rate to decline. Similar statistical laws also underlie the premium computation of insurance companies. It may be found, for instance ... that out of a thousand motor cars a certain percentage is involved in road accidents each year and that such accident involves a certain average cost. Since no definite statement is made about the individual person or the individual event we speak of the probability of an event taking place ... [22]

The laws underlying criminality, therefore, can never state more than the possibility of the occurrence of crime, given the presence of certain conditions (and interactions), whereby this is only one of several possibilities from among which springs the probability of an individual member of society behaving in a particular way. In other words — unless one wishes to fall into the error of a mechanical concept of causality which excludes all accidents — no statement can in fact be made on who will behave in a criminal manner or when or where. [23]

Among the laws governing man's day-to-day behaviour criminological research identifies those which, if present and interacting, make a criminal offence one of the possible modes of behaviour. This realisation then enables socialist society and its State to liquidate criminality systematically by changing its vital conditions.

In terms of method this means that the law-determined connections have to be identified on the basis of exact analyses of individual criminal offences, on the basis of a comprehensive study of a large number of cases, and by abstraction from these. 'To discover a statistical law a large mass of chance occurrences [i.e. criminal offences] must be investigated. The law of large numbers reflects the dialectical connection between chance and necessity.'[24]

From abstraction of the general features from individual data, of the necessary and essential features from a multitude of facts which in the individual case characterise the multiple causal relations as cause and effect or conditions of effect, and from the multiplicity of interactions among causal relations, there emerge the general laws which we may describe as the components of the complex of conditions of an offence.

A circumstance which in one case of criminal action has been shown as its cause may appear merely as the condition in other cases, or vice versa,[25] or, having been an accidential, unique and non-recurrent event, may not occur in other cases at all. Reduction of a diversity to its common denominators, its general, essential and indispensable aspects, presupposes statistics. From these the laws can then be derived by theoretical processing.

In this cognitive procedure we embrace certain connections, next relate them to criminality and its dynamics, combine these numerous components and calculate their correlations by statistical mathematical methods.[26] Moreover, we record the interactions between these definite connections and other phenomena of reality. This is important because the law itself is likewise just one element of the universal interaction.

The recording of law-determined connections requires the development of a system of combinable components with whose aid the structure of the phenomenon of criminality may be revealed. At present, most of the studies have failed to go beyond the details of the manifestations of an offence, or the details of the offender's personality[27] or beyond such very general terms as inadequate attitude to work, lack of discipline and shortcomings in the management of an enterprise. What is needed is components accurately reflecting the reality hidden behind such general labels, components which are capable of quantitative treatment and which will provide information on the internal structure of the offence and, following generalisation and theoretical processing, of the category of similar offences.

Closely linked with these are other shortcomings in the comprehension of reality. The phenomena which we confront in our cognitive process are objectively real. Causality, law and interactions all exist objectively, outside consciousness. This circumstance is still sometimes ignored in the development of the components referred to, which are then instead based on subjective assessments. Thus statistics and analyses of crimes against property sometimes state what percentage of offenders have to be seen as lazy workers or tending towards excessive consumption of alcohol, etc., with the object of determining the offender's attitude to work and, beyond this, his state of consciousness. It would be more correct to develop criteria which could yield information on a person's mode of behaviour towards objective relations (towards work, towards socialist property, etc.) and his ideas on these. But these criteria are not being determined. No precise definition is supplied of what is meant by 'lazy work' or 'excessive consumption of alcohol'. There is no telling whether these terms correctly reflect what they are supposed to cover and express. In what way and to what extent does a certain behaviour deviate from normal behaviour? (Come to that, whose behaviour is normal behaviour?). In practice the circumstances are assessed, in each individual case, on the basis of subjective experience and impressions. This is bound to result in imprecision in the abstraction.

Analyses of the roots of juvenile offences, for instance, frequently point out that a certain percentage of the juveniles came from one-parent families. This, under the heading of difficulties in upbringing or shortcomings in the juvenile's social adjustment as reflected in his offence, is then regarded as a real criterion. The assumption is thus made that this is an objective, general, essential and inevitable correlation. But if the fact that a young person comes from a single-parent family is equated with 'inadequate upbringing' then this is a subjectivist assessment. It is necessary to identify those components which render it possible to make statements in line with objective reality. But this clarification must precede analysis. [28]

These tasks of criminality research presuppose that procedures are applied which: (a) enable the individual offences to be analysed in depth and all connections to be laid bare together with their social and individual conditions (various procedures of interrogation, observation, etc.); (b) enable the frequency, the dynamics and the degree of the various connections to be established (chiefly statistical and mathematical methods); (c) enable laws and interrelationships to be identified (theoretical analysis and generalisation mainly in accordance with materialist-dialectical methods). These three categories also refer to the range of validity of the statements arrived at by these procedures.

The variant listed under (a) allows statements to be made about criminal offences and the phenomena determining them, on the basis of our existing criminological views and concepts. This does not mean that this state of research is lagging behind in importance. As the facts to be recorded are organised according to concepts they are, in a sense, already generalised, classified and systematised. Whenever interrogation takes place by questionnaire additional points arise in connection with the use of these methods and possible sources of error. The result of any research vitally depends on the degree to which the method is mastered and hence on the accuracy of the result obtained. It is a fact that these methods cannot embrace the internal relationships. This can be done only by way of theoretical processing. Referring to Hegel's distinction between intellect and reason, Engels observed:

Hegel's distinction, under which only dialectical thinking is reasonable, has a certain point. All activities of the intellect — induction,

257

deduction, hence also abstraction ... analysis of unfamiliar objects (the mere cracking of a nut is the beginning of analysis), synthesis (clever tricks performed by animals) and, combining the two, experimentation (in the face of new obstacles and in unfamiliar situations) — all these we share with the animals. In their nature all these procedures — i.e. all means of scientific research recognised by ordinary logic — are entirely the same in man and the higher animals. They differ only in degree (i.e. the development of the method in question). The basic features of the method are the same and lead to the same results in man and animals so long as both apply and confine themselves to these elementary methods. Dialectical thought, on the other hand — just because it presupposes the examination of the nature of the concepts themselves — is possible only to man, and then only on a relatively high level of development ... not reaching its full development by modern philosophy until much later ... . [29]

These reflections emphasise the importance of theoretical conclusions. At the same time they show that the different methods must not be absolutely opposed one to the other.

The statistical procedures of the second group (b), for instance, are analytical devices enabling us to identify the common features underlying a multitude of criminal offences. We are dealing here with a generalisation of medium degree. With these methods conclusions are reached about the stability of connections. This is, therefore an intermediate stage on the road to theoretical analysis and generalisation.

As for the statistical methods, it should be pointed out that their full potential is not yet being sufficiently utilised in criminilogical research. At the same time we must always remember their limitations. Marx's remark, quoted by P. Lafargue and frequently cited in statistical works, that 'a science cannot be regarded as fully developed until it has reached a point where it can use mathematics', [30] must not be taken to mean that statistical and mathematical procedures, however useful, can replace a thorough theoretical analysis of the material. They are not sufficient for an understanding of its inner dialectical nature, though that is precisely what is needed for determining the means and methods of an effective struggle against crime. It is in its attitude to this important methodological problem that our socialist position differs essentially from that of bourgeois criminologists; this, too, is a refelction of our divergent view of criminality and its causes. [31]

Theoretical analysis, generalisation and verification, together with the procedures used in all these, are not specific to criminological research. Thus extrapolation, interpolation, deduction and reduction, as well as mathematical dialectics, are used in all scientific disciplines since all these disciplines are concerned with the discovery of natural or social laws. Without the application of Marxist—Leninist philosophy it is impossible to understand the nature of criminality. This is not the place to discuss the problem of those scientists who, while not recognising the dialectical method, come to scientific conclusions whenever they apply it at least unconsciously. As the theoretical procedures[32] are not specific to criminology we may confine ourselves here to the statement that without their application criminological research cannot develop into a real science capable of freeing society from the evil of criminality.

It should also be pointed out that an absolute confrontation of the three listed groups of procedures does damage to research. The first two procedures are applied on the basis of an appropriate theory. That theory determines the starting point of research, the research programme, the contents and the process of a criminological examination, etc. On the other hand, that theory will only be free from subjectivism if it rests upon a strict examination of facts.

Critique of the method of bourgeois criminologists

An examination of the method of bourgeois criminology at this point is intended chiefly to show up its rational elements and to mark out the limits within which certain methodological conclusions and practices can be utilised for criminality research in the German Democratic Republic. In doing so it is useful to concentrate on those criminologists who proceed from the relations between the offender and his circumstances, because we ourselves are concerned with procedures serving the investigation of this area and because, moreover, speculative theories can hardly provide starting points for methods useful in practice.

The reprensentatives of speculative theories[33] in bourgeois criminology for the most part proceed from the view that criminality is rooted in a specific heredity, in an inherited biological peculiarity of the offender, i.e. in certain psychological states detached from society. Upon this view are then based special diagnostic procedures, such as anamnesis for the purpose of prediction, a method which totally or very largely disregards social implications. The assumption that criminality is essentially rooted in parts of an isolated internal system, i.e. in inherited characteristics, logically leads to a disregard of the offender's social relations and their conditioning by the system of society. Because the method is subordinated to this concept it lacks — as its practitioners admit — all 'sociological' procedures.

The representatives of empirically oriented theories in bourgeois criminology, on the other hand, apply a multitude of 'sociological' research procedures which are already highly developed and sophisticated and have furnished a mass of interesting data. However, in examining their methods it is always necessary to ask to what extent these research procedures, the way they are applied, or the views on their limits of application, are based on unscientific doctrines and views of criminality. An uncritical adoption of the research procedures of bourgeois criminologists might lead us to a one-sided or mechanistic view and even into the realm of bourgeois philosophy. At the Ninth Plenary Meeting of the SED Central Committee Hager said:

> The pursuit of the central sociological research programme has revealed important ideological problems ... in particular, a number of our sociologists have shown an uncritical attitude to the terminology and methodology of bourgeois sociology. Such concepts of bourgeois sociology as 'formal group', 'informal group', 'field of tension', 'micro and macro-structures', 'structure line',etc., are being adopted uncritically and described as common currency of sociological and socio-psychological theory ... There is no class-indifferent, non-partisan ideological foundation of sociology that is common to socialism and capitalism. The present critical dialogue with bourgeois sociology must also include the critique of its categories and concepts, though of course rational problems and elements of bourgeois sociological methods and techniques should usefully be applied in our own researches. [34]

We shall now give an example of the method of empirically oriented bourgeois criminologists in order to try to define the theoretical positions associated with it. Mergen in his 'methodology of criminal—biological investigations' [35] provides a comprehensive survey of the criminological research methods of that trend among criminologists whose work has led to some important conclusions about the causes of criminality in West Germany. His exposition may be regarded as representative also of the methods of other West German researchers of the empirical school.

Mergen emphasises the importance of investigation questionnaires for both individual and mass investigations of the causes of criminal offences. They form the basis both of multiple individual investigations and of their subsequent statistical processing. These investigation questionnaires are not identical with our own data-collecting questionnaires (which serve the compilation of data already established) but instead seek to discover various items of information.

The investigation consists of two phases:

1 collection of basic data (environment, heredity, past criminal record, family, etc.),
2 observation and investigation of the examinee, analytical and synthetic processing of the case, and conclusions. [36]

The questionnaires serve analysis and synthesis in both the above phases. They are drawn up in accordance with appropriate correlation systems or problem areas and are completed by scientists of various disciplines and by laymen. The first form is sent to the mayor of the municipality where the examinee was born or is resident. The questions contained in it concern the civic status of the examinee, his occupation, his financial circumstances, his behaviour, his moral qualities and his psychological make-up. In the case of juveniles the questionnaire is adapted to the specific problems of juveniles. This form makes it possible to question any person who may be in a position of providing information about the examinee.

A second form serves the establishment of the examinee's domestic environment, the pre-history of his personality development, of his way of life and of the peculiarities of his personality at the time in question. This questionnaire also asks for a report on his criminal offence, together with conclusions and suggestions. Mergen notes on this point:

> As far as possible, these sociological investigations and inquiries should be made by trained personnel. The form is sociologically oriented and moves about a nucleus consisting of mesological data. The examinee's personality is here related ontogenetically to the general environment surrounding the examinee, and correlations are established with the special environment chosen for himself by the examinee. [37]

A third form is addressed to the prosecutor's office concerned with the case, and supplies various criminological data. These include an extract from the criminal register as well as account of the examinee's criminal offence and his behaviour in the course of the criminal proceedings. This form is suitably modified in the case of minors or juveniles.

The fourth form concerns what is known as scholarity. This is addressed to the inspector of education concerned and provides information on the examinee's physical and mental development, his behaviour and social integration. This form is supplemented by further sociological data. The information provided by it commands a high degree of objectivity as the data are collected and formulated by experienced educationists and psychologists.

A fifth form is addressed to the director of the penal institution and supplies observation of the offender during detention. The questions differ in the case of adults and juveniles.

A sixth form is completed by the prison medical officer. It contains general medical check-up data and analyses, as well as any further examinations and analyses resulting from diagnosis, together with conclusions.

In the second phase the investigations are conducted both analytically and synthetically. According to Mergen they are sub-divided into three main categories:

1 Anamnesis, comprising family anamnesis and personal anamnesis, thus providing a longitudinal section.
2 The present state, comprising the findings and conclusions of clinical and so-called technical examinations, thus representing a cross-section.
3 Synthesis is a compilation of all results, together with conclusions, criminal-biological diagnosis and social prediction.

These three groups are contained in one main questionnaire. This is sub-divided into three sections and is supplemented by simultaneous investigations in different directions. [38]

The methodological procedures described by Mergen, his account of the methods to be applied and his justification of the rôle of statistical analysis are all based on the view that criminal offences are the result of an interaction of criminogenic environmental and dispositional factors. Mergen expressly concludes that sociological methods must on no account be excluded from environmental research. The offender's disposition and environment, he states, must be investigated with the same thoroughness. Nor must such an investigation stop at the findings. Instead the results must be correlated to each other and interrelations discovered. [39]

This view shows Mergen to be proceeding within the framework of the basic formula of bourgeois criminology as developed by Mezger and, so it appears, accepted by most West German criminologists. According to Mezger a crime is the product of the offender's disposition-related and development-determined personality and of his personality-moulding and deed-moulding environment. [40] Mergen's acceptance of this view is clear also from his understanding of the rôle of statistics and its limitations. On this point he has this to say:

Even if, for instance, alcoholism or imbecility, social circumstances or other characteristics have been linked with criminal behaviour by means of this tool, nothing of any substance has thereby been achieved. The real connections between the criminogenic factors, their cross-influences and interactions, their dynamics upon confrontation, etc., all of which are important for criminogenesis, have as yet scarcely been tackled. Thus statistics may find that a high percentage of delinquents comes from a bad social environment without solving the question of the primacy of this characteristic. Did the offender turn criminal because he came from a bad environment or did he get into a bad environment because he was prone to criminality.[41]

The line of investigation, the research method and the manner in which its findings are processed are all determined by Mergen's concept. The above-listed data and their subsequent interpretation reflect the fact that criminal offences are being isolated from the existing capitalist society and from the processes stemming from its foundations. They are, as a matter of principle, investigated from the point of view of the individual offender. Even the investigation of social connections ultimately only serves a better knowledge of the offender. Criminality is seen as the sum of individual isolated and accidental actions. [42]

The procedure and method described by Mergen are applied in a large number of separate criminological studies. [43] These too show that criminality research proceeds solely from the aspect of the offender. Social, physical and biological phenomena are described and understood as isolated more or less independently acting forces, and this assigns to them a character which does not in fact attach to them. Plekhanov first pointed out, in characterising such a theory, that 'the activity of social man is being chopped up and its various aspects and manifestations are being transformed into some special forces which allegedly determine society's social evolution'. [44] It follows from the concept of bourgeois factor theory that the statistical and other exact procedures serving the investigation of social processes are used in order to lend a downright independent character to individual characteristics and groups of characteristics. What really matters is that these procedures should be used as an instrument for the most accurate possible reflection of social processes.

Whenever we refer to the connections between criminality and social processes we mean those basic connections which characterise, shape and determine social life and the development of society itself. The application of Marxist philosophy as a method and simultaneously as the foundation of each individual discipline demands that individual connections should be placed in the context of the general connections, especially of decisive connections. Without a reduction of the discovered connections to decisive ones, i.e. to production relations, it is impossible to proceed beyond the stage of the study of surface phenomena or to discover the decisive laws and nature of criminality. The bourgeois criminologists, however, stop at the application — albeit a highly polished application — of exact procedures, in particular of statistical and mathematical procedures. Their work lacks the next stage — the scientific generalisation of the conclusions arrived at.

West German criminologists frequently demand that criminology should be freed from philosophy and history; this means that a non-historical and society-unrelated approach is being raised to the status of a theory. Deliberately or unconsciously the fact is being overlooked that a specific criminological statement acquires general scientific value not by being torn out of its historical context but only by being placed in it.

West German criminologists have expressed the opinion that the thesis that criminality can be liquidated and that, along with the building of socialist society, it can be systematically forced back, is not scientifically founded and that all criminality research in the GDR is only pursuing the aim of buttressing this thesis. They overlook the fact that we are dealing here not with some narrow criminological conclusion but with the results of a comprehensive scientific analysis of society and its political and economic evolution. The successful struggle against crime presupposes a scientific processing of the accumulated material. But this is primarily a question of the correct system of reference, of overcoming the limitations imposed upon themselves by bourgeois criminologists, such as regarding the existing social conditions as taboo and — often unwittingly — sanctifying them.

Bourgeois criminologist, from their position, are unable to comprehend that the analysis of social developmental processes and their connections with criminality and its developments lead to the scientifically founded view that criminality can be liquidated and that the decisive prerequisites for this are being created by the development of socialist democracy.[45] The scientific sterility of bourgeois criminology is reflected basically in its earlier absolutisation of poverty as a criminogenic factor, and now of prosperity as the soil on which the frightening development of criminality is taking place in the Federal Republic. The view that, on the strength of present knowledge, the earlier thesis of criminality from poverty is no longer tenable is likewise only a half truth. Neither the poverty nor the prosperity of certain sections of the population is the root of the growing criminal infestation of bourgeois-imperialist society. Its causes can be identified only when the social connections, as objectively existing and developing, are investigated and understood.

The statement that bourgeois criminologists ignore the historical aspect does not mean that many among them are not engaged in historical investigations. However, these historical reflections are conducted in isolation from the social soil. They are subordinated to the fundamental positivist position of these criminologists. This is a shortcoming that has marked bourgeois criminology from its very beginnings. Freud, for instance, because of some particularly marked neurological phenomena in bourgeois women who had committed criminal offences, applied certain diagnostic procedures. But his well-known conclusions concerning the causes of such criminality missed the circumstance that the neurological facts discovered by him were connected with the circumstances and the way of life of these women, and that they were in turn linked with the social relations of the bourgeoisie. Although Freud's work reflects an unconsciously historical approach, for instance in the adaptation of his investigation procedures to a changed subject of research, he nevertheless lacked the scientific socio-historical approach.

Measured against the real system of reference which also underlies socialist criminology, the results of bourgeois criminology are no more than a photograph of criminality and its causes. Such a superficial consideration and the theoretical limitations underlying it must result in speculative assumptions or else condemn criminology to impotence and surrender to crime.

Although the research methods applied by the empirically oriented criminologists are all conditioned by a system of reference in line with their basic concepts, which are ultimately focused on the isolated individual, they have in fact developed or adopted a number of methods and techniques which can also be used by us in phenomenological investigations of criminality and which can be fruitful to us provided their application rests on a genuinely scientific foundation. This applies also to those methods which do not belong to criminology proper, such as statistical and mathematical procedures, but which are used by bourgeois criminologists, even though within the limits of their theoretical concepts. The philosophical method, on the other hand, which is so important to socialist criminologists, is rejected by the methodology of bourgeois criminologists; in consequence their results are bound to be limited. That is also why the thesis that it is one of the tasks of criminology either to verify all its findings and individual results by further investigations (i.e. to confirm them as true) or to falsify them (to label them as incorrect hypotheses) cannot be accepted. [46] That thesis is scientific only in so far as it applies to individual data or empirical findings concerning a definite criminal phenomenon. The obligation of verification or falsification exists in all fields of research up to a medium degree of generalisation. However, the thesis is untenable and must be rejected when related to the foundations of criminological theory formulation or to philosophical method. These foundations and this philosophical method are based not merely on the results of a single scientific discipline but also upon the results of all scientific disciplines, and they comprise the laws according to which nature, society and thought develop. Individual criminological results cannot therefore simply falsify those theoretical foundations. Such a demand amounts, at best, to harmful scepticism, or to its philosophical basis, positivism, which impedes an effective struggle against crime.

The methods of bourgeois criminology and the positions underlying them are anchored in its scientific attitude to criminality and to the existing society itself. They are a reflection of the view that criminality is a phenomenon that is eternally linked with the life of society, the price, in a manner of speaking, that has to be paid as the price for the 'freedom' in bourgeois society. The concepts and the methodology are reflections of resignation or surrender in the face of criminality and its social mainsprings. Socialist criminological methodology, on the other hand, springs from the realistic and optimistic view that criminality can be removed from the life of society. This view is based on the historic experience formulated by Marx and Engels as long as a hundred years ago. [47]

The scientific system of reference in criminality research and a few methodological consequences

Contrary to the views of bourgeois criminologists it has been stated that scientific criminality research, if it is to serve the purpose of systematically eliminating criminality, must trace the connections down to the social foundations, to the production relations. Scheler observes on this point:

> The law is thus, first of all, contained in the fact that the multiplicity has a single source. Marx stated that such diverse phenomena as production, distribution, exchange and consumption were all 'links of one totality, diversities within a unity' [Marx/Engels, *Works* (German edition) vol. 13, Berlin 1961, page 630]. The unity of the world, however — hence also of social existence as a totality — consist in its materiality. The materiality of social reality is the foundation of its necessary, essential, inherent connection. The unified determination of social phenomena is based upon the reduction of all

social phenomena and relations to the fundamental material relations. That is why social phenomena cannot be considered or investigated in isolation from each other, in separation from the general foundation of their existence and their interconnection. A scientific comprehension of social phenomena presupposes an analysis of the connection pattern governing the totality of social relations and requires the reduction of all these relations to the simplest and most primordial of relations, the production relations, which fundamentally determine the character of any given social formation. [48]

This represents a basic orientation towards the universality and depth of the relationships to be investigated. It follows, for instance, that an examination of the relationships between offences against property in the construction industry and the individual's way of thinking, habits, criteria of educational or cultural standards, specific working conditions, family circumstances, etc., must not stop at these data. It is necessary instead to comprehend the essential connections down to the basic relations of our society, the production relations.

The importance of this thesis does not, by reducing the components of criminal phenomena to socialist production relations, confine itself to establishing that criminality and the motive forces underlying it are alien to the nature of socialism. We are dealing with a far more complex set of problems, as the following reflections will show:

(a) In our literature we still frequently find studies which confine themselves to comparing criminal phenomena in the GDR with criminal phenomena in the German Federal Republic; such a comparison is unsatisfactory unless it is related to the social foundations prevailing in each of the countries. An isolated comparison of external phenomena amounts to the bourgeois positivist method. The method of comparison naturally presupposes comparable phenomena, i.e. it requires the essential differences to be identified from the start.

(b) The comparison of criminal phenomena or their isolated serial development in the GDR is insufficient to the discovery of the laws underlying them. No comprehensive scientific conclusions can be drawn from the incidence, the structure or the distribution of offences among the various age groups alone. The following examples will illustrate this.

The criminal statistics for 1963 reported a 51·8 per cent share of 14 to 25-year-old offenders in the total crime figures. Broken down into various age groups the figures were: 14 to 16 years, 5·1 per cent; 16 to 18, 8·6 per cent; 18 to 21, 17·7 per cent; 21 to 25, 20·4 per cent. [49]

If these figures were now to be compared — and this is still being done

— with a view to discovering the highest incidence of offences such an approach would be faulty for a number of reasons. For one thing, the rules of comparability are violated by the different lengths of the intervals compared — these vary from two to four years. For another thing, neither the absolute crime figures nor the percentage figures are comparable, for the reason that they do not relate uniformly to the proportions of the various age groups in the overall population. If the frequency of criminal law infringements is related to 100,000 of the population in the above age groups (or to smaller units) we find a totally different picture. The coefficient for these age groups in 1963 was as follows: 14 to 16 years, 1,224; 16 to 18, 2,608; 18 to 21, 2,323; 21 to 25, 1,624.

This shows the main incidence of criminal offences to lie unquestioningly with the age group from 16 to 18. [50] The statistics for 1965 show a similar picture. The figures per 100,000 of the population in the different age groups are: 14 to 16 years, 836; 16 to 18, 2,026; 18 to 21, 2,476; 21 to 25, 1,681. [51]

The computation of the coefficient provides a basis for certain conclusions. Their value, admittedly, is limited as they contain information on the phenomena only and not on their nature.

It must further be remembered that the coefficients thus calculated are based on age groups which, though consecutive, nevertheless reflect different processes. In the case of offenders between 14 and 16 and also between 16 and 18, for instance, account must be taken of the peculiarities of biological and psychological development associated with those age groups; these are changes which bear on the varying degree of maturity among juveniles. The next two age groups are associated with full integration in the production process, which takes place with the completion of the eighteenth year, and also with the earlier attainment of majority, the foundation of a family, etc. It is clear, therefore, that no essential or profound conclusions can be drawn from the coefficients or their comparison.

A scientific analysis requires that the discovered components of offences investigated should be related to the concrete conditions of development in our socialist society and to their reflection in the typical or normal behaviour of GDR citizens. Thus it is necessary to relate conditions underlying crimes against property in the construction industry, committed by offenders between 18 and 21, to the following: first, to inclinations, attitudes and usages: second, to working and living conditions, including the production relations, of young non-offenders of the same age group in the construction industry, and in socialist society generally, as reflected by the information available about our socialist younger generation.

Only such a comparison can correctly reflect reality and enable the significance and functions of the components to be correctly assessed, so that the causes of criminality may be overcome by a comprehensive system of struggle against criminality.

The need to relate the various components to the so-called normal behaviour of socialist man must not be understood to mean that this normal behaviour is some subjectively established 'average'. The normal behaviour cannot, therefore, be determined on just any construction site because the thinking and behaviour of the building workers on such a site may very well reflect a behaviour that is atypical of present-day conditions. Genuine normal behaviour is directly connected with the laws of social evolution; it is the thinking and behaviour of the individual, in line with the attained stage of social development and the requirements springing therefrom. It is manifested, in particular, in the observance and realisation of socialist law and of socialist norms of behaviour.

This so-called normal behaviour is investigated principally by sociologists. But as the required sociological findings are still lacking in many areas the question arises of what data could or should be used at present, alongside and in conjunction with theoretical considerations, within the framework of criminological investigations. Such data are available in the form of the documents and analyses of the Socialist Unity Party of Germany, the State bodies and institutions, and social organisations. These various bodies and institutions possess, for instance, analyses of the evolution of productive forces, the performance and the awareness of the working people in various fields of production and in individual factories. These bodies, furthermore, possess studies of conditions in residential areas. Similarly, use should be made of the statistical data of central and local bodies of the State Central Statistical Board and of other administrative and economic management bodies, since such data can reveal the gradual development of modes of behaviour and consciousness in the individual's production life and outside it. On this basis, and beyond it, the experience of officials working in diverse fields should be generalised and systematised because, in conjunction with other objective data, these allow valid conclusions to be drawn. Furthermore, greater use should be made of the findings of other scientific disciplines. Finally, the judiciary organs and their employees likewise possess a store of useful information. This is gained by the functionaries of judiciary organs mainly through collaboration with other bodies and institutions, by participation in standing committees, etc. Last but not least, the normal behaviour manifests itself in a variety of ways in the criminal proceedings themselves, in the confrontation of the offender with the views of his groups and their demands, and also in connection with the statements of social prosecutors and the acceptance of guarantees for the offender's future good behaviour.

Establishment of the correlation between the various statements and the social law itself within the framework of criminality research makes it possible to achieve a high level of theoretical processing of the regularities discovered. The results achieved to a large extent meet the demand for the development of effective crime prevention. They are indeed the necessary prerequisite of any comprehensive system of crime prevention.

In the field of research into the causes of juvenile crime, for instance, scientific findings have been greatly extended. In a paper on trends in juvenile criminality in Germany and their causes Lekschas comes to the conclusion that the causes of juvenile crime are not in any way special causes whose abolition would by themselves solve the problem.

> The term, in fact, comprises phenomena which emerge in the process of the formation of the juvenile's personality and which result if the development of an 'internal' socialist controlled system of social action is disturbed or deformed in a young person .... [They cause him to] succumb to influences which lead to anti-social, objectively harmful and criminal, or indeed anti-legal behaviour, i.e. to the development within him of views of life which, as 'internal' norms of behaviour, conceal within them the possibility of antisocial or even society-endangering modes of behaviour. Investigation of the causes of juvenile criminality related to the development of personality or to certain negative personality features ... leads us to the problem of young people developing an awareness of social responsibility. This to us seems to be the central problem of the causes of juvenile criminality. This is not an educational problem in the narrow sense but a problem of inter-relations between child and society, or young person and society. [52]

Streit arrived at a similar generalisation: 'The central problem of the causes of juvenile crime is clearly the conflict-accompanied development by young people of an awareness of social responsibility. This is not an educational problem in the narrow sense but a problem of interrelations between growing and developing young people and society'. [53]

Investigations of crimes against property in the construction industry have led to the identification of the problems which must be placed at the centre of any effective crime prevention. Thus it is predominantly young

270

people who appear as the offenders in crimes against property in this sphere of the economy. The roots of their misdemeanour go back to negative influences in their childhood and early youth which disturbed the evolution of the socialist personality of these young people. Inadequate subsequent care by society for the socialist development of these juveniles further promoted these negative features. Additional factors were shortcomings at the construction site, especially in the political and ideological shaping, development and education of the juveniles.

In the area of adult criminality in the construction industry the crucial problem lies chiefly in the inadequate acquisition of socialist habits and views. A positive change in this field requires first of all that industrial management should realise the error of the idea that production can be organised in isolation from human beings. [54] This process is taking place on an increasing scale in connection with the discussion of the new principles of management in socialist enterprises and is conditioned by the requirements of social evolution as a whole.

The tasks of analysis of individual violations of the criminal law

It has already been stated that crime research conducted from a criminological point of view makes different demands also on the analysis of the individual offence, its causes and conditions, from those made by criminal law theory. In the individual criminal proceedings these demands cannot always be met. Moreover, the findings are frequently also unsatisfactory for other reasons. It is a well-known fact that the standard of investigation of definite causal connections by the investigatory authorities is not always up to the requirements of a comprehensive establishment of the roots of an offence. It must always be remembered that all the investigations conducted in the course of criminal proceedings serve one specific aim and have to be concluded within definite time limits, and that the social task of crime prevention cannot be performed, as it were, 'on the offender's back'. This would only make him the object of extraneous interests. At the same time it is necessary to arrive at a social analysis of the vital conditions governing an individual's development, showing how essential external effects are processed by him and why they are processed in a particular way. Criminological research thus requires additional scientific analyses, in which various disciplines and organisations must participate. These would also offset any shortcoming that might exist in an analysis worked out in the course of the criminal proceedings themselves. The development of investigatory models might prove a useful aid to those engaged in investigation for improving the pattern of their inquiries. [55] On the other hand, the use of questionnaires in the collection of background information has also proved most successful.

The 'Juvenile Criminology' research group's questionnaire on the personality and development of juvenile first offenders and recidivists, for instance, elicits the following data on the offender's personality:

(a) Motives of the offender (socially determined causes)	1	To gain prestige and respect
	2	To show off, to impress
	3	Pity
	4	Revenge
	5	Envy
	6	Sexual motives, including jealousy
	7	Permanent conflict with parents
	8	Permanent conflict at place of work
	9	Political and ideological causes
	10	Unknown
Motives of the offender (object-determined causes)	1	Striving for achievement
	2	Striving for possessions
	3	Comfort
	4	Enjoyment
	5	Urge for excitement (adventure)
	6	Immaturity
	7	Sexual curiosity
	8	Urge for independence
	9	Unknown [56]
(b) Offender's social activity	1	Active
	2	Sporadically active
	3	Active only under guidance
	4	Passive/ indifferent
Offender's membership of social organisations	1	No membership
	2	Youth Organisation (FDJ)
	3	Society for Sport and Technology (GST)
	4	Gymnastics and Sport League (DTSB)

	5	Trade Union Association (FDGB)
	6	Political party
Offender's social activity, as assessed by his group	1	Positive
	2	Reserved
	3	Passive
(c) Offender's attitude during the court hearing	1	Tried to be frank about the state of affairs
	2	Tried to gloss it over/belittle it
	3	Tried to deny it/justify it
	4	Tried deliberately to obscure it
Overall impression of the offender's bearing during the court hearing	1	Appropriate
	2	Demonstratively indifferent
	3	Inhibited
	4	Sullen, secretive
	5	Tearful
	6	Importunate
	7	Insolent
	8	Uncontrolled
(d) Offender's present performance at school (vocational school)	1	Above-average overall marks
	2	Average overall marks
	3	Poor overall marks
Showing in his occupation	1	Above-average performance
	2	Average performance
	3	Poor performance
School attendance up to	1	Sixth year
	2	Seventh year
	3	Eighth year
	4	Ninth year
	5	Tenth year
	6	Eleventh or twelfth year
Type of school	1	Primary school
	2	Secondary school
	3	Extended secondary school
	4	Special school
	5	Ancillary school
Offender had to repeat a form	1	Once
	2	Twice
	3	Three or more times

Apprenticeship	1	Completed
	2	Discontinued in its first year
	3	Discontined in the second year
	4	Discontinued in the third year
Reason for discontinuation of apprenticeship	1	Intellectual inadequacy
	2	Lack of interest (dislike of the occupation)
	3	Laziness
	4	Sickness
	5	Other reasons
Grade obtained by offender in his skilled worker's examination	1	Very good/good
	2	Satisfactory
	3	Fair
	4	Failed
Offender's attitude to work and study, as assessed by his workmates	1	Very good
	2	Good
	3	Satisfactory
	4	Unsatisfactory
(e) Did he have the job he wanted?	1	Yes
	2	No
	3	Cannot be established
(f) Does the offender assert himself vis-à-vis others?	1	Yes
	2	Cannot be determined
	3	No
Special characteristics of the offender	1	Frequent running away
	2	Loner — no contact with others
	3	Stay-at-home (tied to his parents)
	4	Stammerer
	5	Bed-wetter
	6	Inhibited, but has contact with others
	7	Inhibited, without contact with others
	8	Boastful, without contact or performance
	9	Leader of a clique with contact with others
	10	Unkempt, neglected

11 Oversexed
12 No special characteristics

What this questionnaire does not cover is, above all, the offender's essential attitudes and habits. Thus we believe that it should cover, on a graduated basis, his attitude to work, to property, to his family, to his workmates, and to the State, as well as a number of supplementary objective control criteria, such as work discipline, leisure activities, behaviour, and family relationships.

This excerpt from the questionnaire shows the lines along which the findings in criminal proceedings ought to be deepened. As the skill of crime experts, prosecutors and judges increases in the sphere of psychology, more particularly forensic psychology, the data on the offender's personality will become more comprehensive and more precise. [57]

Attention should be drawn, however, to a few problems which are of general importance and do not depend on specialised training. It is sometimes the case that the judicial authorities, after correctly determining causal relations and tracing back the chain of events to the causant factors, subsequently line up the phenomena so discovered as if they were a purely mechanical sum of facts. Admittedly, this method reveals a great many correlations, but it does not reflect reality accurately. There is a danger, for instance, that the relationship between external circumstances and the offender's thinking is comprehended too mechanically or that the internal factors (character features and attitudes) are absolutised. The following example will illustrate such a mechanical understanding of the relations between external circumstances and the offender's mind.

In a criminal case in the P. district in 1964 it was established that the offender possessed markedly selfish traits and had not yet understood the meaning of social property. Seeing an electric motor lying about a construction site he had decided to steal it and had realised his intention (this was described in great detail). It was further pointed out that the action had been made easy for him by the fact that the motor had evidently been lying about in the open for a number of weeks, with no one taking any notice of it. The offender had intended to sell the motor. He had shown selfish traits in his earlier development and these had been strengthened by his keeping company with persons who were themselves dominated by the old way of thinking.

Not every criminal action is recorded so fully. This particular account already shows some progress in the analysis of the causes of the offence. On the other hand it still over-simplifies the real state of affairs. It does not reveal how deeply the offender was enmeshed in selfishness, whether he suffered from internal conflict and if so how it developed, or what influences, needs or even positive value concepts and modes of thinking may have been in interaction or dispute with each other. The account still seems ultimately based on the view that the offender's deed-related backward consciousness must be seen as the full cause of the offence.

It should not be overlooked that any such internal mechanism is marked by the processing of perceptions and influences, by a continuous reciprocal reaction to them, including, for instance, the fact that the motor in question was exposed to deterioration and was not being guarded or looked after; and by internalised social value concepts about the firm's property and other attitudes. It is, in fact, a process extending from the perception of the electric motor to the completion of the action. Indeed, if the offender subsequently has 'a conscience' about his action, then this shows that the process of internal debate extends even beyond the offence.

The essential point about these findings is not the listing of the circumstances involved but the interlocking of connections, the interaction, the dialectical unity of all components. These do not exist by themselves, in isolation, but interact with each other and in turn are related to other phenomena, and thus give rise to actions, i.e. also to the offence.

It is important that this aspect should be brought out. To achieve this, the discovery of causal relations, starting from the decision to commit the offence (as their effect) is not sufficient. Causality, applied to the specific research subject, must be understood as embedded in the universal interaction, the universal relations existing in reality. This means that the dialectics of objective and subjective factors — transcending the fundamental and elementary form of causal connection — must be comprehended. [58]

This uncertain approch to the problem becomes obvious, for instance, if the question is asked whether disrupted domestic conditions were the cause of an offender's alcoholism or whether his alcoholism was the cause of the disruption of his domestic circumstances. This is the well-known chicken-and-egg problem. Yet these mutual relationships, reciprocal influences and interactions are still not always taken into account. At the scientific conference of the Institute for Political and Juridical Research of the Walter Ulbricht German Academy for Political Science and Jurisprudence, on fundamental questions of the new GDR Criminal Code in November 1963, it was emphasised:

A far more important part is played by abstraction in the generalisation of the causes of crime. Its material basis must be the individual analyses of the causes of crime in each criminal case. Proceeding from these data abstraction is to be performed by statistical procedures and methods such as analysis, synthesis, induction and reduction.... From our own studies it is well known ... that the causes of criminality are either not established at all or frequently established superficially, incompletely, and too often unsatisfactorily. Exposition of the causes in a criminal file frequently consists of a listing of numerous aspects and facts which are then described as the cause — as it were, a collective cause. The reason for this not infrequent practice is the simple registration of facts connected with the criminal offence .... If, however, the cognitive process concerning the causes of the crime is pursued to 'abstract—concrete' findings ... then a step has been taken towards a thorough and sufficiently comprehensive understanding of the subject, of the complex of numerous aspects which together form the phenomenon. We use the term 'abstract—concrete' understanding because we have moved beyond the listing of facts to a comprehension of their interrelations. [59]

Causality, in fact, is just *one* form of correlation; it is always only one element of the universal correlation and universal interaction, and by itself does not explain the real movement. Only the entire complex of phenomena with its reciprocal effects and interactions produces the criminal offence. The knowledge of these — in their abstract—concrete state — is necessary in each individual case. That is also what the criminal proceedings should aim at.

Marxist philosophical literature generally proceeds from the idea that the cause—effect relation is a specialised case of interaction. Engels writes: 'Only from this universal interaction can we arrive at the true causal relation. In order to understand the individual phenomena we must snatch them from the general correlation and view them in isolation; it is then that the changing movements will emerge, the one as cause and the other as effect'. [60] This makes it clear at the same time that, although every phenomenon is causally determined, the individual causal relation does not embrace the universal interaction but has been isolated or abstracted from it.

The function of reciprocal action is particulary emphasised in the more recent literature. It is pointed out that the thesis according to which the 'cause—effect relation' is a specialised case of the interaction relation is problematical to the extent that cause is linked to irreversibility in time,[61] whereas effect and counter-effect may be entirely reversible. [62] Klaus observes on this point: .

... that the discovery of the cause of an appropriate effect invariably only has the character of a provisional explanation of real events. The provisional character is due to the fact that a discovered cause is in itself only the effect of another as yet undiscovered cause. The abstractness of the endless linear causal chain leads to the theory of a prime mover, and this serves the champions of religion to this day as a foundation for specific forms of the existence of God. It was the great merit of dialectics to have proved that the cause—effect relation is only an abstraction from the infinite number of interlinked reciprocal effects which make up the real world. Genuine causal chains run back into themselves. Effects react backwards upon causes. The linear causal chain is only a specialised case of interaction ... It must be noted that ... in classical mechanics this view has already been abandoned, as a matter of principle, since even the relationship of charge and field postulates the category of interaction ... Most clearly of all this is shown on the plane of the higher kinetics of matter, the plane of biological and social modes of behaviour. [63]

Even Hegel opposed stopping at causality with the argument that interaction and not causality was the ultimate beyond which there was no further tracing back. [64] Engels observes:

The whole of accessible nature represents a system, an overall interrelated pattern of bodies, and by bodies we understand more particularly all material existences ... The fact that the bodies are in a relation with each other includes the view that they act upon one another and that this mutual interaction makes up the movement. [65]

Utilisation of the philosophical category of interaction for the discovery of the causes of crime by the judicial organs in the individual case and for criminality research generally involves various other theoretical questions and practical consequences. To begin with, the demand that attention should be paid to interaction must not be understood to mean that henceforward all correlations must be traced to infinity. The philosophers, in fact, have already indicated such limits as the absolute limit of interaction. The problem thus consists in the fact that with a sufficiently large spatial separation between two events the interaction of these two events becomes sufficiently small. It follows, for one thing, that investigations may confine themselves in their 'spatial' statements to those events or phenomena which are close to each other. These are the connections which are important for crime prevention and for the struggle against crime. Another conclusion is that, for example, with offenders over the

278

age of 25 the great variety of phenomena which influenced them in their childhood and youth need not as a rule be investigated. In any event it is probably advisable, according to the offender's personality and also the different offences, to concentrate on particular essential problem areas in his earlier development. A similar proposal has already been made in connection with adult criminality. [66]

The call for an investigation of the interactions underlying criminal offences leads us straight to the problem of reflection, a problem essential to the realistic judgement of personality development, represented here in the form of the individual's ability to reproduce external influences by internal changes and to react to them. Lenin remarked that it was logical 'to assume that all matter possesses a property related in its nature to perception, the property of reflection'.[67] This property of matter exists in a particular manner in every form of movement of matter. The form which interests us in connection with man's social behaviour is studied in particular by the psychologists in their endeavour to discover the laws governing the determination of human behaviour. An essential foundation of this is the well-known thesis that the process of cognition is determined by external, objective conditions which are 'refracted' by the internal regularities of the process concerned. In other words, external causes act through internal conditions. [68] This thesis illustrates the function of the reflection of objects and processes in the evolution of individuals and society; they have to be investigated up to a point both in the criminal proceedings and in criminality research. [69]

Let us, for the sake of argument, take the influence, to be determined in the criminal proceedings, of the circumstances which were operative at the time of the decision to commit a criminal offence and its execution.

(a) The offence − the situation is here simplified for the sake of clarity − may be a primary consequence of the fact that in the offender's past development no adequately effective system of values and attitudes has developed. That, in turn, is due to a combination of ideological, social and physiological circumstances which resulted in the offender's yielding to the temptations, etc., to which he was exposed at the time in question.

(b) The offence, on the other hand, may equally well be the consequence of the fact that the individual's system of attitudes − though in itself positively developed − was restricted in its effectiveness under the influence of the prevailing situation, for example through alcohol, excitement, slightness of risk, etc., so that a certain need was not deliberately restrained or a desirable objective renounced. [70]

In the former case the external circumstances essentially play the part of the immediate occasion, of the − normally accidental − trigger, whereas in the latter case they perform the decisive function.

The central problem about the practical application of the category of interaction and the concepts of reflection is the correct understanding of the process of the internalisation of external influences. Considerable importance attaches to the findings of investigations into this internalisation. Marxist psychologists, for instance, point out that we cannot simply assume 'that objectively present financial hardships in the family, or the fact that both parents are gainfully employed, or the fact that the offender's parents are divorced, or that the offender is physically handicapped is invariably processed in the same way'. [71] One child, exposed to domestic upheaval, will become indifferent, superficial and undisciplined, whereas another will merely be stimulated by the same conditions into choosing more interesting games without being moulded by them, which means that various other circumstances must act and interact as causes. The characteristics of a person's social behaviour must be understood from as many different aspects as possible, in their interaction with one another and with the social environment. [72]

To comprehend the dialectics of objective and subjective factors also means to determine the true effectiveness of certain external influences. It is still a widespread practice to compile the negative phenomena present in an offender's personality and in his work and life style, and to describe them as a complex of causes of his offence; this is in no way justified.

Only the abolition of such a one-sided approach or shortcoming in the determination of the causes of offences will create those material conditions which are necessary for the abstraction of general laws and the identification of interactions.

In connection with the fact that it is quite frequently 'assumed' that a certain fact in an offender's past was vitally responsible for moulding him, it is necessary to emphasise another advantage of the comprehensive application of Marxist philosophy. On the basis of a deeper personality study — something not yet achieved or even achievable in all criminal proceedings — it is possible to uncover phenomena which are not downright 'negative' but can be shown to be reflected in the offender's personality, to have been internalised by him. Both the consideration of the correlations between external and internal factors and the tracing back of the causes, the drawing of conclusions form internal to external circumstances, may lead to a deeper comprehension of reality.

The practical importance of understanding the interactions and reflections finally lies in the fact that this will make more apparent the connection between the effectiveness of old survivals in the offender's conciousness and the insufficient counter-action of socialist conditions and social forces.

The findings derived from individual criminal proceedings – also in their aspect of the main basis of criminological research – would further gain in value if they could be built into a scientific system. There have been various attempts to do just this. [73] Proceeding from recently developed ideas on the causes of criminality – ideas underlying also the present book – the following system can be outlined:

The first complex embraces the correlations, causal connections and interactions, including reflection, from the angle of the situation in which the criminal offence was committed (generally described as the action situation). These include, first of all, all external conditions which influence the decision to commit the offence, further all those internal conditions in which external circumstances are refracted and which played a part in causing or permitting the flip-over to the decision to commit the offence. This complex thus comprises the external and internal conditions as well as their interaction in so far as they were generally effective 'at the time' of the decision to commit the offence, of rather 'shortly before', as well as those which caused the flip-over into the new situation, i.e. the decision to commit the offence.

The second complex embraces all those conditions which were significant in the development of the offender's personality. This includes all those circumstances which resulted in an inadequate development in the offender of an effective system of values and attitudes.

Such a systematisation of connections, causal relations and interactions more clearly reveals the processes which explain why a specific offence was really committed. It thus increases the value of the data from which criminality research must proceed.

It follows that criminality research, even in the analysis of the individual offence, must be guided by Lenin's doctrine: 'In order really to know a subject it must be comprehended and investigated from all its sides, with all connections and "mediations".'[74] 'Facts, if taken in their totality, in their inter-connection, are not only "stubborn" but also absolutely cogent things. But if individual facts are taken, separated from the whole, separated from their connections, then the data are full of gaps, then they are arbitrarily selected, then what we are doing is merely juggling with data or something even worse. '[75] 'Dialectics demand a comprehensive consideration of interrelations in their specific development, not the tearing out of a small piece of this and a small piece of that'. [76]

Problems of a theoretical generalisation of the results of exact criminality research

The first thing to be done within the framework of criminality research is the abstraction of the general elements from the multiplicity of correlations underlying individual criminal offences; this is done by the processing of a large number of exact analyses of individual cases. This entails a certain data loss in that all those circumstances which are unique in the individual action fade into the background and remain unconsidered. The general element comprises only their common components, those which emerge by constant repetition. It is these that matter. The 'data loss' does not impair the value of the findings. Abstraction thus leads us towards the identification of the underlying laws. The process of ascent from the concrete to the abstract is at the same time the deeper and more complete reflection of reality. [77]

Of particular interest in this connection is the degree of generalisation aimed at. This is determined by the goal of developing means and measures for crime prevention. If, for instance, generalisation is carried at once to such concepts as the 'survivals of the past' then – quite apart from the fact that these concepts are not yet sufficiently clarified – this will scarcely make it possible to devise any specific preventive measures. True, these concepts express a certain relationship towards the socialist social order and a certain historical attitude vis-à-vis those phenomena; but such a stage of generalisation is not suited to specific conclusions. What matters in the identification of general elements among the multiplicity of connections underlying criminal offences is the clear understanding of the relation with the personalities of the offenders, with their individual and social development, and with their conditions of life and work. A solution of the problem, as with any other abstraction, does not lie in subjective arbitrariness but is determined 'by the objective connection itself'. [78] This connection consists in the objective demand for the succesful conduct of a fully developed system of struggle against criminality.

Various other problems attending the identification of these underlying laws are connected with the attribute 'essential'. This relates to those phenomena, including their negative effects, whose liquidation represents an essential prerequisite of a systematic abolition of criminality. Whereas the attributes 'general' and 'necessary' relate to correlations which are relatively constant, the 'essential' correlations determine the character of the offences and reflect the internal relation between criminality and its causes.

The content of the attribute 'essential' can only be clarified for criminality research by a thorough analysis of reality. The only scientific foundation for such an attempt is Marxist—Leninist philosophy. The analysis proves that the phenomena effective as causes of criminality are phenomena alien to the nature of socialism, phenomena which socialist society is compelled to oppose and, in the process of its advance, to overcome. These are, above all, the old, the outlived, everything that impedes progress in the diverse relations of men with one another, within the family, within the work team and in all other groupings with which they directly communicate — impeding elements, therefore, in the so-called macrogroups and in certain respects in their conditions of existence. These phenomena are reflected in attitudes, customs and beliefs, even in the moulded features of character. Particular attention must be devoted to these subjective phenomena within the complex of the causes of criminality. Understanding of these phenomena makes it possible to penetrate deeply negative elements which have become established and in themselves represent an underlying system which must be comprehensively influenced as part of the crime prevention effort in order to overcome the essential components of the causes of criminal offences.

Finally — and this is the point to which investigations must penetrate — criminality reflects what is outdated and what has to be replaced in the economic reality of our own day. This consists of certain features of as yet insufficiently developed production relations in certain spheres or enterprises, and ultimately also in the low state of evolution of productive forces — low, that is, by the yardstick of the state of development of a communist society. [79]

We are therefore dealing with social phenomena related to a particular period in social evolution, to a period when, by comparison with communism, the state of development of the productive forces, educational and cultural standards and the individual's consciousness is lower.[80] The programme of the Communist Party of the Soviet Union therefore states:

> Growing prosperity, rising cultural standards and the consciousness of the working people are creating all the prerequisites of liquidating criminality and of ultimately replacing criminal law penalties by measures of social influencing and education. Under the conditions of socialism anyone who has come off the rails of honest work can again return to useful activity. [81]

The above-named conditions in the social and individual sphere do not exhaust the total number of essential determinants of criminality. They merely emphasise that criminality research, if it is to discover the laws determining criminality, must turn its attention towards essential internal correlations.

This implies that, alongside and in interaction with the essential conditions, there must be further conditions which, though not essential, are nevertheless connected with criminal offences. Researches by the various disciplines concerned with crime reduction and crime prevention must on no account neglect these further conditions. This follows from a realisation of their character and of the dialectics of their relations to the essential conditions of criminality.

This formulation of the problem is not identical with our earlier differentiation between the causes of crime and conditions favouring crime. Researchers have pointed out that these concepts and their differentiation are important for the exploration of the causes of individual offences and moreover characterise the historical position of the various factors. [82] However, the concepts are only conditionally applicable to the overall phenomenon of criminality which is governed by laws of a statistical character. The conditions which must be comprehended other than the essential ones are not reflected with scientific exactitude by the concept of 'favourable conditions'. Their characterisation in line with methodological requirements will be dealt with in greater detail elsewhere.

Some of the conditions which have hitherto been described as 'favourable' are in fact essential for certain criminal phenomena. Among those 'favouring' recidivist offences we have already mentioned the frequently inadequate effectiveness of the educational work of penal organs and work teams. But this circumstance can become absolutely essential for recidivism under our conditions of social development. To characterise these phenomena otherwise would mean to ignore the dialectics existing in reality.

The functions — not to be confused with the characteristic of 'essential' — of individual essential correlations are different for each group of offences and in their general manifestations. These functions require further specific study.

The concept of 'favourable conditions' is intended by its author to carry a different meaning.

The essential conditions and the interaction between them in fact presuppose general effective conditions. These, in a sense, are the wider prerequisites of criminality. They are of a very diverse nature and are not essential because they are not in an inner relation to criminality. [83]

The distinction between essential conditions and general effective conditions, necessary as it is for an understanding of the underlying laws,

284

must not be schematically applied in the programming of criminological researches or in the mapping out of a system of prevention. That is why this book has repeatedly drawn attention to the dialectics between the two. Thus the exploration of a criminal phenomenon will necessarily have to extend to the totality of relations. Only then can the law-determined relations be identified. Any one-sidedness or failure to take account of the complexity of all conditions would be detrimental to an effective prevention. Thus a system of prevention of criminal traffic offences, if it is to be effective, must necessarily make allowance for the general climatic conditions of the different seasons and of natural human dispositions, capabilities and limitations.

Criminality research finally has to take note of two further problems. Investigations in the construction industry, for instance, have shown that wherever men handle articles which they also require for their everyday needs an infinitely higher incidence of crimes against property is encountered than under conditions where they cannot themselves use the articles they work with for the satisfaction of their personal needs. Thus there is hardly any pilfering of building materials at sites where construction uses large-scale panels. There is, therefore, a connection between criminality and the usefulness of the articles handled by the individuals. This is confirmed also by researches in the sphere of trade. There, too, we find a relatively high incidence of crimes against property although these circumstances cannot be described as essential to the existence of criminality. Yet acquaintance with them is important for the development of effective preventive measures.

A relatively special problem arises from the fact that certain socialist relations can lag behind others or undergo deformation under the effect of subjective and objective shortcomings. They may then give rise to conflicts with the law. This aspect was very convincingly formulated at the Twenty-first Congress of the Communist Party of the Soviet Union by the example of the deformation of personal property :

> The concept of prosperity as an unlimited growth of personal property is not our concept; it is a view alien to communism. Personal ownership by the working people of numerous objects as a form of personal need does not run counter to the building of communism so long as it is kept within reasonable limits and does not become an objective in itself. But inflated personal property can in certain circumstances become an obstacle to social progress and in fact sometimes does so; it becomes a breeding ground of customs and practices of private owners and may lead to bourgeois excrescences. [84]

The deformation of socialist relations can give rise to selfish tendencies and strengthen the desire to own more and more, thus excluding others from the utilisation of the property. The wealth of society under socialist conditions therefore grows not primarily through personal property but through socialist property. The prosperity of our people is increasingly based on facilities and on objects of use which are communally enjoyed. The relations existing under such circumstances and the resulting consequences require further investigation. Deformation, however, may arise also in other spheres. Thus it has been observed in some cases that persons entrusted with certain official rights do not apply these in the interest of society. Such people fail to understand that the political rights entrusted to them in a socialist State should serve the interests of society, but instead see them as personal 'power'. This gives rise to the most diverse actions which may bring other people not only into conflict with the official concerned but even with our State and its law.

Systematisation of criminality research

A rich source of investigation data is available in the shape of a large number of analyses of individual criminal phenomena. According to the various aims of different investigations, the manifestations of criminality, their incidence, structure, developmental tendencies and causes were investigated. From all these studies it is clear that the greatest possible importance attaches to the quality of the individual analysis. For one thing, insufficient care in the investigation of an individual case reduces the chosen data base and impairs its representative character, and for another it is the depth of analysis that decides the degree of generalisation or the kind of new knowledge arrived at.

If the investigations are intended merely to lay bare the structure of the criminal phenomena then this is, as a rule, satisfactorily achieved by the findings of the penal organs within the framework of the criminal proceedings, and contained in the files on the case. These files, relating to a large number of proceedings, are more or less the only material basis of the majority of such analyses. For a deeper examination, however, it is necessary to go beyond this collection of data. This applies, in particular, whenever the internal system (beliefs, attitudes, abilities, aspirations, character features, etc.) of offenders guilty of a particular type of crime have to be investigated with a view to developing ways of influencing such persons. To that end, in most cases, only a limited number of offences are investigated. All these considerations, therefore, have a bearing on the choice of areas under examination, of the material, of the methods to be employed, etc.

If the laws governing the correlations underlying the offences are to be discovered then research must not stop at the surface manifestations of criminality. These, in a sense, are only halfway data in the cognitive process, i.e. the way to the understanding of the essence leads through them. This is a general rule of scientific work: the way leads from the manifestation to the substance and from the less deep substance to the deeper substance.[85] This is not to say that establishing the forms of manifestation is not of considerable importance for crime prevention. Indeed, from the time and place of the commission of certain criminal offences conclusions can sometimes be drawn about appropriate protective measures. But these are not the real objective of criminality research. This research, therefore, has the following stages: (a) analysis of the individual case; (b) discovery of the phenomenology of the criminal phenomenon concerned; (c) discovery of the underlying laws and correlations.

As for the first stage, certain requirement have already been referred to. Systematisation of the next two stages, which must also meet the demands of systematic and complex crime prevention, requires the alignment of the various steps to discover the underlying laws with the actual processes of our social reality, the processes by which individuals are moulded and determined in their thoughts and actions. What matters, therefore, is a deep understanding of the real dialectics between criminality and certain phenomena and processes in our reality.

Investigation of the manifestations of criminality (phenomenology) comprises their external shape and development.

In bourgeois criminology, phenomenology is an independent field. Since in the view of bourgeois criminologists the real causes of criminality, and hence its nature, cannot be comprehended — a point which was made earlier — primary importance is attached to the investigation of external phenomena and correlations. We shall not at this point deal with the philosophical basis of such an unscientific view. [86]

Some analyses by the judiciary authorities, in the opinion of the present author, seem to overrate the importance of phenomenological researches. They only deal with criminality in a quantitative way and their conclusions do not specifically allow for the limited validity of such researches. This is not to deny that within the sphere of external phenomena there are correlations which permit of conclusions to be drawn concerning their elimination, as for instance in the above-mentioned high incidence of offences committed in certain places and at certain times.

287

But these are not essential correlations which would lead towards an understanding of regular correlations. Any attempt to work out preventive measures on the basis of particular recorded phenomena alone therefore comes close to the bourgeois point of view which assigns to phenomenology an independent existence.

Hand in hand with this 'practice' goes an over-estimation of methods which, admittedly, are sufficient for the recording of the manifestations of criminality and their development but which are not adequate to the demands of comprehensive scientific criminality research. Any scientific criminality research depends on methods capable of discovering the laws themselves which determine criminality.

At the present moment we still lack a general study of the manifestations of criminality. That is why this problem will be discussed here through the example of crimes against property in the construction industry. The attempt will be made to develop a certain pattern which will be applicable also as a standard for other investigations. Criminological research should always employ standards which ensure uniformity and simplification. A study of the manifestations of offences against property in the construction industry first of all presupposes the discovery of the absolute number of offences in this category of crime and the numerical trend. The absolute totals revealed in criminal statistics about offences against property in the sphere of socialist, personal or private property must then be broken down according to the different social or economic spheres, including that of the construction industry. Since no such breakdown was worked out for the country as a whole during the past few years we must start by looking at the development of this criminal phenomenon from the district level. This may involve some inaccuracies, but these will be susceptible to verification and, if necessary, correction by comparison of the general tendency of crimes against property and their frequency in the district under review with the tendency and frequency on the national scale, as well as by various supplementary considerations.

The absolute total of criminal offences against property in the construction industry reveals but little about their incidence. It is necessary to establish their specific quotient by relating the number of offences against property in the construction industry to the number of workers employed in this industry. Only thus can a clear view be gained of the part played by crimes against property in this area and the trend of such crime.

We are now able to compare this result with specific crime figures in other areas. The absolute total of criminal offences against socialist property is considerably smaller in the construction industry than in industry as a whole. But related to the number of employees it is considerably higher for the construction industry than the average for other industries. Really valid statements, however, can only be made when the quotient has been observed and compared over a prolonged period of time. It would therefore be a mistake to use the quotient thus found for drawing any final conclusions about a favourable or unfavourable trend. The answer to the question about an increase or decrease in criminality depends on further correlations and interactions which cannot be covered statistically. They include, for instance, changes in the law and in the application of criminal law, and the development of relations between individuals, the State and our society, as reflected in the collaboration of citizens in the discovery of criminal offences and the struggle against them.

Investigation of the manifestations further demands the breakdown of offences against property according to their various modes of commission from a legal point of view. It is obvious that criminal offences against socialist property must be treated separately from attacks on other forms of property. Within these areas a further breakdown must be performed according to legal categories. The manifestations of crimes against property in the construction industry must be further subdivided according to the industry's separate spheres (industrial construction, housing, the rural building trade, road and bridge construction, etc.). Further characteristics to be recorded include categories such as giant building sites, building sites using traditional methods, building sites using modern methods, etc.

As far as possible the actual way in which the offences have been committed should be fully recorded. This applies to the nature of the objects to which the offences relate, their material value, the offender's relationship to these objects, the tactics of committing the offences, the techniques by which they are committed, in particular the means and methods applied, data about the time and place of the offence, the material and notional damage, and finally the forms of participation (offender acting singly, several offenders, group offences).

The trend marking the manner in which the offences have been committed must likewise be investigated. Thus, from a declining trend of the material value of the stolen objects certain conclusions may be drawn and starting points formulated for further investigations which may reveal the trend of the nature of these offences. Data concerning the manner in which offences against property have been committed also permit certain conclusions to be drawn concerning the effectiveness of technical measures for their prevention.

Available studies and data do not yet provide a comprehensive picture of how crimes against property in the construction industry are distributed among the various districts, towns, municipalities, parts of cities, residential districts and industrial centres. Individual studies confirm that consideration of this aspect leads to a more rapid understanding of essential connections and hence to the making of changes.

Of considerable importance also is the establishment of correlations connected with the struggle against these offences. They include the quota of discovered offences and their trend, the existence of phenomena indicating latent criminality, the relations between informer and offender, between the informer and the object of the offence, the duration of the offender's criminal activity and any peculiarity of its discovery.

Equally important is the complex of investigations relating to the offender. These include biological, psychological and social factors in so far as they are connected with the commission of the criminal offences. Past studies have concentrated on data about the following factors: the offender's sex and age; family status; number of children; possible separation from his family; living conditions; educational status, subdivided into schooling and attainment of educational objective, vocational training (apprenticeship, conclusion of the apprenticeship, examinations, further education); occupation; social origin; participation in organisations and socialist brigades; voluntary activity; behaviour and reputation in his local neighbourhood; income and material position of the family; duration of the labour relationship; frequency of change of place of work; attitude towards work (laziness at work, abuse of alcohol during working hours, disciplinary punishments; distinctions, norm fulfilment, improvement proposals, etc.); relations as a citizen (re-immigrant, former frontier-crosser, new arrival); previous criminal record (nature of offence, sentence and punishment served); conspicuous habits connected with the offence; peculiarities in the offender's mentality and their relationship to his offence; asocial inclinations or membership in criminal organisations.

In addition, it seems necessary to include data about any concentration of negative phenomena in the offender's work or life, such as numerous previous punishments, educational inadequacies, etc.

Investigation of the various manifestations of criminality requires a certain classification (classifying phenomenology). This comprises the numerical magnitude of criminality, its distribution among the various categories of offences and individual offences, their methods of commission, the grouping of offenders, etc. Moreover, there is a need for the description of the structure of criminality (structural phenomenology). This is not confined — as the use of the word by criminal law scholars might suggest — to the distribution of criminality in terms of offences, age groups, territorial areas, etc. Involved are questions such as professional qualifications of the offender, school attendance and completion of study, family relationships, leisure activities, living conditions, income, working conditions, position within his work group, etc. These data still remain within the framework of the question of the nature of the offence; no statement can as yet be made on the reasons for it. Structural phenomenology, for instance, is unable to answer the question why the authors of certain criminal offences occupy one particular position in their team and not another, why their social or personal relations are structured in one particular way and not in another. The sociometric method, therefore, is not sufficient for the discovery of extensive new knowledge because it covers only the nature of relations. Having said this we have already passed beyond the sphere of phenomenology.

The phenomenon of criminal offences and offender personality — both these are still within the sphere of phenomenological considerations — reveals factors which are linked with (a) the offender's personality development; and   (b) the transition into becoming an offender — the entry into a different state.

The same subdivision is employed also by cause analysis in depth. Thus the knowledge of those essential circumstances which brought about the 'new state' makes it possible, by means of specific measures and influences, to prevent other or further offences and systematically to re-educate the individuals concerned. Methodical procedure — in the study both of the manifestations and of the causes — may be summed up under the concepts of longitudinal section analysis and cross-section analysis. This systematisation is reflected also in such procedures as criminological surveys by questionnaires in which the separate complexes of questions are structured in accordance with this system.

The examination of the causes of criminality, which is based on the data referred to and their systematisation, is similarly a process of increasingly thorough penetration into the correlations of criminality. It begins with the determination of its essential phenomena or the structural determination of its essence. The following account of research procedure will once more illustrate this point.

Structural essence determination proceeds from the various above-listed phenomena or factors or from their frequency distribution. They must first of all be examined as to their significance. By means of correlation computation and other methods the highly significant phenomena and relations are identified. But only their further theoretical penetration makes the essential connections visible. [87] Eventually the question 'why' follows the question 'what for?', i.e. the question about the function of the various essential determinants. Without a knowledge of their specific function in the various criminal manifestations a truly effective struggle against the roots of crime cannot be achieved. Only this 'ultimate' stage of the investigation, the functional essence determination, permits a full comprehension of the possibility of criminal behaviour. [88]

The fundamental realisation underlying this systematisation is the essentially social determination of criminality, contrary to the teachings of bourgeois criminologists who proceed from the dispositional determination of criminality and similar assumptions. This does not mean — as we have pointed out — that the individual sphere can be disregarded. The point is merely that the real dialectics between objective and subjective factors must be understood.

Generally — and hence also with regard to the causes of criminality — it is the objective conditions which are of predominant importance in the dynamics of society. They ultimately also determine the development of the subjective factor. But this is merely the fundamental relationship. No scientific systematisation can ignore the fact that in socialism the relation between the spontaneous and the conscious undergoes a fundamental transformation. Under socialist conditions society becomes a consciously steered entity. This requires particular attention to be paid to the subjective determinant in the complex of the causes of criminality. [89]

The classical authors of Marxism—Leninism as well as the documents of the SED have time and again stressed the growing rôle of the subjective factor in socialist society. Hence the discovery of the essential subjective conditions is gaining increasing importance also in the sphere of the causes of crime, if only to ensure an effective struggle against it. [90] Our considerations must be based on the fact that people consciously change their life style, that consciousness is an active factor supporting the advance of historical progress. Therein lies the socially important aspect of the dialectics of being and consciousness, an aspect of particular importance also in the struggle against crime. The development of consciousness helps the individual to shape his life style and relationships in a socialist way and to mould himself into a socialist personality.

Systematisation must first proceed according to the gnosiological relationship of objective and subjective elements; in this way it ensures that appropriate attention is paid to the significance of the subjective factor. The first concern is the complex of objective causes, since human behaviour is externally determined and society is the decisive system of reference in man's life. That is why in criminality research the specific relations of the offender to his environment, i.e. group relations in the immediate and less immediate spheres, occupy a central place. They exert decisive influence on man's action, and if these relations have not yet become socialist they harbour the possibility that they may trigger faulty behaviour.

In the following reflection we shall emphasise some typical relations which, according to the studies of criminality in the construction industry, reveal aspects essential for the commission of offences. A comprehensive exposition of the rôle of group relations in the existence of criminality and the struggle against it is not possible within the present context. [91]

Investigations of crimes against property in the construction industry show, for instance, the existence of correlations with certain aspects of the offender's relations with so-called macro-groups. This applies in particular to relations which:

(a) Result from the *class origin of the offender*. It has been shown that the frequency of offences is not evenly distributed among offenders from different classes and strata of the population. We find that some classes or strata still often have development problems in connection with their integration into socialist society or else suffer from the after-effects of the disruptive influence of capitalist relations.

(b) Arise from the *grouping of trades among those employed in construction.*

(c) Stem from the *age group*, etc.

As a member of such a 'macro-group' the individual in question is compelled to communicate with the conditions peculiar to these groups, with the group pattern. This includes: (a) the group's material conditions of existence; (b) group-typical norms, values, traditions and forms of co-operation; (c) position vis-à-vis other groups and the resulting contact relations.

Crimes against property in the construction industry are associated with certain aspects or phenomena in the *material* conditions of those employed in construction. Underlying those crimes, in particular, is a subjective desire of the indivual to enrich himself contrary to the law of distribution according to performance, which is valid for our society, to disregard the interests of society, of teams or individuals, or at least to place his personal interest above those of society and his team mates. Group-typical norms, values, forms of co-operation and traditions among employees in construction do not as yet exclude certain survivals, for example in cultural standards. Among construction workers found guilty of criminal offences correlations and interdependences were found to exist between their individual life style, their income and their intellectual and cultural standards, all of which must be seen as clear consequences of the capitalist exploitative order. A statistical analysis of such factors as low educational standard, heavy physical work, the inclination to spend free time in public houses, all proved that the statistical series ran parallel to each other. This suggests that negative phenomena are operative here, which in their interaction contain the possibility of criminal behaviour.

Building methods which are still predominantly based on physical work — this is not the place to examine the reasons for this — naturally do not require a high standard of education. Statistics therefore show a high proportion of such offenders to be unskilled workers, with a relatively large number who failed to reach the eductional level aimed at by schools, etc. This educational standard largely impairs the ability to recognise social connections and requirements, and this in turn favours the preservation or the propagation of wrong attitudes. This physical-labour method of construction in turn impedes the development of socialist relations of the building workers with one another, with their work, with socialist property, with the State or with society.

Mere reference to relations within the macro-groups would fail to bring out the great differences among them. The *closer* plane of reference is between personality and micro-group. It is this that represents the specific system of reference for behaviour orientation. It is through his membership in what are called micro-groups that the individual is confronted with the group-specific conditions which constitute his life style. This embraces the material circumstances, contact partners, social norms and values with which the personality really communicates. The most important micro-groups, also according to criminological research, are the family, the school group, the work team, and leisure groupings (groups of friends, cliques), etc. This systematisation of the various group relationships and the position of the groups — once more subdivided according to the main trends of social development — comprises the true dialectic. It focuses attention on the two correlation systems (external and internal) which in their dialectical conjunction may produce criminality as a functional result.

The complex of subjective conditions which underlies criminality as an important complex of causes, contains a variety of elements. These elements differ from one another in their nature. They are, first, of an ideological nature.

Ideological elements in many respects play a part in crimes against property in the construction industry — our example here. On the other hand, outdated views inherited from capitalist society continue to be effective. In a few cases, however, it has also been possible to identify ideological influences originating in imperialist West Germany. These ideological elements manifest themselves in the form of selfish or individualistic attitudes to certain requirements, social values, etc. Listed among these in analyses, for instance, was the desire to live at the expense of others, or the 'inclination' to work as one's own entrepreneur in order to enrich oneself.

Secondly, particular importance in connection with offences against property in the construction industry attaches to those subjective conditions which must be assigned to human psychology. Among these psychological processes we must list above all certain outdated habits of thought and actions which for the most part have been inherited from capitalism and which, though they reflect conditions no longer existing, have struck firm root. Thus the former custom of construction workers of taking home offcuts or remnants from their place of work, or of working in a particular way regardless of such requirements as economical use of materials, of drinking alcoholic beverages during working time, etc., are all associated with habits of thought which reflect certain modes of action.

The psychological conditions also include the characteristics of the offender. Frequently such offenders are found to be weak-willed, readily influenced or unstable in their personality. There is frequent mention in the analyses of an offender's 'inclination' towards the misuse of alcohol, disregard of his family or readiness to yield to negative influences. It is also found that in certain work teams one of the members, especially strongly rooted in old traditions and ideas, will be the one who 'sets the tone'. An essential part is therefore played by character traits; these must be laid bare to reveal the views and attitudes which underlie them.

It is important, in this context, to oppose the view that one is simply dealing with 'evil people' who have had these characteristics given them, as it were, in the cradle and that they are, therefore, powerless in the face of them. At the same time, the opposite over-simplification must likewise be rejected, i.e. that these characteristics can be positively transformed in a short period of time or even by a single talk with the offender.

These problems eventually lead us to another psychological phenomenon. Blindness to society is determined also by the individual consciousness which, in its content, is a reflection of the social consciousness. However, 'it possesses its own peculiarities which stem from the specific relations and conditions of each individual's life, in a class society primarily from his class association, and also from his education and the political and ideological influences, etc., to which he has been exposed in the course of his life'.[92] The individual consciousness thus plays an important part in the framework of the internal causes of the commission of criminal offences. Turning once more to the example of the construction industry, we find there, compared with other industries, a relatively higher percentage of offenders whose individual consciousness, with all its peculiarities, has not yet reached the general average. In consequence their action is often more strongly determined by specific rudimentary aspects of their working and living conditions. Some part is played by such phenomena as the momentarily low production standard in various branches of construction, shortcomings in management, persisting instances of confusion at building sites, as well as the peculiarities associated with the living conditions of men employed in this industry. All these aspects and phenomena are interlinked in a complex manner, they interact with each other and determine one another. They are not only made more conspicuous by systematisation but they are also more clearly isolated from other phenomena and processes which are not essential for social crime prevention. These consist of the above-mentioned general conditions which need not therefore be systematised in this context.

Notes

[1] Cf. pp. 83 ss., esp. p. 89 of this book; also G. Stiller, 'Theoretische und methodologische Grundlagen der kriminologischen Forschungen in der DDR', Habil. thesis, Potsdam—Babelsberg 1965, pp. 37 ss.

[2] Cf. Stiller, loc. cit,. pp. 140 ss.

[3] Cf. H. Weber, 'Die Gesellschaftswidrigkeit der Vergehen in der Etappe des umfassenden Aufbaus des Sozialismus in der DDR', Habil. thesis, Potsdam—Babelsberg 1965.

[4] The problem of differentiation between criminality as a social phenomenon and a sum of individual offences is discussed elsewhere.

[5] Interesting statements and reflections can be found in H. v. Hentig, *Die unbekannte Straftat*, Berlin—Göttingen—Heidelberg 1964, which contáins data on undiscovered crime under capitalist conditions.

[6] For a critique of these views at the 25th meeting of the GDR State Council cf. *Neue Justiz*, 1966, no. 12, p. 371, and no. 13, p. 385. For the general problems of the objective laws in socialist society cf. H. Scheler, 'Der objektive Charakter der gesellschaftlichen Gesetze im Lichte der Subjekt—Objekt—Dialektik', *Deutsche Zeitschrift für Philosophie,* Special issue 1964, pp. 7 ss., esp. pp. 12 ss.

[7] Cf. H. Harrland/G. Stiller, 'Entwicklung eines umfassenden Systems der Kriminalitätsvorbeugung in der DDR', *Staat und Recht*, 1966, Issue 10, pp. 1609 ss.

[8] Cf. Part I of this book, esp. pp. 33 ss.

[9] Cf. Part I of this book, esp. p. 89.

[10] On the relation between the causal concept and method cf. also R. Hartmann, 'Aufgaben der Jugendkriminologie in der DDR', *Staat und Recht*, Issue 6, pp. 977.

[11] Cf. F. Engels/K. Marx, 'Die Heilige Familie', in: K. Marx/F. Engels, *Werke*, vol. 2, Berlin 1958, p. 138; F. Engels, 'Die Lage der arbeitenden Klasse in England', loc. cit., pp. 356 ss.; F. Engels, 'Zwei Reden in Elberfeld (I), loc. cit., p. 541; V. I. Lenin, 'How Should Competition be Organised?' (German version in) *Werke*, vol. 26, Berlin 1961, pp. 409 ss; also G. Klaus/H. Hiebsch, *Kinderpsychologie*, Berlin 1962, pp. 380 ss.

[12] V. I. Lenin, 'The Collapse of the Second International' (German version in) *Werke*, vol. 21, Berlin 1960, p. 233.

[13] Cf. also G. Stiller, 'Zur Methodologie der Erforschung der Ursachen der Kriminalität und der Verbrechensvorbeugung', *Staat und Recht*, 1963, Issue 10, pp. 1687 ss.

[14] Cf. Part I of this book, esp. p. 60 ss.

[15] Cf. H. Hörz, 'Zum Verhältnis von Kausalität und Determinismus', *Deutsche Zeitschrift für Philosophie*, 1963, Issue 2, p. 157.

[16] Cf. H. Hörz, loc. cit., p. 158.

[17] 'Causality does not exist outside necessity but it is not identical with it and determines also chance phenomena' (Omelyanskiy, quoted by H. Hörz, loc. cit., p. 153).

[18] Cf. the present book, esp. p. 60 ss.

[19] Cf. H. Scheler, 'Der objektive Charakter ...', loc. cit., p. 25.

[20] Cf. the present book, esp. p. 69 ss.

[21] Cf. *Grundlagen der marxistischen Philosophie*, Berlin 1964, pp. 191 ss.

[22] G. Klaus, *Moderne Logik*, Berlin 1964, p. 393.

[23] Criminology would be unable to develop proposals for crime prevention if it oriented itself, in the individual case, towards chance phenomena among the causes; these chance phenomena, after all, are characterised by the fact that they are unique and non-repetitive. On the relation between causality and statistical laws cf. K. Zweiling, 'Einige Gedanken zu Philosophie, Determiniertheit und Kausalität', *Deutsche Zeitschrift für Philosophie*, 1964, Issue 10, pp. 1240 ss.

[24] *Grundlagen der marxistischen Philosophie*, Berlin 1964, pp. 236 ss.

[25] Cf. also I. Holtzbecher/H. Pompoes, 'Ursachen und begünstigende Bedingungen der Kriminalität im Bauwesen', *Neue Justiz*, 1964, no. 5, p. 134.

[26] This requirement is not adequately met by the factors and data covered by criminal statistics, or by their frequency.

[27] Thus a statement that a pupil has failed to reach the eductional

target of the eighth grade does not yet reveal the reasons for this failure. These might be illness, educational problems, lack of intelligence, etc., or a combination of interacting factors.

[28] All analyses in future should state the criteria used for recording a phenomenon as well as the precise meaning of the concepts used whenever these are not generally known.

[29] F. Engels, 'Dialektik der Natur', in: K. Marx/F. Engels, *Werke*, vol. 20, Berlin 1962, p. 491.

[30] Cf. R. Stemmler/H. Becher/G. Reichstein/W. Steglich, *Statistische Methoden im Sport*, Berlin 1965, p. 5.

[31] These problems will be discussed forthwith.

[32] Marxist—Leninist philosophy is not only the ideological foundation of the struggle for social progress but also a universal method of scientific insight. Cf. the critique of statistical formalism in P. Bollhagen, *Soziologische Forschung: Grundsätze und Methoden*, Taschenbuchreihe 'Unser Weltbild' vol. 44, pp. 55 ss.; A. Werbin/A. Furmann, 'Der historische Materialismus im System der Gesellschaftswissenschaften', *Sowjetwissenschaft — Gesellschaftswissenschaftliche Beiträge*, 1966, Issue 8, p. 868. The latter essay shows convincingly that Marxist philosophy — not just materialist dialectics — is the universal method. An unjustified restriction is called for by P. Pares, 'Einige Gedanken zur kriminalpolizeilichen Analyse', *Forum der Kriminalistik* 1966, Issue 10, pp. 11 ss.

[33] Cf. G. Stiller, 'Zu Problemen der Methodologie der Erforschung der Jugendkriminalität' in: *Studien zur Jugendkriminalität*, Berlin 1965, pp. 88 ss.

[34] K. Hager, 'Gesellschaftswissenschaft auf neuen Wegen', (Diskussionsbeitrag auf dem 9. Plenum des ZK der SED), *Neues Deutschland* of 1 May 1965, p. 7.

[35] Cf. A. Mergen, *Methodik kriminalbiologischer Untersuchungen*, Stuttgart 1953.

[36] Cf. loc. cit., p. 29.

[37] Cf. loc. cit., p. 32.

[38] Cf. loc. cit., pp. 38 ss.

[39] Cf. loc. cit., p. 25.

[40] Cf. E. Mezger, *Kriminologie*, Munich und Berlin 1951, p. 5.

[41] Cf. A. Mezger, *Methodik kriminalbiologischer Untersuchungen*, loc. cit., p. 22.

[42] Cf. loc. cit., p. 17.

[43] Cf. A. Bollermann, *Die Kriminalität der Ruhrbergleute*, Bonn 1961; H. Ebardt, *Zur Kriminologie jugendlicher Vermögenstäter*, Hamburg 1965; H. Fuhlendorf, *Die Jugendkriminalität nach dem Kriege*, Hamburg

1960; D. Goos, *Die Kriminalität in Betrieben der Elektroindustrie*, Bonn 1963; E. Haas, *Die Kriminalität in Betrieben der Automobilindustrie einer Grosstadt Norddeutschlands* Bremen 1964.

[44] G. V. Plekhanov, *Selected Philosophical Writings,* vol. II, Moscow 1957, p. 242 (in Russian).

[45] Cf. 'Erklärung des Staatsrates der Deutschen Demokratischen Republik zur Rechtsentwicklung in beiden deutschen Staaten', *Schriftenreihe des Staatsrates der DDR*, 1966, no. 1, pp. 117 ss.

[46] Cf., for instance, H.-J. Schneider, 'Entwicklungstendenzen ausländischer und internationaler Kriminologie', *Juristen-Zeitung*, 1966, 11/12, pp. 369 ss.

[47] Cf. pp. 144 ss. of this book.

[48] H. Scheler, 'Der objektive Character ... ', loc. cit., p. 21.

[49] To be precise, the age groups in the statistics should be not 14 to 16, 16 to 18, etc. but 14 to 15, 16 to 17, 18 to 20, 21 to 24.

[50] This is not the place to discuss the justification of one system of age grouping or another. Certain misgivings have been expressed, e.g. from the point of view of acceleration. Cf. E. M. Yuzbasheva, 'The Statistical Method in Criminal Law Research', *Izvestiya vysshikh uchebnykh zavedeniy — Pravovedeniye,* Leningrad 1964, no. 2, pp. 51 ss.

[51] Cf. H. Harrland, 'Zur Entwicklung der Kriminalität und zu einigen Problemen ihrer wirksamen Bekämpfung', *Neue Justiz*, 1966, no. 20, p. 618.

[52] J. Lekschas, 'Studien zur Bewegung der Jugendkriminalität in Deutschland und zu ihren Ursachen', in: *Studien zur Jugendkriminalität*, Berlin 1965, pp. 9 ss., esp. pp. 64 ss.

[53] Cf. J. Streit, 'Neue Wege zur Verhütung der Jugendkriminalität', *Sozialistische Demokratie* of 28 May 1965, p. 8.

[54] Cf. H. Blüthner/H. Kerst, 'Zu den Ursachen der Eigentumskriminalität im Bauwesen und zu der Vorbeugung bei dieser Kriminalitätserscheinung durch die Organe der sozialistischen Strafrechtspflege', thesis, Potsdam—Babelsberg 1965.

[55] Cf. J. Lekschas, 'Zur Feststellung der Ursachen der Straftat durch die Gerichte', *Neue Justiz*, 1965, no. 15 pp. 478 ss.

[56] This is not the place to discuss the problem of whether the individual questions relate to motives or to attitudes.

[57] The Department for Scientific Criminality Research at the Office of the GDR Prosecutor General has developed a questionnaire designed to investigate recidivist crime in the area of offences against property and offences of violence. This questionnaire, which is a great deal more informative than earlier ones, is attached as an Appendix.

[58] Such an approach is attempted by H. Blüthner, 'Zu den Ursachen der Kriminalität in der DDR', *Neue Justiz*, 1963, no. 19, pp. 620 ss., esp. p. 624. On the causality—interaction relationship cf. H. Hörz, 'Der dialektische Determinismus in Natur und Gesellschaft', *Taschenbuchreihe 'Unser Weltbild'*, no. 34, Berlin 1962, pp. 64, 69, 87.

[59] Grundfragen des Neuen Strafgesetzbuches der DDR, Berlin 1964, pp. 155 ss.

[60] F. Engels, 'Dialektik der Natur', in: K. Marx/F. Engels, *Werke*, vol. 20, Berlin 1962, p. 499.

[61] This means that the cause can never follow the effect in time.

[62] Cf. *Philosophisches Wörterbuch*, Leipzig 1964, p. 597.

[63] G. Klaus, *Kybernetik und Gesellschaft*, Berlin 1964, pp. 18 ss.

[64] Cf. G. W. Hegel, *Enzyklopädie der philosophischen Wissenschaften*, 5th edn, Leipzig 1949, art. 154, pp. 149 ss.

[65] F. Engels, 'Dialektik der Natur', in: K. Marx/F. Engels, *Werke*, vol. 20, Berlin 1962, p. 355.

[66] Cf. J. Lekschas, 'Zur Feststellung der Ursachen ... ', loc. cit., p. 480.

[67] V. I. Lenin, (German version in) *Werke*, vol. 14, Berlin 1962, p. 85.

[68] Cf. S. L. Rubinstein, *Sein und Bewusstsein*, Berlin 1962, p. 37.

[69] Cf. *Philosophisches Wörterbuch*, loc. cit., p. 607.

[70] Cf. J. Helm, 'Einige sozialpsychologische Aspekte der Jugendkriminalität', in: *Psychologie und Rechtspraxis*, Berlin 1965, pp. 24 ss.

[71] J. Mehl, 'Fragen der gerichtspsychologischen Persönlichkeitsgutachtens', in: *Psychologie und Rechtspraxis*, loc. cit., p. 16.

[72] Cf. loc. cit., p. 17.

[73] Cf. pp. 190 ss. of the present book.

[74] V. I. Lenin, 'Once Again on the Subject of the Unions', (German version in) *Werke*, vol. 32, Berlin 1961, p. 85.

[75] V. I. Lenin, 'Statistics and Sociology', (German version in) *Werke*, vol. 23, Berlin 1957, p. 285.

[76] V. I. Lenin, 'Once Again on the Subject of the Unions', loc. cit., p. 82.

[77] Cf. V. I. Lenin, *Philosophical Paralipomena* (German version), Berlin 1954, p. 89.

[78] Cf. K. Zweiling, 'Einige Gedanken zu Philosophie, Determiniertheit und Kausalität', *Deutsche Zeitschrift für Philosophie* 1964, Issue 10, pp. 1240 ss.

[79] Cf. G. Stiller, 'Theoretische und methodologische Grundlagen der kriminologischen Forschungen in der DDR', Habil. thesis, Babelsberg 1965, pp. 68 ss.

[80] Cf. p. 159 ss. of the present book.

[81] *Programme and Statutes of the CPSU* (quoted from the German edition, Berlin 1961, p. 100).

[82] Cf. G. Stiller, 'Ursachen und begünstigende Bedingungen der Straftaten in der DDR und ihre Bekämpfung', *Neue Justiz*, 1964, no. 10, pp. 300 ss.

[83] Cf. especially Part II of the present book. No description of their systematic categorisation is therefore given at this point.

[84] Cf. *Uber die Kontrollziffern für die Entwicklung der Volkswirtschaft der UdSSR in den Jahren 1959 bis 1965,* Berlin 1959, pp. 114 ss.

[85] Cf. *Philosophisches Wörterbuch*, loc. cit., pp. 416 ss.

[86] Cf. also E. Buchholz, 'Der Diebstahl und seine Bekämpfung in der DDR', Habil. thesis, Berlin 1963, p. 276.

[87] This was discussed in the first few chapters of this Part. The main object is the highlighting of the relations between the individual factors and their deepest socio-economic roots, the prevailing production relations, and the various intermediate links.

[88] Cf. also M. Vorwerg, 'Methodische Prinzipien der sozialpsychologischen Forschung', in: *Sozialpsychologie im Sozialismus*, Berlin 1965, pp. 117 ss.

[89] Cf. G.J. Glesermann, 'Objektive Bedingungen und subjektiver Faktor beim Aufbau des Kommunismus', *Sowjetwissenschaft − Gesellschaftwissenschaftliche Beiträge*, 1965, Issue 10, pp. 1005 ss.

[90] Cf. esp. F. Engels, 'Anti-Dühring', in: K. Marx/F. Engels, *Werke*, vol. 20, Berlin 1962, p. 264.

[91] Cf. W. Friedrich, 'Zum Problem der Verhaltensdetermination im Jugendalter', *Jugendforschung*, 1965, Issue 6, p. 11.

[92] *Philosophisches Wörterbuch*, loc. cit., p. 90.

10 Procedures for the Investigation of Criminality and its Causes

The importance of method in criminality research

The correct application of the various procedures for the investigation of criminality and its causes demands not only an acquaintance with the laws and requirements of the building of socialism and with the theory of the causes of criminality, but also a scientific method. By this we mean the manner in which the various procedures are applied in specific criminality investigation, the practical procedures and actions of all those taking part in criminality research, the selection of the research field and information sources, the mapping out of procedural stages, the organisation of the employment of helpers, the drafting of the plan of criminality research and the definition of the steps needed for its realisation.

Available research results show that method has not yet always had the necessary attention devoted to it. Various criminality analyses reveal weaknesses in the preparation of the investigations. Thus, research objectives are still sometimes defined without available relevant research findings being first evaluated. The purpose of any such preliminary evaluation must be to decide whether further researches are to verify or supplement available results or whether specialised investigations will be enough to arrive at new findings. An ill-prepared approach towards criminality research may result in wasted effort or in a situation where available findings, long verified and found correct, are worked out all over again. This aspect of preparation includes the utilisation of the analyses of the Workers' and Peasants' Inspectorate and the Ministry of the Interior. Research plans should therefore invariably ensure that relevant results already available are studied and processed.

Of considerable importance also is the choice of the field of research. Sample studies should be so planned that from their findings conclusions can subsequently be drawn concerning the phenomenon as a whole. Criminality research as a rule aims at statements about certain causes of criminality in specific territorial or social areas, especially economic areas. However, it is only rarely possible to explore a criminal phenomenon in its entirety. That is why sample studies must produce results which allow conclusions to be drawn concerning the phenomenon as a whole. The procedure needed for arriving at such representative statements will be explained in connection with other statistical procedures.

The research field must further be mapped out in accordance with the objectives of a particular research project. Thus, if the prerequisites of a system of crime prevention in cities are to be worked out, then the cities suitable for such a study must be selected. It must be remembered, among other things, that conditions in towns with fewer than 50,000 inhabitants, situated near major cities, are different from conditions in rural areas, that conditions in towns with more than 100,000 inhabitants again differ from those in very large cities like Berlin, Leipzig, etc.

Finally, the field must be sufficiently productive for the research intended. It would therefore be desirable, by means of a pilot test, to establish the absolute figures of crime statistics for the criminal phenomena under consideration in the territory or sphere envisaged, and the period of time to which these figures refer. According to the task in hand the number of criminal cases to be examined, the time span within which they fall, and the territorial extent of the area under investigation must be appropriately adjusted.

It is also important to make sure of the information sources from the very beginning. Thus the quality, and hence the usefulness, of the criminal files must be checked; a decision must be made on what additional conditions should be investigated and what persons should be additionally questioned. It is particularly important in this context to evaluate the documents of the SED, certain analyses of State bodies, and other official data.

Experience gained in criminality research also shows that it is exceedingly important to prepare one's collaborators in criminality research as carefully as possible and to instruct them suitably. These, as a rule, will be employees of the judiciary and they will collect their data on certain criminal phenomena by means of questionnaires. The value of the findings provided by them will depend crucially on the attitude they bring to this task, on their understanding of the need for a high standard of work, and on their knowledge of the problems to be investigated and the methods to be applied.

Various control methods have been developed for assessing the quality of the findings obtained from the questionnaires described above, and for drawing conclusions about the objectivity of the data collected. These methods include not only the sampling procedures to be described later but also various indirect checks. It has, for instance, been found useful to question all staff involved in a survey about their own views on the joint action of the various causes of a criminal offence, the chances of liquidating criminality and the effectiveness of measures taken by the judiciary. The views expressed also provide clues to the care and skill applied to the questionnaire operation. There have been cases of a considerable percentage of questionnaires having to be scrapped because they had not been handled in accordance with instructions. Purposeful preparation and training of the staff involved in the survey will very largely avoid such shortcomings.

This includes the methodical training of all those participating in a survey. Interviewing, for instance, requires a certain scientifically based procedure if all sources of error are to be excluded or at least knowingly allowed for. The standard of those participating, finally, is of vital importance in the choice of the method to be applied in criminality research. Complicated methods presuppose that those applying them actually master them, because otherwise the project might be in jeopardy. The order in which various procedures are to be applied, on the other hand, will depend very largely on the research objective itself.

The experiences made in this field by Czech criminologists — experiences basically coinciding with our own — are worth quoting. B. Kvasnička reports:

> Finally we would like to mention the survey technique. Experience made by the Crime Research Institute in the investigations reported on has led us to believe — and other members of the Institute agree with us — that as a matter of principle the direct collection of survey data cannot be achieved without the participation of a relatively large number of helpers. As, at the time we were mounting the research project, the use of paid outside interviewers was out of the question we had no choice but to base our project on the co-operation of the machinery of the Public Prosecutor's Office. The Regional Public Prosecutor's Offices organised the survey and the staffs on the District Prosecutor's Offices (with the help of a few volunteers from other judiciary bodies and a somewhat larger number of assigned helpers from organisations of the heavy engineering industry) filled in the questionnaires concerned. A check on the results achieved in this way, however, revealed beyond any doubt that this is not a recommendable expedient since the number of wrongly classified cases under certain headings amounted to more than 50%, with the result that we had to spend a great deal of time on their re-classification on the strength of written material and on the manual re-sorting of the data.
>
> The reason for these errors was clearly the lack of interest of the

interviewers. Nothing much can be done about this since such an exercise objectively represents additional work for the officials engaged in the criminal proceedings. Even though, under Article 89, Section 1, Sub-Section f of the criminal code the circumstances which led to an offence or made its commission possible are a mandatory subject of investigation for the record, this does not mean that work to provide research data could be presented as being no more than the discharge of this statutory obligation. The fact is that research frequently — whenever it looks for hitherto unknown factors — must establish circumstances which can be of no significance whatever for the judgement of the individual case, and the time-consuming technical preparation of the various research data quite clearly constitutes a task which in no way follows from the demands of the proceedings themselves. This is true of all such surveys if moreover — as in our project — the data are about criminal cases already concluded; a study of the files and the collection of data from other sources can clearly only serve the purposes of research. In a situation of chronic understaffing (frequently even with unfilled vacancies) this is bound to mean that the majority of the helpers — with the exception of a relatively small number of particularly conscientious and keen ones — cannot arouse a sufficiently great interest in the research project to ensure genuinely valuable results.

We therefore consider it indispensable, in all those cases where a very small sample is insufficient, to employ a team of specially picked and paid outside helpers for criminological surveys. Otherwise, in present circumstances, no serious research can be guaranteed except under great difficulties, and even then it may not be truly effective.[1]

Experience also teaches that it is useful to start the survey as soon as the methods to be used have been decided upon. In this the designing of the questionnaire and its subsequent evaluation represent relatively independent stages which in turn require a specialised procedure. The questionnaires themselves are statistically processed; the problems arising from this fact will be discussed later. At present various far-reaching methods, including testing procedures, are increasingly gaining in importance. These too will be discussed in subsequent sections.

All that has been said about the use of research methods will have made it clear that the success of criminality research must depend on scientifically based methods. Various problems of method will be touched upon in connection with certain procedures. This is important because questions of method play an important part at each stage of research and execution of criminological investigations and also because throughout any research the method applied to it must be constantly checked.

Information in criminality research

Mention has already been made of the special importance which knowledge and selection of information sources have for criminality research. The information problem, however, requires a separate examination since the character of information, its peculiarities and limitations are important questions concerning the research projects themselves.

First of all we must clarify what is to be regarded as information. The specific question is whether the information concept as formulated by cybernetics[2] may be employed. In favour of its employment is the fact that it is sufficiently general to comprise all phenomena which might lead to new knowledge. Also in favour is the fact that, in view of the growing importance of cybernetics and the need to apply it in future also to criminological research, a conceptual agreement would facilitate collaboration. Information, therefore, is anything 'that carries within it traces of any fact or any event, whether already taken place or yet to occur. Information is anything that furnishes data or statements about that fact.'[3] This is a definition from which criminality research should also proceed — at least for the moment.

For the establishment of correlations all phenomena should be regarded as primary sources in so far as they are directly perceptible, i.e. have entered into external reality, have become objectivised. These are, above all, the criminal offences themselves (to be discussed in detail in connection with their manifestations). They include, moreover, the offenders and their complex personalities, as well as other phenomena which provide information about the offender, such as data about his normal social behaviour, about his specific working and everyday conditions, and also any related conflicts in the social sphere, his local environment, etc. These phenomena (primary sources) are to be examined within the framework of criminality research or to be deduced from secondary sources. Secondary sources are all those data which do not themselves reflect or depict a correlation but merely allow for one to be inferred.

Another problem which comprises a series of difficult questions is the recording of subjective processes. These processes are not the result of mechanically operating external circumstances and influences, just as the subjective circumstances do not exert a mechanical reaction upon the external world. In consequence no mechanical conclusions can be drawn from external circumstances about internal processes or characteristics. Whenever individuals are made to supply information on subjective processes it must be remembered that they are themselves subject to social and psychological processes. It is therefore always necessary to verify any information obtained through subjective facts and processes or from subjective secondary sources by checking them against objective criteria. Thus any assessment of an offender's inner attitude should always be confronted with objective phenomena, such as his performance, behaviour vis-à-vis other persons and domestic circumstances. Clarity about the problems connected with the collection, sorting and evaluation of information will ensure that the available material is utilised fully and comprehensively, that possible errors and limitations on information are taken account of and that the researches are thus raised to a higher level.

There is a further problem connected with the criminal offences which represent the principal basic information material for criminality research. The offences, together with their causes and the conditions favouring them are first of all established by the investigatory bodies and subsequently by the Public Prosecutor's Office, the Court, the Conflict Commission or the Arbitration Commission. Quite often, however, not all the information established by the investigatory bodies is essential to the Court's verdict and is therefore not reflected in it. This means in turn that the facts not required by the Court for arriving at its findings are not verified in the course of its proceedings. If one also remembers that the scientific standards of the officials of the various judiciary bodies involved in the analysis vary a good deal it is obvious that the exactitude of the data may be affected by various factors.

Information on actual events is primarily gleaned from the case files. These reflect the law-infringing mode of behaviour and the correlations interconnected with it. It must, however, be remembered that the data contained in these case files often represent secondary sources. These data, therefore, carry various 'sources of error' which might result, for research, in a distorted reflection of reality. It has been pointed out that some investigatory procedures have not yet reached the level of an exact scientific social analysis. From all this, therefore, follows a need to supplement and verify certain data by checking them against objective criteria. Finally one cannot even be sure that correlations not mentioned in the case files may not in fact have been operative. This caution is supported by sampling.

It is clear, therefore, that the case files alone are not sufficient for criminological research. They are, in a sense, a collection of the results of analysis and the evaluation of various information sources or of information itself. They include personal documents of the offender, official documents, scientifically accurate statements, calculations, etc., as well as the verbal statements of the offender, observations by people from his environment, from his teams, etc. These statements and opinions also reflect various individual interests, impressions and assessments. The case files also include other documents which describe, reconstruct, etc., an objective occurrence. These peculiarities of the various documents must be very carefully noted in their evaluation. Criminality research, after all that has been said above, must endeavour to establish objective occurrences as directly as possible. As this is not always feasible it is important that, on a matter of principle, use is made first and foremost of those items of information which are reliable, and which contain the most accurate and truthful statements possible about objective and subjective processes. The greater the number of intermediate reflecting links, the greater the possible degree of divergence from objective reality. An assessment of past analyses and methods suggests that this principle has not invariably been sufficiently observed. It has occasionally been infringed for reasons of expediency and convenience or because of the difficulties of getting hold of the necessary data.

The sources of information can basically be divided into two main categories.[4] On the one hand there is the information gleaned from the criminal proceedings, i.e. the individual case, and hence limited to it; and on the other there is the information which transcends the case and generalises from it. The first group includes any culpable actions, any changes in the external world brought about by the offender's action, the offender's general behaviour in his specific environment, observations by citizens, work teams, etc., on the offence and the offender, the offender's personal documents, the documents of other persons and authorities, and objects connected with the offence. The second group includes chiefly the material resulting from the processing and generalisation of the criminologically significant events and circumstances. Among them are:

(a) The offence-related findings, i.e. the statistical record sheets of the penal organs for the relevant criminal statistics (these are filled in by the bodies which conclude the criminal proceedings and are kept at District Public Prosecutors' Offices), the punched cards to which the findings are transferred from the above-mentioned statistical record sheet (these are kept at the Prosecutor's Office concerned with the case), the statistics generally kept by all criminal judiciary organs; the criminality analyses of judiciary organs;

(b) Information and data relating to social conditions, the laws underlying them and the demands arising from them, i.e. documents of the SED, the mass organisations and the National Front, documents of central and local administrative bodies and their institutions, analyses of Workers' and Peasants' Inspectorates, analyses of economic bodies concerning productivity and work, economic losses and their causes, etc., research results (in particular also those of other scientific disciplines), dissertations, press reports, and statistics published by various State institutions, economic management bodies and the Central Statistical Office.

Such information varies a good deal in its objectivity and validity, and these variations must be allowed for.

The offender's personal documents (letters, remarks on his action, autobiographies, diaries) reflect certain impressions, feelings and moods; they contain assessments and opinions moulded by his state of knowledge, attitude and habit. They are valuable in that they reveal information about his personality.

The value of statements by offenders, members of their families, other citizens, work teams, representatives of State bodies and of social organisations is affected by their attitude to the offence, to the victims, to the object of the offence, etc. The judgement of this circle of individuals is coloured both by certain social influences and by their own state of development. An exact understanding of the specific working and everyday conditions and the social sphere of this circle of persons (in particular of the offenders) very largely depends on the investigator's skill in correctly grasping and also quantifying these conditions in each individual case.[5]

Attention should further be drawn to the fact that the information sources here listed show *peculiarities* in respect of various criminality phenomena and occasionally may prove to be insufficient. Thus, in the case of juvenile criminality recourse will have to be had to additional information resulting from the special peculiarities of juveniles and the specific character of their position in society. Other phenomena will have to be taken into account in connection with sexual offences by persons over 60 and with other offences. In addition, different peculiarities may arise from different circumstances; thus it may at times be advisable or necessary to study the personal files of offenders, to visit certain institutions, or to call for expert opinion.[6]

In connection with these problems of information it should be remembered that documentation is steadily gaining in importance as a source of information in criminality research.

Document analysis in criminality research

Criminality research is based on documents, primarily the resolutions of the Socialist Unity Party of Germany (SED) which, because of their scientific content, high degree of generalisation and seminal character, are of overriding importance to research itself and to crime prevention.

It has already been said that great importance attaches to the evaluation of the case files. These files are interesting both as overall documents and also for the many detailed documents they contain.

Other considerations again require the processing of various official documents in which statistical data, crime categories and their characteristics are examined from various points of view. From the nature and the purpose of these documents, from the point of view under which the statistical data are processed or presented (absolute figures or percentages), etc., conclusions can be drawn about the usefulness they possess for practical workers and scholars in criminality research. A different approach is needed in dealing with the personal documents of the accused and of other persons.

The documents to be analysed may be divided into official and unofficial. The official documents as a rule show a high degree of generalisation and are also objective; however, this must not be understood in an undifferentiated (undialectical) manner and the character of each document must be tested and taken into account. Thus, documents of bourgeois criminologists, official documents on criminality in imperialist countries, etc., may have to be evaluated. But these have repeatedly shown themselves to be biased or even downright 'doctored'. Moreover, official documents from imperialist countries frequently contain statements on the causes of criminality which are based on unscientific theories.

A high degree of generalisation and objectivity is found, for instance, in documents of local administrative bodies in the GDR, in the records of economic bodies and enterprises, of social organisations, etc. But even within this group the informative value of the different documents varies from one to another.

If the causes of crime in an industrial enterprise are to be investigated the totality of the documents in this field must be subjected to analysis. This includes documents on the trends of criminality, on the employees, their material situation and vocational qualifications, development of the productive forces and democratic life within the enterprise, documents on public health, personal staff files, etc. In most cases such document analysis must be supplemented by other procedures, such as interrogation and direct observation. Particular attention must also be paid to the purpose and date of the various documents since these may contain clues on whether certain conditions, indispensable to criminality research, have been disregarded. Additional aspects may also arise from the particular situation at the time.

Unofficial documents sometimes suggest that their authors put particular emphasis on aspects close to their own hearts, aspects which do not meet the requirements of objectivity. Personal documents, in particular, may contain subjective assessments.

Document analysis, even though the limitations on its value must not be overlooked, should be used to a greater extent in criminological research. This is true in particular of the evaluation of the most important official documents which contain statements on the evolution of society in various spheres and areas, on the contradictions operative there and on the forces capable of resolving them. Of particular importance in this connection are statements about typical ideas and behaviour, the so-called normal behaviour of working people. At the same time, the analysis of various unofficial documents (e.g. of offenders, or of persons and teams from the offenders' environment, etc.) should also be intensified because these documents also convey − and in a relatively short space of time − data on the object under investigation, and are capable of enlarging the available fund of knowledge.

The following general observations can be made in connection with document analysis, especially the analysis of criminal case files:

(a) The documents contained in the case file should be viewed and analysed as an intergral whole in order to avoid one-sided assessments. The verdict, for instance, contains only the connections essential for the determination of criminal responsibility, though this does not mean that other connections of significance to criminality research may not have been effective at the time. The totality of conditions can only be understood from a study of all documents, interrogations, expert opinions, letters, the summing up, the indictment, verdict and sentence, etc.

(b) In analysing the individual documents allowance must be made for the special situation which arises, in the case file, from the fact that the most important source of information − the accused or defendant − is being made to answer for a criminal offence and may therefore often attempt to belittle his misdemeanour. The officials of the judiciary, on the other hand, are charged with determining his culpability and holding him accountable. This may create a clash of interest and at times affect the degree of objectivity. In each case, therefore, the relation of the information source to the offence, or the offender, must be taken into consideration.

(c) The documents to be analysed as a rule reflect subjective impressions of events or phenomena, sometimes even coveyed at second or third hand. These persons' degree of intelligence, interests, attitudes and other aspects, however, greatly affect the objectivity of the documents. In this connection it should also be mentioned that investigatory organs are still inclined to reproduce statements by the accused, by witnesses, etc., in the words of the interrogator. This vitiates the degree of objectivity necessary for criminality research.

(d) It must further be remembered that a peculiar problem of the analysis of expert opinion is that specialised knowledge is often required for a full understanding of it. Occasionally, a supplementary questioning of the experts may be necessary. This applies not only to psychological and psychiatric opinions but also, for instance, to expert opinions on road and weather conditions, on economic and other aspects, and also on responsibilities stemming from professional positions. Difficult questions are finally encountered in the evaluation of opinions and assessments made by individuals or teams. These questions have already been dealt with above and therefore will not be discussed here again.

Document analysis is gaining increasing importance in criminological surveys. It is used in conjunction with interviewing, sampling and testing methods. Its place within the system of research procedures therefore requires further scientific clarification.

Criminological surveys

Among the procedures to be discussed the most important are those which make it possible to cover criminality or a category of criminal offences on a national scale, or within a limited territory, or in a social, more particularly economic, sphere. This provides the prerequisites of analysing a multiplicity of offences together with their causes and conditions, and thus of discovering the laws governing their connections which determine criminality in the GDR under present-day conditions of social development. One such procedure is the criminological survey by questionnaire.[7]

This procedure is indispensable because, as we have stated, the information on offences and their roots, as collected by questionnaire, represents valuable primary data for criminality research.

Surveying by questionnaire has been developed into a specialised criminological procedure over the past few years, and it has already proved its worth. The complex of questions contained in the questionnaires has become more comprehensive and more precise, largely thanks to the increasing application of the findings of other scientific disciplines. There is nowadays scarcely a research project which can do without surveys.

First, the function of the survey has to be clarified within the framework of criminological research. The survey serves the compilation of the findings arrived at in the criminal proceedings because these contain information on the offence and its causes. It is not, therefore, concerned with discovering new or supplementary correlations; that is the task of a number of other procedures, including the above-mentioned written or oral interviewing. Nor is the survey concerned with collecting information on the manner in which the criminal proceedings were conducted, on the enlistment of social forces, the effectiveness of the punishment, warranty for good behaviour, suspended sentences, or the application of procedural norms which are necessary to the criminal law expert or the proceedings specialist in order that he can draw conclusions on the performances of the judiciary bodies. Such a demand, occasionally raised by practitioners, mistakes the fact that surveying is a criminological procedure with its special place in the system of methods used by that discipline. Admittedly, certain such conclusions can occasionally be made, for instance in connection with the examination of the causes of recidivism, without impairing the genuinely criminological character of the procedure. Again, there is nothing to prevent other disciplines from applying the survey method to their own purpose or even from linking their own questionnaires with the criminological ones.

The starting point for criminality research, in its attempt to discover the correlations of complex phenomena, is the specific criminal offence. Investigation of the relevant population (the totality of phenomena to be covered) or its parts (in respect of causally operative phenomena and the laws governing relations among them) demands that the examination should start from the individual offence. On this, important information is gained in the criminal proceedings. Their collection and compilation from a criminological point of view by a survey is one of the foundations of new criminological knowledge.

The place of the criminological survey within the system of research procedures stems principally from the fact that the law-determined correlations are of a a statistical character. In consequence, considerable importance attaches to statistical analysis for the discovery of these correlations. Statistical analysis starts from the statistical survey and proceeds to the processing and evaluation of the data thus collected. Such statistical data are provided, above all, by the proceedings themselves; indeed, no other exact research discipline could provide relevant facts and information on a similar scale. The judiciary organs reveal the causes of the criminal action to the extent necessary for the discharge of their own tasks and verify these causes at various stages of the proceedings. Criminological surveying is a form of statistical surveying appropriate to the subject of criminology. Statistical surveys are used by a multiplicity of other scientific disciplines. They supply criminology with a wealth of valuable data.

Opinions continue to differ about the position and importance of criminological surveys. In some quarters the interview is still preferred to the criminological survey. However, the structure of the causes of criminality and the laws governing their correlations can only be approached by way of the phenomenology of the offences. These are the facts which are collected and examined in the course of the criminal proceedings. The interview cannot discharge this task, if only because the establishment of the offence itself is the job of the competent administrative organs, which means that comprehensive information and results can be expected from them alone. Finally, the time lag between the commission of an offence and any possible interview by criminologists would lead to highly unreliable results. Added to this is the fact that the most varied procedures are applied in the criminal proceedings, linked with one another or modified, in order to obtain results optimally corresponding to the facts. Thus interrogation, document analysis, expert opinion and comparison are all used.

A number of bourgeois criminologists stress and indeed over-emphasise the interview method on ideological grounds. The West German sociologist König states:

> There are ... countless procedures for ensuring the direct connection with the data, ranging from simple observation to the strictly controlled experiment. Yet in this series the personal interview occupies a central part which nowadays emerges ever more clearly. Provided it is ... subjected to methodical control, the interview in its various forms will always remain the royal road of practical social research ..[8]

This view conceals the earlier-mentioned temporising position adopted by bourgeois criminologists. If the causes of a social deformation of offenders are to be examined then such an examination must start from the individual in his whole complexity, in his quality of a natural being and as an ensemble of social relations. The research method must match this complexity of the subject, its multi-layered and multi-faceted character. Any one-sided emphasis on the interview runs counter to this demand.

At the same time a warning should be uttered against any overrating of the criminological survey. If scientific results are aimed at, allowing for precise statement to be made on the causes of criminal phenomena and providing for effective preventive measures, then such surveys must be supplemented by other procedures. A number of researchers in scientific institutes, as well as members of the judiciary, have been, and indeed still are, deducing far-reaching statements merely from data obtained by questionnaires and without further verification. Such an absolutisation of the survey must be rejected, especially as until quite recently the questionnaires in use varied a great deal in their degree of sophistication. In certain cases they did not even meet the minimum demands that have to be made on this important tool of research.

This also raises the question of the limitations of the survey method. As we know, not everything that has to be criminologically investigated is in fact revealed in the course of the criminal proceedings. These merely uncover the causes of the offence to the extent necessary for decision on the offender's criminal responsibility, his re-education and the liquidation of the causes and conditions directly operating upon his life, i.e. as a rule the immediate and essential determinants of his culpable behaviour. The social aspects of these determinants, however, cannot be comprehensively investigated in the proceedings. Here then lie the limitations of the data obtained by the survey.

The main objection to the absolutisation of criminological survey by questionnaire, however, is based on the limitations affecting the objectivity, validity and reliability on the results themselves. These further limitations of the survey method emphatically support the need for the application of the whole system of procedures. These particular limitations are connected, among other things, with the degree of objectivity reflected by the various documents in the case file. This point was made earlier in connection with document analysis. The reason why this aspect is once more emphasised is that the evaluation of the questionnaires prepared by our own research team revealed that the relations of the information carrier to the criminal offence, or to the offender, had not been adequately taken into account.

Another problem confronting an absolutisation of the criminological survey by questionnaire stems from the fact that the documents to be analysed and any other information from the criminal proceedings reproduce subjective observations of events or phenomena and are therefore of a reflective character. It is clear, therefore, that the limitations of the documents to be evaluated — the case file — are at the same time the limitations of the survey.

Practical experience also induces us to utter one further warning: the

316

case files or the records of the proceedings also contain statements about negative environmental conditions without any proof of whether, or to what extent, they had any bearing on the offender's action. In such cases there is a danger that the questionnaires might become mere catalogues of all conceivable shortcomings, weaknesses or faults of the offender himself or of certain phenomena in his environment.

While it is necessary to oppose any absolutisation of criminological surveying, it must be stated, on the other hand, that the possibilities provided by the method are still not being fully utilised.

An analysis of recently prepared questionnaires shows that these pursue very diverse purposes. It also shows that available theoretical and methodological experience and knowledge has been applied in them to a greatly varying degree. Some of them suggest that surveys are still not being prepared with the necessary care. Yet such a preparation is of crucial importance to the quality of the results achieved by the method. We shall mention just a few major problems in this context.[9]

Like any other scientific investigation, criminological surveying also proceeds by stages. Each individual stage has its own specific characteristics which must be taken into consideration. This is generally true for methodology and in particular for the preparation of any survey questionnaire.

It is one of the major tasks of criminality research to use available research results for designing a model of the causes of criminality. In addition to the systematic evaluation of all past research results in the field this involves also the inclusion of the findings of criminal statistics and of the analytical work by judiciary bodies. These data are scientifically processed with the object of identifying those systems of correlations on which the criminological survey is focused, in order thus to arrive at definite results for crime prevention.

It might be objected that the criminologist should include all factors in his considerations as he cannot know in advance which correlations may determine a particular criminal phenomenon under present-day conditions. But this is only partially true. For one thing, all criminality research is based on available knowledge and experience, and for another the chosen research subject of itself demands an appropriate narrowing of the questions to be put; finally the ultimate objective — the creation of the prerequisites of preventive measures in a particular direction — affects the preparation of the questionnaire.

Past experience shows that criminal phenomena and their causes must be criminologically studied in three correlation systems. These are: (a) the offender's internal system conditions; (b) the system of internal and external conditions in the actual offence situation: (c) the system of phenomena determining the past development of the offender's personality. The survey is then focused on those phenomena which are connected with the criminal offence.

There is still often uncertainty about the object and the limits of surveying; this is reflected in the fact that all conceivable questions are included in the questionnaire. This may discredit the procedure in the eyes of the practical workers in our judiciary bodies. Whenever available data are insufficient the draft of a survey questionnaire should be tested by a sample investigation. Such a test as a rule will result in both a completion and a shortening of the questionnaire, and in any case also in greater scientific accuracy of the method.

Evaluation of concluded criminal proceedings generally shows that not all the questions included in a questionnaire can be answered from the case file. Such shortcomings, gaps or uncertainties can be remedied only at the cost of considerable work. As a rule, therefore, questionnaires should be linked with pending or current proceedings. Admittedly this can lead to other difficulties, but these are easily dealt with. On the strength of an analysis of available questionnaire material a few hints might be in order on how to improve the contents of survey questionnaires.

It is as a rule difficult to cover in the questionnaire the statements made in the proceedings about the motives behind an offence. In spite of the efforts of judiciary and investigatory organs to explore and define these motives, the results achieved — since we are dealing here with psychological processes — vary a good deal in value. A stronger lead should be given in this direction by psychologists. What we want to define here is the question of what should be included in the questionnaire under the heading of the motive.

In nearly all questionnaires the heading 'motives' also covers personality features and psychological dispositions. The questionnaire used for studying the causes of recidivism among juveniles — otherwise a questionnaire which seems more sophisticated than some — includes among the motives of the offence such concepts as 'personal convenience', 'immaturity' etc. Other questionnaires include 'lack of discipline', 'irresponsibility', 'low opinion of women' and 'because others do it'. The first of these concepts, however, represent personal characteristics which, though they may determine the motivation process, are not in themselves motives of the offence. They lack the characteristics which make a motive. Similarly, disparate concepts are listed among the motives in other studies. Hinderer, for instance, lists among the motives of theft such ideas as personal advantage, the offender's wish to gain prestige among his friends or to harm others, hostility, fear and frank admission of a mistake, or lack of willpower to resist an invitation to commit a criminal offence. [10]

By motive we mean the internal reason that makes an individual take a definite purposive action. Automatic movements, such as are found in offences of negligence, on the other hand, may take place without a motive. The first characteristic of a motive, therefore, is its purposiveness. This characteristic, in consequence, is absent in 'indiscipline' and 'irresponsibility'. These merely express an attitude or perhaps a mode of action. The second characteristic which must be present before we can talk about a motive is that a motive drives the individual towards realisation. This characteristic is likewise absent in certain phenomena which are, therefore, wrongly labelled motives. This is not to gainsay the importance of such phenomena in the motivation process. Personality traits and attitudes do in fact play an important part in this process, and valuable conclusions may be derived from them for the struggle against crime. But they are not motives and therefore should not be described as such.

Another problem arises from the differences in the practical processing of questionnaires designed to explore various attitudes. Thus the questions not only relate to the individual's attitude to work, to social property, society, to the State, etc., but the answers obtained are qualified by value judgements such as 'good' or 'bad'. In other cases the questions about various attitudes are supplemented by a number of indicators. In the former case researchers are clearly guided by the consideration that the questionnaires should only cover the data established during the criminal proceedings; the proceedings themselves, as a rule, scarcely produce any very definite data on attitude. The latter approach can be justified by the argument that it is not enough to establish the mere presence of one attitude or another, since that in itself reveals nothing about how firmly it is rooted in the offender, and that it is therefore difficult to discover any development of attitudes by comparing various criminal phenomena. Much as the latter approach commends itself, it must not be forgotten that the criminal proceedings in themselves can scarcely provide the necessary basis. There is thus no alternative to choosing the former road and, according to the criminal phenomenon in question, using indirect methods for discovering the development of certain processes and also their depth, etc. To that end it is necessary to utilise all the internal and external circumstances that have been established in so far as they relate to the attitude in question. The exact quantities of certain phenomena, in particular attitudes, must be investigated by other methods. They presuppose a quantification of the questions under examination and normally exceed what can be discovered in the course of case proceedings.

Mention should finally be made of a problem which cannot be tackled by statistical or mathematical processing or by subsequent evaluation. That is the problem of how the operation of inter-relations and remote correlations can be highlighted to provide a higher level of theoretical generalisation. Such correlations cannot easily be read from the questions in the questionnaires. There is much to be said for the increasing practice of requiring the criminologist conducting the survey to provide, beyond the collection of individual correlations, a comprehensive presentation of the principal causes and of their function and interrelations in connection with the commission of the criminal offence. This provides valuable supplementary material from which important conclusions can be drawn for the development of a system of preventive measures and social programmes.

Statistical procedures in criminality research

The range of application of statistical procedures

In criminality research the investigation of the individual case is not as a rule focused casuistically, i.e. related just to the one case in question, but statistically, i.e. with a view to subsequent statistical processing of the various correlations, more particularly the causes and conditions of a large number of individual offences. This purpose is served principally by the survey method referred to above. From a large number of questionnaires the general and necessary correlations can be extracted by processing. Only thus can the laws governing the correlations be identified.

Criminality research so far has used statistical methods in a variety of ways in a one-sided manner. Their application was concentrated chiefly on the sphere of criminal statistics. These statistics, compiled by the judiciary bodies, covered all criminality, its trends, the external structure of offences and the measures of penal bodies. Criminal statistics, moreover, contained a number of important elements upon which criminality research must base itself in its further work, e.g. on the offender's personality and its development. Criminal statistics are integrated into the Central Criminal Statistics kept under the direction of the Prosecutor General.

Statistical methods, moreover, have been used in the study of special phenomena and correlation. Such statistical studies have been prepared or conducted either by the penal bodies themselves or by scientific research teams. Harrland reports various examples of statistical studies designed to investigate specialised correlations. [11] Such studies may stem from initial conclusions and suggestions found in the Central Criminal Statistics, or in scientific research data, or even in questions arising from the practical work of penal bodies. Thus it has been found in criminal proceedings that re-settlers from West Germany have relatively often been found to have committed criminal offences. These observations in themselves are not sufficient to decide whether this is a problem of general social significance. This is where statistical procedures can supply the answer. If it were found, for instance, that these citizens have particular difficulties in finding their niche in our community, both at their place of residence and in their work team, that they live in an individualistic way, avoiding socialist teams, and that, on the other hand, our social forces are not making sufficient efforts to enlist them, then this would provide important starting points for preventive work by our penal authorities. Appropriate conclusions might be drawn for more effective integration of such persons in the socialist transformation process. The findings of such statistical procedures might also give rise to specific questions on such subjects as care for re-settlers at reception centres, their accommodation, the work of local bodies, organisations, etc.

These methods are based on the ability of statistics to describe criminality or individual phenomena. The frequency of offences and all countable or measurable phenomena or factors are expressed in percentages, ratios, frequency distributions, mean values, indicators, etc.

Criminality research, however, is also interested in the description and determination of connections. Thus the relations between frequently observed phenomena must be investigated with a view to discovering whether a positive correlation is present, how close it is, etc. The measures for such connections are the correlation coefficient, the regression coefficient, etc. Functional dependence, on the other hand, will rarely be established in criminality research since this, by its nature, presupposes that a definite value of one variable factor is unequivocally associated with the value of a second variable (see diagrams on pages 322 and 323).

These problems will be further elucidated by examples from criminality research. The statistical procedures, moreover, provide the basis for the planning and execution of sample surveys whenever for reasons of time it is not possible to investigate the totality of certain phenomena. Statistical methods are then used to ensure that the sample studied represents a kind of reduced-scale model of the totality (the statistical 'population'). It also makes it possible to calculate the accuracy of inductively derived results.

The large number of statistical procedures and the range of questions to which they can be applied must not lead us to overrate statistically established findings. Marx pointed out that 'the internal law which ... expresses itself in chance occurrences and governs them becomes visible only when these chance occurrances are viewed in vast numbers'.[12] Statistics, therefore, must be supplemented by other methods. Without the application of Marxist philosophy as a method the true causes of criminality cannot be laid bare. On the other hand, it is a mistake to regard statistically obtained results as purely quantitative findings. That would mean negating the dialectical relation between the general and the specific, between essence and appearance. Statistically obtained results, if further processed theoretically, reveal the underlying laws and make it possible to concentrate all forces on their control.

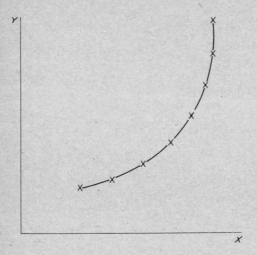

For functional dependence the graphic representation of the pairs of measured values in the co-ordinate system is a line of points which can be extended into a continuous curve.

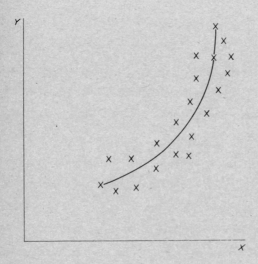

For correlative dependence the graphic representation still shows the points to be grouped along a curve. Compared with functional dependence the points are spread over an area.

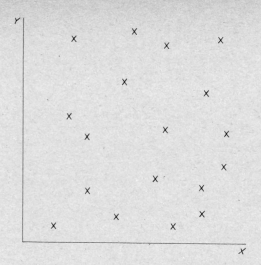

For independence of the examined variables the points are distributed about the entire co-ordinate system.

The laws of statistics have nothing in common with the laws which are investigated by criminologists. It would therefore be a mistake to confuse the 'law of large numbers' — which states that 'the overall effect of a large number of chance factors under certain very general conditions is a result which is almost independent of chance'[13] — with the objective of criminality research, the discovery of the laws determining criminal behaviour. Harrland rightly points out that an equation of these laws would mean adopting the bourgeois point of view. The bourgeois sociologists see the 'law of large numbers' as a kind of 'universal law' or 'fundamental law', and this enables them to avoid any in-depth analysis of essential relations and hence of the real causes of social phenomena and processes.

Another example from bourgeois criminology is the absolutisation of mathematical methods.

Within the framework of empirically oriented theories, mathematical methods have recently been used on an increased scale for the determination of connections existing between various factors. The application of mathematical methods undoubtedly represents progress in criminological research. It also makes it possible to calculate certain functional relationships capable of reflecting correlations more meaningfully. However, certain bourgeois criminologists are concerned not so much with the application of mathematical methods as with the elevation of such functional relationships to the status of a theoretical and methodological principle. They see the ultimate wisdom in those functional relationships instead of in the study of the causes of criminality, and in this way once more demonstrate that they have no intention of investigating the deeper connections rooted in social relations.

This essentially agnostic position is also revealed by the theory of 'relationship', developed under American influence and now apparently widespread among West German criminologists. Middendorf points out that the bourgeois criminologists and sociologists

> to this day know very little about the ultimate background of crime and that, because of this realisation, criminologists and sociologists have lately gone over to avoiding the word 'cause' altogether and instead speak more modestly of a 'functional relationship' between two facts without claiming that their sequential occurrence also represents causality in the meaning of the natural sciences. [14]

This is a clear attempt to draw even the representatives of the empirically oriented theories into the realm of unscientific speculation. Middendorf's 'recommendation' reveals the scientific bankruptcy of his criminological concepts. Any research which deliberately opts out of our investigating causal processes is not only scientifically untenable but also represents a capitulation in the face of crime. The doctrine of 'relationship' has its social roots directly in the imperialist system of society and possesses a reactionary character.

Attention must finally be drawn to another limitation of statistically obtained results. This arises from the fact that statistics reflect certain phenomena and connections, i.e. it is of reflective character. It is therefore necessary to paralyse any factors which might cause reality to be distorted in its statistical reflection. This warning is found also in Soviet literature on the subject. Baydeldinov says: 'The sociologist wishing to subject a social object to statistical analysis must above all ensure that the collected statistical material accurately reflects the quantitative parameters of the object.' [15] Any subjective attitudes must be avoided. This applies both to the scientific and personal preparation of those applying statistical methods and to the problem of accurately defining the concepts used in the statistics. The validity of statistical findings depends on the conditions under which the statistical procedure is employed. Unless this is borne in mind, the figures and results produced will fail to convey a real picture.

Statistical methods make it possible to cover criminality not only as a static picture but also to approach the dynamics of the various processes of criminality. This is done, on the one hand, by periodical statistics, i.e. the collection of data and correlations over a prolonged time-span and at definite fixed periods. On the other, the separate findings are related to their time series. Their movement thus reflects the trend in the development of the phenomenon itself. Some of the factors will disappear, or decline, and new ones will appear. If this pattern is related to other

324

statistical series, e.g. the social structure of society or economic processes and their statistically determined movement, then valuable conclusions may be drawn concerning the progress and future requirement of the struggle against criminality.

Use of statistical procedures in the examination of connections of phenomena from among the complex of the causes of offences

The need to identify and study regular connections between definite criminal phenomena and the factors determining them demands the application of various statistical procedures. Several such statistical procedures have lately been used on an increasing scale in criminality research. Thus, in order to analyse the magnitude and trend of the connection between two characteristics, contingency tables are prepared and the contingency coefficient is calculated. [16] In these, however, separate characteristics are still considered singly, e.g. the correlation between the schooling and the earnings of an offender. In such a case schooling may be covered under certain categories (e.g. 8, 10 or 12 years at school, higher education) and the same applies to the person's income. This makes it possible to draw up contingency tables and to calculate the contingency coefficient. [17] This will presently be explained in greater detail.

A particular rôle among statistical procedures is played by those which serve the investigation of reciprocal relations existing between two or more phenomena subject to random changes. These are procedures for the analysis and quantitative evaluation of statistical correlations. They are covered under the concept of correlation analysis. The various correlation procedures are of particular importance in criminality research because they enable exact statements to be made about the causes of certain criminal phenomena. [18]

The correlation procedures perform three main tasks:

1   They enable hypotheses about connections between certain social phenomena and individual peculiarities of the offender — connections which might have operated as causes — to be tested, as they are able to state whether the interdependence of variations between these connections exceeds the extent of accidental effects.

2   Correlation computations at the same time measure the closeness or completeness of existing connections. They provide comparable numerical values for the closeness of correlations, thus reflecting the examined processes in their quantitative relationships and providing a deeper insight into their nature.

3   On the strength of the calculated closeness of correlations it is possible, by means of appropriate procedures, to assess the factors determining criminal phenomena and thus to make a quantitative distinction between connections and influences essential and inessential to a particular development process. [19]

It is all-important that the statistical procedures applied in correlation analysis should be based on a scientific concept. This means that from the very start the connections to be investigated must be chosen on the basis of theoretical considerations. To divorce the procedures from the theoretical foundations of criminality research would lead to the discovery of useless correlations and to scientifically untenable conclusions. This point needs emphasising if only to exclude the possibility of pseudo-correlations which might result from an accidental parallelism on the quantitative course of two social phenomena. It certainly does not mean that the statistical coverage of the necessary scope of various relationships should be restricted from the outset to an extent that would leave the general connections out of consideration. Discovery of the stability and the regularity of relationships, and eventually the law underlying them, demands a wealth of data. We merely want to avoid correlation computations whose uselessness is obvious from the start.

The application of correlation procedures will now be illustrated by a few examples, and a few technical and conceptual details will be explained. [20] To begin with, the closeness of the connection between two phenomena is described by a numerical term known as the coefficient of correlation (r). It is so designed than in the event of a complete correlation, signifying an unambiguous functional relation, it has the value 1 and in the event of a total absence of any relation it has the value 0. For a complete positive correlation it has the value $+1$ and for a complete negative correlation the value -1. Values of $r \pm 0.5$, disregarding the ratio between the sample of offences examined and the population, express a very loose correlation which might well be accidental. From such a correlation no conclusions should be drawn about a generally valid relationship. Values of 0.6 indicate a perceptible correlation, 0.7 a pronounced correlation and anything higher a very close correlation. [21]

In making a correlation table we are concerned with the distribution of a number of events among the correlation classes of two data series x and y (see Fig. 10.1).

The data series in this case are, along the y axis, the number of previous punishments and, along the x axis, the grade at school after which the offender ceased his school education. If, for instance, an offender who

326

Left school after what grade?

y \ x	4	5	6	7	8	9	10	Total
1	–	–	–	1	3	3	1	8
2	–	1	1	16	5	4	–	27
3	–	8	25	30	12	2	1	78
4	1	3	15	12	1	–	–	32
5	2	1	3	–	–	–	–	6
	3	13	44	59	21	9	2	

(Left axis label: Number of previous punishments)

Fig. 10.1   Example of a correlation table

ceased his schooling after the sixth grade has had three previous convictions, this is what we call an event. The frequency of these events is entered in the table. It can be seen that the data show a roughly normal distribution. That is a prerequisite for the application of certain correlation methods. The most convenient method is the tabulation of correlations by placing a tally in the appropriate space; such a tabulation makes it possible to estimate the correlation in advance (see Fig. 10.2).

With increasingly close correlation the scatter of individual values about the diagonal of the tabular field becomes less. The limit of ideal correlation is reached when each class of y corresponds to only one of x, and vice versa, i.e. when all values lie on the diagonal, indicating a correlation of +1. The other diagonal would correspond to a correlation of $r = -1$. Between these two extremes lie the values encountered in empirical research. The closer their approximation to the limit, the more reliable are the statements. As the coefficient of correlation approximates zero the two data no longer correlate, they are unconnected and permit of no further statement than that of being unconnected.

As for the types and the calculation of the coefficient of correlation, the various methods can be subdivided according to the kind of data to be correlated. These may be represented by quantitative graduated values but may also be present in the form of qualitatively graduated variables.

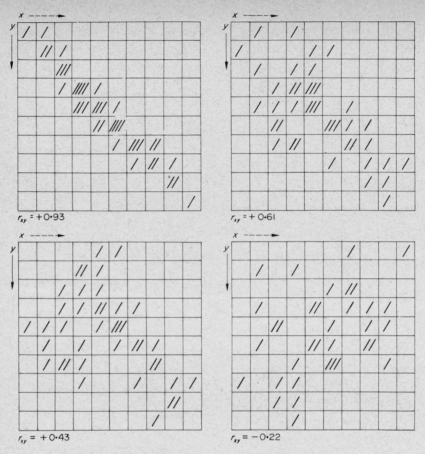

Fig. 10.2   Correlation table by the tally entry method

To quote an example. The political interest of schoolboys can be established by devising the following scale: the political interest of a schoolboy x is great/average/slight. We thus have a variable graduated into three qualitative categories. Another method, however, would be to measure his political knowledge and from the results infer his political interest; i.e. the schoolboy could be asked 12 or 15 questions bearing on his political knowledge and each of his answers could be assessed at 3, 2 or 1; the marks thus scored could be subdivided into quantitative data categories, for instance 0–5, 6–10, 11–15, 16–20, 21–25, etc. In this case we would have a quantitatively graduated set of data.

Attempts should always be made to discover an experimental way of quantifying the two variables to be correlated, since then the generally reliable correlation method of linear value correlation and the tetrachoric four-square coefficient can be used. As, however, it will hardly ever be feasible in our research field to correlate two measurable variables, a detailed explanation of this method will not be given here. Besides, the variables must have a normal distribution. These and similar conditions are frequently not met in phenomena of a living nature. For this reason we shall instead deal at slightly greater length with the so-called free distribution methods.

(i) Correlation measurements based on frequency
If in a sample two data are considered, and both can only be assessed qualitatively (e.g. domestic background: orderly, slack, disorderly; or office holder: yes or no), then we are faced with a case of so-called categorial data connection. For this we can calculate two coefficients.

First, the four-square coefficient of correlation (phi coefficient). To proceed from an example: in a study of aspects of juvenile criminality a comparison was made between juvenile first offenders and recidivists. Apart from numerous other data both groups of offenders clearly showed a difference in the frequency of 'under the influence of drink while committing the offence'. Figure 10.3 shows that recidivists were more frequently and first offenders less frequently under the influence of drink while committing their offence.

	First offenders	Recidivists	Total
Under the influence of drink	(a) 37	(b) 79	118
Not under the influence of drink	(c) 93	(d) 60	153
	130	139	269

Fig. 10.3 Four-square correlation table: distribution of the criterion 'under the influence of drink at the time of the offence' among first offenders and recidivists.

Both variables here are alternatives and qualitatively graduated. The frequencies entered in the four squares are then used in the following formula:

$$\phi = \frac{bc - ad}{\sqrt{(a+b)\,(c+d)\,(a+c)\,(b+d)}} \quad,$$

giving, with our figures,

$$\phi = \frac{79 \times 93 - 37 \times 60}{\sqrt{116 \times 153 \times 130 \times 139}} = 0{\cdot}29.$$

The coefficient for the correlation between the effect of drink and a criminal past is therefore 0·29. In other words, there is a correlation but it is exceedingly slight and lies close to the limit of the interpretable. Admittedly, the phi coefficient is the least favourable among all four-square coefficients, i.e. those calculated by other (here not explained) procedures would lie higher.

The four-square correlation method presupposes a mutually exclusive division of the data. Whenever the data are qualitatively graduated into more than two alternatives then the contingency coefficient (C) is used. This will be shown by another example (Fig. 10.4).

Consideration of the empirical frequency distribution (always the left-hand figure in each square) discloses a trend towards the assessment by

Assessment of performance and attitude by school/place of employment	Number of previous punishments			Total
	1	2	3	
Good	28 (14·8)	12 (16·1)	8 (.......)	48
Average	21 (18·7)	28 (.......)	11 (.......)	60
Poor	9 (24·7)	23 (.......)	48 (.......)	80
	58	63	67	188

Fig. 10.4   Multi-square table for calculation of the contingency coefficient

industrial enterprise or school to worsen with the number of previous sentences. We can verify this trend by comparing the empirical distribution with a theoretical distribution. We arrive at the theoretical distribution by calculating the value for each square — sum of each column multiplied by the sum of each line divided by the overall sum (values in brackets in Fig. 10.4).

For the top left square this would mean $58 \times 48 \div 188 = 14 \cdot 8$. These values are known as the expected frequencies. To calculate the coefficient of contingency we use the following formula:

$$C = \sqrt{\frac{\Sigma\left(\frac{b^2}{e}\right) - N}{\Sigma\left(\frac{b^2}{e}\right)}} \quad , \qquad \text{where}$$

b = observed frequency (numbers outside the brackets in Fig. 10.4)
e = expected frequency (numbers in brackets)
N = number of persons in the sample.

It is clear from the formula that the term $\frac{b^2}{e}$ is calculated for each square and subsequently summed.

The term $\frac{b^2}{e}$ for the top left square in Fig. 10.4 would be $\frac{28^2}{14 \cdot 8}$

The coefficient of contingency embraces only the range from 0—1. It depends on the number of columns and is always smaller than the equivalent measured coefficient of correlation. Its theoretical maximum value, the so-called r equivalent, is calculated according to the formula

$$r \text{ equivalent} = \frac{C}{\sqrt{\frac{m-1}{m}}}$$

where m = number of columns.

The last of the coefficients based on frequency, worth mentioning here, is the biserial coefficient. It is used when one set of data are alternatives and the other are multiple sub-divisions. A few examples are given in Fig. 10.5 below. Further details about these coefficients of correlation can be found in standard textbooks of statistics.

x / y	Office holder Yes	No	x / y	Previous punishments Yes	No	x / y	Family complete Yes	No
Marks for political knowledge			**Performance in his job**			**Number of previous punishments**		
0–8			Very good			1		
9–16			Good			2		
17–24			Indifferent			3		
25–32			Bad			4		
33–40			Very bad			5		

Fig. 10.5   Correlation table for calculating the biserial coefficient of correlation

(ii) Ranking series

Alongside the correlation procedures based on frequency there are some which are based on ranking series. These are known as ranking correlations. Ranking series are found, for instance, when schoolboys are assessed by their teacher in terms of performance and discipline, i.e. when the teacher draws up a series from the best, through the second best, etc., down to the worst. The best known of ranking correlation procedures leads to the determination of the rho coefficient according to Spearman. This will be briefly demonstrated by an example. We have two ranking series concerning five persons in the sample (see Fig. 10.6).

In the x column we enter their average school report marks and in the y column the number of recorded infringements of discipline by each pupil.

We then arrange these figures in two ranking series. Thus we find that pupil A holds the first place in the performance ranking series Rx and the third place in the dicipline ranking series Ry. We now want to establish to what extent the two ranking series resemble each other and whether they correlate. In terms of content the question is: is there a connection be-

VPn	*x* School report average	*y* Recorded infringements of discipline	Rx	Ry	D	D²
A	1·9	4	1	3	−2	4
B	2·6	5	3	4	−1	1
C	3·6	8	5	5	0	0
D	2·2	3	2	2	0	0
E	3·0	1	4	1	3	9

Σ 14

Fig. 10.6 Table for the calculation of the ranking correlation coefficient (rho)

tween good performance and good discipline on the one hand and between bad performance and bad discipline on the other?

The coefficient of ranking correlation is calculated in accordance with the formula

$$\varsigma = 1 - \frac{6 \, \Sigma \, D^2}{N \, (N^2 - 1)}$$

where D = difference in ranking order (ranking position in column Rx minus ranking position in column Ry) and N = number of persons in the sample.

With the figures in our particular example substituted in the formula

$$\varsigma = 1 - \frac{6 \times 14}{5 \times 24} = 1 \cdot 00 - 0 \cdot 70 = 0 \cdot 30,$$

we find that the correlation between the two ranking series is 0·30, i.e. there is a slight connection between performance and discipline.

Having listed a few, though by no means all, possibilities of correlation calculation we want to emphasise again that the choice of the procedure depends on the quality of the data obtained.

Another observation is necessary in this context. Correlation calculation permits an accurate determination of the closeness of connections between phenomena and factors. But this does not mean that one phenomenon is invariably the cause and the other its effect. Such a relationship could statistically be proved only by factor analysis; this involves reducing the investigations to those phenomena which determine other, mutually correlating, factors. Factor analysis is based on the assumption that data correlating with each other within one series can be reduced to a common factor. It is the task of factor analysis, by devising a correlation matrix, to discover the common complexes of causes or factors for any two definite phenomena. Further details may be found in the specialised literature. [22]

Mention should finally be made of a circumstance which is encountered in the calculation of the coefficient of correlation as the uncertainty factor. This follows from the ratio between the number of investigated offences and the population. If the number of investigated offences is very small in relation to the total over a certain period of time, or a certain area, etc., then even a very high coefficient of correlation could be entirely accidental. The greater the sample of investigated offences is in relation to the population, the more reliable is the statement that can be made about the degree of correlation. To allow for this circumstance, a significance test has been developed. This aims at establishing the degree to which the r values of the sample apply to the population as a whole.

The specialised statistical literature contains tables of accidental maximum values (also known as threshold tables) whose data are useful for such a significance test. Generally speaking, a probable error of 5 per cent will still meet the requirements of significance. Thus, if we have investigated 50 criminal offences against socialist property in the construction industry of one region in 1966 and if we expect that the probable error (a) will not exceed 5 per cent, then r will have to be at least 0·27 in order to be beyond accidental effects. [23] If the number of investigated offences is less, say only 10, then r will have to be above 0·58 in order to contain a useful statement. [24]

Particular importance, moreover, attaches to the interpretation of the calculated coefficient of correlation.

The numerical determination of the correlation through the coefficient of correlation is not in itself a valid statement; it is merely a preliminary task and the first stage. The quantitative information on the connection must be supplemented by a qualitative meaningful interpretation. What is meant here is not the effect of such factors as type of interrogation (written, oral, anonymous, etc.), type of questions (on motives, opinions and facts), type of object of questions and the relationship between questioner and respondent, even though a correlation is modified by each of these. What matters is the question: what, from the point of view of the nature of the correlation between the two variables, lies behind the coefficient of correlation? How has it come about? What does it state?

The specialised literature contains various breakdowns and patterns for the interpretation of coefficients of correlation.

To start with, we may refer to a no doubt over-simplified but instructive subdivision, according to which correlations can be interpreted on the following lines:

(a) Unilateral control means that a factor A determines a factor B. Other authors call this a direct connection. The important point is that we are dealing here with direct causality between two data.

(b) Mutual control means that a factor A is caused by a factor B and in turn itself causes this factor B — a pattern tantamount to the concept of dialectical reciprocal action.

(c) Third-party control means that both A and B are caused by a factor C. A variant of this is the indirect correlation. This means, for instance, that although C causes A and B, B additionally determines A because of the effect of C.

(d) Complex control means that the complex of factors $(A + B + C + ... X)$ causes the factor Y. Since this, too, is a case not only of equilibrium among the various causant factors but also of correlations, this pattern can very probably be thought of in terms of indirect correlation, i.e. that A not only causes Y directly but also affects it indirectly through B.

Added to this is the fact that in reality these four possibilities are linked with one another. They can only be artificially isolated.

The 'unravelling' of this (in reality) well-ordered field of factors, put differently, serves the investigation of causes in the social sciences. It is important to know that the separation of the interpretation of the coefficients from their calculation is necessary for the simple reason that one and the same coefficient may be interpreted in different ways. A few examples will illustrate what we mean.

Researches by criminologists into questions of juvenile criminality reveal the existence of a correlation between a father's excessively strict and loveless style of upbringing and the son's recidivism. This means that the fathers of recidivist juveniles are more often excessively strict and loveless in their upbringing methods than the fathers of first offenders. How is one to interpret this correlation? A very persuasive interpretation would be that an over-strict, loveless father is responsible for his son's criminal behaviour. That would be an interpretation in the sense of unilateral control. If, however, one interprets the facts as showing that, on the one hand, an excessively strict style of upbringing drives a young person into criminal behaviour while, on the other hand, a son's criminal behaviour leads to hardening of the paternal attitude, then this would be an interpretation on the lines of mutual control.

The pattern of third-party or even complex control would finally allow of the following interpretation: loveless strictness of the father on the one hand and criminal recidivism of the son on the other both derive from one or more common factors, e.g. social causes, emotional poverty in the family, or other permanent psychological stresses within the family, etc. It is important to remember in all interpretations that the evaluation of statistical data is a scientific activity.

A scientific preparation and evaluation of an empirical survey, however, is possible only on the basis of Marxist—Leninist theory. Even in empirical work and in the statistical evaluation of findings, ideological indifference or a mechanical and uncritical processing of statistical data can lead to a falsification of the results and to harmful consequences. Quantification alone does not yet lead to a scientific approach. On the other hand, the incorrect application and evaluation of empirical and statistical methods in the bourgeois social sciences must not lead us to the conclusion that a rational posing of questions and exact methods and techniques are necessarily unsuitable for our conditions.

Any uncritical attitude, divorced from our class position and from our social conditions, is unscientific and class-unspecific.

(iii) Sampling in criminality research
An important rôle in the examination of a large number of offences whose causes are to be explored is played by sampling.

In the majority of research projects for the discovery of the causes of criminality or of definite criminal phenomena it would be quite impossible to cover the totality (the population) of the criminal offences. Thus the criminal statistics for 1965 record 30,131 criminal offences against socialist property, [25] and these cannot, of course, be criminologically examined in their totality. Neither the manpower nor the facilities necessary for such an enterprise are available, nor would the expense of time and money justify such an investigation. On the other hand, we need the knowledge about the totality of the processes. Even the 4,884 criminal offences recorded within the construction industry for the year 1963 are still too numerous for an in-depth analysis. The best way of analysing mass phenomena, therefore, is the method of sampling, which means that the number of cases and the cases themselves are so chosen that they permit of the necessary conclusions in respect of the totality. The object of sample analysis, therefore, is not to draw conclusions concerning the studied sample but to discover the essential features of the structure of the whole.

Some analyses from which general findings have been derived do not yet meet the prerequisite of the representativeness of the sample. For one thing, the necessity of stating the number of individual cases under analysis is being overlooked. The reader must be able to form a picture of the scope of the material basis and its value. For another, it is not clear whether the selected sample represents a reduced-scale reflection of the population, i.e. whether it may claim to be representative of the whole. This applies, for instance, to studies in which the authors have based themselves on data available to them from central and local penal bodies but have made their selection only from a subject or time-span consideration. In certain studies conclusions are drawn in respect of the phenomenon as a whole, which conveys the impression that the condition of representativeness was met in the sample, but no evidence of this is supplied. In fact one is dealing with a more or less arbitrary selection which then, because of a distorted reflection of reality, in this case of the totality of the phenomenon, also leads to unfounded conclusions whose practical realisation is not sufficiently scientifically grounded. This applies also to studies and analyses which carry the note: '... Investigated through the example of ... criminality in the Region (District) X', without containing any details about the representative character of the data.

These objections, made with the benefit of hindsight, do not mean that such studies are worthless. But their findings necessarily carry a higher degree of relativity, and this must be borne in mind when they are used. If necessary the findings should be verified.

It will rarely be possible to ensure that the sample under examination agrees totally and in every respect with the population. Provided this is borne in mind, it is possible to establish by test whether the deviation lies within the range of accidental fluctuation or goes beyond it. A number of statistical testing procedures (mean value, scatter) are available for this purpose under definite conditions.

Scharbert and Spalteholz in an interesting paper thoroughly justify the representative character of their studies. We shall quote their arguments in detail:

> To begin with, the crime statistics show that the cases of criminal frontier crossing covered by the sample account for about 13% of the total criminality in this category during the period under review. This shows, on the one hand, that restriction to this sample range covers the number of research units necessary for representative sampling and, on the other, that the number of cases of criminal frontier crossing in the Potsdam District during the period under review exhibits the characteristic of mean frequency in relation to other dis-

tricts of the GDR. Existing quantitative deviations between districts lie within margins which do not play a significant part in the characterisation of the total criminological picture but mutually cancel each other out.

By embracing the offences from the Potsdam District a mean is thus obtained which represents the quantitative characteristic of the totality of the offences under review.

As relations of the same order of magnitude exist with regard to general demographic, socio-economic and cultural structures, and since the share of the Potsdam District in various statistical indicators roughly corresponds to its size, it is therefore possible, in respect of the statistics covering the criminal offences under examination and also in respect of essential general social characteristics, to regard the sample as representative of the causes of criminality in respect of criminal crossing of the GDR State frontier during the period under review and hence, from the research results, to draw conclusions which are valid beyond the boundaries of the district. However, this statement is subject to a reservation arising from the assessment of a peculiarity of significance to the subject under investigation.

Because of its geographical position with regard to West Berlin and the numerous resulting historical relationships of individuals — relationships of economic, cultural and family nature — with the area at present belonging to the special territory of West Berlin, and also because the State frontier runs along the Potsdam District and the communications between West Berlin and Western Germany touch the territory of the Potsdam District, the area under investigation is not comparable either with the GDR as a whole or with any of its other districts.

In dealing with the correlations determining the criminal offence of frontier crossing it is therefore necessary to emphasise all those factors and phenomena which result from the peculiarity (e.g. the effect and results of frontier crossing prior to 13 August 1961) if wrong generalisations of these peculiarities are to be avoided.

Provided this reservation is borne in mind — a restriction relevant chiefly to the specific nature of the connections of the offenders with West Berlin and to the possibility of the commission of this offence — it is proper to state that the general relations and trends revealed by the offences covered are not only valid for the territorial area under investigation but also represent essential relations and trends attaching to the totality of such offences, even though modified by a number of special, territorially specific conditions.

This defines the validity both of the investigation and of the area under investigation. [26]

Sampling is therefore used in criminality research whenever the category of the offence, or the specific criminal phenomenon, cannot be investigated in its totality but when analysis of selected offences can reveal reguliarities which also underlie the totality (the statistical 'population'). First of all, given the accuracy of the estimate to be achieved, it is possible to calculate the necessary sample size. [27] If, because of the size of the sample and the cost involved, it is impossible to examine the calculated number of offences care must be taken that, if a smaller number of offences is selected, such a selection is representative of the population and meets both qualitative and quantitative conditions. The representative data must contain all the characteristic elements which constitute the total phenomenon and must, moreover, be present in a sufficient number to exhibit those elements in a definite ratio.

The first question, therefore, is why the representative sample must contain the characteristic elements of the structure of the phenomenon as a whole.

Criminality research is concerned with the discovery of the laws underlying connections and interdependencies; these must first be fully recorded if they are to be correlated with essential social relations in socialist society. On this basis, for instance, the fundamental diversity of criminality or of individual groups is investigated and defined. It is obvious that any sample study which disregards this diversity of criminality, behind which lie qualitative differences in its causes, in its social rôle and in its effects, must lead to wrong conclusions. If, for instance, only the serious cases of offences against property in the construction industry were selected and analysed in order to draw conclusions about crimes against property in the construction industry, then this would inevitably lead to wrong results. Such an analysis – provided other prerequisites were observed – could only permit of conclusions about the totality of serious crimes against property in the construction industry. It would not even be possible without further work to draw conclusions, from such data, about serious crimes against property in other social spheres.

The problem must be solved principally by phenomenological investigation of the various criminal phenomena. The programming of the sample can be based on research data reflecting all the external characteristics of a particular phenomenon. These will include, for instance, statements on the age and sex of the offender, his occupation, the nature of his work, his class origin, his educational standard, his place of work, etc. The offences, for their part, are analysed in respect of their manner of commission, their material and notional consequences, the place of the offence, the time of the offence, etc. These data must be present whenever a decision is made on the structure of the representative sample. In sociological studies agreement between sample and population is demanded in respect of the social position of the individuals forming the subject of the investigation and the structure of their consciousness. [28] As for the structure of consciousness, in the criminological sphere phenomenological statements will be sufficient, since we are concerned here with the deed-related consciousness and since between the offence in its specific shape and the deed-related consciousness there is dialectical connection which permits conclusions to be drawn from the offence to the consciousness. The dialectical connection between an individual's consciousness and his specific working and everyday conditions, moreover, shows that the phenomena characterising these conditions are reflected in his consciousness. Knowledge of the characteristics of these working and everyday conditions, as provided by phenomenology, will — provided the other premises are given — fully meet the qualitative conditions of criminality research.

In the selection of the individual actions to be regarded as representative a number of problems and sources of error have to be considered. To begin with, a lot will depend on precise concepts, their clear contents and their consistent application. It must also be remembered that the conceptual embracing of the phenomena in various respects amounts to disregard of the finer points. A related problem is that 'limits' must not be included in the selection of the data. (There is also the danger that, in certain cases, some phenomena or criteria may be forced into a preconceived pattern.)

Thus, if a subdivision according to place of residence is needed, the data are usually organised only under 'town' or 'country'. Yet everyday conditions and relations are conditioned also according to whether one is dealing with a big city or a small town, with a large or a small municipality, with a municipality in the vicinity of a big city or one located in a predominantly agricultural region, etc. Such essential aspects and phenomena must be considered whenever the research task demands it.

To ensure a representative study it must also be remembered that our society and all social phenomena are not in a static condition but in perpetual movement. Any comparisons must therefore relate to the same period of social evolution. It follows that phenomenological investigations must be supplemented and updated roughly every year. In addition, changes due to the development of society must also be allowed for in the concepts used. Thus, views on the criteria for the structure of the working class and, in consequence, the statistical criteria for inclusion in the category 'worker' have undergone changes. New groups, subgroups, etc., are emerging in the process of social evolution as an expression of its dynamics. Any comparisons must therefore be based on the latest knowledge about the development of society.

Any outline of representativeness would also state what essential phenomena must be embraced in any set of sample data to meet the quantitative requirements of selection. On the one hand, the number must be large enough for the 'law of large numbers' to be sufficiently operative. It is impossible to state a definite number that would meet this requirement. This is not the place to judge the extent to which the 20 per cent principle used in the sampling of election results can provide a general starting point. It certainly does not appear to be acceptable without reservation, considering the very different character of criminological questions, orders of magnitude, etc. Matters are different with the 10 per cent limit mentioned by Osipov. But this must not be applied as a rigid pattern either. [29] Generally speaking, the principle applies that the lowest possible number should be used which still ensures that the qualitative data of the population are represented in the sample.

Equally vital is a correct selection. This must not be coloured by any bias. The sample will correspond to the population only provided that the selection of its individual elements (in our case the individual criminal offences) is made on a random basis. In practice this can be based on an existing punched card index. It is important that each case should have the same chance of being selected. This can be ensured if a certain number of cases are picked out according to an external characteristic; such a characteristic has a purely accidental relation to the structure of the criminal phenomenon under analysis. A definite period of time could provide such a characteristic; it should not, however, be used if the type of crime is in itself determined by time factors. Another external characteristic might be the names of the offenders, since the first letter of an offender's name has no relation to his offence. Yet another possibility is to shuffle the punched cards, then draw out one card at random and thereafter include in the sample every tenth or fifteenth card after it. Finally, using simple procedures, it is possible to make a random selection from a sufficiently shuffled stack of punched cards; care must, however, be taken to ensure that each card has the same chance of being picked.

The selection error can be further reduced by the method of cluster sampling. This means that clusters of units are sampled out of a population in accordance with periods fixed in advance. For instance, out of a set of alphabetically arranged punched cards the first to the tenth, the 100th to the 110th, the 200th to the 210th, etc., will be included in the sample. Sociologists prefer this method to random sampling. [30]

Once a definite quantity has been ensured for criminality research by random sampling the results have to be inspected to see whether they meet the programmed requirements of representativeness in respect of qualitative data. It has to be established whether the individual cases selected are not only sufficiently numerous to ensure that they contain the qualitative data in their proper proportions but also whether a cross-section of the required qualitative data is ensured. If appreciable deviations are found to exist in individual correlations the number of individual cases must either be suitably increased until these deviations cancel each other out or else — if this is not necessary or possible — a certain correction must be applied to the qualitative data by varying the investigation processes.

Yet another problem is connected with the size of the sample of individual cases under investigation. Harrland points out that his remarks on criminality analysis by statistical methods as a general rule refer only to relatively large numbers. The sampling method, he says, is

> not valid for limited scientific investigations of small numbers, such as the study of 100 criminal cases, e.g. the cases of premeditated homicide in the GDR over a period of two years. Under such conditions it is possible, and therefore also necessary, to obtain information on all individual cases coming within the purview of the investigation, and to process these. Needless to say, this changes nothing about the applicability of statistical procedures and methods to such systematic work, or the no doubt considerable value of its findings. [31]

As for the question — frequently asked in this connection — whether it is advisable to use the punched card technique for small numbers, or whether simple counting by means of tabulation would not be sufficient, this cannot be discussed within the scope of the present study. Sociologists take the view that employment of the punched card technique is not justifiable or necessary unless one deals with more than 1,000 individual cases. [32] For quantities below that number the punched card procedure would neither save work nor increase the validity of the results.

Harrland's arguments raise the question of the extent to which it is possible to conclude from small numbers, such as the ones adduced here for criminal homicide, whether the discovered correlations are accidental

342

or whether they are general and necessary for the category of offence studied. This question is of considerable practical importance. On the one hand, there are various types of offence which, by their nature, occur relatively rarely, and on the other, the problem is of growing interest in that the number of such small groups is likely to increase as criminality is gradually reduced. At the present moment the question is important also in the investigation of the causes of offences such as frequent recidivist fraud relating to personal property, serious offences against property committed by offenders from certain economic spheres, e.g. construction, offences against property at the stage of the project study of industrial construction objects, etc. The question is: under what conditions can generally valid conclusions be drawn from a small number of criminal offences?

In connection with the 'law of large numbers', bourgeois literature also speaks of a 'law of small numbers'. [33] This is not the place to decide whether this is justified or whether we are not faced merely with a modified operation of the 'law of large numbers'. Available experience shows that it is only possible on very definite premises to abstract the necessary and stable elements from a relatively small unit. Those premises include that only small numbers are available, that the associated fundamental type — e.g. for specialised questions of offences against social property, the general criminality against socialist property — has been identified and analysed, and that these results are used as a supplement to or as a model and yardstick for the analysis of small numbers. This would suggest that no special law is operative.

Correlations discovered from a small number of criminal offences must in any case be confronted with findings previously arrived at by the application of the 'law of large numbers'.

The magnitude of the number of individual cases to be investigated, moreover, depends on whether we are dealing with a comprehensive or a very narrow set of questions. Thus, in order to explore the deeper connections between criminality and excessive drink or between criminality against property and asocial attitudes, a relatively large number will have to be selected. If, on the other hand, the question concerns the depth of a specific psychological phenomenon, e.g. the connection between a manifestation of private ownership mentality among construction workers and certain conditions in the management of materials by construction enterprises, a smaller number will be sufficient. This follows also from the fact that for a study of this kind only such individual cases are selected as are already known to have revealed this particular correlation.

There is yet another side to the problems we have just discussed — one of particular importance in practice. Area Public Prosecutors, for example, were required to analyse all the offences of deliberate violence and the court's findings on them over a definite, relatively short space of time, to draw from them conclusions for preventive measures, and to assess the effectiveness of such measures. Closer study revealed that within that stipulated space of time only eight such offences had occurred. That, of course, is not an adequate basis for any general conclusions. Too much is expected of an Area Prosecutor's office if it is asked to lay bare the operative causant correlations and interactions and to draw conclusions from them for a general programme of preventive measures within its territory. No general laws can be derived from a mere eight offences. All the practitioner can do here is compile his findings and, without attempting to single out accidental correlations, pass them on to the superior body, the one responsible for a larger unit. Any generalisation can then be performed at district level or perhaps only at national level. [34]

At the same time, the significance of a smaller number of offences within an area can be increased if generalisations made in analyses at district or national level, within the same sphere of problems, are made available to areas. Such information, from the top downwards, as it were, would provide an important prerequisite of scientifically founded conclusions.

In addition, the analytical results of Party, State and economic bodies, of research teams, of scientific studies, etc., should all be utilised to supplement, verify and, if necessary, correct the investigation results achieved at area level.

These reflections support the demand made earlier that each analysis or evaluation of analytical results must state the number of individual cases examined. If absolute figures are omitted from analyses and merely the percentages given, false impressions may be created and mistaken measures based upon them. The validity of percentages — e.g. for the trend in premeditated homicide, an offence relatively rarely committed in the GDR — is slight. Thus, if one case of premedidated homicide occured in a district in 1965 and two such cases were recorded in 1966 it would be downright mistaken to conclude that these figures represent a 100% increase for this type of crime. Such a percentage statement possesses no informative validity.

If, for a small total of criminal offences, the phenomenological data are expressed in percentages, then the decimals should be omitted. The inclusion of, say, two decimals merely suggests an accuracy and precision which, in view of the data available, is not attainable at all. [35]

In conclusion, the experience of criminologists in other socialist coun-

344

tries may prove useful. Kvasnička points out that an examination of the population serves no purpose if, during the period to be investigated — about one year — the specific conditions in certain spheres of society, more particularly in economics, have undergone such modifications that the structure of criminality and its causes has been affected. Even when it is technically possible to study the population such peculiarities must be taken into consideration. In suitable cases it might be possible greatly to reduce the time-span investigated. If that is not possible without serious reservations then one should ask how the scope of the problems under investigation might be narrowed down in order either to eliminate the changes or account for them accurately. Kvasnička moreover recommends another way. He states:

> This danger could be avoided, above all, by the technique of stratified sampling, whereby the individual spheres of society affected by criminality are described as strata and the number of representative samples is chosen from the individual strata not in accordance with the frequency of established criminality within those strata but according to the number of persons belonging to the sphere in question, as indicated, for instance, by their place of work. However, this procedure is technically very difficult: in view of the relatively low frequency of criminality (especially in certain spheres) difficulties might be encountered in particular in selecting a sufficiently large number of samples from a relatively short period — sufficiently large, that is, to ensure all strata are appropriately represented.
>
> We have therefore chosen another procedure which — at the risk of being suspected of a predilection for modish terms — might be described as model sampling. This consists of selecting a sphere of society in which specific deviations are minimal and which, at the same time, in respect of the social relations present within it, most closely approximates to the relations existing in society as a whole, i.e. the relations towards which society is inevitably moving. The samples of a particular type of criminality are then selected for research only from within that sphere, which thus appears as a specific model of society as a whole.
>
> As will be seen, elements of sociological-monographic research are here applied, up to a point, in conjunction with elements of routine statistical procedures. The main obstacle that has to be overcome, before we are sufficiently entitled to extrapolate the results thus obtained also beyond the boundaries of our model sphere, consists in the most thorough possible examination of that sphere with regard

to social relations which might be operative on an appreciable scale in the emergence of criminality. (This includes not only its typicality with regard to the present state of society but also a certain evolution within the given sphere, i.e. its probable typicality in the future, since that is more important if the research results are to be applicable in future.)

In our specific case we were guided in the choice of our model sphere mainly by considerations of the class structure of those employed in it, the technical level of the production process, the qualification of the working people, their movements, wage conditions, production structure, prerequisites of latent criminality, etc. On this basis we came to the conclusion that engineering would represent such a suitable model sphere. Next, in order to eliminate any geographical influences — seeing that it was impossible to conduct the investigations over the entire territory of the Czechoslovak Socialist Republic — we selected our territorial investigation area in such a way that it comprised criminality both in regions with a long tradition of concentrated engineering and some newly set-up enterprises, and that Slovakia and the Border Regions were represented in proper proportion. In consequence, our studies were conducted on the territory of the capital, Prague, and the districts of Central Bohemia, Northern Bohemia, Southern Bohemia, Southern Moravia and Central Slovakia. [36]

(iv) The importance of quantification procedures in criminality research
The social and individual phenomena which make up the complex of the causes of criminal phenomena are as a rule factors which, initially, are not quantifiable. Thus the following factors are listed as conditioning offences against property in construction: (a) low educational and cultural standard of the offender; (b) survival of the view that work serves solely for the acquisition of the individually needed means of subsistence; (c) individualism manifested as team selfishness; (d) survival of the view that in a privately owned enterprise it is permissible to take home personally needed building material or cut-offs; (e) a widespread desire to develop into an independent entrepreneur and to use every possible means for personal profit; (f) a tendency towards indiscipline and an unsatisfactory attitude to work; (g) lack of personal identification with the enterprise, absence of pride in the enterprise; (h) repeated change of employment; (i) a tendency towards excessive drink; (j) widespread loose family ties, the majority of offenders having lived separated from their families for long

346

periods of time, often in primitive barracks; (k) wrong development in childhood, caused chiefly by wrong upbringing by parents; (l) contradictions resulting from shortcomings in planning, frequent misplanning or replanning; (m) contradictions resulting from shortcomings in the management of material resources with frequent waste or deterioration of material, tools and machines, considerable stocks in excess of plan, absence of clear responsibility for material management, construction site discipline, etc.; (n) lack of activity by social institutions and organisations at various building sites, especially dispersed ones; (o) indifference towards statutory regulations applying to building sites — industrial safety, etc.; (p) inadequate supervision of work, accountancy, building sites and workers.

The majority of these factors varies in weighting within the different groups of offences against property. Others are susceptible of accurate quantification. Thus, 'repeated change of employment' could be, and should be, further subdivided into, say, three to five jobs, five to ten jobs, more than ten jobs, in a year.

In line with the general requirement, each phenomenon must be conceptually defined and, if at all possible, quantified. This applies also to such 'factors' as shortcomings in management, bad family relations, survivals of outdated ideas in the offender's consciousness, etc. Unless this is done the analysis will be superficial and fail to penetrate to the real roots of the criminal offences.

Of particular interest to us is the first group of phenomena. The problem is how the listed findings, such as 'low educational and cultural standard' or 'unsatisfactory attitude to work' can be measured. Mensuration would make it easier, among other things, to develop scientifically founded and precise crime prevention measures and also to identify any changes produced in the offender by educational influences and other measures, or by a relapse, or generally by the passage of time.

A number of different procedures have therefore been developed for the quantitative representation of social and individual phenomena. Their usefulness consists in presenting non-numerical phenomena quantitatively.

Not all the phenomena in question are equally susceptible to quantification. This applies particularly to views, ideas, habits and other psychological processes. Quantitative representation of social phenomena is generally more difficult than that of natural phenomena. This difficulty, however, is not sufficiently met by qualifying the attitude of offenders to work as very good, good, adequate, bad or very bad. These grades lack the prerequisites of quantitative classification. It is therefore advisable to look for symptoms derived from the phenomena which are a quantitative reflection of the phenomena themselves. This will enable the researcher to determine the quantity in question by indirect methods. The derivation of such symptoms, their evaluation and the ascertainment of their magnitude are subject to certain rules. However, before we discuss the various problems of quantification a few general questions have to be dealt with concerning the listing of symptoms or criteria (indicators) in which a phenomenon (index) becomes manifest. [37]

In criminality research, especially in the study of juvenile criminality, it is important to know how a person who has become an offender spends his free time. This is directly related to his intellectual and cultural standard and to the type of influences to which he is exposed. Leisure-time behaviour reflects the influence which family, work teams, etc., had or failed to have on the offender. If this phenomenon is measured and the result related to the use of leisure time by a socialist individual typical of our stage of the evolution of society, some valuable indications may be deduced for the development of a system of crime prevention.

Revealing studies on this subject are available in the field of juvenile research.[38] A team of specialists is examining the problems of 'leisure activities and leisure guidance of young people', thus ensuring that all essential aspects are duly considered also in the methodological field. The indicators used by this research team should also be applied in criminality research since normal behaviour and deviation from normal behaviour can only be examined on a unified basis.[39] This work, moreover, should make a direct contribution to a positive shaping of the leisure time of young people.

In a supplment to the periodical *Problems of Peace and Socialism*, Staykov relates his experience in connection with an analysis of leisure-time activity. He shows how the type of leisure activity and its periodicity was established by interview. To define the type of activity, twenty-nine indicators were developed, ranging from social activity, aspects of education, cultural activity, participation in sports, various hobbies, life within the family, participation in entertainments, all the way to passive recreation, religious cultic activities and pointless time-killing. This example of a quantitative classification of this phenomenon also provides certain hints for some investigations of criminality. However, the question of the obstacles in the way of leisure activity appropriate to the ideas of the respondent — a question raised in the same study — is tailored more towards general sociological investigations. For the purposes of criminality research it would be more important to find out from the respondents why they spend their free time in the manner described by them and why they do not make use of the various opportunities of socialist leisure activity.

Various methodological findings can also be derived from measurements of the industrial enterprise climate by sociological research teams. These findings are of particular interest if they have a bearing on the detection of correlations between certain criminal phenomena and particular phenomena of the enterprise climate. Investigation of crime against property in the construction industry has also revealed connections with certain negative elements of the enterprise climate. The variously listed shortcomings in the management of the construction process, ignorance of long-term construction plans, diverse shortcomings in the management of materials and the organisation of labour, as well as a low degree of class consciousness among certain sections of the labour force are all listed among the factors determining the climate in an industrial enterprise. An interesting compilation of such factors and aspects in which the enterprise climate is reflected, as well as of procedures to ascertain them, will be found in Armélin's essay 'An Analysis of the Industrial Enterprise Climate is Badly Needed'.[40]

A difficult question is the definition of motivation structure, for instance, in offences against property. It is made more difficult by the fact that various categories of offences against property reveal specialised or modified motivations. Investigations in the construction industry have shown that the motive behind thefts connected with spare-time work has been the construction worker's desire to act as an independent entrepreneur and his striving for an unjustifiably high income. This is not the place to examine whether the motives listed in each individual case have in fact been the determinants of the decision to commit the offence. We have already pointed out that there is such a thing as habitual motivation. Frequently the individual concerned will not have been clear about his own motives at the time of decision and will have produced them subsequently. Moreover, motives can change, and what are called substitute motives may be given by the offender.[41] Scientific studies of offences against property in the construction industry generally list the offender's desire to enrich himself. But such a statement neither fully reveals the motivation process nor the differentiation of motives, with the result that statements concerning the deed-related consciousness and the offender's state of consciousness cannot be sufficiently well founded.

More recent attempts to penetrate deeper into the motivation structure of offenders against property — admittedly in the industrial sphere — were made by Buchholz and, following him, Knobloch. Knobloch lists the following motives for the 330 criminal offences examined by him.

(a) Appropriation of money or goods for the purpose of leading an extravagant or parasitical life, or being in a position to continue an increased consumption of alcohol; (b) acquisition of valuables as a basis for illicit work; (c) personal requirement in household, garden, etc.; (d) appropriation of money or valuables in order to maintain relations with women or men; (e) satisfaction of expensive requirements, or inability to manage with the means available to him; (f) cupidity and striving for money or valuables at any price; (g) habitual enrichment, resulting from an outdated tradition; (h) satisfaction of the need for personal assertion; (i) attempt to escape from a difficulty in which the offender finds himself either culpably or innocently; (j) other motives. [42]

Knobloch further points out that this study comprises only those motives which were decisive in the ripening of the decision to commit the deed and in the execution of the offence.

The advance represented by this analysis over more general statements is obvious. However, an analysis of psychological processes and a compilation of appropriate indicators should not confine itself to motives as listed by the penal organs but on relevant studies by psychologists. Only then will it be possible to arrive at clearer formulations of the various motives, to avoid overlapping, and to allow qualitative and quantitative differences to emerge clearly. Thus, the motive, or rather cluster of motives, listed under (a) above appears as a kind of general motive and seems inadequately differentiated from, for instance, the motives listed under (d), (e) and (f).

The findings of psychology are still not being adequately considered in our criminal law practice. In consequence, researches are very frequently based on different questions, different labels are used for the motives, and their systematisation is performed solely on the basis of their frequency or the particular researcher's personal experience. Buchholz distinguishes three main ideological-psychological trends which, by and large, agree with the findings of criminal law research. [43] Manecke lists the following motives of offences against property: (a) acquisition of specific items of use; (b) opportunity to lead a profligate life; (c) opportunity to lead a parasitical life; (d) creation of a temporary or permanent additional source of income; (e) avarice and cupidity. [44] Differences in systematisation of motives make it difficult to compare studies.

To arrive at a uniform basis it would be desirable to develop a model. This should take into consideration the fact that motives are qualitatively differentiated in psychology. Thus a person's needs are distinguished from his interests and these in turn from his ideals. The hierarchy of motivation, rising from lower motives to higher ones, should be taken into account in systematising the motives of offences against property. [45] Another well-known distinction of motives is that between material and moral stimuli. Detection of these motives and their interaction will reveal, above all, an individual's attitude to work.

The creation of such categories of motives might make it easier for criminological research to comprehend the motivation process in its full depth. The decision to commit a criminal offence against socialist property is only rarely an instantaneous decision in which a particular motive dominates and mobilises the elements in the offender's consciousness to the point of decision. More often the offender passes through a state of tension in which powerful emotional elements are also operative, though these are still being lost in criminological analyses. It would also be possible to identify the interrelationships of internal and external agents upon the motivation process, in particular the formation of the motive. Thus the life-style demands associated with the motive of acquisition of money in order to meet expensive requirements are socially determined. Discovery of the entire internal process and its social conditioning will lead to a new quality of knowledge on the causes of criminal offences and make it possible to map out new paths for the complex struggle against such phenomena. Of particular interest in this connection are the various quantification procedures. They cannot be discussed here in detail and reference must be made to the available literature. [46]

The essence of these procedures lies in the fact that numbers are assigned to the object under investigation. If, for instance, attitudes are to be measured then numbers must express the extent of a particular attitude. The various indicators and numbers must not be chosen arbitrarily but according to special rules. This is an important theoretical and methodological problem which must be solved on the basis of the foundations discussed in the first chapter. No technique, however, is a substitute for a scientific selection of the indicators. Even in the bourgeois literature we can read:

> In this forest of methods the researcher must not lose sight of the facts, since a scale is composed of indicators. The first and foremost problem of behaviour measurement is the compilation of a series of clear, carefully formulated indicators covering the area in question. A jumble of casually invented indicators, which are then dropped into the funnel of some quantification technique, must lead to muddled results. [47]

Formal considerations to be borne in mind in quantification techniques include the determination of the number of indicators, the avoidance of ambiguities, and the unit of measurement. [48]

From what we have said it is obvious that the value of the results depends on the selection of the indicators. This selection must ensure that all the indicators essential for the area under review are included. This is possible only on the basis of a theoretical foundation and an appropriate analysis of the sphere to be investigated. It is first necessary to determine which essential indicators lend a particular phenomenon its characteristic features.

In the Soviet literature on the quantitative representation of qualitative data concerning an individual's attitude to work the following indicators are listed: fulfilment of his work norm; improvement of his own skills; quality of his work; possibility of his being entrusted with responsible work; possible refusal of work assigned to him; participation in the innovator's movement; proposals and requests designed to improve work organisation; observed changes in his attitude to work over the past few years; possible social or administrative reprimand for his behaviour within or outside the work process; work discipline; participation in rationalisation and invention schemes. [49]

These indicators are subdivided into categories of answers so that graduated measurements can be performed. The above-quoted selection of indicators admittedly, and wrongly, avoids inclusion of internal motives, of the part played by working morale and hence the individual's attitude to work. This aspect must not be excluded from an individual's relationship to his work. [50]

The necessary assignment of numbers may be made in a variety of ways. In the quantification of social phenomena the most common method will be a conditional assignment of numbers. [51]

One of the advantages of quantification procedures is that they reflect contradictory ideas and attitudes in the various numerical data. This circumstance makes it possible — as is demonstrated in the listed literature — to penetrate more deeply into the contradictoriness of objective and subjective processes.

Of particular interest is the problem of measuring moral factors, e.g. attitude to work. This is not yet sufficiently clarified. Given that the individuals concerned have an option of different behaviour within the production process, an option guided by their attitude, then their behaviour, e.g. their economic performance and its amount, will be a measure of their attitude to work. [52] These options of behaviour must first of all be examined since they form the framework for quantification.

Finally, an important part in the definition of indicators and the selection of quantification procedures is played also by the peculiarities of various work spheres. Proceeding from the dialectical connection between work performance and work concept, the indicators to be chosen, for instance, in the construction industry, are norm fulfilment, utilisation of working time, economical use of materials, attitude towards squandering of materials, participation in measures to improve skills, etc. Utilisation of all possibilities of quantifying certain phenomena is certain to lead to a substantial deepening of knowledge in criminality research.

In conclusion, mention should be made of the most essential conditions to be met by the selected indicators to ensure an objective reflection of degrees of behaviour. The *Introduction to Sociological Research* has this to say on the subject:

(a) The indicators must include the essential behaviour data with regard to a social object.
(b) The indicators must unambiguously reflect the degrees of behaviour covered by them.
(c) The indicators must make it possible to compare degrees of behaviour between individuals.
(d) The indicators must comprise the entire essential behaviour with regard to a social object, from positive to negative behaviour. [53]

Interviewing in criminality research

Interviewing is used on a considerable scale in all disciplines investigating social or individual processes. The different forms of interviewing are studied by sociologists, economists, psychologists, educationists, jurists and increasingly also criminologists. It is important, first of all, to dissociate oneself from the view that interviewing is the 'queen of methods'. If, for instance, the reasons for the demoralisation of certain individuals are examined, then — as has been explained — researches must start with the individual in his whole complexity, as a natural creature and as an ensemble of social relations. This complexity of the individual must be matched by a complexity of procedures. Interviewing is only one method among many.

Bourgeois literature passes over in silence the shortcomings arising from the bias of the above view, and the consequences which result therefrom for an accurate comprehension of reality. The only substantial sources of error are the prejudices and convictions of the respondents. Thus Scheuch writes: 'The validity of an answer is always in jeopardy whenever the information intended by the respondent deviates from the views held by the interviewer on the social acceptability of an answer.'[54] No doubt this may give rise to certain errors. But this is not the essence of the matter.

To reject an absolutisation of interviewing does not mean that this procedure should not be used. Indeed it holds an important place within the system of procedures. In criminality research in the GDR it has now an assured place. One way of using the written interview technique, for instance, is for the researcher to address his questions to a particular circle of persons from whom he wants replies. This is a type of multiple interview. These respondents may be offenders within a particular category of offence, interviewed for instance at a detention centre, or work teams which had offenders among their members, or the husbands or wives of offenders, or their parents, or even officials of economic and administrative institutions, etc.

The areas to which the questions refer and where suitable results may be achieved are (a) of objective and (b) of subjective character.

(a) Includes data on the offences and the phenomena determining them, data on the environment, related to working, living and other everyday conditions, as well as on the offender's behaviour at and outside his place of work. Such behaviour, in turn, may refer to criminal offenders or simply to typical aspects of individuals in our socialist system.

(b) Includes:

(i) Motivations.

(ii) Assessments and judgements. The appropriate questions may be addressed to the offender or to other persons in order to ascertain how they judge or assess certain events. From their answers, their attitudes may be ascertained under various different heads. So far this possibility has not been adequately used in criminality research, though it is especially useful for increasing the effectiveness of preventive measures. It is worth considering whether this might not provide a way to an early identification of persons socially at risk, whose ideas and actions should be acted upon within the framework of crime prevention.

(iii) The emotional life of the offender. This aspect of the personality of criminal offenders has likewise so far been insufficiently studied. It should not, however, be neglected since from the ability to process experience — both negative and positive — conclusions may be drawn concerning an individual's readiness and willingness to integrate in the building of socialism and in his teams and groups.

(iv) Ideas concerning preventive measures. Questions on this subject are important because they may provide the answer to how certain measures of crime prevention are 'taken' by present or past offenders, or by other persons and groupings. However, all these possibilities can only be exhausted if the questions asked are representative and if all opportunities are used for a quantitative representation of the phenomena concerned.

The suggested use of a questionnaire for interviewing a multiplicity of persons presupposes an awareness of the limitations and of the value of such statements, as well as its harmonisation with the above-mentioned procedures of criminality research. The system and method of interviewing has not so far been developed by socialist researchers. [55] The criminality researcher must distinguish between interviews serving mass surveys and individual interrogation. This differentiation is not identical with the consideration of whether a multiplicity of questions – or indeed all the complexes of questions envisaged by the research task – are to be included, or only certain specialised issues. Either of these may apply to mass surveys or to individual surveys.

Individual interrogation – unless it forms part of a mass survey – primarily serves the verification or control of certain findings. The conclusions drawn from individual interrogation are valid only in connection with the results of that individual case. Individual interrogation therefore, in criminality research, presupposes the use of other research procedures. Their most important form is the interview, structured upon a conversation plan and conducted either as an individual or a group interview. This will be discussed later.

The technique of questioning, both in mass surveys and in individual surveys, is invariably subordinated to the subject and the research aim in question. These will also decide whether the questions are to be posed in writing or orally, or in combination. It is also worth noting that questioning techniques must not be underestimated. Whether or not the procedure will yield useful results depends very largely on the mastery of the technique. [56]

Interviewing is useful not only for the registration of external phenomena; it also provides a chance of discovering subjective connections and penetrating into the interdependences between objective and subjective phenomena.

Supplemented by the results of other procedures, interviewing provides a close approach to regular correlations by covering the causal connections and interactions between various phenomena and by leading the researcher to important data for ascertaining the closeness of correlations. [57] The results of interviewing are evaluated chiefly by statistical processing, whereby a variety of statistical procedures can be applied. Interviewing is thus an important prerequisite of criminological discovery and theoretical generalisation.

The procedure is applicable to the exploration of a criminal phenomenon both if the problem has not yet been clearly delineated and whenever analysis in depth of clearly delineated correlations is called for. Such analysis will lead to a more accurate exploration of correlations already known to exist.

Interviewing, finally, is a preliminary procedure for comprehensive investigations. Such a preliminary questioning makes use of the knowledge of a multiplicity of people concerning what correlations to select, whom to subject to a comprehensive questioning, and how to formulate the questions accurately. In this way shortcomings and sources of error can be identified in good time and eliminated.

In criminality research the questioning of a large number of persons by questionnaire has proved useful. In this connection a number of principles must be borne in mind:

(a) If the respondent can remain anonymous this will, as a rule, be beneficial to the result. In sociology the findings of anonymous interrogations are assessed more highly than those where the respondent has to give his name.

(b) It is advisable to mix 'introductory' questions with problem questions in the questionnaire. The purpose of the 'introductory' question is the promotion of a willingness to reveal all one's knowledge in answering the questions. The problem questions must not be confused with the problems to be solved by the investigation; these must be translated into the questions to be addressed to the respondents, so that their replies may provide clues for tackling the problem under investigation.

(c) The problem under investigation should be approached from different directions in the questionnaire. This enables the answers to be checked and increases their validity.

(d) The questionnaires contain questions of knowledge, questions of opinion and questions of motivation. Questions of opinion are normally introduced with the words 'What do you think ...'; the motivation questions with the words 'Why do you ...'. Leading questions must not be asked.

(e) It has been found useful to include in a questionnaire both open-ended and closed questions. Sociologists suggest that one-third of the questions should be open-ended and two-thirds closed. The point to remember about open-ended questions is that they are difficult to categorise and to enumerate; indeed this may prove altogether impossible. With closed questions, on the other hand, there is a greater risk that the answer may be steered into a particular direction. At the same time their informative validity is greater since the replies — which are either Yes or No — are relatively less depent on the intellectual level of the respondent.

(f) The questions must be the same for all the addressees of the questionnaire. Likewise, if the same circle of persons is re-interrogated after a certain lapse of time, the continuity of the questions should be preserved. This will more clearly reveal any trend or shift in emphasis.

It is important that universal standards should be established for written and oral interviewing. These should be worked out on the grounds of the existing literature and experience, in collaboration with psychologists and educationists, since their structure will be determined less by logical than by psychological aspects. Criminality research further demands that the questionnaires for the principal manifestations of criminality, and occasionally also for certain complexes of causes, should differ from one another. Studies of crime against property in the construction industry, for instance, have revealed different areas of problems for offenders under 25 and over 25. With the younger offenders it was shown that in the majority of cases their faulty development started in childhood. Questions must therefore be framed to produce answers on why a personality was formed in a particular way, or why no sufficiently effective system of moral or social attitudes has developed in the offender's ontogenesis. Among the older offenders a relatively consolidated positive system of attitudes was found to exist in the majority of cases. Here, then, a complex of questions must be designed to discover why the effectiveness of that system was inhibited, or what effect the present situation had on it, etc.

Needless to say, not all problems can be tackled by interviewing. Questionnaires and other forms of interrogation have their limitations and these must be borne in mind:

(a) There is the chance of the question being misinterpreted by the respondent.

(b) There is also the chance of the respondent lacking a sufficiently serious attitude to the interview.

(c) There is the chance of insufficient rapport between the questioner and the respondent, and this may impair his readiness to co-operate.

(d) There are differences in the respondents' adaptability to the suspected intentions of the questioner.

(e) With closed questions there is occasionally an enforced subordination of the respondents' views to the formulation of the question.

(f) It is extremely difficult to cover motives.

(g) With open-ended questions, in particular, there is the possibility that the evaluator may understand and interpret the answers differently from how they were given or intended.

Generally speaking, the limitations of all questioning methods arise from the fact that they inevitably deal with a 'subjective' source of in-

357

formation, and also from the fact that the results of interviews, even if combined with those of other procedures, are no substitute for a theoretical processing of the entire material. [58]

Questionnaires, finally, should be compiled with an eye to the requirements of subsequent processing and evaluation techniques. Organising the processing of the collected data has sometimes caused difficulties in the past. Thus, if it is intended to transfer the results to Hollerith cards then it must be remembered that these cards have 80 columns and that within these columns the figures range from 0 to 9. It is therefore necessary to devise primary and sub-questions and in so doing bear in mind the numerical possibilities of a Hollerith card. Machine-processing of questionnaires, and the use of mechanical methods generally, calls for preliminary coding and standardisation. These problems are more fully discussed in the relevant literature. [59]

The application of procedures in individual investigations and of testing procedures in criminality research

The procedures and techniques discussed in the preceding sections serve the investigation of mass phenomena. Their applicability and their limitations have been viewed from that angle. Occasional reference, however, has also been made to the fact that some of them — e.g. oral or written interviewing — are suitable also as testing or verifying procedures. The first question to answer, therefore, is why testing procedures are necessary in criminality research.

Criminality research proceeds from a multiplicity of individual cases. The connections of individual criminal offences are analysed and then viewed in their totality. The exactitude and validity of the general analysis, therefore, depend to an appreciable extent on the standard of the analysis of the individual phenomenon. That is why it is necessary, within limits, to verify the correctness of the individual analysis. A second (repeat) analysis of the same phenomenon should, whenever possible, use a different procedure from the one used the first time, in order to pinpoint inaccuracies and, if necessary, correct them. This practice also permits conclusions to be drawn relating to the procedure used in the first analysis, its limitations or shortcomings, as well as, in consequence, conclusions concerning the entire material.

Criminality analysis aims at the discovery of definite laws and interactions. Its findings provide the scientific basis for crime prevention. The correctness of the results of criminality research is thus ultimately reflected in criminality trends. This practical confirmation, however, cannot be derived from criminal statistics alone. It requires instead the use of analytical procedures ranging from the statistical registration of criminality trends to the questioning of individuals about their views on the effectiveness of preventive measures. This is a complicated form of testing since a multiplicity of factors operate here, and criminality trends, as well as any changes in them, do not depend only on the effectiveness of certain preventive measures and methods. The verification of research findings in the practical struggle against criminality is as yet largely unexplored territory. This aspect of testing the effectiveness of crime prevention methods cannot be discussed here in any detail; it should be made the subject of a special study.

The importance of the quality of the individual investigation for the results of criminality research also makes it necessary to use certain procedures for supplementing available data. Time and again gaps are found to exist in the examination of the various aspects of the personality of offenders and in analyses of their working and everyday conditions. The data sometimes do not cover certain connections which have already been proved to be essential in a large number of other offences. To collect such supplementary information is very time-consuming. Moreover, it is difficult to bridge the usually considerable time-span between the offence and the supplementary investigations. This frequently reduces the value of such supplementary data. Many things look different to a person after the passage of time. Such supplementary data are also subject to a great variety of influences. Yet they cannot be avoided. What matters, therefore, is that the findings should be used with all appropriate care and caution.

Some of the principal procedures for individual examination and verification will now be discussed — not only from the point of view of subsequent testing and supplementation of the data, but also in order to ensure that a high standard is achieved in the original examination.

Important forms of individual questioning are the interview and exploration. The interview is conducted according to an exact pattern of questions laid down beforehand. This pattern must be followed in all interrogations serving the testing procedure. It is mapped out in writing in advance. The interviewer must endeavour to keep closely within the boundaries of his questions. This does not, of course, exclude 'planned' digressions but these should only serve to lead the respondent to the subject or to establish a better rapport with him. In an interview in which two strangers come face to face it is important that a relationship of trust is created between the partners. Sometimes it may be useful to assure the respondent that this anonymity will be respected. The results of an interview depend very largely on the quality of the pattern of questions. Experience gained in this field has been evaluated in the literature. [60] The interview must be so conducted that the answers can be quantified in order to ensure comparability with the original investigation. The interview may cover facts, experiences of the respondent himself or of other persons, subjective processes, and certain working and everyday conditions. The general limitations are the same as for other procedures in which human beings are the source of information. It should, however, be remembered that limitations also stem from the strict pattern of the questions. Whether or not the possibilities of an interview are fully exhausted must depend to a great extent on the interviewer's experience.

Exploration is a systematically conducted but seemingly informal exploratory conversation. In such a conversation the planned questions or complexes of questions are touched upon, but their order emerges from the situation. Exploration, too, is concerned with the establishment of objective or subjective connections and phenomena. This form of conversation offers a particularly favourable chance of a deeper understanding of subjective processes, motives and views. The method is thus superior to the interview and to the written survey. Prerequisites of successful exploration are the creation of an appropriate atmosphere and the questioner's adaptation to the respondent, in particular to his linguistic capabilities. It is not advisable to take notes during a conversation; the results should be entered later in the exploration record. The value of exploration depends on a number of factors which must be borne in mind.

Exploration results are only susceptible of qualitative evaluation. They cannot easily be subjected to a standard yardstick. Conditions differ too much from one conversation to another.

The results of exploration depend greatly on the explorer's skill. The method requires the application of psychological knowledge and experience and some experimenting is advisable before embarking on exploration. Particularly useful results are yielded in the areas of opinion and motivational research.

Exploration deepens the researcher's understanding, reveals new connections to him and sharpens his eye for the problems under investigation. Frequently new questions emerge from it. This is where the direct contact between the researcher and the information source proves valuable.

However, exploration should not be employed as the sole procedure. Its general limitations require that its findings be tested by objective criteria. Exploration of any considerable number of persons requires an appropriate reciprocal moderation and mutual understanding between the explorers. [61]

The kind and number of persons selected for exploration must depend on its objective. If it aims at supplementing available data then the choice of the persons to be questioned presents no difficulties. In all verification procedures the principle of random sampling should be applied.

Yet another procedure is observation. In the interview and in exploration the researcher appears in an active rôle, proceeding in accordance with a predetermined plan. This is not the case with observation. Although this, too, is performed systematically, the researcher does not interfere in the evolution of certain processes. This procedure, generally described as participating observation, is subdivided into external and internal observation. External observation is principally observation of behaviour. It can cover individuals or groups, but groups must be small enough to be surveyable by the observer. External observation may be concerned also with a person's receptivity. Thus, by travelling in a car at a given speed and in appropriate traffic conditions the receptivity and capacity of observation of a driver has been tested. [62]

Internal observation means that the researcher is himself within the group whose behaviour or development he wishes to examine. This participation in the work and the life of the individual enables him to understand certain important processes and connections. Thus it is possible by internal observation to verify the function of connections. It must, however, be remembered that a work team, for instance, may develop within the process of work and of neutral interaction so that, in certain circumstances, a different assessment may result. The experience of psychologists should be drawn upon in this respect. [63] What we have said of other procedures applies also to observation: it should not be the only method used but requires supplementation.

The above-mentioned forms of participating observation are conducted according to a predetermined plan. They have nothing in common with casual observation, which is of little value as a scientific procedure. The most that casual observation can yield is suggestions leading to a deliberate and systematic procedure.

It is vital for observation that the objectivity of the observer should be assured and that he should follow events from a distance. Whether he grasps reality as it is or receives a distorted picture of it depends on just that. On no account must the researcher approach the examination with the prejudice that it cannot yield anything new or that it will not get him anywhere. [64] Psychologists point out that observation yields valuable results, especially when it concentrates on significant situations. What situations are significant to individual researchers must depend on their research task. [65]

A method similar to exploration is that of indirect attitude analysis. It, too, serves the verification of results achieved. Its peculiarity lies in the fact that it examines attitudes indirectly. The idea is to avoid the distortion produced by direct questions. Direct questioning, as psychologists know, invariably contains the risk of a particular effect being triggered. Indirect attitude analysis, on the other hand, can make use of different techniques. Instead of a questionnaire, for instance, it is possible to use a test sorting of cards which contain statements thought to apply to the individual in question, etc.

The experiment must be distinguished from the observation discussed above. Whereas observation covers a phenomenon in its development, the experiment first examines, takes into consideration or even sets up its own conditions. The relevant literature — even that of bourgeois sociology and psychology — contains some valuable hints concerning its application. [66] König states that various procedures are developed to control the various factors, and here lies the greatest difficulty for the application of experimental methods in social research. In principle it is possible to differentiate between the case where the researcher so compiles his experimental groups that, with the exception of the independent variable, they are entirely identical in all other factors judged relevant, and that case where the effect of disturbing variables is controlled in accordance with probability theory. Thus, from a basic totality one selects two groups according to a random procedure on the assumption that the interfering variable will affect both groups in the same random way and thus become calculable.

König further states that the most common objection to experiment is that the results achieved cannot be tranferred to social reality because of the artificial character of the experimental set-up. Quite apart from the fact that experiments are also possible under the conditions of a normal environment, this objection overlooks the fact that any accurate testing of hypotheses invariably presupposes very special artifical situations; even the law of gravity disregards the density of air. The relatively rare use of experiments seems to be due much more to the absence of any very accurate theories in the sphere of sociology. [67]

It is not yet possible to outline adequately the range of application of experiment in criminal research. It may well be that it can be used for testing the effectiveness of certain preventive measures. But that problem lies outside the questions discussed here. It seems, however, that the experiment is needed also for testing special hypotheses, where it can help to verify the assumed rôle and function of a particular relation or of particular relations. Kuzmin has reported his experiences in this field. [68] This source is useful also for defining the limitations of experiment.

The testing procedures also include the comparative method. This can be applied in a variety of contexts. Thus the comparative analysis of historical materials may serve the deduction of underlying laws. In our context it can help to compare research results from different disciplines. If the correctness of results is to be tested in this manner, this presupposes a comparability of the data. This is of particular importance. Comparability applies both to the qualitative and to the quantitative aspects. In consequence, criminality analyses are comparable if they agree in their characteristic data and in all significant indices.

The cases so far discussed all show the peculiarity that the results obtained from a small number of criminal offences are to be tested as to their representative character in respect of the main group of that particular type of criminality. Comparability finally presupposes that a unified way of coding is used in different examination procedures.

The comparative method should also be applied in all cases where individual investigations have been performed by different procedures. This could yield important conclusions concerning the standard of these investigations.

The test can be useful in criminality research in a number of different ways. To begin with, it is suitable for the checking of questionnaires. In mass surveys it has proved desirable to discuss the draft questionnaires first with experts and then with a group of selected persons. Only thus can the necessary maturity of the questionnaire be guaranteed. The same applies to data collection forms.

At the International Symposium on Problems of Juvenile Criminality and of its Control, Szabó reported on the application of the test method in personality research. It was used for examining the effect of a complicated educational situation upon the personality of a juvenile. What was examined was not the pattern of the circumstances but their effect on the individual's personality. The studies were concentrated mainly on elucidating the motives which preceded the various phenomena. [69] The test was finally applied to checking a causal model. The research team concerned had worked out a model of the complex of phenomena determining a particular type of crime. They then used the test method to verify this research model. Only then did they proceed to mass investigations designed to yield the required information concerning the entire population. [70]

The sociometric procedure can also play a certain part in criminality research. This procedure – also known as sociometrics – has recently been repeatedly and extensively discussed. [71] It is, however, generally agreed that it merely provides an insight into the relations within a team or a group. Thus the partner selection test in a particular relationship may show the relations in which the members of the group stand to one another; but it cannot explain why the relations are as they are. That would require other procedures yet.

The above-mentioned procedures — whose listing here makes no claim to completeness — are applicable both to environment studies and to the exploration of the man—environment communication. The procedures also serve the examination of the specific character of certain internalisation processes. [72]

Both in individual examinations of criminal offences and in the testing of results the separate psychological aspects of offenders and the procedures for their analysis are of considerable importance. This emerges directly from the dialectical—materialist personality theory. In connection with the above-mentioned procedures of observation, questioning, testing, etc., the question arises as to what criteria are to be used in measuring the quality of the diagnostical procedures.

The principal quality criteria are objectivity, reliability and validity. These are, as it were, the basis of assessment from an operational point of view and must invariably be supplemented by a verification of the subject contents of the diagnosis. [73]

A procedure is said to possess objectivity if it leads to results which are independent of the person of the evaluator. The greater the scope for evaluation or decision-making by the evaluator, the greater is the risk that, because of subjective factors in the evaluator, identical phenomena will be differently assessed. That, of course, would impair objectivity. It follows that observation, interviewing, intelligence tests, etc., each carry a different degree of objectivity. The measure of the objectivity of a procedure is the coefficient of objectivity r_{obj}. It is based on the following definition:

Objectivity is the mean degree to which the assessments of several independent evaluators on the test performance of a random sample correlate with one another.

The coefficient of objectivity is calculated as follows:

(a) A diagnostic procedure (test or questionnaire) is applied to a random sample.

(b) Several assessors assess the data independently of one another.

(c) The degree of agreement of the values of any two assessors is calculated as r_{obj} according to the following diagram:

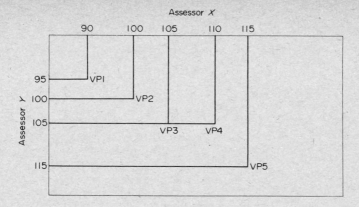

The assessor X, on the strength of a test performance, assigns to VP1 the value 90, while the assessor Y, using the same data, assesses the same VP at 95. For absolute objectivity the values of all samples would have to lie on the diagonal of the diagram (in the above example VP2, VP3, VP5). The more they deviate from it, the lesser the objectivity of the procedure. The coefficient of objectivity — like any other coefficient of correlation in multi-square tables — is calculated according to the formula:

$$r_{obj} = \frac{N\Sigma X \times Y - \Sigma X \times \Sigma Y}{\sqrt{[N\Sigma X^2 - (\Sigma X)^2] \times [N\Sigma Y^2 - (\Sigma Y)^2]}}$$

The more closely r_{obj} approximates the value +1, the more objective is the procedure. If more than two evaluators are involved r_{obj} is calculated by comparing pairs and working out the mean of the results. [74] It should be clearly emphasised that the criterion of objectivity is only one of the quality criteria. The value of a method cannot therefore be judged only according to whether it satisfies or does not satisfy this criterion.

The objectivity of a research result should be tested not only for each psycho-diagnostic procedure but for each case of criminality investigation, and should be justified by the researcher or the author of any published study. Scharbert and Spalteholz have this to say on the subject:

Difficulties in meeting the demand for objectivity were encountered in particular in cases when the findings arrived at in court or during preliminary proceedings diverged from the results obtained in our investigations. Thus the summing-up reports of investigation departments, indictments and verdict justifications frequently contained the same stereotyped phrases about the offender's ideological attitudes which frequently were neither factually justified nor proved but — as an analysis of the material revealed — had first been subjectively interpreted from objective facts and then taken over in bulk from one account to another. In a number of cases assessments about negative ideological views were attested and justified merely by evidence that the persons concerned prior to 13 August 1961 had frequently visited West Berlin or had been following West German radio and television programmes. By the systematic application of differentiated examination methods it was possible in such cases to resolve such discrepancies and correct over-simplified conclusions. In all other instances an approximate agreement or correlation of result series from different assessors was achieved thanks to clear evaluation instructions and by determining a sufficient number of invariables. As a result the investigation attained an adequate degree of unambiguousness. [75]

By reliability of a diagnostic procedure we mean that repeated application of the same procedure within a short space of time will produce identical results. A number of mathematical procedures have also been developed to determine reliability; these will be found in the specialised literature. Inadequate reliability may be due to a number of reasons — insufficient objectivity of the tests, insufficient stability of the procedure, and finally insufficient constancy of the material under investigation.

Reliability should also be tested and justified in all criminality researches. Scharbert and Spalteholz make the following points with this quality criterion of diagnostic procedures:

The demand concerning the accuracy of our study was the one most difficult to meet: reliability has to be assessed as more or less incomplete. This is due, on the one hand, to the fact that ascertainment of reliability requires a repetition of the investigation under identical conditions, which was not possible in view of the specific nature of the subject under investigation and also, in some cases, the special situation of the individuals in the sample, in that they were in custody. On the other hand, it was due to the objectives of the study itself: the conditioning factors associated with the offence of criminal frontier crossing are diverse in character and origin even in simple cases and require the application of diversified investigation methods. As for a generally reliable method, which would adequately meet the various spheres involved in the criminal decisions of young people — as yet no such method exists in criminology. There are no preliminary studies or similar investigations which would render possible a comparison or a critique of methods. Above all, it is not yet certain whether, and to what extent, the relationships and data to be covered both sociologically and psychologically can be netted by the same investigatory trawl and with bracketed methods. Empirical investigation is not only an indispensable preliminary for generalisations and systematisations but also a criminological attempt whose results cannot yet be reliable in every respect. This reservation about the reliability of our study concerns in particular its diagnostic passages, which cannot be more than starting points or base lines for the psychological assessment of the offender's personality; and the description of functional connections between the subjective and objective factors among the causes of the offences, since these — as mentioned above — had frequently to be obtained by interpolation and for that reason alone cannot lay claim to a high degree of reliability. Other elements of the investigation, such as those concerned with the study of objective everyday conditions, social attitudes and ideological opinions, as well as motivation and decisions, possess a substantially higher degree of reliability. [76]

The validity of a procedure is the degree to which it really measures what it is supposed to measure. Statements on the validity of a result are made in relation to specific practical problems to whose solution the procedure in question is to be applied. This is why the result must be related to a criterion outside the procedure. This is difficult, however, as such criteria are frequently only relative themselves. In that case the principle of validity states that a procedure is the better validated the more completely its findings agree with the criterion significant for the objective in question. The lesser this agreement, the less valid is the information coveyed by the procedure. Validity can be calculated by various mathematical methods.

Demands concerning validity must likewise be made on all criminality research. A differentiated and bracketed application of different procedures simultaneously can meet the requirements resulting from the complex nature of the determinants of the offences investigated, the frequently complex systems of interdependences of subjective and objective elements which, as social phenomena, at the same time are of mass character. Because of this procedural technique and of the validity of the covered population the content of the study is correlated with the essential qualitative parameters of the subject and in consequence will usually be regarded as sufficiently valid. [77]

The criteria of objectivity, reliability and validity provide an important basis for accurately assessing the value of various procedures and of the results achieved by them. Important as these procedures are in their scientific application, they must not be handled in blind faith. It is important to remember their limitations and, whenever possible, replace less reliable procedures by more reliable ones. [78]

Berger makes the demand that in all sociological researches the validity, reliability and accuracy of the data observed should be tested by mathematical and statistical methods. He states:

> The concepts of validity, reliability and accuracy are key concepts of statistical analysis. They are important not only in the evaluation of the observational data but equally important in any kind of statistical analysis. The method by which the empirical material has been collected is irrelevant.
>
> Validity of the results means that the empirically gained results must correspond to social reality, i.e. to social conditions. The results of the study, therefore, are valid only if the real circumstances are reflected in them. This presupposes a reliable measuring of the data.
>
> Reliability of the results means that identical results have been obtained under the same conditions by the same methods and techniques. Reliable results are, therefore, present only when the investigation, including evaluation, has been conducted accurately.
>
> Accuracy of the results means that the range of error in the collection and evaluation of the research data must be kept relatively low. The greater the selection and the less the differences between the sample and the population, the more accurate the results become. It must be remembered, however, that as the selection increases so do the sources of error in the evaluation of the data. Care should, therefore, be taken to see that both the range of error due to selection and the range of error due to technical evaluation are kept relatively low.[79]

Notes

[1] V. Kvasnička, 'Some Methodological and Technical Experiences of Criminological Research', *Právník*, 1966, pp. 266 ss. (in Czech).

[2] Cf. I. A. Poletayev, *Kybernetik*, Berlin 1962, p. 14.

[3] Ibid.

[4] Cf. H. Berger, *Methoden industriesoziologischer Untersuchungen*, Berlin 1965, pp. 72 ss., esp. pp. 73 ss.; H. Jetzschmann/H. Kallabis/

R. Schulz/H. Taubert, *Einführung in die soziologische Forschung*, Berlin 1966, pp. 77 ss.

⁵ Cf. also A. Kudlik, 'Über die Methoden der Untersuchung der Ursachen der Kriminalität', in *Aktuelle Beiträge zur Staats- und Rechtswissenschaft aus den sozialistischen Bruderländern*, Potsdam−Babelsberg 1963, Issue 4, pp. 28 ss.

⁶ Cf. also H. Berger, 'Zur Anwendung verschiedener Erhebungsmethoden bei der soziologischen Forschung', *Wissenschaftliche Zeitschrift der Humboldt-Universität zu Berlin*, 1964, pp. 838 ss.

⁷ The use of the term questionnaire is somewhat misleading since the data survey does not in fact involve any questioning. In its proper meaning the questionnaire is used for the written interview, a procedure which differs considerably from the data-compiling survey performed with the aid of the data 'questionnaires' discussed in this section.

⁸ R. König, 'Das Interview − Formen, Technik, Auswertung', in: *Praktische Sozialforschung*, vol. I, Cologne 1957, p. 27.

⁹ Cf. also H. Blüthner/G. Stiller, 'Rolle und Grenzen der kriminologischen Erhebung im System der kriminologischen Forschungsmethoden', *Staat und Recht*, 1967, Issue 5, pp. 769 ss.

¹⁰ Cf. H. Hinderer, 'Der Täter in seiner Beziehung zur Straftat und zur Gesellschaft und die persönlichkeitsbedingten Grenzen der strafrechtlichen Verantwortlichkeit', Habil. thesis, Halle−Wittenberg 1966, p. 203.

¹¹ Cf. H. Harrland, 'Die Bedeutung der Kriminalstatistik für die Leitung des Kampfes gegen die Kriminalität, ihre Funktionen, ihre Organisation und ihre Arbeitsweise', thesis, Halle−Wittenberg 1963, pp. 166 ss.

¹² K. Marx, *Das Kapital*, Dritter Band, in: K. Marx/F. Engels, *Werke*, vol. 25, Berlin 1964, p. 836.

¹³ A. N. Kolmogorov, quoted by H. Harrland, 'Die Bedeutung der Kriminalstatistik für die Leitung des Kampfes gegen die Kriminalität, ihre Funktionen, ihre Organisation und ihre Arbeitsweise', thesis, Halle−Wittenberg 1963, p. 108.

¹⁴ W. Middendorf, *Soziologie des Verbrechens*, Cologne−Düsseldorf, 1959, p. 222; the same author in: *Recht der Jugend*, 1961, Issue 4, p. 59; the same author in: *Kriminalistik*, 1960, p. 271.

¹⁵ L. Baydeldinov, 'Einige Fragen der statistischen Untersuchung der sozialen Wirklichkeit', *Sowjetwissenschaft−Gesellschaftswissenschaftliche Beiträge*, 1962, Issue 11, p. 1200.

¹⁶ Cf. H. Haubenschild, 'Zum Persönlichkeitsstatus Jugendlicher in den Jugendwerkhöfen der DDR', thesis, Berlin 1966, p. 424; other examples listed in J. Jetzschmann/H. Kallabis/R. Schulz/H. Taubert, *Einführung in*

die soziologische Forschung, loc. cit., pp. 160 ss.

[17] Cf. H. Jetzschmann/H. Kallabis/R. Schulz/H. Taubert, ibid.

[18] Cf. loc. cit., pp. 202 ss. Thus, e.g., the closeness of the correlation between two data is assessed either direct or by percentages and as a rule overestimated.

[19] Cf. loc. cit., pp. 206 ss.

[20] Use is made here of an as yet unpublished study by H. Dettenborn.

[21] Cf. P. Flaskemper, *Allgemeine Statistik — Theorie, Technik und Geschichte der sozialwissenschaftlichen Statistik*, Hamburg 1959, p. 167; cf. also E. Förster, 'Zur Anwendung der Korrelations-und Regressions-analyse in der Ökonomie', *Wissenschaftliche Zeitschrift der Humboldt-Universität zu Berlin*, 1964, pp. 559 ss.

[22] Cf. esp. H. Berger, *Methoden industriesoziologischer Untersuch-ungen*, Berlin 1965, pp. 53 ss.

[23] Cf. E. Weber, *Grundriss der biologischen Statistik*, 4th edn, Jena 1961, p. 525.

[24] Cf. also E. Förster/F. Egermayer, *Korrelations- und Regressions-analyse*, Berlin 1966, pp. 231 ss., esp. p. 267.

[25] Cf. H. Harrland, 'Zur Entwicklung der Kriminalität und zu einigen Problemen ihrer wirksamen Bekämpfung', *Neue Justiz*, 1966, no. 20, p. 615.

[26] K. - O. Scharbert/W. Spalteholz, 'Die verbrecherischen Grenzüber-schreitungen Jugendlicher und Heranwachsender in ihren Erscheinungs-formen sowie in ihrer sozialen und psychischen Determiniertheit', thesis, Babelsberg 1966, pp. 37 ss.

[27] Cf. J. Jetzschmann/H. Kallabis/R. Schulz/H. Taubert, *Einführung in die soziologische Forschung*, Berlin 1966, p. 145.

[28] Cf. B. A. Gruschin, 'Probleme der Repräsentation bei der Erfor-schung der öffentlichen Meinung', *Deutsche Zeitschrift für Philosophie*, 1964, pp. 808 ss.

[29] Cf. V. Yadov, 'Aus der Arbeit des soziologischen Laboratoriums der Leningrader Universität', *Sowjetwissenschaft — Gesellschaftswissenschaft-liche Beiträge*, 1964, Issue 10, p. 1118.

[30] Cf. H. Jetzschmann/H. Kallabis/R. Schulz/H. Taubert, *Einführung in die soziologische Forschung* Berlin 1966, p. 140.

[31] H. Harrland, 'Die Bedeutung der Kriminalstatistik für die Leitung des Kampfes gegen die Kriminalität, ihre Funktionen, ihre Organisation und ihre Arbeitsweise', thesis, Halle—Wittenberg 1963, p. 43.

[32] Cf. H. Berger, 'Zur Methodologie und Methodik der soziologischen Forschungen', Fragen der marxistischen Soziologie, *Wissenschaftliche*

Zeitschrift der Humboldt-Universität zu Berlin, 1964, Special volume I, p. 67.

[33] Cf. W. Sauer, *Kriminologie,* Berlin 1950, p. 18.

[34] Thus one of the shortcomings of the analysis of violent crime, compiled in the Halle District in 1963, was the drawing of 'conclusions' from exceedingly small numbers of cases.

[35] Cf. also E. Weber, *Grundriss der biologischen Statistik* Jena 1948, p. 19. Cf. also M. Benjamin, 'Mathematische Methoden in der staatlichen Leitung', *Staat und Recht,* 1965, Issue 6, pp. 899 ss., esp. p. 903.

[36] V. Kvasnička, 'Some Methodological and Technical Experiences of Criminological Research', *Právník* 1966, pp. 266 ss. (in Czech).

[37] Cf. 'Bericht über das Kolloqium zu Fragen der marxistischen Jugendforschung', *Jugendforschung, Informationsbulletin des Wissenschaftlichen Beirats für Jugendforschung beim Amt für Jugendfragen,* 1966, Issue 7.

[38] Cf. G. Röblitz, 'Jugendforschung im Freizeitbereich als Problem und Aufgabe', *Jugendforschung, Informationsbulletin des Wissenschaftlichen Beirats für Jugendforschung',* 1965, Issue 4, pp. 1 ss.

[39] Cf. G. Röblitz, 'Zur Ermittlung und Einteilung des Freizeitverhaltens', *Theorie und Praxis der Körperkultur,* 1962, Issue 7; by the same author, 'Tätigkeitsprotokoll als Verfahren zur Ermittlung des Freizeitverhaltens von Jugendlichen', *Wissenschaftliche Zeitschrift der Deutschen Hochschule für Körperkultur,* 1964, Issue 2.

[40] Cf. P. Armélin, *Die Wirtschaft,* 1965, no. 2 Appendix, pp . 8 ss.

[41] For the reliability of motivation statements cf. H.-D. Schmidt, 'Einige Prinzipien und Techniken der Befragung und Vernehmung', in: *Psychologie und Rechtspraxis,* Berlin 1965, p. 108.

[42] Cf. G. Knobloch, 'Über die Beweggründe von Tätern bei Straftaten gegen das sozialistische Eigentum in Industriebetrieben', *Schriftenreihe der Deutschen Volkspolizei,* 1965, Issue 5, p. 449.

[43] Cf. E. Buchholz, 'Der Diebstahl und seine Bekämpfung in der DDR', Habil. thesis, Berlin 1963, pp. 277 ss.

[44] Cf. K. Manecke, 'Zu einigen Fragen der Theorie der Ursachen der allgemeinen Kriminalität in der DDR', unpublished manuscript, p. 11.

[45] Cf. G. Rosenfeld, *Zur Theorie der Lernmotivation*, Berlin 1964.

[46] Cf. I. Krasemann, 'Einige Bemerkungen zur Quantifizierung gesellschaftlicher Erscheinungen', *Deutsche Zeitschrift für Philosophie,* 1964, Issue 12, pp. 1429 ss., esp. p. 1431 and the literature listed there; H. Jetzschmann/H. Kallabis/R. Schulz/H. Taubert, *Einführung in die soziologische Forschung*, Berlin 1966, pp. 170 ss.

[47] B. F. Green, quoted by I. Krasemann, 'Einige Bemerkungen ...', loc. cit. , p. 1433.

[48] Cf. I. Krasemann, 'Einige Bemerkungen ...', loc. cit., pp. 1434 ss. and the literature listed there.

[49] Cf. A. G. Zdravomyslov, quoted by I. Krasemann, loc. cit., p. 1437.

[50] H. Deutschländer, 'Zur Quantifizierung gesellschaftlicher Erscheinungen, speziell ideologisch-moralischer Prozesse', *Deutsche Zeitschrift für Philosophie*, 1965, Issue 5, p. 607; cf. also A. G. Zdravomyslov/ V. A. Yadov, 'Erfahrungen aus einer konkreten Untersuchung des Verhältnisses zur Arbeit', *Sowjetwissenschaft—Gesellschaftswissenschaftliche Beiträge*, 1964, Issue 10, pp. 1017 ss.

[51] Cf. H. Deutschländer, 'Zur Quantifizierung ...', loc. cit., p. 607; I. Krasemann, 'Einige Bemerkungen ... ', pp. 1438 ss.; E. Weckesser, 'Die schriftliche Befragung in der konkret-soziologischen Forschung', *Deutsche Zeitschrift für Philosophie*, 1964, Issue 1, pp. 80 ss; H.-D. Schmidt, *Empirische Forschungsmethoden der Pädagogik*, Berlin 1962, pp. 106 ss.

[52] It is important to emphasise this aspect since, given an outdated technology, it is quite possible for production results to be low even though the workers have a positive attitude to work.

[53] H. Jetzschmann/H. Kallabis/R. Schulz/H. Taubert, *Einführung in die soziologische Forschung*, loc. cit., p. 172.

[54] E. K. Scheuch, in: R. König, *Handbuch der empirischen Sozialforschung*, vol. I, Stuttgart 1962, p. 179; on this set of problems cf. also H. Berger, 'Zur Methodologie und Methodik der soziologischen Forschung', *Fragen der marxistischen Soziologie, Wissenschaftliche Zeitschrift der Humboldt-Universität zu Berlin*, 1964, Special volume I, pp. 55 ss.

[55] Cf. K. Braunreuther, 'Einige theoretische und praktische Aspekte der marxistischen Soziologie', *Fragen der marxistischen Soziologie, Wissenschaftliche Zeitschrift der Humboldt-Universität zu Berlin*, 1964, Special volume I, p. 25.

[56] Cf. K. Braunreuther, loc. cit., p. 26, and H. Berger, 'Zur Methodologie und Methodik der soziologischen Forschung', *Fragen der marxistischen Soziologie, Wissenschaftliche Zeitschrift der Humboldt-Universität zu Berlin*, 1964, Special volume I, p. 56.

[57] Cf. K. Marx, 'Fragebogen für Arbeiter', in: K. Marx/F. Engels, *Werke*, vol. 19, Berlin 1962, pp. 230 ss.

[58] On interviewing cf. W. Friedrich, 'Die Befragungsmethode — ein notwendiges Arbeitsmittel der marxistischen Jugendforschung', *Deutsche Zeitschrift für Philosophie*, 1963, Issue 10, pp. 1240 ss; H.-D. Schmidt, *Empirische Forschungsmethoden der Pädagogik*, Berlin 1962, pp. 41 ss.; E.-H. Berwig/H. Senf/W. Vier, 'Forschungsmethodische Fragen einer

Untersuchung zum Stand des politisch-moralischen Bewusstseins und Verhaltens von Schülern und Lehrlingen', *Pädagogik*, 1964, Issue 2, pp. 122 ss.; G. V. Osipov et al., 'Marxistische Soziologie und koncrete soziologische Forschung', *Sowjetwissenschaft—Gesellschaftswissenschaftliche Beiträge*, 1963, Issue 2, p. 149; V. Yadov, 'Aus der Arbeit des soziologischen Laboratoriums der Leningrader Universität', *Sowjetwissenschaft—Gesellschaftswissenschaftliche Beiträge*, 1964, Issue 10, p. 1119; E. Weckesser, 'Die schriftliche Befragung in der konkret-soziologischen Forschung', loc. cit., pp. 80 ss. Weckesser above all demonstrates the consequences resulting from ignorance about the technique of constructing a questionnaire. Cf. also R. Frenzel, 'Zur Ausarbeitung konkret-soziologischer Methoden für die Untersuchung bestimmter Verbrechensarten (insbesondere Fragebogen und Täterbefragung)', *Staat und Recht*, 1963, Issue 12, pp. 1988 ss.; R. Schulz/O. Eisenblätter, 'Jugend in der technischen Revolution', *Jugendforschung*, 1965, Issue 3, pp. 2 ss.

[59] Cf. V. E. Tsugunov, 'The Use of Cybernetic and Mathematical—Analytical Machines in Specific Sociological Research', *Sovetskoye gosudarstvo i pravo*, 1964, No. 11, pp. 98 ss.

[60] Cf. H.-D. Schmidt, *Empirische Forschungsmethoden der Pädagogik*, Berlin 1962, pp. 41 ss.; by the same author, 'Einige Prinzipien und Techniken der Befragung und Vernehmung', in: *Psychologie und Rechtspraxis*, Berlin 1965, pp. 106 ss.; on interviewing techniques esp. pp. 111 ss.; W. Friedrich/A. Kossakowski, *Zur Psychologie des Jugendalters*, Berlin 1962, pp. 179 ss.

[61] Cf. H.-D. Schmidt, *Empirische Forschungsmethoden der Pädagogik*, Berlin 1962, pp. 48 ss.; on the techniques cf. esp. pp. 50 ss.

[62] The perceptivity of a person can also be computed by the methods of information theory; cf. L. B. Itelson, 'Über die Anwendung der mathematischen und kybernetischen Methoden in der pädagogischen Forschung', *Psychologische Beiträge* Abt. II, Issue 3, Berlin 1963, pp. 3 ss.

[63] Cf. esp. H. Kallabis, 'Zur Dialektik der sozialistischen Bewusstseinsbildung und Problemen der Forschung', *Deutsche Zeitschrift für Philosophie*, 1963, Issue 1, p. 49.

[64] Cf. H.-D. Schmidt, *Empirische Forschungsmethoden der Pädagogik*, loc. cit., pp. 74 ss.

[65] Y. S. Kuzmin, 'Zum Problem der Sozialpsychologie', *Sowjetwissenschaft—Gesellschaftswissenschaftliche Beiträge* 1964, Issue 4, p. 415; cf. also K. Braunreuther, 'Einige theoretische und praktische Aspekte der marxistischen Soziologie', loc. cit., p. 23.

[66] Cf. A. G. Zdravomyslov/V. A. Yadov, 'Erfahrungen aus einer konkreten Untersuchung des Verhältnisses zur Arbeit', loc. cit., p. 1021.

[67] Cf. R. König, 'Soziologie', in: *Das Fischer Lexikon*, Frankfurt/M. 1960, p. 200.

[68] Cf. Y. S. Kuzmin, 'Zum Problem der Sozialpsychologie', loc. cit., pp. 414 ss.

[69] Cf. A. Szabó, 'Theoretische Probleme der Methodologie der sozialistischen Kriminologie und technische Fragen der kriminologischen Forschung', in: *Jugendkriminalität und ihre Bekämpfung in der sozialistischen Gesellschaft*, Berlin 1965, p. 99.

[70] Cf. ibid.

[71] Cf. M. Vorwerg, 'Röntgenbild vom Kollektiv', *Neues Deutschland* of 24 June 1964, p. 6; I. Helm/E. Kasielke, 'Bei der Beurteilung der Tat eines Jugendlichen die aktuelle sozialpsychologische Situation berücksichtigen', *Forum der Kriminalistik*, 1965, Issue 1, pp. 30 ss.; I. S. Kuzmin, 'Zum Problem der Sozialpsychologie', loc. cit., p. 416; M. Lupke/D. Seidel, 'Internationales Symposium über die Bekämpfung der Jugendkriminalität in der sozialistischen Gesellschaft', *Schriftenreihe der Deutschen Volkspolizei*, 1964, Issue 12, p. 1293; W. Bachmann, 'Zur Psychologie des Kollektivs', *Deutsche Zeitschrift für Philosophie*, 1964, Issue 5, pp. 574 ss.; H. Horstmann, 'Die soziometrische Utopie J. L. Morenos in ihrer Beziehung zur Spontaneität der kapitalistischen Gesellschaft', *Deutsche Zeitschrift für Philosophie*, 1964, Special issue, p. 109.

[72] Cf. esp. I. S. Kuzmin, 'Zum Problem der Sozialpsychologie', loc. cit., p. 412; H. Hiebsch/M. Vorwerg, 'Versuch einer Systematisierung des sozialpsychologischen Forschungsbereichs', *Deutsche Zeitschrift für Philosophie*, 1964, Issue 5, p. 552; H. Hiebsch/M. Vorwerg, 'Über Gegenstand, Aufgaben und Methoden der marxistischen Sozialpsychologie', *Deutsche Zeitschrift für Philosophie*, 1963, Issue 5, pp. 593 ss.

[73] This section essentially reproduces the exposition of G. Clauss, 'Zur Standardisierung psychodiagnostischer Verfahren', *Probleme und Ergebnisse der Psychologie*, 1964, Issue 9, pp. 7 ss. Clauss himself proceeds from Lienert and other psychologists and also uses Vorwerg's critique of the views of bourgeois authors.

[74] On the use of qualitative criteria in written interviews cf. 'Bericht über das Kolloquium zu Fragen der marxistischen Jugendforschung', *Jugendforschung, Informationsbulletin des Wissenschaftlichen Beirats für Jugendforschung beim Amt für Jugendfragen*, 1966, Issue 7.

[75] Cf. K. - O. Scharbert/W. Spalteholz, 'Die verbrecherischen Grenzüberschreitungen Jugendlicher und Heranwachsender in ihren Erscheinungsformen sowie in ihrer sozialen und psychischen Determiniertheit,' thesis, Babelsberg 1966, p. 31.

[76] Cf. loc. cit., p. 32.

[77] Cf. loc. cit., p. 33.

[78] On the various mathematical procedures cf. esp. G. Clauss, 'Zur Standardisierung psychodiagnostischer Verfahren', *Probleme und Ergebnisse der Psychologie*, 1964, Issue 9, pp. 11 ss., pp. 20 ss.; on validity, reliability and accuracy of results cf. also H. Berger, 'Zur Methodologie und Methodik der soziologischen Forschung', loc. cit., p. 80.

[79] H. Berger, *Methoden industriesoziologischer Untersuchungen*, loc. cit., p. 80.

Appendix to Part IV

Data Questionnaire

Office of the Prosecutor General of the German Democratic Republic, Department for Criminality Research
Ref: IX   390-3/66

Questionnaire for the Examination of Recidivism in Criminal Offences against Property and Violent Offences

---

Reference of Public Prosecutor .... Questionnaire No ....
Area ....
District ....
Name and forename of offender ....
Date of birth ....
Permanent address ....
Short outline of case ....
....
Criminal laws violated ....
Case finally concluded on ....
by summary judgement ....
....
Substance of concluding decision ....
....
Present whereabouts of offender:
Place of employment and work, residence or social welfare institution ....
....
                          date ....
Questionnaire filled in by: name ....
                          office ....

When completed this questionnaire must be sent to the Prosecutor General of the GDR, Department for Criminality Research

PART I

Manifestation of most recent criminal offence

1   Card category

2   Offence for which most recent sentence was passed
(In the event of multiple offences the most serious individual offence should be listed; in the event of repeated offences that individual action should be listed which most clearly characterises the offence)

Offences involving robbery
01   Robbery, Art. 249, Section I, Criminal Code
02   Robbery, Art. 249, Section II, Cr. C.
03   Major robbery, Art. 250, Section I, Cr. C.
04   Major robbery, Art. 250, Section II, Cr. C.
Sexual offences
11   Indecent assault, Art. 176, Section I, Cr. C.
12   Indecent assault, Art. 176, Section II, Cr. C.
13   Rape, Art. 177, Section I, Cr. C.
14   Rape, Art. 177, Section II, Cr. C.
Offences against the person
21   Bodily injury, Art. 223, Cr. C.
22   Dangerous bodily injury, Art. 223a, Cr. C.
23   Maltreatment of dependants, Art. 223b, Cr. C.
24   Bodily injury under Art. 223a in conjunction with Art. 228, Cr. C.
25   Grave bodily injury, Art. 224, Cr. C.
26   Grave bodily injury, Art. 224, in conjunction with Art. 228, Cr. C.
27   Deliberate grave bodily injury, Art. 225, Cr. C.
28   Bodily injury resulting in death, Art. 226, Cr. C.
Offences to the detriment of social property under the Supplemental Criminal Law
31   Theft under Art. 29, S. Cr. L. (242 Cr. C.)
32   Theft under Art. 30, S. Cr. L. (242 ss. Cr. C.)
33   Embezzlement under Art. 29, S. Cr. L. (246 Cr. C.)
34   Embezzlement under Art. 30, S. Cr. L. (246 Cr. C.)
35   Fraud under Art. 29, S. Cr. L. (263 Cr. C.)
36   Fraud under Art. 30, S. Cr. L. (263 Cr. C.)
37   Breach of confidence Art. 29, S. Cr. L. (266 Cr. C.)
38   Breach of confidence Art. 30, S. Cr. L. (266 Cr. C.)

Other offences to the detriment of social property
41   Receiving
42   Habitual receiving
43   Damage to property
44   Unauthorised use of vehicles
Theft and embezzlement to the detriment of personal and private property
51   Theft, Art. 242, Cr. C.
52   Major theft, Art. 243, Section I, Cr. C.
53   Major theft, Art. 243, Section II, Cr. C.
54   Recidivist theft, Art. 244, Section I, Cr. C.
55   Recidivist theft, Art. 244, Section II, Cr. C.
56   Embezzlement, Art. 246, Section I, Cr. C.
57   Embezzlement, Art. 246, Section II, Cr. C.
Fraud and breach of confidence to the detriment of personal and private property
61   Fraud, Art. 263, Section I, Cr. C.
62   Fraud, Art. 263, Section II, Cr. C.
63   Fraud, Art. 263, Section IV, Cr. C.
64   Fraud, Art. 263, Section V, Cr. C.
65   Recidivist fraud, Art. 264, Section I, Cr. C.
66   Recidivist fraud, Art. 264, Section II, Cr. C.
67   Breach of confidence, Art. 266, Section I, Cr. C.
68   Breach of confidence, Art. 266, Section II, Cr. C.
Other offences damaging personal and private property
71   Receiving
72   Habitual receiving
73   Damage to property
74   Unauthorised use of vehicles

3   Of how many separate actions was the offence composed?

State number:

4   How many independent offences were committed by the offender?

State number:

5   The most serious offence resulted in personal injury which was

1   Severe
2   Moderate

3 Slight
4 None
5 Not established

6 Amount of material damage in GDR marks

(Only to be completed for offences against property)
    State amount:

7 Specific occasion for commission of the offence (predominantly)

1 Restraints weakened by drink
2 Personal quarrel
3 Irritation over the behaviour of the damaged person
4 Incitement by third parties (instigators)
5 Acute shortage of money
6 Irresponsible behaviour of the victim
7 Others
8 Not established

8 Offender's motives (socially oriented)

1 Striving for prestige and recognition
2 Revenge, envy
3 Conflicts at work
4 Conflicts at home
5 Conflicts at school
6 Conflicts with friends
7 Irritation over the behaviour of State bodies
8 Others
9 Not established

9 Offender's motives (object-oriented)

1 Striving for possessions, love of luxury
2 Striving for a comfortable life
3 Urge for adventure
4 Jealousy
5 Urge for sexual gratification
6 Economic difficulties, own fault
7 Economic difficulties – no fault of his own
8 Others
9 Not established

10   Mode of commission

1   By violence against persons
2   By violence against property
3   By deception (e.g. forged papers)
4   By violence against persons and property

11   The offence was committed

1   At the offender's place of work
2   In the immediate vicinity of his place of work
3   At the offender's home (or temporary address)
4   In the immediate vicinity of his home
5   At a place where the offender was for a short period (e.g. construction or assembly sites)
6   At a place visited by the offender in the course of his work (e.g. as a regular driver)
7   At a place visited by the offender in passing (e.g. as a work-shy element, vagrant, or after absenting himself from an educational or social welfare institution)

12   Form of participation

1   Sole offender
2   Participant
3   Instigator
4   Assistant
5   Member of a group or gang
6   Instigator in a group or gang

13   State of completion

1   Attempt, offender being apprehended before completion
2   Attempt, offender being disturbed before completion
3   Attempt, completion being prevented by victim's resistance
4   Attempt, completion being impossible for other reasons
5   Completion

14   Time of commission of offence

1   0600 to 1200
2   1200 to 1800
3   1800 to 2200

4   2200 to 0100
5   0100 to 0400
6   0400 to 0600
7   Unknown

15   Peculiarities of the time of commission

The offence was committed
1   during working time
2   during free time
3   on leave, during holiday time

16   Day of the offence

1   Sunday/holiday
2   Working day
3   Pay day

17   Place of the offence

1   Offender's home
2   Victim's home
3   Department stores, sales centres, kiosks, stores
4   Enterprises and construction sites
5   Public transport
6   Public institutions
7   Streets, squares
8   Taverns
9   Isolated spots

18   The offence was committed

1   At the District centre
2   At the Area centre
3   In a town under Area administration
4   In a rural community

19   Who suffered damage from offences against property, according to industries or their enterprises; damaged form of property and preferred objects

Offences against property in industry
01   Ore, potash, metallurgy, smelting

02 Coal and power
03 Chemicals
04 Heavy engineering
05 Motor engineering, shipbuilding
06 Other metal-processing industries
07 Electrical engineering
08 Foodstuffs industry
09 Light industry

Construction

10 Industrial building
11 Urban and residential building
12 Rural building
13 Building materials industry
14 Maintenance and repair of existing buildings

Transport and communications

20 Post office
21 Railways
22 Haulage and removal enterprises
23 Other transport enterprises, such as shipping on lakes and inland waterways, municipal transport enterprises, etc.

Agriculture

30 Agricultural production co-operatives and craft production co-operatives
31 State farms and other socialist estates
32 Motor and tractor stations and repair centres
33 Trade centres for agricultural needs and rural trade co-operatives
34 State bulk purchase enterprises for agricultural products
35 Forestry
36 Fisheries
37 Other agriculture

Trade

40 State retail trade
41 State department store associations
42 Co-operative retail trade
43 Socialist wholesale trade
44 Commission business
45 Private trade
46 Socialist catering and hotel establishments
47 Private catering establishments

Other spheres

50 Banks, savings banks, insurance firms

51 Parties and mass organisations
52 Central and local State bodies
53 Health service, educational and cultural institutions
54 Municipal housing administration and workers' housing construction co-operative
55 Municipal service enterprises
56 State oil and petrol stations
57 Coal trade
58 Lottery and pools, State circuses, sideshows, etc.

Semi-State enterprises
60 In industry
61 In construction
62 In transport and communications
63 In agriculture and forestry
64 In trade
65 In other spheres of the economy

Craft production co-operatives
70 Vehicle repair and building
71 Radio, TV and electrical appliance repair, electrical installations
72 Building and ancillary building crafts
73 Other production or service crafts

20 *Nature of property damaged*

1 State property
2 Co-operative property
3 Property of semi-State enterprises
4 Property of private enterprises, individual craftsmen and tradesmen
5 Property of parties and social organisations
6 Personal property of citizens

21 *Preferred object of offences against property*

1 Money
2 Articles of use and consumption
3 Foodstuffs
4 Drink and tobacco
5 Building materials
6 Material for electrical and sanitary installations
7 Articles of equipment

8   Tools

9   Others

22 Was the offender under the influence of drink at the time of the offence?

1   Greatly

2   Moderately

3   Slightly

4   No

5   Unknown

23 Offender was assessed as follows under Art. 4 of the Juvenile Court Law (JGG) or Art. 51 of the Criminal Code (StGB)

1   Art. 4 JGG positive

2   Art. 4 JGG negative

3   Art. 51, Section I, St. G. B. positive

4   Art. 51, Section II, St. G. B. positive

5   Art. 51, Sections I and II, St. G. B. negative

6   Offender was not assessed

24 The offence was favoured by

1   Disorder and slackness

2   Lack of supervision and vigilance

3   Inadequate protection of the attacked object, although such protection was called for

4   Inadequate personnel selection and insufficiently skilled personnel

5   Irresponsible behaviour of the damaged party

25 These circumstances were

1   Deliberately exploited by the offender

2   Not deliberately exploited by the offender

26 Offender was ascertained

0   By evaluation of test series, card indexes, clues and expert opinions

1   By the employment of tracker dogs

2   By statements of witnesses who saw or observed the offender

3   By operational measures such as patrols and observation

      (a) by members of the security organisations
      (b) by direct enlistment of citizens

4   By a check on certain groups of people
5   By confidential tip-offs
6   In connection with the clearing-up of other offences
7   By the questioning of accomplices
8   In other ways
9   Cannot be deduced

Knowledge of the offender's action was gained, as non-participants, by

27 *Prior to the commission of the offence*

1   Family members
2   Colleagues at work
3   Officials and superiors
4   Friends or close acquaintances
5   Other persons

28 *After the commission of the offence*

1   Family members
2   Colleagues at work
3   Officials and superiors
4   Friends or close acquaintances
5   Other persons

29 *The above-named*

1   Informed the investigatory authority
2   Informed the Public Prosecutor or
3   Other official quarters concerned with the investigation
4   Initially tried to protect the offender by keeping their knowledge to themselves

30 *Offender's behaviour during investigation*

1   Immediately confessed when ascertained as a suspect
2   Initial deception about the facts or course of action
3   Initial pretence of another offender
4   Initial denial of the offence without detailed deception
5   Stubborn denial of the offence until completion of investigation

31 Attitude to the offence during court proceedings

1 Frank exposition of facts and genuine repentance
2 Frank exposition of facts without realisation of guilt (e.g. attempt at justification, recalcitrance)
3 Stubborn continuation of disguising attempts begun during preliminary investigations
4 Development of new deception manoeuvres after confession during preliminary investigations (withdrawal of confession)

The following measures were taken for the removal of discovered law infringements or other shortcomings in management

32 By the investigating body

1 Written report to the manager of the damaged enterprise
2 To the superior body (Association of nationally owned enterprises, etc.)
3 To the local administrative bodies
4 To the central bodies through the Ministry of the Interior
5 Other measures

33 By the Public Prosecutor

1 Demand for investigation
2 Protest against the law infringements and shortcomings discovered in management
3 Other measures

34 By the court

1 Issue of court criticism addressed to the manager of the damaged enterprise or institution
2 To superior economic managements
3 To State bodies (outside the juridical sphere)

35 Participation of social forces in the investigations preceding the court proceedings

1 Conversations with offender's team mates to assess his personality and to prepare for participation in court proceedings
2 Conversations with social forces in offender's home neighbourhood (National Front Committee, Committee for Order and

Security, sports organisations, etc.) to assess the offender's personality and to prepare for participation in court proceedings

3   Combination of 1 and 2

36 Duration of preliminary investigations (from start of case against known persons to conclusion)

1   Up to 2 weeks
2   Up to 1 month
3   Up to 2 months
4   Up to 3 months
5   Over 3 months

37 Offender was under detention pending investigation

1   Up to 1 month
2   Up to 2 months
3   Up to 3 months
4   Up to 4 months
5   Up to 5 months
6   Up to 6 months
7   Over 6 months
8   Not under detention pending investigation

38 Duration of proceedings from start of case against known person until legal validity of finding

1   Up to 2 months
2   Up to 3 months
3   Up to 4 months
4   Up to 5 months
5   Up to 6 months
6   Up to 9 months
7   Over 9 months

39 Enlistment of social forces in the preliminary investigations to discover favourable conditions

1   Conversations with offender's team mates to assess his personality and to discover favourable conditions
2   Conversations with social forces in offender's home neighbourhood to assess his personality and to discover favourable conditions
3   Combination of 1 and 2

40   *The court proceedings were conducted*

1   Publicly in court
2   In camera
3   In court with a limited invited public
4   Before an extended public at the offender's work place
5   Before an extended public in the town or rural municipality

41   *Participating in the court proceedings was a social prosecutor*

1   From the offender's work team
2   From his home neighbourhood
3   From other spheres

42   *A social defending counsel*

1   From the offender's work team
2   From his home neighbourhood
3   From other spheres

43   *Other social forces participating*

1   Representatives of the offender's work team
2   Representatives of social forces from his home neighbourhood
3   Representatives of his work team and from his residential area

44   *The evaluation of the proceedings took place before*

1   Workers of the enterprise where the offender was employed, or the enterprise damaged
2   The public of his home neighbourhood
3   At his place of work and in his home neighbourhood

45   *Type and extent of punishment*

Non-custodial punishment
01   Public reprimand
02   Public reprimand combined with a fine
Suspended sentence up to 6 months
11   By itself
12   With prohibition to change place of work
13   With good behaviour warranty
14   With prohibition to change place of work and good behaviour warranty

Suspended sentence from 6 months to 1 year
21 By itself
22 With prohibition to change place of work
23 With good behaviour warranty
24 With prohibition to change place of work and good behaviour
    warranty
Suspended sentence from 1 to 2 years
31 By itself
32 With prohibition to change place of work
33 With good behaviour warranty
34 With prohibition to change place of work and good behaviour
    warranty
Imprisonment
41 Imprisonment up to 3 months
42 Imprisonment from 3 to 6 months
43 Imprisonment from 6 months to 1 year
44 Imprisonment from 1 to 2 years
45 Imprisonment from 2 to 3 years
46 Imprisonment for more than 3 years
Imprisonment with hard labour
51 Hard labour up to 2 years
52 Hard labour up to 3 years
53 Hard labour up to 5 years
54 Hard labour up to 7 years
55 Hard labour up to 10 years
56 Hard labour over 10 years
Punishments and educational measures for juveniles
61 Custodial treatment up to 6 months
62 Custodial treatment from 6 months to 1 year
63 Custodial treatment from 1 to 2 years
64 Custodial treatment for more than 2 years
65 Suspended sentence of up to 6 months
66 Suspended sentence from 6 months to 1 year
67 Suspended sentence for more than 1 year
68 Institutional education
69 Other educational measures
Fines as the principal punishment
71 Up to 150 marks
72 Up to 300 marks
73 Up to 500 marks

74   Up to 1,000 marks
75   Over 1,000 marks

46   *Fines as additional punishment*

1   Up to 150 marks
2   Up to 300 marks
3   Up to 500 marks
4   Up to 1,000 marks
5   Over 1,000 marks

47   *Payment of damages under Art. 268, Criminal Procedure Law*

1   Claim for damages not made, or not made in time, by the damaged party
2   Damages awarded in principle
3   Amount of damages laid down
4   Application rejected

48   *Assigned to category of punishment*

1   Cat. I
2   Cat. II
3   Cat. III

49   *Period of probation in the event of suspended sentence*

1   1 year
2   1 to 2 years
3   2 to 3 years
4   3 to 4 years
5   4 to 5 years

Type of other offences multiply committed by the offender

50   *The other offences relate to:*

0   Predominantly offences against State and social property
1   Predominantly offences against private and personal property
2   Predominantly offences against State organs and public security
3   Predominantly frontier violations
4   Predominantly offences against persons
5   Predominantly sexual offences with violence

6   Predominantly other sexual offences
7   Predominantly offences against the economy
8   Predominantly traffic offences
9   Various offences, without any marked specialisation

51   Amount of ascertained material damage caused by the other offences

1   Up to 50 marks
2   Up to 100 marks
3   Up to 300 marks
4   Up to 500 marks
5   Up to 1,000 marks
6   Up to 5,000 marks
7   Over 5,000 marks

52   Were the other offences predominantly committed in connection with the offender's job? If yes, state nature

(Specific designation, e.g. sales centre manager, accountant, professional driver, etc.)
1   Yes
2   No

53   Did the offender predominantly act

1   Alone?
2   As an accomplice?
3   As instigator?
4   As assistant?
5   As a member of a group or gang?

54   Was the offender predominantly under the influence of drink?

1   Yes
2   No
3   Not established

55   Predominant motives of the offences

1   Desire to enrich himself
2   Desire for a comfortable and easy life
3   Material difficulties which were of his own making
4   Material difficulties through no fault of his own

5 Desire for status
6 Urge for adventure
7 Unbridled sexual desire
8 Sexual curiosity
9 Others

56 *Predominant mode of commission*

1 By violence against persons
2 By violence against property
3 By deception (e.g. forged papers)
4 By violence against persons and property

PART II

Picture of offender's personality

57 *Offender's age at the time of his most recent offence*

1 Under 16
2 Under 18
3 Under 21
4 Under 25
5 Under 30
6 Under 40
7 Under 50
8 Under 60
9 Over 60

58 *Schooling*

1 Up to the 4th grade
2 Up to the 6th grade
3 Up to the 7th grade
4 Up to the 8th grade
5 Up to the 9th grade
6 Up to the 10th grade
7 Up to the 11th grade
8 Up to the 12th grade

59 Type of school

1 Primary school
2 Polytechnic secondary school
3 Extended secondary school
4 Special school (auxiliary school)

60 Technical and Higher Education

1 Technical College course completed
2 Technical College course not completed
3 University course completed
4 University course not completed

61 Vocational training

1 Vocational training completed at time of offence
2 Vocational training cut short without final examination
3 No vocational training started after school
4 Offender still undergoing vocational training at time of offence
5 Offender still at general or secondary school at time of offence
6 Offender at specialised school or university at time of offence

62 Field of vocational training

1 Industry
2 Construction
3 Transport/Haulage
4 Agriculture
5 Trade
6 Service enterprises
7 Craft enterprises
8 Others

63 At the time of his offence the offender was working

1 In the trade he was trained for
2 In another trade as a trainee
3 In another trade as an unskilled worker

64 Sector of the economy in which the offender was employed at the time of his most recent offence, as a (enter detailed description)

1 Industry

2   Construction
3   Transport/Haulage
4   Agriculture
5   Trade
6   Service facilities
7   Areas outside material production

65   Property relation encountered by offender in his work

1   State
2   Co-operative
3   Semi-State
4   Private
5   Private wholesale
6   Small artisan, private craftsman

66   Position in the production process

1   Under training
2   Untrained worker
3   Trained worker
4   Office worker without vocational qualifications
5   Office worker with vocational qualifications
6   Craftsman
7   Brigade leader, master craftsman, middle management
8   Senior management
9   Independent

67   At the time of his offence the offender did not paticipate in the production process

1   Housewife
2   Old-age pensioner
3   Schoolchild/student
4   Temporarily unemployed
5   Prolonged illness
6   Work-shy

68   Offender's labour discipline

1   Irregular work attendance
2   Occasional slacking
3   Frequent slacking

4   Follows no regular occupation
5   Predominantly unemployed

69   *Is poor work discipline predominantly due to excessive drink?*

1   Yes
2   No
3   Not established

70   *Earnings at the time of his most recent offence*

1   Up to 200 marks per month
2   Up to 300 marks per month
3   Up to 400 marks per month
4   Up to 600 marks per month
5   Up to 800 marks per month
6   Up to 1,000 marks per month
7   Over 1,000 marks per month

71   *Family status*

1   Single
2   Married
3   Widowed
4   Divorced
5   Separated

72   *Family circumstances*

1   Living alone with parents
2   Living alone with relations
3   Living alone as a lodger
4   With his family with parents or relations
5   With his family in a flat of his own
6   Living alone in a flat of his own
7   Living in hostels
8   Living with his fiancée or regular girl friend
9   Living with another woman

73   *Dependent children living in offender's household*

1   One child
2   Two children

3   Three children
4   Four children
5   More than four children
6   None

74   Dependent children living outside the offender's household

1   One child
2   Two children
3   More than two children
4   None

75   Living conditions

1   Sufficiently large flat in reasonable state of repair
2   Flat too small but in reasonable order
3   Sufficiently large but dilapidated flat
4   Flat too small and moreover dilapidated

76   The offender was predominantly brought up

01   By his natural parents
02   By step-parents
03   By his natural mother and stepfather
04   By his natural father and stepmother
05   By his natural mother alone
06   By his natural father alone
07   By his stepmother alone
08   By his stepfather alone
09   By foster or adoptive parents
10   By a foster-mother alone
11   By a foster-father alone
12   By his grandparents or one grandparent
13   By brothers or sisters
14   By other relations
15   In a children's home
16   Frequent change of persons in charge

77   The offender's parents

1   Are divorced
2   Are separated
3   Father died while offender was a child
4   Mother died while offender was a child

78 Offender was accommodated in Youth Welfare institutions

1 Up to one year
2 Up to three years
3 Up to five years
4 Over five years

79 How many moves while accommodated in Youth Welfare institutions?

1 One move
2 Two moves
3 Three moves
4 More than three moves
5 No moves

80 Offender first came to the notice of Youth Welfare as

1 A schoolboy under 14
2 A juvenile under 18
3 Did not come to its notice
4 Not ascertainable

81 Offender came to the notice of Youth Welfare because of

1 Offence-prone behaviour in childhood
2 Criminal actions
3 Educational difficulties
4 Other misbehaviour
5 Failure of persons responsible for his upbringing

82 Offender entered the GDR from West Germany or West Berlin after 1956

1 New immigrant
2 Re-settler

83 Time elapsed between immigration and first offence in GDR

1 Up to 6 months
2 Up to 1 year
3 Up to 2 years
4 Over 2 years

84   Offender already had a criminal record when he entered the GDR

1   Yes
2   No

85   Predominant leisure activities of offender

1   Frequent attendance in taverns
2   Visits to cultural and sports events
3   Loafing about public places
4   Active sport
5   Hobbies, stamp collecting, etc.
6   Cinema, radio, television
7   Spare-time or relief work for reward
8   Not ascertained

86   Association with work-shy elements, persons with criminal records and other persons at social risk

1   Yes
2   No
3   Not ascertainable

PART III

Recidivist offences

87   How many court sentences have been passed on the recidivist?

1   One
2   Two
3   Three
4   Four
5   Five
6   More than five

88   Prior to his most recent offence the offender appeared before

1   Conflict Commission or Abitration Commission
2   Court

89 His previous punishments relate to

1   Predominantly offences against social property
2   Predominantly offences against private and personal property
3   Predominantly offences against State organs and public security
4   Predominantly frontier violations
5   Predominantly offences against the person
6   Predominantly sexual offences
7   Predominantly offences against the economy
8   Predominantly traffic offences
9   Various offences without any marked specialisation

90 Resulting from his previous punishments the offender has been

1   At Juvenile Labour Centres
2   At a Juvenile Re-education Centre
3   At a penal institution
4   Only punishments not involving custodial treatment

91 Total time spent by the recidivist at the Juvenile Labour Centre, the Juvenile Re-education Centre, or a penal institution

1   Up to 1 year
2   Up to 18 months
3   Up to 2 years
4   Up to 3 years
5   Up to 5 years
6   Up to 8 years
7   Up to 10 years
8   Over 10 years

92 Time elapsed between first and second previous punishments

1   Less than 6 months
2   From 6 months to 1 year
3   From 1 to 2 years
4   Over 2 years

93 Time elapsed between second and third previous punishments

1   Less than 6 months
2   From 6 months to 1 year
3   From 1 to 2 years
4   Over 2 years

94   *Time elapsed between third and fourth previous punishments*

1   Less than 6 months
2   From 6 months to 1 year
3   From 1 to 2 years
4   Over 2 years

95   *Time elapsed between fourth and fifth previous punishments*

1   Less than 6 months
2   From 6 months to 1 year
3   From 1 to 2 years
4   Over 2 years

96   *Offender received suspended sentences for previous offences*

1   Once
2   Twice
3   More than twice

97   *Offender received custodial sentences for previous offences*

1   Once
2   Twice
3   Three times
4   More than three times

98   *When given custodial sentences the offender was allowed conditional postponement under Art. 346, Criminal Procedure Law*

1   Once
2   Twice
3   More than twice

99   *Offender's age at the time of his first offence*

1   Under 16
2   Under 17
3   Under 18
5   Under 21
6   Under 25
7   Over 25

100 *Time elapsed between last previous punishment and most recent offence when offender was at liberty*

1   Up to 3 months
2   From 3 to 6 months
3   From 6 months to 1 year
4   From 1 to 2 years
5   Over 2 years

101 *The court sentence preceding the most recent offence was*

A custodial sentence
01   Up to 6 months
02   From 6 months to 1 year
03   From 1 to 2 years
04   Over 2 years
A suspended sentence
11   Up to 6 months
12   From 6 months to 1 year
13   From 1 to 2 years
A fine as the principal punishment
21   Up to 150 marks
22   Up to 300 marks
23   Up to 500 marks
24   Up to 1,000 marks
25   Over 1,000 marks
Punishments or measures for juveniles
31   Custodial treatment of up to 6 months
32   Custodial treatment from 6 months to 1 year
33   Custodial treatment from 1 to 2 years
34   Custodial treatment of over 2 years
35   Suspended sentence
36   Education at a centre
37   Other educational measures

102 *Offender was prematurely released from serving a custodial sentence*

1   On conditional postponement
2   By the amnesty decree of October 1964

103   The offender became culpable again

1   Before expiry of his probationary period in case of suspended sentence
2   Before expiry of his probationary period in case of remission on parole
3   After expiry of his probationary period
4   Within a year of discharge on the grounds of the amnesty decree

104   After his release the offender

1   Had a job assigned to him and took it up
2   Looked for a job himself
3   Had a job assigned to him but looked for one himself
4   Did not take up a job assigned to him
5   Did not have a job assigned to him and did not look for one himself

105   The job

1   Was what the offender wanted
2   Was not what the offender wanted

106   The job

1   Was in line with the offender's training
2   Required a higher degree of training than possessed by the offender
3   Required a lesser degree of training than possessed by the offender
4   Offender was placed in an unfamiliar occupation

107   The job assigned to, or taken up by, the offender after his release, compared with his work prior to detention, represented

1   A financial improvement
2   A financial drop
3   No financial change

108   His previous punishments were known

1   To his personnel department
2   To his team mates
3   In his home neighbourhood
4   To his personnel department and his team mates

5   To his team mates and in his home neighbourhood
6   To his personnel department and in his home neighbourhood
7   To his personnel department, his team. mates and in his home neighbourhood
8   To none of those from 1 to 7

109   Did the offender slack in the job assigned to him?

1   Occasionally
2   Frequently
3   Continually
4   Soon gave up the job again

110   The offender slacked

1   Because he was work-shy
2   Because he was not sufficiently rested due to consumption of alcohol
3   Because he earned more doing spare-time and occasional jobs

111   Did the offender commit his most recent offence immediately after release (e.g. while still en route to his place of residence or shortly after his arrival there)?

1   Yes
2   No

112   In the opinion of the official completing this form, is the offender's recidivism due predominantly

1   To his inadequate upbringing
2   To shortcomings in his re-integration
3   To his personality
4   To a combination of the listed factors
5   To a combination of 1 and 2
6   To a combination of 1 and 3
7   To a combination of 2 and 3
8   Cannot be judged

Enclosure 1

Short assessment of the specific causes, conditions and immediate occasions of the offence (e.g. what circumstances made the offender once more decide to commit an offence)

Enclosure 2

Notes on other factors, not covered in data questionnaire

Enclosure 3

As far as can be judged from the file, how did the offender assess the educational or re-educational process?
    by the investigatory body
    by the Public Prosecutor and the court
    by the serving of his punishment
    by his team mates and his enterprise
(state briefly)

How did the offender assess his re-integration process (e.g. what problems were there in choosing a place of work, finding accommodation, and what support did he receive; what was his contact with his team mates and how did they treat him)?

Index

Accountability, significance of, in criminology 201-17
Acquinas, Thomas 140
Adultery 179
Age of offender and criminological personality 227-8
Aggression 179-80
American criminologists 120, 128, 130
Amusement parks, people resorting to objectionable 166-7
Armélin, P. 349

Bader, Karl Siegfried 119
Bauer, Fritz 207
Baumann, Jürgen 122
Bavcon, Ljubo 74-6, 81-3
Beccaria, Cesare (Marchese di) 109, 131-2
Begging 126
Behaviour, offender's consciousness relating to 212-17
Behaviour stereotypes 191
Being and Consciousness (Rubinstein) 3
Benjamin, Michael 64
Berger, H. 368
Bernal, John Desmond 27
Beydeldinov, L. 324
Biserial coefficients 331-2
Blackmail 180
Bodily injury, *see* offences against the person
Böhme, Karl-Martin 31
Bourgeois criminology 6, 27-8, 107-33: preliminary observations 107-9; in a bourgeois society 109-14; conflicting trends in 114-23; methods of 123-8; is it at a cross-roads? 128-33
Buchholz, Erich 32, 64, 349
Building industry, offences against 30; *see also* property offences against

Carnegie Fund for International Peace 118
Case files as a source of information 308-9, 312
Causal relationship 60
Cause *vis-à-vis* condition 93
Central Statistical Office 310, 320
Choice, freedom of 203-5
Class Struggle and Crime (Streit) 30
Cohen, Albert K. 121, 124
Communal or private ownership? 139-50
Coefficient contingency 325-31
Coefficient of correlation 333-5
Coefficient of objectivity 364-5
Communist Party of the Soviet Union (CPSU) 5, 70-1
Concentration camps 131
Conditional criminals 226
Consciousness of offender, content and form of 212-17
Constitution, East German 9
Contingency coefficient 325-31
Council for Constitutional and Law Research 20

Crèches, shortage of 153
Crimes: against GDR 12-13, 111, 159-60; against humanity 12; against peace 12; undetected 249; *see also under* offences
Criminal code 1, 9, 15, 225, 276
Criminal proceedings, personality analysis in 223-42
Criminality: as a mass phenomenon 74-5; causes of and procedures for investigation into 303-68, (importance of method 303-6; information available 307-10; document analysis 311-13; criminological surveys 313-20; statistical procedure 320-53; and how it is used 325-53; interviewing 353-8; application and testing 358-68); eight general conclusions made as to 87-90; is it a sickness? 208; research and the theoretical problems of 247-96; (unit and methods of 248-53; philosophical premises 253-71; critique of bourgeois criminologists 259-66; system of reference and methodological consequences 266-71; tasks of analysis of individual violations of criminal law 271-81; problems disclosed, 282-5; systematisation of, 286); restricting function of order, 166-8
Criminals: are they born so? and are they insane? 225; extent of, in Germany in 1939 111
Criminal statistics 33, 93-4, 111, 116, 267-8, 320-53
Criminological personality research 224-9; *see also under* personality
Criminology: as a social science, 50-4; is it a pure empirical scien-

ce? 57; rôle of 50; task in, defined 43-4; *see also* social criminology
Cultural standards, rôle of 168-74
Cybernetics 307

Data, heads of inquiry for, in past investigations 290-1; heads in present questionnaire 369-404
Death sentence 111, 116, 131
Decree of the State Council (1961) 145, 155
Deed-relationship 229
Dierl, Otto 31
Discovered offences and non-detection 249
Drewitz, Fritz 215
Drunkenness as a cause of doing a criminal act 88, 276
Dzykonski, K. 239

Economy, objective contradictions in 174-7
Egotism 128-9
Einheit (journal) 155
Eisenhüttenstadt 164
Ellenberger, H. 109
Engels, Friedrich 3, 28-30, 58, 69, 71, 78, 84, 139, 156, 201, 204, 232, 257-8, 266, 277-8
Environment 189, 225
Execution, *see* death sentence
Exner, Franz 116-18
Exploitative States 142
Extortion 206

Fascism, *see* Nazi period
Fedoseyev, P.N. 5-6
Feix, Gerhard 30, 92, 227-8
Feuerbach, Paul Johann Anselm 109, 110, 190

Fichte, Johann Gottlieb 132, 140
Finkelnburg, Karl 117, 119
First offenders 229, 272-5
Flogging 115-16
Four-square coefficient of correlation 329
Fraud 126
Freedom, significance of, in criminology 201-17
Free-will 203
Frenzel, Rudi 228
Frequency of crime, correlation measurements based on 329
Freud, Sigmund 46, 265

Gangsterism 120, 121, 130
German Academy for Constitutional Law and Jurisprudence (DASR) 19
German Democratic Republic, social conditions of criminality in present day 159-81
Gertsenson, Aleksey A. 46, 122
Glueck, Eleanor 43, 125, 128
Glueck, Sheldon 125, 128
Göllnitz, Gerhard 31, 217
Göppinger, Hans E. 109
Gotha programme (Marx) 146
Graphs dealing with functional dependence, correlative dependence, and independence 322-3
Grathenauer, Kurt 30
Griebe, Walter 30

Habitual criminals 130, 226, 228, 272-5, 399-404
Hager, Kurt 8
Hahn, Eric 196
Harrland, Harri 33, 320, 342
Hartmann, Richard 31-3, 92, 123

Hegel, G.W.F. 51, 57, 110, 113, 132, 140, 257, 278
Hellmer, Joachim 7, 18-19, 131, 189
Hentig, Hans von 120
Hiebsch, Hans 161-2, 192
Hinderer, Hans 229-30
Hinze, Peter 215
Hippies 166-7
Hollerith cards 358
Homicidal offences 30, 59, 118
Hommel, Karl Ferdinand 109, 131
Homosexuality 180
Hörz, Herbert 2, 60, 62-3, 65, 68, 69, 93, 96, 99
Human personality 189: *see also under* personality

Incomes, variation of, as a factor in criminality 175-6
Institute for Criminal Law (Humboldt University) 33
Individual, importance of basic ideological attitude of the 160-1
Information, bases of, investigating criminality 307-10
International Symposium (on juvenile crime) 363
Interviewing to obtain data for criminological surveys 314-15, 353-8; *see also* questionnaire
Introduction to Sociological Research 353

Jaensch, Erich 225
Jäger, Günther 30
Jäger, Herbert 122
Jameson, Samuel Haig 130
Jung, Karl 225
Juvenile Court Convention (eleventh at Münster) 132

Juvenile Criminology Research Group's Questionnaire 272-5
Juveniles 31, 33, 44, 46, 48, 50, 101, 120-1, 125, 225, 227, 310, 363

Kallabis, Heinz 146
Kant, Immanuel 110, 132, 140
Klaus, Georg 194, 254-5, 277-8
Klusener, Eckbert 33
Knobloch, Gerhard 32, 349-50
Komin Industrial Area 165
König, R. 315, 363
Kraft, Otto 30
Kretschmer, Ernst 225
Kudryavtsev, V.N. 216
Kurella, Alfred 169-70
Kuzmin, Y.S. 363
Kvasnička, B. 305-6, 345

Labour protection, offences involving 31
Lafargue, P. 258
Lander, Hans-Jürgen 58, 72-5
Lange, Richard 84-5, 207-8
Latent offenders 226
Leading questions in interviews 356
Leisure: activities during, must be meaningful 48; as a basis to perform criminal acts 171-3, 348
Lekschas, John 32-3, 92, 205, 228, 270
Liepmann, Moritz 118-19
Listz, Franz von 112
Livestock, offences against 30-1
Lombrosian school 115, 225
Loose, Wolfgang 203, 205, 239
Lorenz, Werner 118
Luther, Horst 92
Lutzke, Arno 33, 92

MacNamara, Donald E.J. 130
Manecke, Kurt 31, 92, 98, 350
Mannheim, Hermann 129
Marat, Jean-Paul 29
Marcus, Franz 116
Marxist—Leninist Theory 1-10, 14, 19, 28-30, 58-9, 71, 79-81, 155-6, 190, 253-4, 266, 283
Mathematical methods 323
Mehlan, Karl-Heinz 31
Mergen, Armand 34-5, 46, 117, 119, 122, 133, 260-3
Merkel, Adolf 112
Mettin, Harry 228
Meyer, Fritz 126-7
Mezger, E and A. 262-3
Middendorf, W. 324
Ministry of the Interior, analyses from 303
Mittelstädt, Otto 115
Morality, the basis of socialist 179
Moscow Consultation, Document of 13
Moscow Declaration (1960) 143
Motives, investigating 318-19, 349-50
Multi-square table for contingency coefficients 320

Nass, Gustav 131
Nazi period 116-19, 131
Negative Social Group Relations, the rôle of 161-6
Notes on the Theory of Causes, Conditions and Circumstances of Criminality in the GDR (Hartmann and Lekschas) 32-3
Nowa Huta 165
Nuremberg Race Laws 116

Objectivity, coefficient of 364-5

Offence, Criminal and Criminological, differentiated 33-40

Offences: against the person 59, 88, 111; against property, see Property, offences against; against the State 12-13, 111, 159, 160; categories of, not the best basis for criminological study 159; economic 173-7; homicidal 30, 59, 118; see also crimes; and under Individual offences, e.g. traffic offences

Offenders: can they be typecast? 224; first 229, 272-5; heads of inquiry made in past investigations 290-1

Ontogenesis 194, 203

Orschekowski, Walter 31

Osipov 341

Ownership, private or commercial? 139-50

People's Court 116

Personal Documents (of offender) as a source of data 310-12

Personality: analysis in criminal proceedings 229-42, 393-9; criminological research into 223-42; dialectical process of development of 189-99; foundations of research into 189-99; what does is want? 237; what is it? 238; what is it capable of? 238

Petasch, Werner 33

Peters, Hans 132

Phylogenesis 203

Pitaval 109

Plato 140

Plekhanov, G.V. 263

Polak, Karl 155-6, 163

Poland 165

Position of the Working Class in England, The, (Engels) 28

Potential offenders 130

Poverty as a cause of criminality 264-5

Praedial offences 30-1

Predictions of criminal behaviour 124-7, 189

Preventive detention 116, 131

Prisons, a breeding place for crime? 118

Problems of Peace and Socialism, (periodical) 348

Professional criminals, see habitual criminals

Professional immorality 126

Property, offences against 30, 111, 159, 174-5, 177, 293, 346-7

Prostitution 178

Psychology vis-à-vis criminology 41

Public Authority, resistance to 126

Public opinion as a tool to combat crime 162-3

Punishment or education 154-5, 163

Quantification procedures in criminological research 346-53

Quensel, Stephan 72, 121

Questionnaires: authors' opinion as to missing questions in 275; form of, in investigations into criminality 377-406 (Part I Manifestation of most recent offence 378-93; Part II Picture of offender's personality, 393-9; Part III Recidivism 399-404); importance of investigative 260-2, 272, 304-5, 313-14, 356-8

Quetelet, L.A.J. 109, 117

Rabe, Rolf 228
Ranking correlations 332-3
Rape 177
Recidivism, what leads to? 126, 309-404; see also habitual criminals
Reckless, Walter 128-9
Reik, Theodor 46
Reinhold, O. 152
Reinwald, Paul 46
Relationship, theory of 324
Renneberg, Joachim 205, 226, 228
Research Group for Juvenile Criminology 46
Responsibility, significance of in criminology 201-17
Robbery 206
Römer, Axel 30
Rowdyism 48; see also gangsterism
Rubinstein, S.L. 3, 89, 195, 201, 202-4, 208, 216, 231, 237-8
Rubnice industrial area 165

Sahre, Hans 31
Sampling in criminality research 336-46
Schaff, Adam 78-80
Scharbert, K.-O. 337-8, 365
Scheler, H. 266-7
Scheuch, E.K. 353-4
Schubert, Ladislav 147
Schubert, Rolf 33, 89
Schuler, Erich 147
Schüler-Springorum, Horst 123-4
Schwartz, Gert 31
Schwartz, Hanns 31
Schwedt, oil centre of 164
Science in History (Bernal) 27
Scientific Advisory Council for Criminality Research 32, 46, 54
Scientific Criminality Research,
Dept. of 32, 46, 54
SED, see Socialist Unity Party of Germany
Selfishness as a cause of criminality 277-8; see also egotism
Sexologists 125
Sexual offences 30, 59, 84, 159, 163, 177-80, 227, 310
Sieverts, Rudolf 123-4
Skaberné, Bronislav 74-6, 81-3
Socialist criminology 27-54; development of 27-33; the subject of 33-46; task of 46-54; theory of causes of, in 57-102 (dialectical determinism in 57-68; law concept, significance of, in 68-83; concepts 83-91; internal structure of 92-102)
Socialist Unity Party of Germany (SED) 2, 5, 8, 19, 47, 58, 70, 71, 143, 146, 156, 171, 176, 209, 254, 260, 269, 292, 311
Society, its nature and character 190
Sociology vis-à-vis criminology 41
Sociometrics 363-4
Spalteholz, W. 337-8, 365-7
Spare time, as a basis to perform criminal acts 48, 171-3, 348
Special problems connected with sexual norms 177-80
Spranger, Eduard 191
Squandering offences 31
Starvation (as a punishment) 115-16
State Central Statistical Board 269
Statistical Procedure when investigating criminality 320-53
Statistical record sheets as a source of data 309-10
Staykov 348

Stiller, Gerhard 8, 33, 64, 92, 95
Streit, Josef 30, 270
Sutherland, Edwin H. 120
Szabó, Andras 30, 34, 35, 40, 42, 45, 94, 122, 363
Szewczyk, Hans 31, 217

Tally method of preparing correlation table 328
Tetrachoric four-square coefficient 328-9
Theft 59, 206
Time, a factor in criminality 93-4
Traffic offences 33
Types of offenders, can and should they be categorised? 224

Ulbricht, Walter 65, 155, 176, 192-3, 209
Undetected crime 249

Vodopivec, Katja 74-6, 81-3

Walczak, Stanislav 165
War and Criminality in Germany (Liepmann) 118
War crimes 12
Weber, Hans 30
Wegner, Arthur 122
West German Criminological Society 132
Wilhelm, Kaiser 117
Work, people having no regular 166-7
Workers' and Peasants' Inspectorate 303, 310

Youth, shortage of facilities for 153
Youth Problems, Dept. for 46, 54
Youthwork, *see* Juveniles
Yugoslavia, social problems in 74-7, 83